## DATE DUE

# THE CONTEMPORARY SHAKESPEARE SERIES

## VOLUME VII

King Henry The Sixth,
Part One

\*

King Henry The Sixth,
Part Two

\*

King Henry The Sixth,
Part Three

\*

King John

\*

Pericles

\*

Titus Andronicus

## Edited by A. L. Rowse

### Modern Text with Introduction

UNIVERSITY PRESS OF AMERICA

2

Copyright © 1987 by A.L. Rowse

University Press of America,® Inc.

4720 Boston Way
Lanham, MD 20706

3 Henrietta Street
London WC2E 8LU England

**Library of Congress Cataloging-in-Publication Data**
(Revised for vol. 7)

Shakespeare, William, 1564-1616.
  The contemporary Shakespeare series.

  Contents: v. 1. Hamlet ; Julius Caesar ; The
merchant of Venice ; A Midsummer night's dream ;
Romeo and Juliet ; The tempest — v. 2. As you like
it ; Coriolanus ; King Lear : King Richard the
Second ; Twelfth night — [etc.] — v. 7. King
Henry VI, part one ; King Henry VI, part two ;
King Henry VI, part three ; Titus Andronicus ;
Pericles ; King John.

   I. Rowse, A. L. (Alfred Leslie), 1903-
II. Title.
PR2754.R67   1984b        822.3'3        84-5105
ISBN 0-8191-3947-5 (alk. paper)

The plays in this volume are also available individually in
paperbound editions from University Press of America.

Book design by Leon Bolognese

# WHY A CONTEMPORARY SHAKESPEARE?

T he starting point of my project was when I learned both from television and in education, that Shakespeare is being increasingly dropped in schools and colleges because of the difficulty of the language. In some cases, I gather, they are given just a synopsis of the play, then the teacher or professor embroiders from his notes.

This is deplorable. We do not want Shakespeare progressively dropped because of superfluous difficulties that can be removed, skilfully, conservatively, keeping to every line of the text. Nor must we look at the question statically, for this state of affairs will worsen as time goes on and we get further away from the language of 400 years ago—difficult enough in all conscience now.

We must begin by ridding our mind of prejudice, i.e. we must not pre-judge the matter. A friend of mine on New York radio said that he was 'appalled' at the very idea; but when he heard my exposition of what was proposed he found it reasonable and convincing.

Just remember, I do not need it myself: *I live in the Elizabethan age*, Shakespeare's time, and have done for years, and am familiar with its language, and his. But even for me there are still difficulties—still more for modern people, whom I am out to help.

Who, precisely?

Not only students at school and in college, but all readers of Shakespeare. Not only those, but all viewers of the plays, in the theatre, on radio and television— actors too, who increasingly find pronunciation of the words difficult, particularly obsolete ones—and there are many, besides the difficulty of accentuation.

The difficulties are naturally far greater for non-English-speaking peoples. We must remember that he is our greatest asset, and that other peoples use him a great deal in learning our language. There are no Iron Curtains for him—though, during Mao's Cultural Revolution in China, he was prohibited. Now that the ban has been lifted, I learn that the Chinese in thousands flock to his plays.

Now, a good deal that was grammatical four hundred years ago is positively ungrammatical today. We might begin by removing what is no longer good grammar.

For example: plural subjects with a verb in the singular:

'*Is* Bushy, Green and the earl of Wiltshire dead?' Any objection to replacing 'is' correctly by 'are'? Certainly not. I notice that some modern editions already correct—

These high wild hills and rough uneven ways
Draw*s* out our miles and make*s* them wearisome

to 'draw' and 'make', quite sensibly. Then, why not go further and regularise this Elizabethan usage to modern, consistently throughout?

Similarly with archaic double negatives—'Nor shall you not think neither'—and double comparatives: 'this

is more worser than before.' There are hundreds of instances of what is now just bad grammar to begin with.

There must be a few thousand instances of superfluous subjunctives to reduce to simplicity and sense. Today we use the subjunctive occasionally after 'if', when
we say 'if it be'. But we mostly say today 'if it is'. Now
Shakespeare has hundreds of subjunctives, not only
after if, but after though, although, unless, lest,
whether, until, till, etc.

I see no point whatever in retaining them. They only
add superfluous trouble in learning English, when the
great appeal of our language as a world-language is
precisely that it has less grammar to learn than almost
any. Russian is unbelievably complicated. Inflected
languages—German is like Latin in this respect—are
really rather backward; it has been a great recommendation that English has been more progressive in this
respect in simplifying itself.

Now we can go further along this line: keep a few subjunctives, if you must, but reduce them to a minimum.

Let us come to the verb. It is a great recommendation
to modern English that our verbs are comparatively
simple to conjugate—unlike even French, for example.
In the Elizabethan age there was a great deal more of
it, and some of it inconsistent in modern usage. Take
Shakespeare's,

'Where is thy husband now? Where be thy brothers?'

Nothing is lost by rendering this as we should today:

Where is your husband now? Where are your brothers?

And so on.

The second and third person singular—all those
shouldsts and wouldsts, wilts and shalts, haths and
doths, have become completely obsolete. Here a vast

simplification may be effected—with no loss as far as I can see, and with advantages from several points of view.

For example, 'st' at the end of a word is rather difficult to say, and more difficult even for us when it is succeeded by a word beginning with 'th'. Try saying, 'Why usurpedst thou this?' Foreigners have the greatest difficulty in pronouncing our 'th' anyway—many never succeed in getting it round their tongues. Many of these tongue-twisters even for us proliferate in Shakespeare, and I see no objection to getting rid of *superfluous* difficulties. Much easier for people to say, 'Why did you usurp this?'—the same number of syllables too.

This pre-supposes getting rid of almost all thous and thees and thines. I have no objection to keeping a few here and there, if needed for a rhyme—even then they are sometimes not necessary.

Some words in Shakespeare have changed their meaning into the exact opposite: we ought to remove that stumbling-block. When Hamlet says, 'By heaven, I'll make a ghost of him that *lets* me', he means *stops*; and we should replace it by stops, or holds me. Shakespeare regularly uses the word 'owe' where we should say own: the meaning has changed. Take a line like, 'Thou dost here usurp the name thou ow'st not': we should say, 'You do here usurp the name you own not', with the bonus of getting rid of two ugly 'sts'.

The word 'presently' in the Elizabethan age did not mean in a few minutes or so, but immediately—instantly has the same number of syllables. 'Prevent' then had its Latin meaning, to go before, or forestall. Shakespeare frequently uses the word 'still' for always or ever.

Let us take the case of many archaic forms of words, simple one-syllable words that can be replaced without the slightest difference to the scansion: 'sith' for since, 'wrack' for wreck, 'holp' for helped, 'writ' for wrote, 'brake' for broke, 'spake' for spoke, 'bare' for bore, etc.

These give no trouble, nor do a lot of other words that he uses: 'repeal' for recall, 'reproof' for disproof, 'decline' for incline. A few words do give more trouble. The linguistic scholar, C. T. Onions, notes that it is sometimes difficult to give the precise meaning Shakespeare attaches to the word 'conceit'; it usually means thought, or fancy, or concept. I do not know that it ever has our meaning; actually the word 'conceited' with him means ingenious or fantastic, as 'artificial' with Elizabethans meant artistic or ingenious.

There is a whole class of words that have completely gone out, of which moderns do not know the meaning. I find no harm in replacing the word 'coistrel' by rascal, which is what it means—actually it has much the same sound—or 'coil' by fuss; we find 'accite' for summon, 'indigest' for formless. Hamlet's word 'reechy', for the incestuous kisses of his mother and her brother-in-law, has gone out of use: the nearest word, I suppose, would be reeky, but filthy would be a suitable modern equivalent.

In many cases it is extraordinary how little one would need to change, how conservative one could be. Take Hamlet's famous soliloquy, 'To be or not to be.' I find only two words that moderns would not know the meaning of, and one of those we might guess:

> . . .When he himself might his *quietus* make
> With a bare bodkin? Who would *fardels* bear. . .

'Quietus' means put paid; Elizabethans wrote the Latin 'quietus est' at the bottom of a bill that was paid—when it was—to say that it was settled. So that you could replace 'quietus' by settlement, same number of syllables, though not the same accentuation; so I would prefer to use the word acquittance, which has both.

'Fardels' means burdens; I see no objection to rendering, 'Who would burdens bear'—same meaning, same number of syllables, same accent: quite simple. I expect all the ladies to know what a bodkin is: a long pin, or skewer.

Now let us take something really difficult—perhaps the most difficult passage to render in all Shakespeare. It is the virtuoso comic piece describing all the diseases that horseflesh is heir to, in *The Taming of the Shrew*. The horse is Petruchio's. President Reagan tells me that this is the one Shakespearean part that he played—and a very gallant one too. In Britain last year we saw a fine performance of his on horseback in Windsor Park alongside of Queen Elizabeth II—very familiar ground to William Shakespeare and Queen Elizabeth I, as we know from *The Merry Wives of Windsor*.

Here is a headache for us: Petruchio's horse (not President Reagan's steed) was 'possessed with the glanders, and like to mose in the chine; troubled with the lampass, infected with the fashions, full of windgalls, sped with spavins, rayed with the yellows, past cure of the fives, stark spoiled with the staggers, begnawn with the bots; swayed in the back, and shoulder-shotten; near-legged before, and with a half-cheeked bit, and a headstall of sheep's leather', etc.

What on earth are we to make of that? No doubt it raised a laugh with Elizabethans, much more familiarly acquainted with horseflesh than we are; but I doubt if Hollywood was able to produce a nag for Reagan that qualified in all these respects.

Now, even without his horsemanship, we can clear one fence at the outset: 'mose in the chine'. Pages of superfluous commentary have been devoted to that word 'mose'. There was no such Elizabethan word: it was simply a printer's misprint for 'mourn', meaning dripping or running; so it suggests a running sore. You would need to consult the *Oxford English Dictionary*, compiled on historical lines, for some of the words, others like 'glanders' country folk know and we can guess.

So I would suggest a rendering something like this: 'possessed with glanders, and with a running sore in the back; troubled in the gums, and infected in the glands; full of galls in the fetlocks and swollen in the joints; yellow with jaundice, past cure of the strangles; stark spoiled with the staggers, and gnawed by worms; swayed in the back and shoulder put out; near-legged before, and with a half-cheeked bit and headgear of sheep's leather', etc. That at least makes it intelligible.

Oddly enough, one encounters the greatest difficulty with the least important words and phrases, Elizabethan expletives and malapropisms, or salutations like God 'ild you, Godden, for God shield you, Good-even, and so on. 'God's wounds' was Elizabeth I's favourite swearword; it appears frequently enough in Victorian novels as 'Zounds'— I have never heard anyone use it. The word 'Marry!', as in the phrase 'Marry come up!' has similarly gone out, though a very old gentleman at All Souls, Sir Charles Oman, had heard the phrase in the back-streets of Oxford just after the 1914-18 war. 'Whoreson' is frequent on the lips of coarse fellows in Shakespeare: the equivalent in Britain today would be bloody, in America (I suppose) s.o.b.

Relative pronouns, who and which: today we use who for persons, which for things. In Elizabethan times the two were hardly distinguished and were interchangeable. Provokingly Shakespeare used the personal relative 'who' more frequently for impersonal objects, rivers, buildings, towns; and then he no less frequently uses 'which' for persons. This calls out to be regularised for the modern reader.

Other usages are more confusing. The word 'cousin'

was used far more widely by the Elizabethans for their kin: it included nephews, for instance. Thus it is confusing in the English History plays to find a whole lot of nephews—like Richard III's, whom he had made away with in the Tower of London—referred to and addressed as cousins. That needs regularisation today, in the interests of historical accuracy and to get the relationship clear. The word 'niece' was sometimes used of a grandchild—in fact this is the word Shakespeare used in his will for his little grand-daughter Elizabeth, his eventual heiress who ended up as Lady Barnard, leaving money to her poor relations the Hathaways at Stratford. The Latin word *neptis*, from which niece comes also meant grandchild—Shakespeare's grammar-school education at Stratford was in Latin, and this shows you that he often thought of a word in terms of its Latin derivation.

Malapropisms, misuse of words, sometimes mistaking of meanings, are frequent with uneducated people, and sometimes not only with those. Shakespeare transcribed them from lower-class life to raise a laugh, more frequently than any writer for the purpose. They are an endearing feature of the talk of Mistress Quickly, hostess of the Boar's Inn in East Cheapside, and we have no difficulty in making out what she means. But in case some of us do, and for the benefit of non-native English speakers, I propose the correct word in brackets afterwards: 'You have brought her into such a canaries [quandary]. . .and she's as fartuous [virtuous] a civil, modest wife. . .'

Abbreviations: Shakespeare's text is starred—and in my view, marred—by innumerable abbreviations, which not only look ugly on the page but are sometimes difficult to pronounce. It is not easy to pronounce 'is't', or 'in't', or 'on't', and some others: if we cannot get rid of them altogether they should be drastically reduced. Similarly with 'i'th'', 'o'th'', with which the later plays are liberally bespattered, for "in the" or "of the."

We also have a quite unnecessary spattering of apos-
trophes in practically all editions of the plays—"d' for
the past participle, e.g. 'gather'd'. Surely it is much
better to regularise the past participle 'ed', e.g. gathered;
and when the last syllable is, far less frequently, to be
pronounced, then accent it, gatherèd.

This leads into the technical question of scansion,
where a practising poet is necessary to get the accents
right, to help the reader, and still more the actor. Most
people will hardly notice that, very often, the frequent
ending of words in 'ion', like reputation, has to be pronounced with two syllables at the end. So I propose to accent this when necessary, e.g. reputatiòn. I have noticed
the word 'ocean' as tri-syllabic, so I accent it, to help,
oceàn. A number of words which to us are monosyllables
were pronounced as two: hour, fire, tired; I sometimes
accent or give them a dieresis, either hoùr or fïre. In New
England speech words like prayèr, thëre, are apt to be
pronounced as two syllables—closer to Elizabethan
usage (as with words like gotten) than is modern speech
in Britain.

What I notice in practically all editions of Shakespeare's
plays is that the editors cannot be relied on to put the accents in the right places. One play edited by a well
known Shakespearean editor had, I observed, a dozen accents placed over the wrong syllables. This is under-
standable, for these people don't write poetry and do not
know how to scan. William Shakespeare knew all about
scanning, and you need to be both familiar with Elizabethan usage and a practising traditional poet to be able
to follow him.

His earlier verse was fairly regular in scansion, mostly
iambic pentameter with a great deal of rhyme. As time
went on he loosened out, until there are numerous irregular lines—this leaves us much freer in the matter of
modernising. Our equivalents should be rhythmically as

close as possible, but a strait-jacket need be no part of the
equipment. A good Shakespearean scholar tells us, 'there
is no necessity for Shakespeare's lines to scan absolutely.
He thought of his verse as spoken rather than written and
of his rhythmic units in terms of the voice rather than
the page.'

There is nothing exclusive or mandatory about my project. We can all read Shakespeare in any edition we like—
in the rebarbative olde Englishe spelling of the First
Folio, if we wish. Any number of conventional academic
editions exist, all weighed down with a burden of notes,
many of them superfluous. I propose to make most of
them unnecessary—only one occasionally at the foot of
very few pages. Let the text be freed of superfluous difficulties, remove obstacles to let it speak for itself, while
adhering conservatively to every line.

We really do not need any more editions of the Plays
on conventional lines—more than enough of those exist
already. But *A Contemporary Shakespeare* on these
lines—both revolutionary and conservative—should be a
help to everybody all round the world—though especially
for younger people, increasingly with time moving away
from the language of 400 years ago.

# King Henry The Sixth, Part One

# INTRODUCTION

The first thing to be noticed about the trilogy of *Henry VI* is its sheer spaciousness. Its vast scope and planning—covering that long reign, the wars in France and its loss, the career of Joan of Arc, the Wars of the Roses in England with the malign career of Richard of Gloucester to link up with *Richard III*—bear out what Robert Greene foresaw and envied in the euphoric confidence of the actor with the provincial accent, who could turn his hand to anything, and was now turning dramatist to compete with the university wits and eventually write them off the page (if not the stage).

The Elizabethans had a great appetite for Chronicles, the heightened self-consciousness of the nation sharpening their interest in its past. Holinshed's and Hall's were the most noteworthy, providing a rich quarry for stories which could be turned to account for the stage, while Hall's provided the unity and direction of theme: the unity achieved by the Tudors in bringing together Lancaster and York, after the disastrous split within the royal family and the conflict for power between parties which it released.

This is foreshadowed in the *First Part,* though it is mainly concerned with the ups and downs of the war in France. Thus this rather sprawling first play is given a certain centricity by the kind of duel waged between the English hero, Talbot, and Joan of Arc, the French heroine as to whose unique personality both English and French were unjust. To the medieval English she was a witch; nor could the French understand her. The Elizabethans could not be expected to get her right; Shakespeare is ambivalent about her, scathing at one moment (as with Shylock) and then his essential humanity breaks through (as it did with the Jew). In the end he concedes her sainthood:

> No, misconceived! Joan of Arc has been
> A virgin from her tender infancy,
> Chaste and immaculate in very thought,
> Whose maiden blood, thus rigorously effused,
> Will cry for vengeance at the gates of heaven.

St Joan has indeed had her revenge.

Talbot had his apotheosis with the patriotic Elizabethans. The relation with his son, the contest between the two as to which should escape from overwhelming forces when neither would fly and both were killed, provided a couple of the best scenes in the play and appealed greatly at the time. Thomas Nash testifies, 'how it would have joyed brave Talbot—the terror of the French—to think that he should triumph again on the stage, and have his bones new embalmed with the tears of ten thousand spectators at least at several times, who imagine they behold him fresh bleeding.' It was precisely this success that inspired Robert Greene's envy to an attack on the actor newly turned dramatist, with a parody of a line from him. Some years later, in the very personal Epilogue to *Henry V,* he himself testified to the popularity this early trilogy won him: of Henry VI,

> Whose state so many had the managing—

polite and prudent as ever, for actually it was that king's imbecility and incapacity that lost him the throne—

That they lost France and made his England bleed:
Which oft our stage has shown.

It is easy to criticise the tyro's first experiment in historical drama. Dr Johnson does so fairly, while showing how
silly critics' suppositions were that it was not Shakespeare's
work. He pointed out that 'the diction, the versification,
and the figures, are Shakespeare's . . . From mere inferior-
ity nothing can be inferred; in the productions of wit there
will be inequality. Of every author's works one will be the
best, and one will be the worst.' And of course a writer's
immature work is not to be condemned by the standard of
his mature achievement—an obvious reason too for establishing its chronological order.

Then Johnson proceeds to a just criticism: 'the truth is
that they have not sufficient variety of action, for the
incidents are too often of the same kind.' Shakespeare
remedied this later with his creative admixture of history
with fiction, the tragic with the comic. And these plays are
too long—for modern production they need considerable
cutting; a recent recension of all three in one was presented
on the English stage with success.

We must remember too that these are early Elizabethan
theatre, and recall the circumstances of the time. Hence
the naif patriotic boasting of a young people who felt
themselves (rightly) to be up-and-coming in those years
soon after the Armada, and the abuse of the French—
who gave as good as they got in return. To the Elizabethans the French were 'a fickle, wavering nation', with
their decades of civil and religious war, and the quick
chops and changes in the course of it. An Elizabethan
audience was no less mercurial, and would have no
difficulty in accepting the improbably speedy turn-abouts
of the Countess of Auvergne or the Duke of Burgundy in
the play: they did not go to the theatre for what was
probable after all, but for what was exciting. Plenty of

that, with all the fighting, executions, murders, with some witchcraft thrown in.

We may find the classic stichomythia, the line-by-line retorts or exchanges of insults tedious—Elizabethans evidently did not, for the dramatist was well aware of what was 'over-tedious', and at one point laughs at a long recital of titles as being so. Some of the lines strike us as bathetic; then we know Shakespeare could often be casual, at another moment write up something exceptionally fine. We must not ignore the possibility of revision either, of his writing in bits and pieces later.

Nor are we far from his association with Marlowe, from whom we have a line:

Like captives bound to a triumphant car;

and an image:

A statelier pyramid to her I'll rear
Than Rhodope's of Memphis ever was.

Above all, we are close to his winning the patronage of Southampton which resulted in the Sonnets and *Venus and Adonis*. In Suffolk's wooing of Margaret of Anjou for Henry's Queen, while falling for her himself, we have a couplet which is virtually repeated in both:

She's beautiful, and therefore to be wooed;
She's a woman, therefore to be won.

In 1591 Southampton, still under-age, ran away across Channel to join Essex's campaign in Normandy in aid of Henry of Navarre. Normandy was all the news, the player turning playwright cashed in on it—so like him; this annoyed Greene but is likely to have had a part in recommending Shakespeare to Southampton and winning his patronage. No doubt about the dates: we are in the years 1591 and 1592, when both the early Sonnets and *Venus and Adonis* were written.

Personal touches? The first line of the play—'Hung be the heavens with black'—has become familiar, because it describes the contemporary practice of draping the stage with black when a tragedy was to the fore, the heavens being the penthouse roof decorated with stars (thus all the more often pointed at in the drama of the time). We see the countryman devoted to sports—such a contrast with Marlowe:

> Between two hawks, which flies the higher pitch;
> Between two dogs [i.e. hounds] which has the deeper
>     mouth . . .
> Between two horses, which does bear him best;
> Between two girls, which has the merriest eye . . .

And we have a passage again to attest his particular devotion to deer-hunting and special knowledge of deer. Are we to see anything personal in his reflection—

>         what is wedlock forcèd but a hell,
>   An age of discord and continual strife?

He always speaks well of marriage based on affection; his own family life at Stratford jogged on well enough, for all his double life in London and his being away most of the time. He was a family man, as ambitious to rehabilitate his family's standing at Stratford as he was to make his mark in literature.

We notice his regular turning to the classics for apt illustrations and comparisons in the unlikely ambiance of English and French history. Talbot's son, bent on death, is somewhat improbably an Icarus; Suffolk's journey to procure Margaret for Queen (without any dowry) is compared to Paris's raid on Greece,

With hope to find the like event in love
But prosper better than the Trojan did.

In these early plays we find several times over the words
'conster' for construe, or 'misconster'—evidently the contemporary pronunciation. No less evidently school background. Naturally, teaching was pragmatic rather than
precise; Nero is spoken of, in contemporary terms, as playing
on the lute, when it should have been a lyre.

The actor-commencing-author's inveterate addiction to
punning takes elementary forms here, shortly to receive
an extraordinary sophistication and intellectualisation,
with his experience of the Southampton circle, in come-
dies like *Love's Labour's Lost*. One may give an example of
the way an archaic use of a simple preposition may con-
fuse meaning:

Choked with ambition *of* the meaner sort—

he clearly means *by* the meaner sort, and I have modernised
it accordingly. A few archaic forms, 'thee' and 'thine', have
been retained where necessary for rhyme—no point in
ruthless pedantic consistency where Shakespeare cared nothing for it at all.

# CHARACTERS

KING HENRY THE SIXTH

DUKE OF GLOUCESTER, Lord Protector, uncle of the King

DUKE OF BEDFORD, Regent of France, uncle of the King

DUKE OF EXETER, Thomas Beaufort, great-uncle of
the King

BISHOP OF WINCHESTER, Henry Beaufort, great-uncle of
the King, later Cardinal

DUKE OF SOMERSET, John Beaufort, formerly Earl

RICHARD PLANTAGENET, later Duke of York

EARL OF WARWICK

EARL OF SALISBURY

William de la Pole, EARL OF SUFFOLK

LORD TALBOT, later Earl of Shrewsbury

JOHN TALBOT, his son

EDMUND MORTIMER, Earl of March

SIR WILLIAM GLANSDALE

SIR THOMAS GARGRAVE

SIR JOHN FASTOLF

SIR WILLIAM LUCY

WOODVILLE, Lieutenant of the Tower of London

MAYOR OF LONDON

VERNON

BASSET

A LAWYER of the Temple

A PAPAL LEGATE

CHARLES, Dauphin and later King of France

REIGNIER, Duke of Anjou and titular King of Naples

DUKE OF ALENÇON

BASTARD OF ORLEANS

DUKE OF BURGUNDY

GENERAL of the French army at Bordeaux

20

GOVERNOR of Paris
MASTER GUNNER of Orleans
A BOY, son of the Master Gunner
SHEPHERD, father of Joan la Pucelle
JOAN LA PUCELLE, Joan of Arc
MARGARET, daughter of Reignier, later Henry VI's Queen
COUNTESS OF AUVERGNE

Lords, wardens, messengers, heralds, soldiers, servants, officers, sentinels, gentlemen, gaolers, attendants, courtiers, ambassadors, fiends (Joan la Pucelle's familiars)

# Act I

## SCENE I
## Westminster Abbey.

*Dead march. Enter the funeral of King Henry the Fifth,*
*attended by the Duke of Bedford, the Duke of Gloucester,*
*the Duke of Exeter, the Earl of Warwick, the Bishop of*
*Winchester, and the Duke of Somerset; with heralds*

BEDFORD
  Hung be the heavens with black, yield day to night!
  Comets, importing change of times and states,
  Brandish your crystal tresses in the sky,
  And with them scourge the bad revolting stars
  That have consented unto Henry's death—
  King Henry the Fifth, too famous to live long!
  England never lost a king of so much worth.
GLOUCESTER
  England never had a king until his time.
  Virtue he had, deserving to command;
  His brandished sword did blind men with its beams;
  His arms spread wider than a dragon's wings.
  His sparkling eyes, replete with wrathful fire,
  More dazzled and drove back his enemies
  Than midday sun fierce bent against their faces.
  What should I say? His deeds exceed all speech;
  He never lifted up his hand but conquered.
EXETER
  We mourn in black; why mourn we not in blood?
  Henry is dead and never shall revive.
  Upon a wooden coffin we attend;

And death's dishonourable victory
We with our stately presence glorify,
Like captives bound to a triumphant car.
What? Shall we curse the planets of mishap
That plotted thus our glory's overthrow?
Or shall we think the subtle-witted French
Conjurers and sorcerers that, afraid of him,
By magic verses have contrived his end?

WINCHESTER
He was a king blessed of the King of Kings.
Unto the French the dreadful Judgement Day
So dreadful will not be as was his sight.
The battles of the Lord of Hosts he fought;
The Church's prayers made him so prosperous.

GLOUCESTER
The Church? Where is it? Had not churchmen prayed,
His thread of life had not so soon decayed.
None do you like but an effeminate prince,
Whom like a schoolboy you may overawe.

WINCHESTER
Gloucester, whate'er we like, you are Protector
And look to command the Prince and realm.
Your wife is proud; she holds you well in awe
More than God or religious churchmen may.

GLOUCESTER
Name not religion, for you love the flesh;
And never throughout the year to church you go,
Except it be to pray against your foes.

BEDFORD
Cease, cease these jars, and rest your minds in peace;
Let's to the altar. Heralds, wait on us.     *Exeunt heralds*
Instead of gold, we'll offer up our arms,
Since arms avail not, now that Henry's dead.
Posterity, await for wretched years,
When at their mothers' moistened eyes babes shall suck,
Our isle be made a marish (marsh) of salt tears,

And none but women left to wail the dead.
Henry the Fifth, your ghost I invoke;
Prosper this realm, keep it from civil broils;
Combat with adverse planets in the heavens!
A far more glorious star your soul will make
Than Julius Caesar or bright—

*Enter First Messenger*

FIRST MESSENGER
My honourable lords, health to you all!
Sad tidings bring I to you out of France,
Of loss, of slaughter, and discomfiture:
Guienne, Champaigne, Rheims, Rouen, Orleans,
Paris, Gisors, Poitiers, are all quite lost.
BEDFORD
What say you, man, before dead Henry's corpse?
Speak softly, or the loss of those great towns
Will make him burst his lead and rise from death.
GLOUCESTER
Is Paris lost? Is Rouen yielded up?
If Henry were recalled to life again,
These news would cause him once more yield the ghost.
EXETER
How were they lost? What treachery was used?
FIRST MESSENGER
No treachery, but want of men and money.
Among the soldiers this is mutterèd,
That here you maintain several factions;
And while a field should be dispatched and fought,
You are disputing of your generals.
One would have lingering wars with little cost;
Another would fly swift, but wants then wings;
A third thinks, without expense at all,
By guileful fair words peace may be obtained.
Awake, awake, English nobility!

Let not sloth dim your honours new-begot.
Cropped are the flower-de-luces in your arms;
Of England's coat one half is cut away.                    *Exit*

EXETER
Were our tears wanting to this funeral,
These tidings would call forth their flowing tides.

BEDFORD
Me they concern; Regent I am of France.
Give me my steelèd coat; I'll fight for France.
Away with these disgraceful wailing robes!
Wounds will I lend the French, instead of eyes,
To weep their intermissive miseries.

*Enter another Messenger*

SECOND MESSENGER
Lords, view these letters full of bad mischance.
France is revolted from the English quite,
Except some petty towns of no import.
The Dauphin Charles is crownèd king in Rheims;
The Bastard of Orleans with him is joined;
Reignier, Duke of Anjou, does take his part;
The Duke of Alençon flies too to his side.                 *Exit*

EXETER
The Dauphin crownèd king? All fly to him?
O, whither shall we fly from this reproach?

GLOUCESTER
We will not fly but to our enemies' throats.
Bedford, if you are slack, I'll fight it out.

BEDFORD
Gloucester, why doubt you of my forwardness?
An army have I mustered in my thoughts,
Wherewith already France is overrun.

*Enter another Messenger*

THIRD MESSENGER
  My gracious lords, to add to your laments,
  Wherewith you now bedew King Henry's hearse,
  I must inform you of a dismal fight
  Betwixt the stout Lord Talbot and the French.
WINCHESTER
  What? Wherein Talbot overcame, is it?
THIRD MESSENGER
  O, no; wherein Talbot was overthrown.
  The circumstance I'll tell you more at large.
  The tenth of August last this dreadful lord,
  Retiring from the siege of Orleans,
  Having full scarce six thousand in his troop,
  By three and twenty thousand of the French
  Was round encompassèd and set upon.
  No leisure had he to enrank his men;
  He wanted pikes to set before his archers;
  Instead whereof, sharp stakes plucked out of hedges
  They pitchèd in the ground confusedly
  To keep the horsemen off from breaking in.
  More than three hours the fight continuèd,
  Where valiant Talbot, above human thought,
  Enacted wonders with his sword and lance.
  Hundreds he sent to hell, and none durst stand him;
  Here, there, and everywhere enraged he slew.
  The French exclaimed the devil was in arms;
  All the whole army stood agazed on him.
  His soldiers, spying his undaunted spirit,
  'A Talbot! A Talbot!' crièd out amain,
  And rushed into the bowels of the battle.
  Here had the conquest fully been sealed up
  If Sir John Fastolf had not played the coward.
  He, being in the vanguard, placed behind
  With purpose to relieve and follow them,
  Cowardly fled, not having struck one stroke.
  Hence grew the general wreck and massacre;

Enclosèd were they with their enemies.
A base Walloon, to win the Dauphin's grace,
Thrust Talbot with a spear into the back,
Whom all France, with their chief assembled strength,
Durst not presume to look once in the face.

BEDFORD

Is Talbot slain? Then I will slay myself,
For living idly here in pomp and ease,
While such a worthy leader, wanting aid,
Unto his dastard foemen is betrayed.

THIRD MESSENGER

O, no, he lives, but taken prisoner,
And Lord Scales with him, and Lord Hungerford;
Most of the rest slaughtered or taken too.

BEDFORD

His ransom there is none but I shall pay.
I'll hale the Dauphin headlong from his throne;
His crown shall be the ransom of my friend;
Four of their lords I'll change for one of ours.
Farewell, my masters; to my task will I.
Bonfires in France forthwith I am to make
To keep our great Saint George's feast with now.
Ten thousand soldiers with me I will take,
Whose bloody deeds shall make all Europe quake.

THIRD MESSENGER

So you had need, for Orleans is besieged;
The English army is grown weak and faint;
The Earl of Salìsbury craves supply
And hardly keeps his men from mutiny,
Since they, so few, watch such a multitude.          *Exit*

EXETER

Remember, lords, your oaths to Henry sworn,
Either to quell the Dauphin utterly
Or bring him in obedience to your yoke.

BEDFORD

I do remember it, and here take my leave
To go about my preparatiòn.                          *Exit*

GLOUCESTER
    I'll to the Tower with all the haste I can
    To view the artillery and munitiòn,
    And then I will proclaim young Henry king.      *Exit*
EXETER
    To Eltham will I, where the young King is,
    Being ordained his special governor,
    And for his safety there I'll best devise.
                            *Exeunt all but Winchester*
WINCHESTER
    Each has his place and function to attend;
    I am left out; for me nothing remains.
    But long I will not be Jack out of office.
    The King from Eltham I intend to steal
    And sit at chiefest stern of public weal.      *Exit*

## SCENE II
## Before Orleans.

*Flourish. Enter Charles the Dauphin, Alençon, and*
*Reignier, with drum and soldiers*

CHARLES
    Mars' true moving, even as in the heavens
    So in the earth, to this day is not known.
    Late did he shine upon the English side;
    Now we are victors, upon us he smiles.
    What towns of any moment but we have?
    At pleasure here we lie, near Orleans;
    At times the famished English, like pale ghosts,
    Faintly besiege us one hour in a month.
ALENÇON
    They want their porridge and their fat bull-beeves.
    Either they must be dieted like mules

And have their provender tied to their mouths,
Or piteous they will look, like drownèd mice.

REIGNIER
Let's raise the siege. Why live we idly here?
Talbot is taken, whom we used to fear.
Remains now none but mad-brained Salisbury,
And he may well in fretting spend his gall;
Nor men nor money has he to make war.

CHARLES
Sound, sound alarum; we will rush on them.
Now for the honour of the forlorn French!
Him I forgive my death that should kill me
When he sees me go back one foot or fly.          *Exeunt*

*Alarum. Enter Charles, Alençon, and Reignier, defeated*

CHARLES
Who ever saw the like? What men have I!
Dogs! Cowards! Dastards! I would ne'er have fled
But that they left me amid my enemies.

REIGNIER
Salisbury is a desperate homicide;
He fights as if one weary of his life.
The other lords, like lions wanting food,
Do rush upon us as their hungry prey.

ALENÇON
Froissart, a countryman of ours, records
England all Olivers and Rolands bred
During the time Edward the Third did reign.
More truly now may this be verified;
For none but Samsons and Goliaths does
It send forth yet to skirmish. One to ten!
Lean raw-boned rascals! Who would e'er suppose
They had such courage and audacity?

CHARLES
Let's leave this town; for they are hare-brained slaves,

And hunger will enforce them to be more eager.
Of old I know them; rather with their teeth
The walls they'll tear down than forsake the siege.
REIGNIER
I think by some odd engines or device
Their arms are set like clocks, still to strike on;
Else never could they hold out as they do.
By my consent, we'll even let them alone.
ALENÇON
Be it so.

*Enter the Bastard of Orleans*

BASTARD
Where's the Prince Dauphin? I have news for him.
CHARLES
Bastard of Orleans, thrice welcome to us.
BASTARD
It seems your looks are sad, your cheer appalled.
Has the late overthrow wrought this offence?
Be not dismayed, for succour is at hand.
A holy maid hither with me I bring,
Which, by a vision sent to her from heaven,
Ordainèd is to raise this tedious siege
And drive the English forth the bounds of France.
The spirit of deep prophecy she has,
Exceeding the nine sibyls of old Rome:
What's past and what's to come she can descry.
Speak, shall I call her in? Believe my words,
For they are certain and infallible.
CHARLES
Go, call her in.                              *Exit Bastard*
                    But first, to try her skill,
Reignier, stand you as Dauphin in my place;
Question her proudly, let your looks be stern;
By this means shall we sound what skill she has.

*Enter Joan la Pucelle and the Bastard*

REIGNIER
  Fair maid, is it you will do these wondrous feats?
PUCELLE
  Reignier, is it you that think so to beguile me?
  Where is the Dauphin? Come, come from behind;
  I know you well, though never seen before.
  Be not amazed, there's nothing hidden from me.
  In private will I talk with you apart.
  Stand back, you lords, and give us leave awhile.
REIGNIER
  She takes upon her bravely at first dash.
PUCELLE
  Dauphin, I am by birth a shepherd's daughter,
  My wit untrained in any kind of art.
  Heaven and Our Lady gracious has it pleased
  To shine on my contemptible estate.
  Lo, while I waited on my tender lambs
  And to sun's parching heat displayed my cheeks,
  God's Mother deignèd to appear to me;
  And in a vision full of majesty
  Willed me to leave my base vocatiòn
  And free my country from calamity;
  Her aid she promised and assured success.
  In complete glory she revealed herself;
  And whereas I was black and swart before,
  With those clear rays which she infused on me
  That beauty am I blessed with which you may see.
  Ask me what question you can possible,
  And I will answer unpremeditated.
  My courage try by combat, if you dare,
  And you shall find that I exceed my sex.
  Resolve on this: you shall be fortunate
  If you receive me for your warlike mate.

CHARLES

You have astonished me with your high terms.
Only this proof I'll of your valour make:
In single combat you shall buckle with me,
And if you vanquish, then your words are true;
Otherwise I renounce all confidence.

PUCELLE

I am prepared; here is my keen-edged sword,
Decked with five flower-de-luces on each side,
Which at Touraine, in Saint Katherine's churchyard,
Out of a great deal of old iron I chose forth.

CHARLES

Then come, in God's name; I fear no woman.

PUCELLE

And while I live, I'll never fly from a man.

*They fight, and Joan la Pucelle overcomes*

CHARLES

Stay, stay your hands; you are an Amazon,
And fight indeed with the sword of Deborah.

PUCELLE

Christ's Mother helps me, else I were too weak.

CHARLES

Whoe'er helps you, 'tis you that must help me.
Impatiently I burn with your desire;
My heart and hands you have at once subdued.
Excellent Pucelle, if your name is so,
Let me your servant and not sovereign be;
It is the French Dauphin sues to you.

PUCELLE

I must not yield to any rites of love,
For my profession's sacred from above.
When I have chasèd all your foes from hence,
Then will I think upon a recompense.

CHARLES
Meantime look gracious on your prostrate thrall.

REIGNIER
My lord, I think, is very long in talk.

ALENÇON
Doubtless he shrives this woman to her smock;
Else ne'er could he so long protract his speech.

REIGNIER
Shall we disturb him, since he keeps no mean?

ALENÇON
He may mean more than we poor men do know;
These women are shrewd tempters with their tongues.

REIGNIER
My lord, where are you? What decide you on?
Shall we give over Orleans or no?

PUCELLE
Why, no, I say; distrustful miscreants,
Fight till the last gasp; I'll be your guard.

CHARLES
What she says, I'll confirm; we'll fight it out.

PUCELLE
Assigned am I to be the English scourge.
This night the siege assuredly I'll raise.
Expect Saint Martin's summer, halcyon days,
Since I have enterèd into these wars.
Glory is like a circle in the water
Which never ceases to enlarge itself
Till by broad spreading disperses it to naught.
With Henry's death the English circle ends;
Dispersèd are the glories it included.
Now am I like that proud insulting ship
Which Caesar and his fortune bore at once.

CHARLES
Was Mahomet inspirèd with a dove?
You with an eagle are inspirèd then.
Helen, the mother of great Constantine,

Nor yet Saint Philip's daughters were like you.
Bright star of Venus, fallen down on the earth,
How may I reverently worship you enough?

ALENÇON
Leave off delays, and let us raise the siege.

REIGNIER
Woman, do what you can to save our honours;
Drive them from Orleans and be immortalized.

CHARLES
Presently we'll try. Come, let's away about it.
No prophet will I trust if she proves false.          *Exeunt*


# SCENE III
## Before the Tower of London.

*Enter Gloucester, with his servingmen in blue coats*

GLOUCESTER
I am come to survey the Tower this day;
Since Henry's death, I fear dishonesty.
Where are these warders that they wait not here?
Open the gates! It is Gloucester that calls.

*Servingmen knock*

FIRST WARDER (*within*)
Who's there that knocks so imperiously?

FIRST SERVINGMAN
It is the noble Duke of Gloucester.

SECOND WARDER (*within*)
Whoever he is, you may not be let in.

FIRST SERVINGMAN
Villains, answer you so the Lord Protector?

FIRST WARDER (*within*)
The Lord protect him! So we answer him.
We do no otherwise than we are willed.

GLOUCESTER
  Who willèd you? Or whose will stands but mine?
  There's none Protector of the realm but I.
  Break up the gates; I'll be your warranty.
  Shall I be flouted thus by dunghill grooms?

*Gloucester's men rush at the Tower gates, and Woodville*
*the Lieutenant speaks within*

WOODVILLE (*within*)
  What noise is this? What traitors have we here?
GLOUCESTER
  Lieutenant, is it you whose voice I hear?
  Open the gates; here's Gloucester that would enter.
WOODVILLE (*within*)
  Have patience, noble Duke; I may not open;
  The Cardinal of Winchester forbids.
  From him I have express commandment
  That you nor any of yours shall be let in.
GLOUCESTER
  Faint-hearted Woodville, prize you him before me?
  Arrogant Winchester, that haughty prelate,
  Whom Henry, our late sovereign, ne'er could brook?
  You are no friend to God or to the King.
  Open the gates, or I'll shut you out shortly.
SERVINGMEN
  Open the gates unto the Lord Protector,
  Or we'll burst them open if you come not quickly.

*Enter Winchester and his men in tawny coats*

WINCHESTER
  How now, ambitious Humphrey, what means this?
GLOUCESTER
  Polled priest, do you command me to be shut out?

WINCHESTER

I do, you most usurping false betrayer,
And not Protector of the King or realm.

GLOUCESTER

Stand back, you manifest conspirator,
You that contrived to murder our dead lord;
You that give whores indulgences to sin.
I'll toss you in your broad cardinal's hat
If you proceed in this your insolence.

WINCHESTER

Nay, stand you back; I will not budge a foot.
This be Damascus; be you cursèd Cain,
To slay your brother Abel, if you will.

GLOUCESTER

I will not slay you, but I'll drive you back.
Your scarlet robes as a child's bearing-cloth
I'll use to carry you out of this place.

WINCHESTER

Do what you dare; I beard you to your face.

GLOUCESTER

What? Am I dared and bearded to my face?
Draw, men, for all this privilegèd place;
Blue coats to tawny coats! Priest, beware your beard;
I mean to tug it and to cuff you soundly.
Under my feet I stamp your cardinal's hat;
In spite of Pope or dignities of Church,
Here by the cheeks I'll drag you up and down.

WINCHESTER

Gloucester, you will answer this before the Pope.

GLOUCESTER

Winchester goose![1] I cry a rope, a rope!
Now beat them hence; why do you let them stay?

---

[1] A reference to venereal disease, for the brothels in Southwark were on the Bishops' property.

You I'll chase hence, you wolf in sheep's array.
Out, tawny coats! Out, scarlet hypocrite!

*Here Gloucester's men beat out the Cardinal's men. Enter*
*the Mayor of London, and his officers*

MAYOR
Fie, lords, that you, being supreme magistrates,
Thus contumeliously should break the peace!
GLOUCESTER
Peace, Mayor, you know little of my wrongs:
Here's Beaufort, that regards nor God nor King,
Has here distrained the Towèr to his use.
WINCHESTER
Here's Gloucester, a foe to citizens;
One that still motions war and never peace,
O'ercharging your free purses with large fines;
That seeks to overthrow religiòn,
Because he is Protector of the realm,
And would have armour here out of the Tower,
To crown himself king and suppress the Prince.
GLOUCESTER
I will not answer you with words, but blows.

*Here they skirmish again*

MAYOR
Naught rests for me in this tumultuous strife
But to make open proclamatiòn.
Come, officer, as loud as ever you can,
Cry.
OFFICER   All manner of men assembled here in arms this
day against God's peace and the King's, we charge and
command you, in his highness' name, to repair to your
several dwelling-places, and not to wear, handle, or use
any sword, weapon, or dagger henceforward, upon pain
of death.

GLOUCESTER
  Cardinal, I'll be no breaker of the law;
  But we shall meet and break our minds at large.
WINCHESTER
  Gloucester, we'll meet to your cost, be sure;
  Your heart-blood I will have for this day's work.
MAYOR
  I'll call for clubs if you will not away.
  This Cardinal's more haughty than the devil.
GLOUCESTER
  Mayor, farewell; you do but what you may.
WINCHESTER
  Abominable Gloucester, guard your head;
  For I intend to have it ere long.
  *Exeunt Gloucester and Winchester with their servingmen*
MAYOR
  See the coast cleared, and then we will depart.
  Good God, these nobles should such stomachs bear!
  I myself fight not once in forty year.      *Exeunt*

# SCENE IV
## Orleans.

*Enter the Master Gunner of Orleans and his Boy*

MASTER GUNNER
  Boy, you know how Orleans is besieged
  And how the English have the suburbs won.
BOY
  Father, I know; and oft have shot at them,
  However unfortunate I missed my aim.
MASTER GUNNER
  But now you shall not. Be you ruled by me.
  Chief master gunner am I of this town;
  Something I must do to procure me grace.

The Prince's spies have now informèd me
How the English, in the suburbs close intrenched,
Used through a secret grate of iron bars
In yonder tower to overpeer the city;
And thence discover how with most advantage
They may vex us with shot or with assault.
To intercept this inconvenience,
A piece of ordnance against it I have placed;
And even these three days have I watched
If I could see them. Now do you watch,
For I can stay no longer.
If you spy any, run and bring me word,
And you shall find me at the Governor's.              *Exit*
BOY
Father, I warrant you; take you no care;
I'll never trouble you if I may spy them.             *Exit*


*Enter Salisbury and Talbot on the turrets with Sir William*
*   Glansdale, Sir Thomas Gargrave, and soldiers*


SALISBURY
Talbot, my life, my joy, again returned?
How were you handled being prisoner?
Or by what means got you to be released?
Discourse, I pray you, on this turret's top.
TALBOT
The Duke of Bedford had a prisoner
Called the brave Lord Ponton de Santrailles;
For him was I exchanged and ransomèd.
But with a baser man-of-arms by far
Once, in contempt, they would have bartered me;
Which I, disdaining, scorned, and cravèd death
Rather than I would be so vile esteemed.
In fine, redeemed I was as I desired.
But, O, the treacherous Fastolf wounds my heart;
Whom with my bare fists I would execute,
If I now had him brought into my power.

SALISBURY
  Yet tell you not how you were entertained.
TALBOT
  With scoffs and scorns and contumelious taunts;
  In open market-place produced they me
  To be a public spectacle to all.
  'Here', said they, 'is the terror of the French,
  The scarecrow that affrights our children so.'
  Then broke I from the officers that led me,
  And with my nails digged stones out of the ground
  To hurl at the beholders of my shame.
  My grisly countenance made others fly;
  None durst come near for fear of sudden death.
  In iron walls they deemed me not secure;
  So great fear of my name among them spread
  That they supposed I could rend bars of steel
  And break in pieces posts of adamant.
  Wherefore a guard of chosen shot I had
  That walked about me every minute while;
  And if I did but stir out of my bed,
  Ready they were to shoot me to the heart.

*Enter the Boy with a linstock*

SALISBURY
  I grieve to hear what torments you endured;
  But we will be revenged sufficiently.
  Now it is supper-time in Orleans;
  Here, through this grate, I count each one
  And view the Frenchmen how they fortify.
  Let us look in; the sight will much delight you.
  Sir Thomas Gargrave and Sir William Glansdale,
  Let me have your express opinions
  Where is best place to make our battery next.

GARGRAVE
    I think at the north gate; for there stand lords.
GLANSDALE
    And I here, at the bulwark of the bridge.
TALBOT
    For aught I see, this city must be famished
    Or with light skirmishes enfeeblèd.

*They shoot. Salisbury and Gargrave fall down*

SALISBURY
    O Lord, have mercy on us, wretched sinners!
GARGRAVE
    O Lord, have mercy on me, woeful man!
TALBOT
    What chance is this that suddenly has crossed us?
    Speak, Salisbury; at least, if you can, speak.
    How fare you, mirror of all martial men?
    One of your eyes and your cheek's side struck off?
    Accursèd tower! Accursèd fatal hand
    That has contrived this woeful tragedy!
    In thirteen battles Salisbury overcame;
    Henry the Fifth he first trained to the wars.
    While any trump did sound or drum struck up,
    His sword never left striking in the field.
    Yet live you, Salisbury? Though your speech does fail,
    One eye you have to look to heaven for grace;
    The sun with one eye yet views all the world.
    Heaven, be you gracious to none alive
    If Salisbury wants mercy at your hands!
    Sir Thomas Gargrave, have you any life?
    Speak unto Talbot. Nay, look up to him.
    Bear hence his body; I will help to bury it.
                *Exeunt attendants with Gargrave's body*
    Salisbury, cheer your spirit with this comfort,
    You shall not die until—

He beckons with his hand and smiles on me,
As who should say 'When I am dead and gone,
Remember to avenge me on the French.'
Plantagenet, I will; and like you, Nero,
Play on the lute, beholding the towns burn.
Wretched shall France be only in my name.

*Alarum, thunder and lightning*

What stir is this? What tumult's in the heavens?
Whence comes this alarum and the noise?

*Enter a Messenger*

MESSENGER
My lord, my lord, the French have gathered head.
The Dauphin, with one Joan la Pucelle joined,
A holy prophetess new risen up,
Is come with a great power to raise the siege.

*Salisbury lifts himself up and groans*

TALBOT
Hear, hear how dying Salisbury does groan.
It irks his heart he cannot be revenged.
Frenchmen, I'll be a Salisbury to you.
Pucelle or pussel (trollop), Dolphin or dogfish,
Your hearts I'll stamp out with my horse's heels
And make a quagmire of your mingled brains.
Convey me Salisbury into his tent,
And then we'll try what these dastard Frenchmen dare.
                    *Alarum. Exeunt with Salisbury's body*

# SCENE V
## The same.

*Alarum. Talbot pursues Charles the Dauphin. Then enter Joan la Pucelle, driving Englishmen before her, and exeunt. Enter Talbot*

TALBOT
  Where are my strength, my valour, and my force?
  Our English troops retire, I cannot stay them;
  A woman clad in armour chases them.

*Enter Joan la Pucelle*

  Here, here she comes. *(To Pucelle)* I'll have a bout with
    you.
  Devil or devil's dam, I'll conjure you.
  Blood will I draw on you—you are a witch—
  And straightway give your soul to him you serve.
PUCELLE
  Come, come, 'tis only I that must disgrace you.

*They fight*

TALBOT
  Heavens, can you suffer hell so to prevail?
  My breast I'll burst with straining of my courage,
  And from my shoulders crack my arms asunder,
  But I will chastise this high-minded strumpet.

*They fight again*

PUCELLE
  Talbot, farewell; your hour is not yet come.
  I must go victual Orleans forthwith.

*A short alarum. Then she enters the town with soldiers*

> Overtake me if you can; I scorn your strength.
> Go, go, cheer up your hungry-starvèd men;
> Help Salisbury to make his testament.
> This day is ours, as many more shall be.                    *Exit*

TALBOT
> My thoughts are whirlèd like a potter's wheel;
> I know not where I am nor what I do.
> A witch by fear, not force, like Hannibal,
> Drives back our troops and conquers as she lists.
> So bees with smoke and doves with noisome stench
> Are from their hives and houses driven away.
> They called us, for our fierceness, English dogs;
> Now, like to whelps, we crying run away.

*A short alarum*

> Hark, countrymen! Either renew the fight
> Or tear the lions out of England's coat;
> Renounce your soil, give sheep in lions' stead.
> Sheep run not half so treacherous from the wolf,
> Or horse or oxen from the leopard,
> As you fly from your oft-subduèd slaves.

*Alarum. Another skirmish*

> It will not be. Retire into your trenches.
> You all consented unto Salisbury's death,
> For none would strike a stroke in his revenge.
> Pucelle is entered into Orleans
> In spite of us or aught that we could do.
> O, would I were to die with Salisbury!
> The shame hereof will make me hide my head.
>                        *Exit Talbot. Alarum. Retreat*

# SCENE VI
## The same.

*Flourish. Enter, on the walls, Joan la Pucelle, Charles,*
*Reignier, Alençon, and soldiers*

PUCELLE
　Advance our waving colours on the walls;
　Rescued is Orleans from the English.
　Thus Joan la Pucelle has performed her word.

CHARLES
　Divinest creature, Astraea's daughter,
　How shall I honour you for this success?
　Your promises are like Adonis' garden,
　That one day bloomed and fruitful was the next.
　France, triumph in your glorious prophetess!
　Recovered is the town of Orleans.
　More blessèd hap did never befall our state.

REIGNIER
　Why ring not out the bells throughout the town?
　Dauphin, command the citizens make bonfires
　And feast and banquet in the open streets
　To celebrate the joy that God has given us.

ALENÇON
　All France will be replete with mirth and joy
　When they shall hear how we have played the men.

CHARLES
　'Tis Joan, not we, by whom the day is won;
　For which I will divide my crown with her,
　And all the priests and friars in my realm
　Shall in procession sing her endless praise.
　A statelier pyramid to her I'll rear
　Than Rhodope's of Memphis ever was.
　In memory of her, when she is dead,
　Her ashes, in an urn more precioùs
　Than the rich-jewelled coffer of Darius,

Transported shall be at high festivals
Before the kings and queens of France.
No longer on Saint Denis will we cry,
But Joan la Pucelle shall be France's saint.
Come in, and let us banquet royally
After this golden day of victory.          *Flourish. Exeunt*

# Act II

## SCENE I
## Orleans.

*Enter a French Sergeant, with two Sentinels*

SERGEANT
  Sirs, take your places and be vigilant.
  If any noise or soldier you perceive
  Near to the walls, by some apparent sign
  Let us have knowledge at the court of guard.
SENTINEL
  Sergeant, you shall.                     *Exit Sergeant*
              Thus are poor servitors,
  When others sleep upon their quiet beds,
  Constrained to watch in darkness, rain, and cold.

*Enter Talbot, Bedford, Burgundy, and soldiers, with
                  scaling-ladders*

TALBOT
  Lord Regent, and redoubted Burgundy,
  By whose approach the regions of Artois,
  Walloon, and Picardy are friends to us,
  This happy night the Frenchmen are secure,
  Having all day caroused and banqueted;
  Embrace we then this opportunity,
  As fitting best to quittance their deceit,
  Contrived by art and baleful sorcery.
BEDFORD
  Coward of France! How much he wrongs his fame,

Despairing of his own arm's fortitude,
To join with witches and the help of hell!

BURGUNDY

Traitors have never other company.
But what's that Pucelle whom they term so pure?

TALBOT

A maid, they say.

BEDFORD                 A maid? And be so martial?

BURGUNDY

Pray God she prove not masculine ere long,
If underneath the standard of the French
She carries armour as she has begun.

TALBOT

Well, let them practise and converse with spirits.
God is our fortress, in whose conquering name
Let us resolve to scale their flinty bulwarks.

BEDFORD

Ascend, brave Talbot; we will follow you.

TALBOT

Not all together; better far, I guess,
That we do make our entrance several ways;
That, if it chances one of us does fail,
The other yet may rise against their force.

BEDFORD

Agreed; I'll to yon corner.

BURGUNDY                    And I to this.

TALBOT

And here will Talbot mount, or make his grave.
Now, Salisbury, for you, and for the right
Of English Henry, shall this night appear
How much in duty I am bound to both.

FIRST SENTINEL

Arm, arm! The enemy does make assault!

*The English scale the walls, cry 'Saint George! A Talbot!',*
                                        *and exeunt*

*The French leap over the walls. Enter the Bastard, Alençon,*
*Reignier, half dressed*

ALENÇON
  How now, my lords? What, all unready so?
BASTARD
  Unready? Ay, and glad we escaped so well.
REIGNIER
  'Twas time, I think, to wake and leave our beds,
  Hearing alarums at our chamber doors.
ALENÇON
  Of all exploits since first I followed arms
  Ne'er heard I of a warlike enterprise
  More venturous or desperate than this.
BASTARD
  I think this Talbot is a fiend of hell.
REIGNIER
  If not of hell, the heavens sure favour him.
ALENÇON
  Here comes now Charles. I wonder how he sped.

*Enter Charles and Joan la Pucelle*

BASTARD
  Tut, holy Joan was his defensive guard.
CHARLES
  Is this your cunning, you deceitful dame?
  Did you at first, to flatter us with it,
  Make us partakers of a little gain
  That now our loss might be ten times so much?
PUCELLE
  Wherefore is Charles impatient with his friend?
  At all times will you have my power alike?
  Sleeping or waking must I ever prevail,
  Or will you blame and lay the fault on me?
  Improvident soldiers! Had your watch been good,
  This sudden mischief never could have fallen.

CHARLES
  Duke of Alençon, this was your default
  That, being captain of the watch tonight,
  Did look no better to that weighty charge.
ALENÇON
  Had all your quarters been as safely kept
  As that whereof I had the government,
  We had not been thus shamefully surprised.
BASTARD
  Mine was secure.
REIGNIER                  And so was mine, my lord.
CHARLES
  And for myself, most part of all this night
  Within her quarter and my own precinct
  I was employed in passing to and fro
  About relieving of the sentinels.
  Then how or which way should they first break in?
PUCELLE
  Question, my lords, no further of the case,
  How or which way; 'tis sure they found some place
  But weakly guarded, where the breach was made.
  And now there rests no other shift but this:
  To gather our soldiers, scattered and dispersed,
  And lay new platforms to endamage them.

  *Alarum. Enter an English Soldier, crying* 'A Talbot! A
  Talbot!' *They fly, leaving their clothes behind*

SOLDIER
  I'll be so bold to take what they have left.
  The cry of 'Talbot' serves me for a sword;
  For I have loaded me with many spoils,
  Using no other weapon but his name.          *Exit*

## SCENE II
### Orleans. In the town.

*Enter Talbot, Bedford, Burgundy, a Captain, and soldiers*

BEDFORD
   The day begins to break and night is fled,
   Whose pitchy mantle overveiled the earth.
   Here sound retreat and cease our hot pursuit.

*Retreat sounded*

TALBOT
   Bring forth the body of old Salisbury
   And here advance it in the market-place,
   The middle centre of this cursèd town.

*Enter a funeral procession with Salisbury's body*

   Now have I paid my vow unto his soul;
   For every drop of blood was drawn from him
   There have at least five Frenchmen died tonight.
   And that hereafter ages may behold
   What ruin happened in revenge of him,
   Within their chiefest temple I'll erect
   A tomb, wherein his corpse shall be interred.
   Upon which, so that everyone may read,
   Shall be engraved the sack of Orleans,
   The treacherous manner of his mournful death,
   And what a terror he had been to France.
   But, lords, in all our bloody massacre,
   I muse we met not with the Dauphin's grace,
   His new-come champion, virtuous Joan of Arc,
   Nor any of his false confederates.
BEDFORD
   It is thought, Lord Talbot, when the fight began,

Roused on the sudden from their drowsy beds,
They did among the troops of armèd men
Leap over the walls for refuge in the field.

BURGUNDY
Myself, as far as I could well discern
For smoke and dusky vapours of the night,
Am sure I scared the Dauphin and his trull,
When arm in arm they both came swiftly running,
Just like a pair of loving turtle-doves
That could not live asunder day or night.
After things are set in order here,
We'll follow them with all the force we have.

*Enter a Messenger*

MESSENGER
All hail, my lords! Which of this princely train
Call you the warlike Talbot, for his acts
So much applauded through the realm of France?

TALBOT
Here is the Talbot; who would speak with him?

MESSENGER
The virtuous lady, Countess of Auvergne,
With modesty admiring your renown,
By me entreats, great lord, you would vouchsafe
To visit her poor castle where she lies,
That she may boast she has beheld the man
Whose glory fills the world with loud report.

BURGUNDY
Is it even so? Nay, then I see our wars
Will turn unto a peaceful comic sport,
When ladies crave to be encountered with.
You may not, my lord, despise her gentle suit.

TALBOT
Never trust me then; for when a world of men
Could not prevail with all their oratory,

Yet has a woman's kindness overruled;
And therefore tell her I return great thanks
And in submission will attend on her.
Will not your honours bear me company?

BEDFORD

No, truly, it is more than manners will;
And I have heard it said unbidden guests
Are often welcomest when they are gone.

TALBOT

Well, then, alone, since there's no remedy,
I mean to prove this lady's courtesy.
Come hither, captain. (*He whispers*) You perceive my
    mind?

CAPTAIN

I do, my lord, and mean accordingly.

*Exeunt*

# SCENE III
## The castle of Auvergne.

*Enter the Countess of Auvergne and her Porter*

COUNTESS

Porter, remember what I gave in charge,
And when you have done so, bring the keys to me.

PORTER

Madam, I will.                                    *Exit*

COUNTESS

The plot is laid; if all things fall out right,
I shall as famous be by this exploit
As Scythian Tomyris by Cyrus' death.
Great is the rumour of this dreadful knight,
And his achievements of no less account.
Fain would my eyes be witness with my ears,
To give their judgement of these rare reports.

*Enter the Messenger and Talbot*

MESSENGER
   Madam, according as your ladyship desired,
   By message craved, so is Lord Talbot come.
COUNTESS
   And he is welcome. What? Is this the man?
MESSENGER
   Madam, it is.
COUNTESS   Is this the scourge of France?
   Is this the Talbot so much feared abroad
   That with his name the mothers still their babes?
   I see report is fabulous and false.
   I thought I should have seen some Hercules,
   A second Hector, for his grim aspèct
   And large proportion of his strong-knit limbs.
   Alas, this is a child, a silly dwarf!
   It cannot be this weak and wrinkled shrimp
   Should strike such terror to his enemies.
TALBOT
   Madam, I have been bold to trouble you;
   But since your ladyship is not at leisure,
   I'll sort some other time to visit you.

                                              *Going*
COUNTESS
   What means he now? Go ask him whither he goes.
MESSENGER
   Stay, my Lord Talbot; for my lady craves
   To know the cause of your abrupt departure.
TALBOT
   Indeed, because she's in a wrong belief,
   I go to certify her Talbot's here.

*Enter the Porter with keys*

COUNTESS
  If you are he, then are you prisoner.
TALBOT
  Prisoner? To whom?
COUNTESS                  To me, blood-thirsty lord;
  And for that cause I lured you to my house.
  Long time your shadow has been thrall to me,
  For in my gallery your picture hangs.
  But now the substance shall endure the like,
  And I will chain these legs and arms of yours
  That have by tyranny these many years
  Wasted our country, slain our citizens,
  And sent our sons and husbands captivate.
TALBOT
  Ha, ha, ha!
COUNTESS
  Laugh you, wretch? Your mirth shall turn to moan.
TALBOT
  I laugh to see your ladyship so foolish
  To think that you have aught but Talbot's shadow
  Whereon to practise your severity.
COUNTESS
  Why, are you not the man?
TALBOT                  I am indeed.
COUNTESS
  Then have I substance too.
TALBOT
  No, no, I am but shadow of myself.
  You are deceived. My substance is not here;
  For what you see is but the smallest part
  And least proportion of humanity.
  I tell you, madam, were the whole frame here,
  It is of such a spacious lofty pitch
  Your roof were not sufficient to contain it.
COUNTESS
  This is a riddling merchant then for once;

He will be here, and yet he is not here.
How can these contrarieties agree?
TALBOT
That will I show you presently.

*He winds his horn. Drums strike up. A peal of ordnance.*
*Enter soldiers*

How say you, madam? Are you now persuaded
That Talbot is but shadow of himself?
These are his substance, sinews, arms, and strength,
With which he yokes at your rebellious necks,
Razes your cities, and subverts your towns
And in a moment makes them desolate.
COUNTESS
Victorious Talbot, pardon my abuse.
I find you are no less than fame has bruited,
And more than may be gathered by your shape.
Let my presumption not provoke your wrath,
For I am sorry that with reverence
I did not entertain you as you are.
TALBOT
Be not dismayed, fair lady, nor misconstrue
The mind of Talbot as you did mistake
The outward composition of his body.
What you have done has not offended me;
Nor other satisfaction do I crave
But only, with your patience, that we may
Taste of your wine and see what eats you have;
For soldiers' stomachs always serve them well.
COUNTESS
With all my heart, and think me honourèd
To feast so great a warrior in my house.          *Exeunt*

# SCENE IV
## The Temple Garden.

*Enter Richard Plantagenet, Warwick, Somerset, Suffolk,*
*Vernon, and a Lawyer*

RICHARD

Great lords and gentlemen, what means this silence?
Dare no man answer in a case of truth?

SUFFOLK

Within the Temple Hall we were too loud;
The garden here is more convenient.

RICHARD

Then say at once if I maintained the truth;
Or else was wrangling Somerset in the error?

SUFFOLK

Faith, I have been a truant in the law
And never yet could frame my will to it;
And therefore frame the law unto my will.

SOMERSET

Judge you, my lord of Warwick, then between us.

WARWICK

Between two hawks, which flies the higher pitch;
Between two dogs, which has the deeper mouth;
Between two blades, which bears the better temper;
Between two horses, which does bear him best;
Between two girls, which has the merriest eye,
I have perhaps some shallow spirit of judgement;
But in these nice sharp quibbles of the law,
Good faith, I am no wiser than a daw.

RICHARD

Tut, tut, here is a mannerly forbearance.
The truth appears so naked on my side
That any purblind eye may find it out.

SOMERSET

And on my side it is so well apparelled,

So clear, so shining, and so evident,
That it will glimmer through a blind man's eye.
RICHARD
Since you are tongue-tied and so loth to speak,
In dumb significants proclaim your thoughts.
Let him that is a true-born gentleman
And stands upon the honour of his birth,
If he supposes that I have pleaded truth,
From off this briar pluck a white rose with me.
SOMERSET
Let him that is no coward and no flatterer,
But dare maintain the party of the truth,
Pluck a red rose from off this thorn with me.
WARWICK
I love no colours; and, without all colour
Of base insinuating flattery,
I pluck this white rose with Plantagenet.
SUFFOLK
I pluck this red rose with young Somerset,
And say with that I think he held the right.
VERNON
Stay, lords and gentlemen, and pluck no more
Till you conclude that he upon whose side
The fewest roses are cropped from the tree
Shall yield the other in the right opinion.
SOMERSET
Good Master Vernon, it is well objected;
If I have fewest, I subscribe in silence.
RICHARD
And I.
VERNON
Then, for the truth and plainness of the case,
I pluck this pale and maiden blossom here,
Giving my verdict on the white rose side.
SOMERSET
Prick not your finger as you pluck it off,

Lest, bleeding, you do paint the white rose red,
And fall on my side so against your will.

VERNON

If I, my lord, for my opinion bleed,
Opinion shall be surgeon to my hurt
And keep me on the side where ever I am.

SOMERSET

Well, well, come on; who else?

LAWYER *(to Somerset)*

Unless my study and my books are false,
The argument you held was wrong in you;
In sign whereof I pluck a white rose too.

RICHARD

Now, Somerset, where is your argument?

SOMERSET

Here in my scabbard, meditating that
Shall dye your white rose in a bloody red.

RICHARD

Meantime your cheeks do counterfeit our roses;
For pale they look with fear, as witnessing
The truth on our side.

SOMERSET                    No, Plantagenet,
'Tis not for fear, but anger, that your cheeks
Blush for pure shame to counterfeit our roses,
And yet your tongue will not confess your error.

RICHARD

Has not your rose a canker, Somerset?

SOMERSET

Has not your rose a thorn, Plantagenet?

RICHARD

Ay, sharp and piercing, to maintain its truth,
While your consuming canker eats its falsehood.

SOMERSET

Well, I'll find friends to wear my bleeding roses,
That shall maintain what I have said is true
Where false Plantagenet dares not be seen.

RICHARD
  Now, by this maiden blossom in my hand,
  I scorn you and your fashion, peevish boy.
SUFFOLK
  Turn not your scorns this way, Plantagenet.
RICHARD
  Proud Pole, I will, and scorn both him and you.
SUFFOLK
  I'll turn my part thereof into your throat.
SOMERSET
  Away, away, good William de la Pole!
  We grace the yeoman by conversing with him.
WARWICK
  Now, by God's will, you wrong him, Somerset;
  His grandfather was Lionel Duke of Clarence,
  Third son to the third Edward, King of England.
  Spring crestless yeomen from so deep a root?
RICHARD
  He bears him on the place's privilege,
  Or durst not for his craven heart say thus.
SOMERSET
  By Him that made me, I'll maintain my words
  On any plot of ground in Christendom.
  Was not your father, Richard Earl of Cambridge,
  For treason executed in our late king's days?
  And by his treason stand not you attainted,
  Corrupted, and exempt from ancient gentry?
  His trespass yet lives guilty in your blood,
  And till you are restored you are a yeoman.
RICHARD
  My father was attachèd, not attainted,
  Condemned to die for treason, but no traitor;
  And that I'll prove on better men than Somerset,
  Were growing time once ripened to my will.
  For your partaker Pole, and you yourself,
  I'll note you in my book of memory

To scourge you for this apprehensiòn.
Look to it well and say you are well warned.

SOMERSET

Ah, you shall find us ready for you still;
And know us by these colours for your foes,
For these my friends in spite of you shall wear.

RICHARD

And, by my soul, this pale and angry rose,
As cognizance of my blood-drinking hate,
Will I for ever, and my faction, wear
Until it withers with me to my grave,
Or flourish to the height of my degree.

SUFFOLK

Go forward, and be choked with your ambition!
And so farewell until I meet you next.                    *Exit*

SOMERSET

Have with you, Pole. Farewell, ambitious Richard. *Exit*

RICHARD

How I am braved and must perforce endure it!

WARWICK

This blot that they object against your house
Shall be wiped out in the next parliament,
Called for the truce of Winchester and Gloucester;
And if you are not then created York,
I will not live to be accounted Warwick.
Meantime, in signal of my love to you,
Against proud Somerset and William Pole,
Will I upon your party wear this rose.
And here I prophesy: this brawl today,
Grown to this faction in the Temple garden,
Shall send between the red rose and the white
A thousand souls to death and deadly night.

RICHARD

Good Master Vernon, I am bound to you
That you on my behalf would pluck a flower.

VERNON
In your behalf ever will I wear the same.
LAWYER
And so will I.
RICHARD
Thanks, gentle sir.
Come, let us four to dinner. I dare say
This quarrel will drink blood another day.      *Exeunt*

# SCENE V
## The Tower of London.

*Enter Mortimer, brought in a chair, and Gaolers*

MORTIMER
Kind keepers of my weak decaying age,
Let dying Mortimer here rest himself.
Even like a man new halèd from the rack,
So fare my limbs with long imprisonment;
And these grey locks, the followers of Death,
Nestor-like agèd in an age of care,
Argue the end of Edmund Mortimer.
These eyes, like lamps whose wasting oil is spent,
Wax dim, as drawing to their exigent;
Weak shoulders, overborne with burdening grief,
And pithless arms, like a withered vine
That droops its sapless branches to the ground.
Yet are these feet, whose strengthless stay is numb,
Unable to support this lump of clay,
Swift-wingèd with desire to get a grave,
As knowing I no other comfort have.
But tell me, keeper, will my nephew come?
GAOLER
Richard Plantagenet, my lord, will come.
We sent unto the Temple, unto his chamber;
And answer was returned that he will come.

MORTIMER
    Enough; my soul shall then be satisfied.
    Poor gentleman, his wrong does equal mine.
    Since Henry Monmouth first began to reign,
    Before whose glory I was great in arms,
    This loathsome sequestration have I had;
    And even since then has Richard been obscured,
    Deprived of honour and inheritance.
    But now the arbitrator of despairs,
    Just Death, kind umpire of men's miseries,
    With sweet enlargement does dismiss me hence.
    I would his troubles likewise were expired,
    That so he might recover what was lost.

*Enter Richard Plantagenet*

GAOLER
    My lord, your loving nephew now is come.
MORTIMER
    Richard Plantagenet, my friend, is he come?
RICHARD
    Ay, noble uncle, thus ignobly used,
    Your nephew, late despisèd Richard, comes.
MORTIMER
    Direct my arms I may embrace his neck
    And in his bosom spend my latter gasp.
    O, tell me when my lips do touch his cheeks,
    That I may kindly give one fainting kiss.
    And now declare, sweet stem from York's great stock,
    Why did you say of late you were despised?
RICHARD
    First, lean your agèd back against my arm,
    And in that ease I'll tell you my disease.
    This day an argument upon a case
    Some words there grew between Somerset and me;

Among which terms he used his lavish tongue
And did upbraid me with my father's death;
Which obloquy set bars before my tongue,
Else with the like I had requited him.
Therefore, good uncle, for my father's sake,
In honour of a true Plantagenet,
And for alliance' sake, declare the cause
My father, Earl of Cambridge, lost his head.

MORTIMER
That cause, fair nephew, that imprisoned me
And has detained me all my flowering youth
Within a loathsome dungeon, there to pine,
Was cursèd instrument of his decease.

RICHARD
Discover more at large what cause that was,
For I am ignorant and cannot guess.

MORTIMER
I will, if now my fading breath permits
And death approaches not ere my tale is done.
Henry the Fourth, grandfather to this king,
Deposed his nephew Richard, Edward's son,
The first-begotten and the lawful heir
Of Edward king, the third of that descent.
During whose reign the Percys of the north,
Finding his usurpation most unjust,
Endeavoured my advancement to the throne.
The reason moved these warlike lords to this
Was because—young Richard thus removed,
Leaving no heir begotten of his body—
I was the next by birth and parentage.
For by my mother I derivèd am
From Lionel Duke of Clarence, third son
To King Edward the Third; whereas he
From John of Gaunt does bring his pedigree,
Being but fourth of that heroic line.
But mark: as in this haughty great attempt

They labourèd to plant the rightful heir,
I lost my liberty, and they their lives.
Long after this, when Henry the Fifth,
Succeeding his father Bolingbroke, did reign.
Your father, Earl of Cambridge then, derived
From famous Edmund Langley, Duke of York,
Marrying my sister that your mother was,
Again, in pity of my hard distress,
Levied an army, thinking to redeem
And have installed me in the diadem.
But, as the rest, so fell that noble earl,
And was beheaded. Thus the Mortimers,
In whom the title rested, were suppressed.

RICHARD

Of which, my lord, your honour is the last.

MORTIMER

True, and you see that I no issue have,
And that my fainting words do warrant death.
You are my heir. The rest I wish you gather;
But yet be wary in your studious care.

RICHARD

Your grave admonishments prevail with me.
But yet I think my father's execution
Was nothing less than bloody tyranny.

MORTIMER

With silence, nephew, be you politic.
Strong fixèd is the house of Lancaster
And like a mountain, not to be removed.
But now your uncle is removing hence,
As princes do their Courts when they are cloyed
With long continuance in a settled place.

RICHARD

O uncle, would some part of my young years
Might but redeem the passage of your age!

MORTIMER

You do then wrong me, as that slaughterer does

Which gives so many wounds when one will kill.
Mourn not, unless you sorrow for my good;
Only give order for my funeral.
And so farewell, and fair be all your hopes,
And prosperous be your life in peace and war!   *He dies*
RICHARD
And peace, no war, befall your parting soul!
In prison have you spent a pilgrimage,
And like a hermit overpassed your days.
Well, I will lock his counsel in my breast;
And what I do imagine, let that rest.
Keepers, convey him hence, and I myself
Will see his burial better than his life.
                    *Exeunt Gaolers, with Mortimer's body*
Here dies the dusky torch of Mortimer,
Choked with ambition by the meaner sort.
And for those wrongs, those bitter injuries,
Which Somerset has offered to my house,
I doubt not but with honour to redress;
And therefore haste I to the parliament,
Either to be restorèd to my blood
Or make my ill the advantage of my good.          *Exit*

# Act III

## SCENE I
### Westminster. The Parliament House.

*Flourish. Enter the King, Exeter, Gloucester, Winchester,
Warwick, Somerset, Suffolk, Richard, and others.
Gloucester offers to put up a bill. Winchester
snatches it, tears it*

WINCHESTER
  Come you with deep premeditated lines?
  With written pamphlets studiously devised?
  Humphrey of Gloucester, if you can accuse
  Or aught intend to lay unto my charge,
  Do it without invention, suddenly;
  As I with sudden and extemporal speech
  Purpose to answer what you can object.
GLOUCESTER
  Presumptuous priest, this place commands my patience,
  Or you should find you have dishonoured me.
  Think not, although in writing I preferred
  The manner of your vile outrageous crimes,
  That therefore I have forged, or am not able
  Verbatim to rehearse the method of my pen.
  No, prelate; such is your audacious wickedness,
  Your lewd, pestiferous, and dissentious pranks,
  As very infants prattle of your pride.
  You are a most pernicious usurer;
  Froward by nature, enemy to peace,
  Lascivious, wanton, more than well beseems
  A man of your profession and degree.

And for your treachery, what is more manifest,
In that you laid a trap to take my life,
As well at London Bridge as at the Tower?
Besides, I fear me, if your thoughts were sifted,
The King, your sovereign, is not quite exempt
From envious malice of your swelling heart.

WINCHESTER
Gloucester, I do defy you. Lords, deign now
To give me hearing what I shall reply.
If I were covetous, ambitious, or perverse,
As he will have me, how am I so poor?
Or how haps it I seek not to advance
Or raise myself, but keep my wonted calling?
And for dissension, who prefers yet peace
More than I do, unless I am provoked?
No, my good lords, it is not that offends;
It is not that that has incensed the Duke:
It is because no one should sway but he,
No one but he should be about the King;
And that engenders thunder in his breast
And makes him roar these accusations forth.
But he shall know I am as good—

GLOUCESTER                                          As good?
You bastard of my grandfather!

WINCHESTER
Ay, lordly sir; for what are you, I pray,
But one imperious in another's throne?

GLOUCESTER
Am I not Protector, saucy priest?

WINCHESTER
And am not I a prelate of the Church?

GLOUCESTER
Yes, as an outlaw in a castle keeps,
And uses it to patronage his theft.

WINCHESTER
Unreverent Gloucester!

GLOUCESTER                  You are reverend
  Touching your spiritual function, not your life.
WINCHESTER
  Rome shall remedy this.
WARWICK                         Roam thither then.
  My lord, it were your duty to forbear.
SOMERSET
  Ay, so the Bishop is not overborne.
  I think my lord should be religious,
  And know the office that belongs to such.
WARWICK
  I think his lordship should be humbler;
  It befits not a prelate so to plead.
SOMERSET
  Yes, when his holy state is touched so near.
WARWICK
  State holy or unhallowed, what of that?
  Is not his grace Protector to the King?
RICHARD  (aside)
  Plantagenet, I see, must hold his tongue,
  Lest it be said 'Speak, fellow, when you should;
  Must your bold verdict enter talk with lords?'
  Else would I have a fling at Winchester.
KING
  Uncles of Gloucester and of Winchester,
  The special watchmen of our English weal,
  I would prevail, if prayèrs might prevail,
  To join your hearts in love and amity.
  O, what a scandal is it to our crown
  That two such noble peers as you should jar!
  Believe me, lords, my tender years can tell
  Civil dissension is a viperous worm
  That gnaws the bowels of the commonwealth.

      A noise within: 'Down with the tawny coats!'

What tumult is this?
WARWICK                    An uproar, I dare warrant,
  Begun through malice of the Bishop's men.

*A noise again: 'Stones! Stones!' Enter the Mayor*

MAYOR
  O my good lords, and virtuous Henry,
  Pity the city of London, pity us!
  The Bishop and the Duke of Gloucester's men,
  Forbidden late to carry any weapon,
  Have filled their pockets full of pebble stones
  And, banding themselves in contrary parts,
  Do pelt so fast at one another's pate
  That many have their giddy brains knocked out.
  Our windows are broken down in every street
  And we, for fear, compelled to shut our shops.

*Enter Servingmen of Gloucester and*
*Winchester in skirmish*

KING
  We charge you, on allegiance to ourself,
  To hold your slaughtering hands and keep the peace.
  Pray, uncle Gloucester, mitigate this strife.
FIRST SERVINGMAN   Nay, if we are forbidden stones, we'll
  fall to it with our teeth.
SECOND SERVINGMAN
  Do what you dare, we are as resolute.

*Skirmish again*

GLOUCESTER
  You of my household, leave this peevish broil
  And set this unaccustomed fight aside.

THIRD SERVINGMAN
    My lord, we know your grace to be a man
    Just and upright, and for your royal birth
    Inferior to none but to his majesty;
    And before we will suffer such a prince,
    So kind a father of the commonweal,
    To be disgracèd by an inkhorn mate,
    We and our wives and children all will fight
    And have our bodies slaughtered by your foes.
FIRST SERVINGMAN    Ay, and the very parings of our nails
    shall pitch a field when we are dead.

*They begin to skirmish again*

GLOUCESTER
    Stay, stay, I say!
    And if you love me, as you say you do,
    Let me persuade you to forbear awhile.
KING
    O, how this discord does afflict my soul!
    Can you, my lord of Winchester, behold
    My sighs and tears and will not once relent?
    Who should be pitiful if you are not?
    Or who should study to prefer a peace
    If holy churchmen take delight in broils?
WARWICK
    Yield, my Lord Protector, yield, Winchester,
    Unless you mean with obstinate repulse
    To slay your sovereign and destroy the realm.
    You see what mischief, and what murder too,
    Have been enacted through your enmity.
    Then be at peace, unless you thirst for blood.
WINCHESTER
    He shall submit, or I will never yield.
GLOUCESTER
    Compassion on the King commands me stoop,

Or I would see his heart out ere the priest
Should ever get that privilege of me.

WARWICK

Behold, my lord of Winchester, the Duke
Has banished moody discontented fury,
As by his smoothèd brows it does appear;
Why look you still so stern and tragical?

GLOUCESTER

Here, Winchester, I offer you my hand.

KING

Fie, uncle Beaufort, I have heard you preach
That malice was a great and grievous sin;
And will not you maintain the thing you teach,
But prove a chief offender in the same?

WARWICK

Sweet King! The Bishop has a kindly rebuke.
For shame, my lord of Winchester, relent;
What, shall a child instruct you what to do?

WINCHESTER

Well, Duke of Gloucester, I will yield to you.
Love for your love and hand for hand I give.

GLOUCESTER (aside)

Ay, but, I fear me, with a hollow heart.
(To them) See here, my friends and loving countrymen:
This token serves us for a flag of truce
Between ourselves and all our followers.
So help me God, as I dissemble not.

WINCHESTER

So help me God—(aside) as I intend it not.

KING

O loving uncle, kind Duke of Gloucester,
How joyful am I made by this contràct!
Away, my masters! Trouble us no more,
But join in friendship, as your lords have done.

FIRST SERVINGMAN    Content; I'll to the surgeon's.
SECOND SERVINGMAN    And so will I.
THIRD SERVINGMAN    And I will see what physic the
    tavern affords.                    *Exeunt Servingmen and Mayor*
WARWICK
    Accept this scroll, most gracious sovereign,
    Which in right of Richard Plantagenet
    We do exhibit to your majesty.
GLOUCESTER
    Well urged, my Lord of Warwick; for, sweet prince,
    Now if your grace marks every circumstance,
    You have great reason to do Richard right,
    Especially for those occasiòns
    At Eltham Place I told your majesty.
KING
    And those occasions, uncle, were of force;
    Therefore, my loving lords, our pleasure is
    That Richard be restorèd to his blood.
WARWICK
    Let Richard be restorèd to his blood;
    So shall his father's wrongs be recompensed.
WINCHESTER
    As will the rest, so wills then Winchester.
KING
    If Richard will be true, not that alone
    But all the whole inheritance I give
    That does belong unto the House of York,
    From whence you spring by lineal descent.
RICHARD
    Your humble servant vows obedience
    And humble service till the point of death.
KING
    Stoop then and set your knee against my foot;
    And in requital of that duty done
    I girt thee with the valiant sword of York.
    Rise, Richard, like a true Plantagenet,
    And rise created princely Duke of York.

RICHARD
    And so thrive Richard as your foes may fall!
    And as my duty springs, so perish they
    That grudge one thought against your majesty!
ALL
    Welcome, high prince, the mighty Duke of York!
SOMERSET *(aside)*
    Perish, base prince, ignoble Duke of York!
GLOUCESTER
    Now will it best avail your majesty
    To cross the seas and to be crowned in France.
    The presence of a king engenders love
    Among his subjects and his loyal friends,
    As it disanimates his enemies.
KING
    When Gloucester says the word, King Henry goes;
    For friendly counsel cuts off many foes.
GLOUCESTER
    Your ships already are in readiness.
                    *Sennet. Flourish. Exeunt all but Exeter*
EXETER
    Ay, we may march in England or in France,
    Not seeing what is likely to ensue.
    This late dissension grown between the peers
    Burns under feignèd ashes of forged love
    And will at last break out into a flame.
    As festered members rot but by degree
    Till bones and flesh and sinews fall away,
    So will this base and envious discord breed.
    And now I fear that fatal prophecy
    Which in the time of Henry named the Fifth
    Was in the mouth of every sucking babe:
    That Henry born at Monmouth should win all
    And Henry born at Windsor should lose all;
    Which is so plain that Exeter does wish
    His days may finish ere that hapless time.          *Exit*

## SCENE II
## Before Rouen.

*Enter Joan la Pucelle disguised, with four soldiers with
sacks upon their backs*

PUCELLE
   These are the city gates, the gates of Rouen,
   Through which our policy must make a breach.
   Take heed, be wary how you place your words;
   Talk like the vulgar sort of market-men
   That come to gather money for their corn.
   If we have entrance, as I hope we shall,
   And then we find the slothful watch but weak,
   I'll by a sign give notice to our friends,
   That Charles the Dauphin may encounter them.
FIRST SOLDIER
   Our sacks shall be a means to sack the city,
   And we be lords and rulers over Rouen.
   Therefore we'll knock.

*They knock*

WATCH *(within)*
   *Qui là?* (Who's there?)
PUCELLE
   *Paysans, la pauvre gens de France,* (Peasants, poor French
    *folk*)
   Poor market folks that come to sell their corn.
WATCH *(opening the gates)*
   Enter, go in; the market bell is rung.
PUCELLE
   Now, Rouen, I'll shake your bulwarks to the ground.
                       *Exeunt into the city*

*Enter Charles, the Bastard, Alençon, Reignier, and soldiers*

CHARLES
    Saint Denis bless this happy stratagem,
    And once again we'll sleep secure in Rouen.

BASTARD
    Here entered Pucelle and her accomplices.
    Now she is there, how will she specify
    Here is the best and safest passage in?

REIGNIER
    By thrusting out a torch from yonder tower,
    Which, once discerned, shows what her meaning is:
    No way to that, for weakness, which she entered.

*Enter Joan la Pucelle on the top, thrusting out*
*a torch burning*

PUCELLE
    Behold, this is the happy wedding torch
    That now joins Rouen unto her countrymen,
    But burning fatal to the Talbotites.        *Exit*

BASTARD
    See, noble Charles, the beacon of our friend;
    The burning torch in yonder turret stands.

CHARLES
    Now shine it like a comet of revenge,
    A prophet to the fall of all our foes!

REIGNIER
    Defer no time; delays have dangerous ends.
    Enter and cry 'The Dauphin!' instantly,
    And then do execution on the watch.
        *Alarum. They storm the gates and exeunt*

*An alarum. Enter Talbot from within the town*

TALBOT
    France, you shall rue this treason with your tears,

If Talbot but survives your treachery.
Pucelle, that witch, that damnèd sorceress,
Has wrought this hellish mischief unawares,
That hardly we escaped the pride of France.          *Exit*

*An alarum. Bedford brought in sick in a chair*
*Enter Talbot and Burgundy without; within, Joan la*
*Pucelle, Charles, the Bastard, Alençon, and Reignier on*
*the walls*

PUCELLE
Good morrow, gallants, want you corn for bread?
I think the Duke of Burgundy will fast
Before he'll buy again at such a rate.
'Twas full of weeds; do you like the taste?
BURGUNDY
Scoff on, vile fiend and shameless courtesan!
I trust ere long to choke you with your own,
And make you curse the harvest of that corn.
CHARLES
Your grace may starve, perhaps, before that time.
BEDFORD
O, let no words, but deeds, revenge this treason!
PUCELLE
What will you do, good greybeard? Break a lance,
And run a-tilt at death within a chair?
TALBOT
Foul fiend of France and hag of all despite,
Encompassed with your lustful paramours,
Becomes it you to taunt his valiant age
And twit with cowardice a man half dead?
Damsel, I'll have a bout with you again,
Or else let Talbot perish with this shame.
PUCELLE
Are you so hot, sir? Yet, Pucelle, hold your peace.
If Talbot does but thunder, rain will follow.

*The English whisper together in counsel*

God speed the parliament; who shall be the Speaker?
TALBOT
Dare you come forth and meet us in the field?
PUCELLE
Perhaps your lordship takes us then for fools,
To try if indeed our own be ours or no.
TALBOT
I speak not to that railing Hecatè,
But unto you, Alençon, and the rest.
Will you, like soldiers, come and fight it out?
ALENÇON
Signor, no.
TALBOT
Signor, hang! Base muleteers of France!
Like peasant footboys do they keep the walls
And dare not take up arms like gentlemen.
PUCELLE
Away, captains! Let's get us from the walls,
For Talbot means no goodness by his looks.
God bye, my lord; we came but to tell you
That we are here.                    *Exeunt from the walls*
TALBOT
And there will we be too ere it be long,
Or else reproach be Talbot's greatest fame!
Vow, Burgundy, by honour of your house,
Pricked on by public wrongs sustained in France,
Either to get the town again or die.
And I, as sure as English Henry lives
And as his father here was conqueror,
As sure as in this late betrayèd town
Great Coeur-de-lion's heart was buried,
So sure I swear to get the town or die.
BURGUNDY
My vows are equal partners with your vows.

TALBOT
> But, ere we go, regard this dying prince,
> The valiant Duke of Bedford. Come, my lord,
> We will bestow you in some better place,
> Fitter for sickness and for crazy age.

BEDFORD
> Lord Talbot, do not so dishonour me;
> Here will I sit, before the walls of Rouen,
> And will be partner of your weal or woe.

BURGUNDY
> Courageous Bedford, let us now persuade you.

BEDFORD
> Not to be gone from hence; for once I read
> That stout Pendragon in his litter sick
> Came to the field and vanquishèd his foes.
> I think I should revive the soldiers' hearts,
> Because I ever found them as myself.

TALBOT
> Undaunted spirit in a dying breast!
> Then be it so. Heavens keep old Bedford safe!
> And now no more ado, brave Burgundy,
> But gather we our forces out of hand
> And set upon our boasting enemy.
> > > > *Exeunt all but Bedford and attendants*

*An alarum. Enter Sir John Fastolf and a Captain*

CAPTAIN
> Whither away, Sir John Fastolf, in such haste?

FASTOLF
> Whither away? To save myself by flight.
> We are likely to have the overthrow again.

CAPTAIN
> What, will you fly and leave Lord Talbot?

FASTOLF                                                    Ay,
> All the Talbots in the world, to save my life.        *Exit*

CAPTAIN
    Cowardly knight, ill fortune follow you!          *Exit*

*Retreat. Pucelle, Alençon, and Charles enter
from the town and fly*

BEDFORD
    Now, quiet soul, depart when heaven please,
    For I have seen our enemies' overthrow.
    What is the trust or strength of foolish man?
    They that of late were daring with their scoffs
    Are glad and fain by flight to save themselves.

*Bedford dies and is carried in.
An alarum. Enter Talbot, Burgundy, and English soldiers*

TALBOT
    Lost and recovered in a day again!
    This is a double honour, Burgundy.
    Yet heavens have glory for this victory!
BURGUNDY
    Warlike and martial Talbot, Burgundy
    Enshrines you in his heart and there erects
    Your noble deeds as valour's monuments.
TALBOT
    Thanks, gentle Duke. But where is Pucelle now?
    I think her old familiar is asleep.
    Now where's the Bastard's braves and Charles's taunts?
    What, downcast? Rouen hangs her head for grief
    That such a valiant company are fled.
    Now will we take some order in the town,
    Placing therein some expert officers,
    And then depart to Paris to the King,
    For there young Henry with his nobles lie.
BURGUNDY
    What wills Lord Talbot pleases Burgundy.

TALBOT
But yet, before we go, let's not forget
The noble Duke of Bedford, late deceased,
But see his exequies fulfilled in Rouen.
A braver soldier never couchèd lance;
A gentler heart did never sway in court.
But kings and mightiest potentates must die,
For that's the end of human misery.                    *Exeunt*

## SCENE III
## Outside Rouen.

*Enter Charles, the Bastard, Alençon, Joan la Pucelle,*
*and soldiers*

PUCELLE
Dismay not, princes, at this accident,
Nor grieve that Rouen is so recoverèd.
Care is no cure, but rather còrrosive,
For things that are not to be remedied.
Let frantic Talbot triumph for a while
And like a peacock sweep along his tail;
We'll pull his plumes and take away his train,
If Dauphin and the rest will be but ruled.
CHARLES
We have been guided by you hitherto,
And of your cunning had no diffidence;
One sudden foil shall never breed distrust.
BASTARD
Search out your wit for secret policies,
And we will make you famous through the world.
ALENÇON
We'll set your statue in some holy place,
And have you reverenced like a blessèd saint.
Employ you then, sweet virgin, for our good.

PUCELLE
　　Then thus it must be; this does Joan advise:
　　By fair persuasions, mixed with sugared words,
　　We will entice the Duke of Burgundy
　　To leave the Talbot and to follow us.
CHARLES
　　Ay, surely, sweeting, if we could do that,
　　France were no place for Henry's warriors,
　　Nor should that nation boast it so with us,
　　But be extirpèd from our provinces.
ALENÇON
　　For ever should they be expulsed from France,
　　And not have title of an earldom here.
PUCELLE
　　Your honours shall perceive how I will work
　　To bring this matter to the wishèd end.

*Drum sounds afar off*

　　Hark, by the sound of drum you may perceive
　　Their powers are marching unto Paris-ward.

*Here sound an English march*

　　There goes the Talbot with his colours spread,
　　And all the troops of English after him.

*Here sound a French march*

　　Now in the rearward come the Duke and his;
　　Fortune in favour makes him lag behind.
　　Summon a parley; we will talk with him.

*Trumpets sound a parley*

CHARLES
  A parley with the Duke of Burgundy!

*Enter Burgundy and troops*

BURGUNDY
  Who craves a parley with the Burgundy?
PUCELLE
  The princely Charles of France, your countryman.
BURGUNDY
  What say you, Charles? for I am marching hence.
CHARLES
  Speak, Pucelle, and enchant him with your words.
PUCELLE
  Brave Burgundy, undoubted hope of France,
  Stay, let your humble handmaid speak to you.
BURGUNDY
  Speak on; but be not over-tedious.
PUCELLE
  Look on your country, look on fertile France,
  And see the cities and the towns defaced
  By wasting ruin of the cruel foe;
  As looks the mother on her lowly babe
  When death does close his tender-dying eyes.
  See, see the pining malady of France;
  Behold the wounds, the most unnatural wounds,
  Which you yourself have given her woeful breast.
  O, turn your edgèd sword another way;
  Strike those that hurt, and hurt not those that help!
  One drop of blood drawn from your country's bosom
  Should grieve you more than streams of foreign gore.
  Return you therefore with a flood of tears,
  And wash away your country's stainèd spots.
BURGUNDY (*aside*)
  Either she has bewitched me with her words,
  Or nature makes me suddenly relent.

PUCELLE

Besides, all French and France exclaim on you,
Doubting your birth and lawful progeny.
Who join you with but with a lordly nation
That will not trust you but for profit's sake?
When Talbot has set footing once in France,
And fashioned you that instrument of ill,
Who then but English Henry will be lord,
And you be thrust out like a fugitive?
Call we to mind, and mark but this for proof:
Was not the Duke of Orleans your foe?
And was he not in England prisoner?
But when they heard he was your enemy,
They set him free without his ransom paid,
In spite of Burgundy and all his friends.
See then, you fight against your countrymen,
And join with them will be your slaughtermen.
Come, come, return; return, you wandering lord;
Charles and the rest will take you in their arms.

BURGUNDY *(aside)*

I am vanquished. These haughty words of hers
Have battered me like roaring cannon-shot
And made me almost yield upon my knees.
*(To them)* Forgive me, country, and sweet countrymen!
And, lords, accept this hearty kind embrace.
My forces and my power of men are yours.
So farewell, Talbot; I'll no longer trust you.

PUCELLE

Done like a Frenchman—*(aside)* turn and turn again.

CHARLES

Welcome, brave Duke. Your friendship makes us fresh.

BASTARD

And does beget new courage in our breasts.

ALENÇON

Pucelle has bravely played her part in this,
And does deserve a coronet of gold.

CHARLES
    Now let us on, my lords, and join our powers,
    And seek how we may prejudice the foe.      *Exeunt*

## SCENE IV
## Paris. The royal palace.

*Enter the King, Gloucester, Winchester, Richard Duke of*
*York, Suffolk, Somerset, Warwick, Exeter, Vernon, Basset,*
*and other courtiers. Then enter Talbot, with soldiers*

TALBOT
    My gracious prince, and honourable peers,
    Hearing of your arrival in this realm,
    I have awhile given truce unto my wars
    To do my duty to my sovereign,
    In sign whereof this arm that has reclaimed
    To your obedience fifty fortresses,
    Twelve cities, and seven wallèd towns of strength,
    Beside five hundred prisoners of esteem,
    Lets fall his sword before your highness' feet,

*He kneels*

    And with submissive loyalty of heart
    Ascribes the glory of his conquest got
    First to my God and next unto your grace.
KING
    Is this the Lord Talbot, uncle Gloucester,
    That has so long been resident in France?
GLOUCESTER
    Yes, if it please your majesty, my liege.
KING
    Welcome, brave captain and victorious lord!
    When I was young—as yet I am not old—

I do remember how my father said
A stouter champion never handled sword.
Long since we were resolvèd of your truth,
Your faithful service, and your toil in war;
Yet never have you tasted our reward
Or been rewarded with so much as thanks,
Because till now we never saw your face.
Therefore stand up, and for these good deserts
We here create you Earl of Shrewsbury;
And in our coronation take your place.

  *Sennet. Flourish. Exeunt all but Vernon and Basset*

VERNON

Now, sir, to you, that were so hot at sea,
Disgracing of these colours that I wear
In honour of my noble lord of York,
Dare you maintain the former words you spoke?

BASSET

Yes, sir, as well as you dare patronage
The envious barking of your saucy tongue
Against my lord the Duke of Somerset.

VERNON

Fellow, your lord I honour as he is.

BASSET

Why, what is he? As good a man as York.

VERNON

Hark you, not so. In witness take you that.

*He strikes him*

BASSET

Villain, you know the law of arms is such
That whoso draws a sword 'tis present death,
Or else this blow should broach your dearest blood.
But I'll unto his majesty and crave
I may have liberty to avenge this wrong,
When you shall see I'll meet you to your cost.

VERNON
   Well, miscreant, I'll be there as soon as you,
   And after meet you sooner than you would.      *Exeunt*

# Act IV

## SCENE I
## The same.

*Enter the King, Gloucester, Winchester, Richard Duke of York, Suffolk, Somerset, Warwick, Talbot, Exeter, the Governor of Paris, and others*

GLOUCESTER
Lord Bishop, set the crown upon his head.
WINCHESTER
God save King Henry, of that name the sixth!
GLOUCESTER
Now, Governor of Paris, take your oath:

*The Governor kneels*

That you elect no other king but him,
Esteem none friends but such as are his friends,
And none your foes but such as shall pretend
Malicious practices against his state.
This shall you do, so help you righteous God.
*Exeunt Governor*

*Enter Fastolf*

FASTOLF
My gracious sovereign, as I rode from Calais
To haste unto your coronatiòn,
A letter was delivered to my hands,
Written to your grace from the Duke of Burgundy.

TALBOT
    Shame to the Duke of Burgundy and you!
    I vowed, base knight, when I did meet you next
    To tear the Garter from your craven's leg,

                    *He plucks it off*

    Which I have done, because unworthily
    You were installèd in that high degree.
    Pardon me, princely Henry, and the rest:
    This dastard, at the Battle of Patay,
    When, but in all, I was six thousand strong,
    And when the French were almost ten to one,
    Before we met or even a stroke was given,
    Like to a trusty squire did run away.
    In which assault we lost twelve hundred men.
    Myself and divers gentlemen besides
    Were there surprised and taken prisoners.
    Then judge, great lords, if I have done amiss,
    Or whether well such cowards ought to wear
    This ornament of knighthood, yea or no!
GLOUCESTER
    To say the truth, this fact was infamous,
    And ill beseeming any common man,
    Much more a knight, a captain, and a leader.
TALBOT
    When first this Order was ordained, my lords,
    Knights of the Garter were of noble birth,
    Valiant and virtuous, full of haughty courage,
    Such as were grown to credit by the wars;
    Not fearing death nor shrinking for distress,
    But always resolute in most extremes.
    He then that is not furnished in this sort
    Does but usurp the sacred name of knight,
    Profaning this most honourable order,
    And should, if I were worthy to be judge,

Be quite degraded, like a hedge-born swain
That does presume to boast of gentle blood.

KING

Stain to your countrymen, you hear your doom.
Be packing therefore, you that were a knight;
Henceforth we banish you on pain of death.

*Exit Fastolf*

And now, Lord Protector, view the letter
Sent from our uncle Duke of Burgundy.

GLOUCESTER (*reads*)

What means his grace that he has changed his style?
No more but plain and bluntly 'To the King'?
Has he forgotten he is his sovereign?
Or does this churlish superscriptiòn
Pretend some alteration in good will?
What's here? *I have, upon especial cause,*
*Moved with compassion of my country's wreck,*
*Together with the pitiful complaints*
*Of such as your oppression feeds upon,*
*Forsaken your pernicious factiòn,*
*And joined with Charles, the rightful King of France.*
O, monstrous treachery! Can this be so?
That in alliance, amity, and oaths
There should be found such false dissembling guile?

KING

What? Does my uncle Burgundy revolt?

GLOUCESTER

He does, my lord, and has become your foe.

KING

Is that the worst this letter does contain?

GLOUCESTER

It is the worst, and all, my lord, he writes.

KING

Why then, Lord Talbot there shall talk with him
And give him chastisement for this abuse.
How say you, my lord; are you not content?

TALBOT

Content, my liege? Yes; but that I am forestalled,
I should have begged I might have been employed.

KING

Then gather strength and march unto him straight;
Let him perceive how ill we brook his treason,
And what offence it is to flout his friends.

TALBOT

I go, my lord, in heart desiring ever
You may behold confusion of your foes.                *Exit*

*Enter Vernon and Basset*

VERNON

Grant me the combat, gracious sovereign.

BASSET

And me, my lord, grant me the combat too.

RICHARD

This is my servant; hear him, noble prince.

SOMERSET

And this is mine; sweet Henry, favour him.

KING

Be patient, lords, and give them leave to speak.
Say, gentlemen, what makes you thus exclaim,
And wherefore crave you combat, or with whom?

VERNON

With him, my lord, for he has done me wrong.

BASSET

And I with him, for he has done me wrong.

KING

What is that wrong whereof you both complain?
First let me know, and then I'll answer you.

BASSET

Crossing the sea from England into France,
This fellow here with envious carping tongue
Upbraided me about the rose I wear,

Saying the sanguine colour of the leaves
Did represent my master's blushing cheeks,
When stubbornly he did deny the truth
About a certain question in the law
Argued betwixt the Duke of York and him
With other vile and ignominious terms.
In confutation of which rude reproach,
And in defence of my lord's worthiness,
I crave the benefit of law of arms.

VERNON
And that is my petition, noble lord;
For though he seems with forged invention
To set a gloss upon his bold intent,
Yet know, my lord, I was provoked by him,
And he first took exception at this badge,
Pronouncing that the paleness of this flower
Portrayed the faintness of my master's heart.

RICHARD
Will not this malice, Somerset, be left?

SOMERSET
Your private grudge, my lord of York, will out,
Though never so cunningly you smother it.

KING
Good Lord, what madness rules in brainsick men,
When for so slight and frivolous a cause
Such factious emulations shall arise!
Good cousins both, of York and Somerset,
Quiet yourselves, I pray, and be at peace.

RICHARD
Let his dissension first be tried by fight,
And then your highness shall command a peace.

SOMERSET
The quarrel touches none but us alone;
Between ourselves let us decide it then.

RICHARD
There is my pledge; accept it, Somerset.

VERNON
  Nay, let it rest where it began at first.
BASSET
  Confirm it so, my honourable lord.
GLOUCESTER
  Confirm it so? Confounded be your strife,
  And perish you with your audacious prate!
  Presumptuous vassals, are you not ashamed
  With this immodest clamorous outrage
  To trouble and disturb the King and us?
  And you, my lords, I think you do not well
  To bear with their perverse objectiòns,
  Much less to take occasion from their mouths
  To raise a mutiny between yourselves.
  Let me persuade you take a better course.
EXETER
  It grieves his highness. Good my lords, be friends.
KING
  Come hither, you that would be combatants.
  Henceforth I charge you, as you love our favour,
  Quite to forget this quarrel and the cause.
  And you, my lords, remember where we are—
  In France, among a fickle, wavering nation.
  If they perceive dissension in our looks
  And that within ourselves we disagree,
  How will their grudging stomachs be provoked
  To wilful disobedience, and rebel!
  Besides, what infamy will there arise
  When foreign princes shall be certified
  That for a toy, a thing of no regard,
  King Henry's peers and chief nobility
  Destroyed themselves and lost the realm of France!
  O, think upon the conquest of my father,
  My tender years, and let us not forgo
  That for a trifle that was bought with blood!

Let me be umpire in this doubtful strife.
I see no reason, if I wear this rose,

*He puts on a red rose*

That anyone should therefore be suspicious
I more incline to Somerset than York;
Both are my kinsmen, and I love them both.
As well they may upbraid me with my crown
Because, indeed, the King of Scots is crowned.
But your discretions better can persuade
Than I am able to instruct or teach;
And, therefore, as we hither came in peace,
So let us still continue peace and love.
Cousin of York, we institute your grace
To be our Regent in these parts of France;
And, good my lord of Somerset, unite
Your troops of horsemen with his bands of foot;
And like true subjects, sons of your progenitors,
Go cheerfully together and digest
Your angry choler on your enemies.
Ourself, my Lord Protector, and the rest
After some respite will return to Calais;
From thence to England, where I hope ere long
To be presented, by your victories,
With Charles, Alençon, and that traitorous rout.
*Flourish. Exeunt all but Richard Duke of York, Warwick,*
*Exeter, Vernon*

WARWICK
My lord of York, I promise you, the King
Prettily, I thought, did play the orator.
RICHARD
And so he did; but yet I like it not,
In that he wears the badge of Somerset.
WARWICK
Tush, that was but his fancy; blame him not;
I dare presume, sweet prince, he thought no harm.

RICHARD
   Well, if I thought he did—but let it rest;
   Other affairs must now be managèd.

                                  *Exeunt all but Exeter*

EXETER
   Well did you, Richard, to suppress your voice;
   For, had the passions of your heart burst out,
   I fear we should have seen deciphered there
   More rancorous spite, more furious raging broils,
   Than yet can be imagined or supposed.
   But howsoever, no simple man that sees
   This jarring discord of nobility,
   This shouldering of each other in the Court,
   This factious bandying of their favourites,
   But that it does presage some ill event.
   'Tis much when sceptres are in children's hands;
   But more when envy breeds unkind division.
   There comes the ruin, there begins confusion.    *Exit*

# SCENE II
## Before Bordeaux.

*Enter Talbot, with trump and drum, before Bordeaux*

TALBOT
   Go to the gates of Bordeaux, trumpeter;
   Summon their general unto the wall.

*Trumpet sounds. Enter the General aloft with his men*

   English John Talbot, captains, calls you forth,
   Servant in arms to Harry King of England;
   And thus he would: open your city gates,
   Be humble to us, call my sovereign yours
   And do him homage as obedient subjects,

And I'll withdraw me and my bloody forces.
But if you frown upon this proffered peace,
You tempt the fury of my three attendants,
Lean famine, quartering steel, and climbing fire;
Which in a moment even with the earth
Shall lay your stately and air-braving towers,
If you forsake the offer of their love.

GENERAL

You ominous and fearful owl of death,
Our nation's terror and their bloody scourge!
The period of your tyranny approaches.
On us you can not enter but by death;
For I protest we are well fortified,
And strong enough to issue out and fight.
If you retire, the Dauphin, well appointed,
Stands with the snares of war to tangle you.
On either hand then there are squadrons pitched
To wall you from the liberty of flight;
And no way can you turn you for redress
But death does front you with apparent spoil
And pale destruction meets you in the face.
Ten thousand French have taken the sacrament
To aim their dangerous artillery
Upon no Christian soul but English Talbot.
Lo, there you stand, a breathing valiant man
Of an invincible unconquered spirit!
This is the latest glory of your praise
That I, your enemy, endue you with;
For ere the glass that now begins to run
Finishes the process of its sandy hour,
These eyes that see you now well colourèd
Shall see you withered, bloody, pale, and dead.

*Drum afar off*

Hark, hark! The Dauphin's drum, a warning bell,

Sings heavy music to your timorous soul;
And mine shall ring your dire departure out.

*Exit with his men*

TALBOT

He fables not; I hear the enemy.
Out, some light horsemen, and survey their wings.
O, negligent and heedless discipline!
How are we parked and bounded in a pale—
A little herd of England's timorous deer,
Mazed with a yelping kennel of French curs!
If we are English deer, be then in blood;
Not rascal-like to fall down with a pinch,
But rather, moody-mad and desperate stags,
Turn on the bloody hounds with heads of steel
And make the cowards stand aloof at bay.
Sell every man his life as dear as mine,
And they shall find dear deer of us, my friends.
God and Saint George, Talbot and England's right,
Prosper our colours in this dangerous fight!     *Exeunt*

# SCENE III
## A plain in Gascony.

*Enter Richard Duke of York, with trumpet and soldiers.*
*Enter a Messenger*

RICHARD

Have not the speedy scouts returned again
That dogged the mighty army of the Dauphin?

MESSENGER

They are returned, my lord, and give it out
That he has marched to Bordeaux with his troops
To fight with Talbot; as he marched along,
By your espials were discoverèd
Two mightier troops than that the Dauphin led,

Which joined with him and made their march for
   Bordeaux.
RICHARD
   A plague upon that villain Somerset,
   That thus delays my promisèd supply
   Of horsemen that were levied for this siege!
   Renownèd Talbot does expect my aid,
   And I am held up by a traitor villain
   And cannot help the noble chevalier.
   God comfort him in this necessity!
   If he miscarries, farewell wars in France.

*Enter Sir William Lucy*

LUCY
   You princely leader of our English strength,
   Never so needful on the earth of France,
   Spur to the rescue of the noble Talbot,
   Who now is girdled with a waist of iron
   And hemmed about with grim destructiòn.
   To Bordeaux, warlike Duke! To Bordeaux, York!
   Else farewell Talbot, France, and England's honour.
RICHARD
   O God, that Somerset, who in proud heart
   Does stop my cornets, were in Talbot's place!
   So should we save a valiant gentleman
   By forfeiting a traitor and a coward.
   Mad ire and wrathful fury make me weep
   That thus we die while rèmiss traitors sleep.
LUCY
   O, send some succour to the distressed lord!
RICHARD
   He dies, we lose; I break my warlike word;
   We mourn, France smiles; we lose, they daily get;
   All due to this vile traitor Somerset.

LUCY
  Then God take mercy on brave Talbot's soul
  And on his son, young John, who two hours since
  I met in travel toward his warlike father.
  This seven years did not Talbot see his son,
  And now they meet where both their lives are done.
RICHARD
  Alas, what joy shall noble Talbot have
  To bid his young son welcome to his grave?
  Away! Vexation almost stops my breath
  That sundered friends greet in the hour of death.
  Lucy, farewell; no more my fortune can
  But curse the cause I cannot aid the man.
  Maine, Blois, Poitiers, and Tours are won away,
  Because of Somerset and his delay.

                                *Exit with his soldiers*

LUCY
  Thus, while the vulture of sedition
  Feeds in the bosom of such great commanders,
  Sleeping neglection does betray to loss
  The conquest of our scarce-cold conqueror,
  That ever-living man of memory,
  Henry the Fifth. While they each other cross,
  Lives, honours, lands, and all hurry to loss.       *Exit*


# SCENE IV
## The same.

*Enter Somerset, with his army, and a Captain of Talbot's*

SOMERSET
  It is too late; I cannot send them now.
  This expedition was by York and Talbot
  Too rashly plotted. All our general force
  Might with a sally of the very town

Be buckled with. The over-daring Talbot
Has sullied all his gloss of former honour
By this unheedful, desperate, wild adventure.
York set him on to fight and die in shame,
That, Talbot dead, great York might bear the name.

CAPTAIN
Here is Sir William Lucy, who with me
Set from our o'ermatched forces forth for aid.

*Enter Sir William Lucy*

SOMERSET
How now, Sir William, whither were you sent?

LUCY
Whither, my lord? From bought and sold Lord Talbot,
Who, ringed about with bold adversity,
Cries out for noble York and Somerset
To beat assailing death from his weak legions.
And while the honourable captain there
Drops bloody sweat from his war-wearied limbs,
And, in advantage lingering, looks for rescue,
You, his false hopes, the trust of England's honour,
Keep off aloof with worthless emulation.
Let not your private discord keep away
The levied succours that should lend him aid,
While he, renownèd noble gentleman,
Yields up his life unto a world of odds.
Orleans the Bastard, Charles, Burgundy,
Alençon, Reignier compass him about,
And Talbot perishes by your default.

SOMERSET
York set him on; York should have sent him aid.

LUCY
And York as fast upon your grace exclaims,
Swearing that you withhold his levied host,
Collected for this expedition.

SOMERSET
   York lies; he might have sent and had the horse.
   I owe him little duty, and less love,
   And take foul scorn to fawn on him by sending.
LUCY
   The fraud of England, not the force of France,
   Has now entrapped the noble-minded Talbot.
   Never to England shall he bear his life,
   But dies betrayed to fortune by your strife.
SOMERSET
   Come, go; I will dispatch the horsemen straight;
   Within six hours they will be at his aid.
LUCY
   Too late comes rescue. He is taken or slain;
   For fly he could not, if he would have fled;
   And fly would Talbot never, though he might.
SOMERSET
   If he is dead, brave Talbot, then adieu!
LUCY
   His fame lives in the world, his shame in you.   *Exeunt*

# SCENE V
## Near Bordeaux.

*Enter Talbot and his son*

TALBOT
   O young John Talbot, I did send for you
   To tutor you in stratagems of war,
   That Talbot's name might be in you revived
   When sapless age and weak unable limbs
   Should bring your father to his drooping chair.
   But, O, malignant and ill-boding stars!
   Now you are come unto a feast of death,
   A terrible and unavoided danger.

Therefore, dear boy, mount on my swiftest horse,
And I'll direct you how you shall escape
By sudden flight. Come, dally not, be gone.
JOHN
Is my name Talbot, and am I your son?
And shall I fly? O, if you love my mother,
Dishonour not her honourable name
To make a bastard and a slave of me.
The world will say he is not Talbot's blood
That basely fled when noble Talbot stood.
TALBOT
Fly, to revenge my death if I am slain.
JOHN
He that flies so will never return again.
TALBOT
If we both stay, we both are sure to die.
JOHN
Then let me stay, and, father, do you fly.
Your loss is great, so your respect should be;
My worth unknown, no loss is known in me.
Upon my death the French can little boast;
In yours they will; in you all hopes are lost.
Flight cannot stain the honour you have won;
But mine it will, that no exploit have done.
You fled for vantage, everyone will swear;
But if I bow, they'll say it was for fear.
There is no hope that ever I will stay
If the first hour I shrink and run away.
Here on my knee I beg mortality
Rather than life preserved with infamy.
TALBOT
Shall all your mother's hopes lie in one tomb?
JOHN
Ay, rather than I'll shame my mother's womb.
TALBOT
Upon my blessing I command you go.

JOHN
  To fight I will, but not to fly the foe.
TALBOT
  Part of your father may be saved in thee.
JOHN
  No part of him but will be shame in me.
TALBOT
  You never had renown, and can not lose it.
JOHN
  Yes, your renownèd name; shall flight abuse it?
TALBOT
  Your father's charge shall clear you from that stain.
JOHN
  You cannot witness for me being slain.
  If death is so apparent, then both fly.
TALBOT
  And leave my followers here to fight and die?
  My age was never tainted with such shame.
JOHN
  And shall my youth be guilty of such blame?
  No more can I be severed from your side
  Than can yourself yourself in twain divide.
  Stay, go, do what you will—the like do I;
  For live I will not if my father die.
TALBOT
  Then here I take my leave of you, fair son,
  Born to eclipse your life this afternoon.
  Come, side by side together live and die,
  And soul with soul from France to heaven fly.   *Exeunt*

## SCENE VI
## The same.

*Alarum. Talbot's son is hemmed about
and Talbot rescues him*

TALBOT
Saint George and victory! Fight, soldiers, fight!
The Regent has with Talbot broken his word
And left us to the rage of France's sword.
Where is John Talbot? Pause, and take your breath;
I gave you life and rescued you from death.
JOHN
O twice my father, twice am I your son!
The life you gave me first was lost and done
Till with your warlike sword, despite of fate,
To my determined time you gave new date.
TALBOT
When from the Dauphin's crest your sword struck fire,
It warmed your father's heart with proud desire
Of bold-faced victory. Then leaden age,
Quickened with youthful heart and warlike rage,
Beat down Alençon, Orleans, Burgundy,
And from the pride of Gallia rescued thee.
The ireful Bastard Orleans, that drew blood
From you, my boy, and had the maidenhood
Of your first fight, I soon encounterèd,
And, interchanging blows, I quickly shed
Some of his bastard blood. And in disgrace
Bespoke him thus: 'Contaminated, base,
And misbegotten blood I spill of thine,
Mean and right poor, for that pure blood of mine
Which you did force from Talbot, my brave boy.'
Here, purposing the Bastard to destroy,
Came in strong rescue. Speak, your father's care;
Are you not weary, John? How do you fare?

Will you yet leave the battle, boy, and fly,
Now you are sealed the son of chivalry?
Fly, to revenge my death when I am dead;
The help of one stands me in little stead.
O, too much folly is it, well I wot (know),
To hazard all our lives in one small boat.
If I today die not with Frenchmen's rage,
Tomorrow I shall die with crippling age.
By me they nothing gain now if I stay;
'Tis but the shortening of my life one day.
In you your mother dies, our household's name,
My death's revenge, your youth, and England's fame.
All these, and more, we hazard by your stay;
All these are saved if you will fly away.

JOHN
The sword of Orleans has not made me smart;
These words of yours draw lifeblood from my heart.
On that advantage, bought with such a shame,
To save a paltry life and slay bright fame,
Before young Talbot from old Talbot fly,
The coward horse that bears me fall and die!
And liken me to the peasant boys of France,
To be shame's scorn and subject of mischance!
Surely, by all the glory you have won,
Then if I fly, I am not Talbot's son;
Then talk no more of flight; it is no boot (use);
If son to Talbot, die at Talbot's foot.

TALBOT
Then follow you your desperate sire of Crete,
You Icarus; your life to me is sweet.
If you will fight, fight by your father's side;
And, commendable proved, let's die in pride.　　*Exeunt*

## SCENE VII
### The same.

*Alarum. Enter old Talbot, led by a Servant*

TALBOT
Where is my other life? My own is gone.
O, where's young Talbot? Where is valiant John?
Triumphant Death, smeared with captivity,
Young Talbot's valour makes me smile at you.
When he perceived me shrink and on my knee,
His bloody sword he brandished over me,
And like a hungry lion did commence
Rough deeds of rage and stern impatiènce.
When my angry protector stood alone,
Tendering my ruin and assailed of none,
Dizzy-eyed fury and great rage of heart
Suddenly made him from my side to start
Into the clustering battle of the French.
And in that sea of blood my boy did drench
His over-mounting spirit; and there died
My Icarus, my blossom, in his pride.

*Enter soldiers carrying John Talbot*

SERVANT
O my dear lord, lo where your son is borne!
TALBOT
You grinning Death, which laugh us here to scorn,
Anon from your insulting tyranny,
Coupled in bonds of perpetuity,
Two Talbots, wingèd through the yielding sky,
In your despite shall escape mortality.
O you whose wounds become hard-featured Death,
Speak to your father ere you yield your breath!
Brave Death by speaking, whether he will or no;

Imagine him a Frenchman, and your foe.
Poor boy! He smiles, I think, as who should say
'Had Death been French, then Death had died today.'
Come, come, and lay him in his father's arms.
My spirit can no longer bear these harms.
Soldiers, adieu! I have what I would have,
Now my old arms are young John Talbot's grave.

*He dies*

*Enter Charles, Alençon, Burgundy, the Bastard, and*
*Joan la Pucelle*

CHARLES
Had York and Somerset brought rescue in,
We should have found a bloody day of this.
BASTARD
How the young whelp of Talbot's, raging wood,
Did flesh his puny sword in Frenchmen's blood!
PUCELLE
Once I encountered him and thus I said:
'You maiden youth, be vanquished by a maid.'
But with a proud majestical high scorn
He answered thus: 'Young Talbot was not born
To be the pillage of a wanton wench.'
So, rushing in the bowels of the French,
He left me proudly, as unworthy fight.
BURGUNDY
Doubtless he would have made a noble knight.
See where he lies inhearsèd in the arms
Of the most bloody nurser of his harms.
BASTARD
Hew them to pieces, hack their bones asunder,
Whose life was England's glory, Gallia's wonder.
CHARLES
O, no, forbear! For that which we have fled
During the life, let us not wrong it dead.

*Enter Lucy with a French herald*

LUCY

Herald, conduct me to the Dauphin's tent,
To know who has obtained the glory of the day.

CHARLES

On what submissive message are you sent?

LUCY

Submission, Dauphin? 'Tis a mere French word;
We English warriors know not what it means,
I come to know what prisoners you have taken
And to survey the bodies of the dead.

CHARLES

For prisoners ask you? Hell our prison is.
But tell me whom you seek.

LUCY

Where is the great Alcides of the field,
Valiant Lord Talbot, Earl of Shrewsbury,
Created for his rare success in arms
Great Earl of Washford, Waterford, and Valence,
Lord Talbot of Goodrich and Urchinfield,
Lord Strange of Blackmere, Lord Verdun of Alton,
Lord Cromwell of Wingfield, Lord Furnival of Sheffield,
The thrice-victorious Lord of Falconbridge,
Knight of the noble Order of Saint George,
Worthy Saint Michael, and the Golden Fleece,
Great Marshal to Henry the Sixth
Of all his wars within the realm of France?

PUCELLE

Here's a silly stately style indeed!
The Turk, that two and fifty kingdoms has,
Writes not so tedious a style as this.
Him that you magnify with all these titles
Stinking and flyblown lies here at our feet.

LUCY

Is Talbot slain, the Frenchmen's only scourge,

Your kingdom's terror and black Nemesis?
O, were my eyeballs into bullets turned,
That I in rage might shoot them at your faces!
O that I could but call these dead to life!
It were enough to fright the realm of France.
Were but his picture left among you here,
It would amaze the proudest of you all.
Give me their bodies, that I may bear them hence
And give them burial as beseems their worth.

PUCELLE
I think this upstart is old Talbot's ghost,
He speaks with such a proud commanding spirit.
For God's sake, let him have them; to keep them here,
They would but stink and putrefy the air.

CHARLES
Go take their bodies hence.

LUCY
I'll bear them hence; but from their ashes shall be reared
A phoenix that shall make all France afeard.

CHARLES
So we are rid of them, do with them what you will.
And now to Paris in this conquering vein!
All will be ours, now bloody Talbot's slain.        *Exeunt*

# Act V

## SCENE I
## Westminster. The royal palace.

*Sennet. Enter the King, Gloucester, and Exeter*

KING
Have you perused the letters from the Pope,
The Emperor, and the Earl of Armagnac?
GLOUCESTER
I have, my lord, and their intent is this:
They humbly sue unto your excellence
To have a godly peace concluded of
Between the realms of England and of France.
KING
How does your grace affect their motiòn?
GLOUCESTER
Well, my good lord, and as the only means
To stop effusion of our Christian blood
And establish quietness on every side.
KING
Ay, indeed, uncle; for I always thought
It was both impious and unnatural
That such inhumanity and bloody strife
Should reign among professors of one faith.
GLOUCESTER
Besides, my lord, the sooner to effect
And surer bind this knot of amity,
The Earl of Armagnac, near knit to Charles,
A man of great authority in France,
Proffers his only daughter to your grace
In marriage, with a large and sumptuous dowry.

KING
  Marriage, uncle? Alas, my years are young,
  And fitter are my study and my books
  Than wanton dalliance with a paramour.
  Yet call the ambassadors; and, as you please,
  So let them have their answers every one.
  I shall be well content with any choice
  Tends to God's glory and my country's weal.

  *Enter Winchester, in cardinal's habit, with Legate*
  *and ambassadors*

EXETER *(aside)*
  What, is my lord of Winchester installed,
  And called unto a cardinal's degree?
  Then I perceive that will be verified
  Henry the Fifth did sometime prophesy:
  'If once he comes to be a cardinal,
  He'll make his cap co-equal with the crown.'
KING
  My Lords Ambassadors, your various suits
  Have been considered and debated on.
  Your purpose is both good and reasonable,
  And therefore are we certainly resolved
  To draw conditions of a friendly peace,
  Which by my lord of Winchester we mean
  Shall be transported presently to France.
GLOUCESTER *(to the Armagnac ambassador)*
  And for the proffer of my lord your master,
  I have informed his highness so at large
  As, liking of the lady's virtuous gifts,
  Her beauty, and the value of her dower,
  He does intend she shall be England's Queen.
KING
  In argument and proof of which contràct,

Bear her this jewel, pledge of my affection.
And so, my Lord Protector, see them guarded
And safely brought to Dover, where enshipped,
Commit them to the fortune of the sea.

*Exeunt all but Winchester and the Legate*

WINCHESTER
Stay, my Lord Legate. You shall first receive
The sum of money which I promisèd
Should be delivered to his holiness
For clothing me in these grave ornaments.

LEGATE
I will attend upon your lordship's leisure.

*He steps aside*

WINCHESTER
Now Winchester will not submit, I trust,
Or be inferior to the proudest peer.
Humphrey of Gloucester, you shall well perceive
That neither in birth or for authority
The Bishop will be overborne by thee.
I'll either make you stoop and bend your knee
Or sack this country with a mutiny.          *Exeunt*

# SCENE II
## A plain in Anjou.

*Enter Charles, Burgundy, Alençon, the Bastard, Reignier,
and Joan la Pucelle*

CHARLES
These news, my lords, may cheer our drooping spirits:
'Tis said the stout Parisians do revolt
And turn again unto the warlike French.

ALENÇON
     Then march to Paris, royal Charles of France,
     And keep not back your powers in dalliance.
PUCELLE
     Peace be among them, if they turn to us;
     Else ruin combat with their palaces!

*Enter a Scout*

SCOUT
     Success unto our valiant general,
     And happiness to his accomplices!
CHARLES
     What tidings send our scouts? I pray you speak.
SCOUT
     The English army, that divided was
     Into two parts, is now conjoined in one,
     And means to give you battle suddenly.
CHARLES
     Somewhat too sudden, sirs, the warning is,
     But we will presently provide for them.
     I trust the ghost of Talbot is not there.
BURGUNDY
     Now he is gone, my lord, you need not fear.
PUCELLE
     Of all base passions fear is most accursed.
     Command the conquest, Charles, it shall be thine,
     Let Henry fret and all the world repine.
CHARLES
     Then on, my lords; and France be fortunate!     *Exeunt*

## SCENE III
### Before Angiers.

*Alarum. Enter Joan la Pucelle*

PUCELLE
  The Regent conquers and the Frenchmen fly.
  Now help, you charming spells and amulets;
  And you choice spirits that admonish me,
  And give me signs of future accidents;

*Thunder*

  You speedy helpers that are substitutes
  Under the lordly monarch of the North,
  Appear and aid me in this enterprise!

*Enter fiends*

  This speedy and quick appearance argues proof
  Of your accustomed diligence to me.
  Now, you familiar spirits that are called
  Out of the powerful regions under earth,
  Help me this once, that France may get the field.

*They walk, and speak not*

  O, hold me not with silence over-long!
  Where I was wont to feed you with my blood,
  I'll lop a member off and give it you
  In earnest of a further benefit,
  So you do condescend to help me now.

*They hang their heads*

No hope to have redress? My body shall
Pay recompense, if you will grant my suit.

*They shake their heads*

Cannot my body nor blood-sacrifice
Entreat you to your wonted furtherance?
Then take my soul—my body, soul, and all,
Before England shall give the French the fall.
                                    *They depart*
See, they forsake me! Now the time is come
That France must drop her lofty-plumèd crest
And let her head fall into England's lap.
My ancient incantations are too weak,
And hell too strong for me to buckle with.
Now, France, your glory droops unto the dust.      *Exit*

*Burgundy and Richard Duke of York fight hand to hand.*
*York then fights with Joan la Pucelle and overcomes her.*
*The French fly*

RICHARD
Damsel of France, I think I have you fast.
Unchain your spirits now with spelling charms,
And try if they can gain your liberty.
A goodly prize, fit for the devil's grace!
See how the ugly witch does bend her brows
As if, with Circe, she would change my shape!
PUCELLE
Changed to a worse shape you can not be.
RICHARD
O, Charles the Dauphin is a proper man;
No shape but his can please your dainty eye.
PUCELLE
A plaguing mischief light on Charles and you!
And may you both be suddenly surprised
By bloody hands in sleeping on your beds!

RICHARD

Fierce cursing hag! Enchantress, hold your tongue!

PUCELLE

I pray you give me leave to curse awhile.

RICHARD

Curse, miscreant, when you come unto the stake.

*Exeunt*


*Alarum. Enter Suffolk, holding Margaret's hand*

SUFFOLK

Be what you will, you are my prisoner.

*He gazes on her*

O fairest beauty, do not fear or fly!

For I will touch you but with reverent hands;

I kiss these fingers for eternal peace,

And lay them gently on your tender side.

Who are you? Say, that I may honour you.

MARGARET

Margaret my name, and daughter to a king,

The King of Naples, whosoever you are.

SUFFOLK

An earl I am and Suffolk am I called.

Be not offended, nature's miracle;

You are allotted to be taken by me.

So does the swan her downy cygnets save,

Keeping them prisoner underneath her wings.

Yet, if this servile usage once offend,

Go and be free again as Suffolk's friend.

O, stay! *(Aside)* I have no power to let her pass;

My hand would free her, but my heart says no.

As plays the sun upon the glassy stream,

Twinkling another counterfeited beam,

So seems this gorgeous beauty to my eyes.

Fain would I woo her, yet I dare not speak.
I'll call for pen and ink, and write my mind.
Fie, de la Pole, disable not yourself.
Have you not a tongue? Is she not here?
Will you be daunted at a woman's sight?
Ay, beauty's princely majesty is such
Confounds the tongue and makes the senses rough.

MARGARET
Say, Earl of Suffolk, if your name is so,
What ransom must I pay before I pass?
For I perceive I am your prisoner.

SUFFOLK *(aside)*
How can you tell she will deny your suit
Before you make a trial of her love?

MARGARET
Why speak you not? What ransom must I pay?

SUFFOLK *(aside)*
She's beautiful, and therefore to be wooed;
She is a woman, therefore to be won.

MARGARET
Will you accept of ransom, yea or no?

SUFFOLK *(aside)*
Fool, remember that you have a wife.
Then how can Margaret be your paramour?

MARGARET
I were best to leave him, for he will not hear.

SUFFOLK
There all is marred; there lies a cooling card.

MARGARET
He talks at random. Sure the man is mad.

SUFFOLK
And yet a dispensation may be had.

MARGARET
And yet I would that you would answer me.

SUFFOLK
I'll win this Lady Margaret. For whom?
Why, for my king! Tush, that's a wooden thing!

MARGARET
  He talks of wood. It is some carpenter.
SUFFOLK *(aside)*
  Yet so my fancy may be satisfied
  And peace establishèd between these realms.
  But there remains a scruple in that too;
  For though her father is the King of Naples,
  Duke of Anjou and Maine, yet is he poor,
  And our nobility will scorn the match.
MARGARET
  Hear you, captain? Are you not at leisure?
SUFFOLK *(aside)*
  It shall be so, disdain they never so much.
  Henry is youthful and will quickly yield. —
  *(To her)* Madam, I have a secret to reveal.
MARGARET *(aside)*
  What though I am enthralled? He seems a knight
  And will not any way dishonour me.
SUFFOLK
  Lady, deign to listen to what I say.
MARGARET *(aside)*
  Perhaps I shall be rescued by the French,
  And then I need not crave his courtesy.
SUFFOLK
  Sweet madam, give me hearing in a cause —
MARGARET *(aside)*
  Tush, women have been captivate ere now.
SUFFOLK
  Lady, wherefore talk you so?
MARGARET
  I cry you mercy, 'tis but *quid* for *quo* (tit for tat).
SUFFOLK
  Say, gentle Princess, would you not suppose
  Your bondage happy, to be made a queen?

MARGARET
 To be a queen in bondage is more vile
 Than is a slave in base servility;
 For princes should be free.
SUFFOLK                        And so shall you,
 If happy England's royal King is free.
MARGARET
 Why, what concerns his freedom unto me?
SUFFOLK
 I'll undertake to make you Henry's queen,
 To put a golden sceptre in your hand
 And set a precious crown upon your head,
 If you will condescend to be my—
MARGARET                          What?
SUFFOLK
 His love.
MARGARET
 I am unworthy to be Henry's wife.
SUFFOLK
 No, gentle madam; I unworthy am
 To woo so fair a dame to be his wife
 And have no portion in the choice myself.
 How say you, madam? Are you so content?
MARGARET
 If my father pleases, I am content.
SUFFOLK
 Then call our captains and our colours forth!
 And, madam, at your father's castle walls
 We'll crave a parley to confer with him.

 *Sound a parley. Enter Reignier on the walls*

 See, Reignier, see your daughter prisoner.
REIGNIER
 To whom?

SUFFOLK     To me.
REIGNIER                Suffolk, what remedy?
  I am a soldier and unapt to weep
  Or to exclaim on fortune's fickleness.
SUFFOLK
  Yes, there is remedy enough, my lord.
  Consent, and for your honour give consent,
  Your daughter shall be wedded to my king,
  Whom I with pain have wooed and won thereto.
  And this her easy-held imprisonment
  Has gained your daughter princely liberty.
REIGNIER
  Speaks Suffolk as he thinks?
SUFFOLK                          Fair Margaret knows
  That Suffolk does not flatter, face, or feign.
REIGNIER
  Upon your princely warrant I descend
  To give you answer of your just demand.

                                    *Exit from the walls*
SUFFOLK
  And here I will expect your coming.

          *Trumpets sound. Enter Reignier below*


REIGNIER
  Welcome, brave Earl, into our territories;
  Command in Anjou what your honour pleases.
SUFFOLK
  Thanks, Reignier, happy for so sweet a child,
  Fit to be made companion with a king.
  What answer makes your grace unto my suit?
REIGNIER
  Since you do deign to woo her little worth
  To be the princely bride of such a lord,
  Upon condition I may quietly
  Enjoy my own, the country Maine and Anjou,

Free from oppression or the stroke of war,
My daughter shall be Henry's, if he pleases.

SUFFOLK

That is her ransom. I deliver her,
And those two counties I will undertake
Your grace shall well and quietly enjoy.

REIGNIER

And I again, in Henry's royal name,
As deputy unto that gracious king,
Give you her hand for sign of plighted faith.

SUFFOLK

Reignier of France, I give you kingly thanks,
Because this is in traffic of a king.
(*Aside*) And yet I think I could be well content
To be my own attorney in this case.
(*To them*) I'll over then to England with this news
And make this marriage to be solemnized.
So, farewell, Reignier. Set this diamond safe
In golden palaces, as it becomes.

REIGNIER

I do embrace you as I would embrace
The Christian prince King Henry, were he here.

MARGARET

Farewell, my lord. Good wishes, praise, and prayers
Shall Suffolk ever have of Margaret.

*She is going*

SUFFOLK

Farewell, sweet madam. But hark you, Margaret—
No princely commendations to my king?

MARGARET

Such commendations as become a maid,
A virgin, and his servant, say to him.

SUFFOLK

Words sweetly placed and modestly directed.

But, madam, I must trouble you again—
No loving token to his majesty?

MARGARET
Yes, my good lord: a pure unspotted heart,
Never yet tainted with love, I send the King.

SUFFOLK
And this with it.

*He kisses her*

MARGARET
That for yourself. I will not so presume
To send such peevish tokens to a king.
*Exeunt Reignier and Margaret*

SUFFOLK
O, were you for myself! But, Suffolk, stay;
You may not wander in that labyrinth:
There Minotaurs and ugly treasons lurk.
Solicit Henry with her wondrous praise.
Bethink you on her virtues that surmount,
And natural graces that extinguish art;
Repeat their semblance often on the seas,
That, when you come to kneel at Henry's feet,
You may bereave him of his wits with wonder.
*Exit*

# SCENE IV
## York's camp.

*Enter Richard Duke of York, Warwick, a Shepherd, and
Joan la Pucelle, guarded*

RICHARD
Bring forth that sorceress condemned to burn.

SHEPHERD

    Ah, Joan, this kills your father's heart outright.

    Have I sought every country far and near,

    And, now it is my chance to find you out,

    Must I behold your timeless cruel death?

    Ah, Joan, sweet daughter Joan, I'll die with you!

PUCELLE

    Decrepit miser! Base ignoble wretch!

    I am descended of a gentler blood;

    You are no father nor any friend of mine.

SHEPHERD

    Out, out! My lords, so please you, 'tis not so.

    I did beget her, all the parish knows.

    Her mother that lives yet can testify

    She was the first fruit of my bachelorship.

WARWICK

    Graceless, will you deny your parentage?

RICHARD

    This argues what her kind of life has been,

    Wicked and vile; and so her death concludes.

SHEPHERD

    Fie, Joan, that you will be so obstinate!

    God knows you are a collop of my flesh,

    And for your sake have I shed many a tear.

    Deny me not, I pray you, gentle Joan.

PUCELLE

    Peasant, be gone!—You have suborned this man

    Of purpose to obscure my noble birth.

SHEPHERD

    'Tis true, I gave a noble to the priest

    The morn that I was wedded to her mother.

    Kneel down and take my blessing, good my girl.

    Will you not stoop? Now cursèd be the time

    Of your nativity! I would the milk

    Your mother gave you when you sucked her breast

    Had been a little ratsbane for your sake.

Or else, when you did keep my lambs a-field,
I wish some ravenous wolf had eaten you.
Do you deny your father, cursèd drab?
O, burn her, burn her! Hanging is too good.          *Exit*

RICHARD

Take her away; for she has lived too long,
To fill the world with vicious qualities.

PUCELLE

First let me tell you whom you have condemned:
Not one begotten of a shepherd swain,
But issued from the progeny of kings;
Virtuous and holy, chosen from above
By inspiration of celestial grace
To work exceeding miracles on earth.
I never had to do with wicked spirits.
But you, that are polluted with your lusts,
Stained with the guiltless blood of innocents,
Corrupt and tainted with a thousand vices,
Because you want the grace that others have,
You judge it straight a thing impossible
To compass wonders but by help of devils.
No, misconceivèd! Joan of Arc has been
A virgin from her tender infancy,
Chaste and immaculate in very thought,
Whose maiden blood, thus rigorously effused,
Will cry for vengeance at the gates of heaven.

RICHARD

Ay, ay. Away with her to execution!

WARWICK

And hark you, sirs; because she is a maid,
Spare for no faggots; let there be enough . . .
Place barrels of pitch upon the fatal stake,
That so her torture may be shortenèd.

PUCELLE

Will nothing turn your unrelenting hearts?
Then, Joan, discover your infirmity,

That warrants yet by law to be your privilege.
I am with child, ye bloody homicides.
Murder not then the fruit within my womb,
Although you hale me to a violent death.

RICHARD
Now heaven forfend! The holy maid with child?

WARWICK
The greatest miracle that ever you wrought!
Is all your strict preciseness come to this?

RICHARD
She and the Dauphin have been juggling.
I did imagine what would be her refuge.

WARWICK
Well, go to; we'll have no bastards live,
Especially since Charles must father it.

PUCELLE
You are deceived; my child is none of his:
It was Alençon that enjoyed my love.

RICHARD
Alençon, that notorious Machiavel?
It dies then if it had a thousand lives.

PUCELLE
O, give me leave, I have deluded you.
'Twas neither Charles nor yet the Duke I named,
But Reignier, King of Naples, that prevailed.

WARWICK
A married man! That's most intolerable.

RICHARD
Why, here's a girl! I think she knows not well,
There were so many, whom she may accuse.

WARWICK
It's sign she has been liberal and free.

RICHARD
And yet, indeed, she is a virgin pure!
Strumpet, your words condemn your brat and you.
Use no entreaty, for it is in vain.

PUCELLE
    Then lead me hence; with whom I leave my curse:
    May never glorious sun reflex its beams
    Upon the country where you make abode;
    But darkness and the gloomy shade of death
    Environ you, till mischief and despair
    Drive you to break your necks or hang yourselves!

*Exit, guarded*

RICHARD
    Break you in pieces and consume to ashes,
    You foul accursèd minister of hell!

*Enter Winchester with attendants*

WINCHESTER
    Lord Regent, I do greet your excellence
    With letters of commission from the King.
    For know, my lords, the states of Christendom,
    Moved with remorse of these outrageous broils,
    Have earnestly implored a general peace
    Between our nation and the aspiring French;
    And here at hand the Dauphin and his train
    Approach now to confer about some matter.

RICHARD
    Is all our travail turned to this effect?
    After the slaughter of so many peers,
    So many captains, gentlemen, and soldiers,
    That in this quarrel have been overthrown
    And sold their bodies for their country's benefit,
    Shall we at last conclude effeminate peace?
    Have we not lost most part of all the towns,
    By treason, falsehood, and by treachery,
    Our great progenitors had conquerèd?
    O Warwick, Warwick! I foresee with grief
    The utter loss of all the realm of France.

WARWICK
  Be patient, York. If we conclude a peace,
  It shall be with such strict and severe covenants
  As little shall the Frenchmen gain thereby.

  *Enter Charles, Alençon, the Bastard,*
  *Reignier, and attendants*

CHARLES
  Since, lords of England, it is thus agreed
  That peaceful truce shall be proclaimed in France,
  We come to be informèd by yourselves
  What the conditions of that league must be.
RICHARD
  Speak, Winchester; for boiling choler chokes
  The hollow passage of my poisoned voice,
  By sight of these our baleful enemies.
WINCHESTER
  Charles, and the rest, it is enacted thus:
  That, in regard King Henry gives consent,
  Of mere compassion and of lenity,
  To ease your country of distressful war
  And suffer you to breathe in fruitful peace,
  You shall become true liegemen to his crown,
  And, Charles, upon condition you will swear
  To pay him tribute and submit yourself,
  You shall be placed as viceroy under him,
  And still enjoy your regal dignity.
ALENÇON
  Must he be then as shadow of himself?
  Adorn his temples with a coronet,
  And yet, in substance and authority,
  Retain but privilege of a private man?
  This proffer is absurd and reasonless.
CHARLES
  'Tis known already that I am possessed

With more than half the Gallian territories,
And therein reverenced for their lawful king.
Shall I, for lucre of the rest unvanquished,
Detract so much from that prerogative
As to be called but viceroy of the whole?
No, Lord Ambassador; I'll rather keep
That which I have than, coveting for more,
Be cast from possibility of all.

RICHARD
Insulting Charles, have you by secret means
Used intercession to obtain a league,
And, now the matter grows to compromise,
Stand you aloof upon comparison?
Either accept the title you usurp,
Of benefit proceeding from our king
And not of any challenge of desert,
Or we will plague you with incessant wars.

REIGNIER (aside to Charles)
My lord, you do not well in obstinacy
To cavil in the course of this contràct.
If once it is neglected, ten to one
We shall not find like opportunity.

ALENÇON (aside to Charles)
To say the truth, it is your policy
To save your subjects from such massacre
And ruthless slaughters as are daily seen
By our proceeding in hostility;
And therefore take this compact of a truce,
Although you break it when your pleasure serves.

WARWICK
How say you, Charles? Shall our condition stand?

CHARLES
It shall;
Only reserved you claim no interest
In any of our towns of garrison.

RICHARD
    Then swear allegiance to his majesty:
    As you are knight, never to disobey
    Nor be rebellious to the crown of England—
    You, nor your nobles, to the crown of England.

*Charles and the French nobles kneel and acknowledge the
                sovereignty of Henry*

    So, now dismiss your army when you please;
    Hang up your ensigns, let your drums be still,
    For here we entertain a solemn peace.          *Exeunt*


# SCENE V
## Westminster. The royal palace.

*Enter Suffolk, in conference with the King,
        Gloucester, and Exeter*

KING
    Your wondrous rare description, noble Earl,
    Of beauteous Margaret has astonished me.
    Her virtues, gracèd with external gifts,
    Do breed love's settled passions in my heart.
    And like as rigour of tempestuous gusts
    Provokes the mightiest hulk against the tide,
    So am I driven by breath of her renown
    Either to suffer shipwreck or arrive
    Where I may have fruition of her love.
SUFFOLK
    Tush, my good lord, this superficial tale
    Is but a preface of her worthy praise.
    The chief perfections of that lovely dame,
    Had I sufficient skill to utter them,
    Would make a volume of enticing lines

Able to ravish any dull conception.
And, which is more, she is not so divine,
So full replete with choice of all delights,
But with as humble lowliness of mind
She is content to be at your command—
Command, I mean, of virtuous chaste intents,
To love and honour Henry as her lord.

KING

And otherwise will Henry never presume.
Therefore, my Lord Protector, give consent
That Margaret may be England's royal Queen.

GLOUCESTER

So should I give consent to flatter sin.
You know, my lord, your highness is betrothed
Unto another lady of esteem.
How shall we then dispense with that contràct
And not deface your honour with reproach?

SUFFOLK

As does a ruler with unlawful oaths,
Or one that at a triumph, having vowed
To try his strength, forsakes even the lists
By reason of his adversary's odds.
A poor earl's daughter is unequal odds,
And therefore may be broken without offence.

GLOUCESTER

Why, what, I pray, is Margaret more than that?
Her father is no better than an earl,
Although in glorious titles he excels.

SUFFOLK

Yes, my lord, her father is a king,
The King of Naples and Jerusalem,
And of such great authority in France
As his alliance will confirm our peace
And keep the Frenchmen in allegiance.

GLOUCESTER

And so the Earl of Armagnac may do,

Because he is near kinsman unto Charles.

EXETER

Beside, his wealth does warrant a liberal dower,
Where Reignier sooner will receive than give.

SUFFOLK

A dower, my lords? Disgrace not so your king
That he should be so abject, base, and poor
To choose for wealth and not for perfect love.
Henry is able to enrich his queen,
And not to seek a queen to make him rich.
So worthless peasants bargain for their wives,
As market-men for oxen, sheep, or horse.
Marriage is a matter of more worth
Than to be dealt in by attorneyship;
Not whom we will, but whom his grace affects,
Must be companion of his nuptial bed.
And therefore, lords, since he affects her most,
It most of all these reasons binds us then
In our opinions she should be preferred.
For what is wedlock forcèd but a hell,
An age of discord and continual strife?
Whereas the contrary brings us bliss
And is a pattern of celestial peace.
Whom should we match with Henry, being a king,
But Margaret, that is daughter to a king?
Her peerless features, joinèd with her birth,
Approve her fit for none but for a king;
Her valiant courage and undaunted spirit,
More than in women commonly is seen,
Will answer our hope in issue of a king.
For Henry, son unto a conqueror,
Is likely to beget more conquerors,
If with a lady of so high resolve
As is fair Margaret he is linked in love.
Then yield, my lords, and here conclude with me
That Margaret shall be Queen, and none but she.

KING

    Whether it is through force of your report,
My noble lord of Suffolk, or for that
My tender youth was never yet assailed
With any passion of inflaming love,
I cannot tell. But this I am assured,
I feel such sharp dissension in my breast,
Such fierce alarums both of hope and fear,
As I am sick with working of my thoughts.
Take therefore shipping; post, my lord, to France;
Agree to any covenants, and procure
That Lady Margaret does deign to come
To cross the seas to England and be crowned
King Henry's faithful and anointed queen.
For your expenses and sufficient charge,
Among the people gather up a tenth.
Be gone, I say; for till you do return
I rest perplexèd with a thousand cares.
And you, good uncle, banish all offence:
If you do censure me by what you were,
Not what you are, I know it will excuse
This sudden execution of my will.
And so conduct me where, from company,
I may resolve and ruminate my grief.                    *Exit*

GLOUCESTER

    Ay, grief, I fear me, both at first and last.

             *Exeunt Gloucester and Exeter*

SUFFOLK

    Thus Suffolk has prevailed; and thus he goes,
As did the youthful Paris once to Greece,
With hope to find the like event in love
But prosper better than the Trojan did.
Margaret shall now be Queen, and rule the King;
But I will rule both her, the King, and realm.        *Exit*

# King Henry The Sixth, Part Two

# INTRODUCTION

D r Johnson found the *Second Part of King Henry VI*
the best of the three, and indeed it has more variety
than the other two. In it also we hear the authentic
demotic voice of Shakespeare in the scenes of Cade's
rebellion, the voice of the people, which he always renders
absurd and comic, good-humouredly but dismissively. It
follows straight on the heels of the *First Part* and belongs
to 1591–2. We know how rapidly he wrote, sometimes
casually enough, just versifying the Chronicles, here mainly
Holinshed. All the same, as Professor Sisson sums up—after
the long and rather profitless controversy about this early
trilogy, 'it is difficult to deny the control of one guiding
hand in the long series of these plays.' He means that they
are authentic early Shakespeare. We need add only that
they are too long, and for modern production need cutting;
in reading them at full length we can all learn something.

The play begins with the King's reception of his wife,
Margaret of Anjou, whom Suffolk had wooed for him in
France, when they fell for each other. Henry is still not
much more than a boy, unfit for the job of king, unable to
keep order in the nursery: a medieval king needed to be
tough in the struggle for survival and in the snake-pit of
politicians. He is more fit to be a cleric, as Margaret
says—and she is an unsatisfied woman. To us Henry's
character is more sympathetic: he always tries for peace

and to keep people together, he is humane but not strong enough for them. This sharpens the conflict of party, and we have too many slanging-matches of politicians.

Besides the personal animosities and in-fighting for power and wealth, there was a real issue: how and when to bring the war in France to a close? It was difficult to make peace in circumstances of defeat. Cardinal Beaufort headed the peace-party, and he receives grave injustice in the play: true, he was too rich and grasping, but he was able and right—and cardinals were not popular in England. Humphrey, Duke of Gloucester, his nephew, headed the war-party and was therefore popular—'good Duke Humphrey'; a light-weight, the people could understand *him*.

He was let down by his wife, the silly Duchess who went in for witchcraft against the King's life: this was factual history, and the sorcery, incantations, raising of a spirit, add a new element of appeal to the play. On the other hand, there is no warrant for supposing that Humphrey was murdered: blaming his death on Beaufort is quite unjust—and Dr Johnson found the Cardinal's death-bed scene truly affecting.

We have the fall of the overweening Suffolk—not much sympathy for him, though his real crime was that he made peace without honour in France and Margaret's marriage, which turned out badly—and his capture and decapitation in the Channel. There is much lopping off of heads, though this gets worse with the Wars of the Roses, with the beginning of which the *Second Part* ends.

Best of all, as we begin to appreciate very early in Shakespeare's work, is what he himself invents: the scenes in which Jack Cade appears, though his rebellion was historical enough, with the Duke of York already plotting his challenge for the crown.[1] In these scenes we hear the actor's marvellous ear for the idiom, the turns of thought,

---

[1] cf my *Bosworth Field and the Wars of the Roses,* 123–5.

of the people. Characteristically enough, Cade is libelled, besmirched and eventually betrayed by his own people. His last reflection on them is, 'was ever feather so lightly blown to and fro as this multitude?' It is precisely the same image which the King has reason to use in the next play—evidently what Shakespeare himself thought, commonplace with Elizabethans who had no illusions on the subject.

The sixteenth century had been thoroughly alarmed by the Peasants' Revolt in Germany and the appalling experiment in communism in Münster, which even threw the weighty Luther off his balance and rendered him quite hysterical. Cade promises his followers, 'henceforward all things shall be in common.' The portrait of the mob occurs in similar terms consistently all through Shakespeare— his was the regular Elizabethan governing-class point of view—and the impracticality of communism is exposed again at the end in *The Tempest*.

He touches off typical wiseacres' arguments, such as he had heard and registered. A smith testifies to Cade's lordly birth, 'because he made a chimney in my father's house, and the bricks are alive at this day to testify it; therefore deny it not.' Lord Say could speak French. Thus Cade: 'the Frenchmen are our enemies: can he that speaks with the tongue of an enemy be a good councillor, or no? . . . Answer if you can.' They all answer no—'and therefore we'll have his head'—and did. What Cade's new deal amounted to in practice was sacking the Inns of Court—'the first thing we do, let's kill all the lawyers.' The next thing is 'to break open the gaols and let out the prisoners.' Cade:

And you that love the commons, follow me.
Now show yourselves men; 'tis for liberty.

It cannot be said that William Shakespeare loved the commons or had any illusions about liberty.

They on the other hand have no use for letters and book-learning. Because a clerk can read and write Cade has him hanged 'with his pen and inkhorn about his neck.' Lord Say has 'most traitorously corrupted the youth of the realm in erecting a grammar school; and whereas before, our forefathers had no other books but the score and the tally, you have caused printing to be used.' And so on. It is all levelled to make fun of the people, and it is very funny; but there is an edge to it, and we need not doubt what William Shakespeare thought. England has had to wait some four hundred years for the grammar schools to go down under the pressure for egalitarianism.

Of personal touches we have images from the theatre as always. Gloucester's Duchess, given an affecting part at the end:

> being a woman, I will not be slack
> To play my part in Fortune's pageant.

Gloucester himself:

> But mine is made the prologue to their play;
> For thousands more, that yet suspect no peril,
> Will not conclude their plotted tragedy.

Classical references are much to the fore: Aeneas bearing old Anchises; Medea cutting young Absyrtus into gobbets [*Titus Andronicus* is not far away]; Ajax Telamonius spending his fury on sheep and oxen; Althea's fatal brand; Ascanius unfolding the tale of burning Troy to Dido; quotations from Cicero ('sweet Tully') and Caesar's *Commentaries*. Though the range of reading may not be wide, the references are, and testify to the undying impression his grammar school training had had—sufficient to last him for his career as a writer, though evidently he kept his reading up in contemporary literature.[2]

Familiar touches from contemporary life have a personal ring; bear-baiting, for example:

Oft have I seen a hot over-weening cur
Run back and bite, because he was withheld,
Which, being suffered with the bear's fell paw,
Has clapped his tail between his legs and cried.

Or there is the affecting visuality of this:

And as the butcher takes away the calf,
And binds the wretch and beats it when it strains,
Bearing it to the bloody slaughterhouse . . .
And as the dam runs lowing up and down,
Looking the way her harmless young one went,
And can do naught but wail her darling's loss . . .

John Aubrey has been absurdly discounted for saying that Shakespeare's father was a butcher, when he was a glover; but of course an Elizabethan glover would take a hand in butchering. Neighbours told Aubrey that as a boy William helped in his father's trade, and 'when he killed a calf he would do it in a high style, and make a speech.' It is in character.

Something is made of Warwick's crest,

The rampant bear chained to the ragged staff—

which became Leicester's, and was much in evidence all round Warwickshire. To my ear the image of 'rich hangings in a homely house' recalls Shakespeare's mother's home, the Ardens' house at Wilmcote, for—quite exceptionally—

---

[2] cf my *What Shakespeare Read and Thought.*

there the farmhouse was hung with a large number of arras hangings.

The language of this play offers no difficult problems in modernising. Why retain Killingworth, as many editions do, for well known Kenilworth; or Sylla for Sulla? (Silly.) Or such an archaic form as 'denayed', for simply denied? The word 'censure' offers a little difficulty, for in Elizabethan times it meant opinion or judgement, not unfavourable, the more restricted sense today. Shakespeare was quite inconsistent in using the personal relative 'who' for which, and vice versa for the impersonal, where today we follow a consistent usage, and—in a modern text—it is an advantage to do so.

A number of footnotes are provided, mainly to explain Latin phrases.

# CHARACTERS

King Henry the Sixth

Margaret of Anjou, Henry's Queen

Duke of York, Richard Plantagenet

Edward  } sons of the Duke of York
Richard  }

Humphrey, Duke of Gloucester, uncle of the King

Duchess of Gloucester, Eleanor Cobham

Cardinal Beaufort, Bishop of Winchester, great-uncle
of the King

Duke of Suffolk

Duke of Somerset

Duke of Buckingham

Earl of Salisbury

Earl of Warwick

Lord Clifford

Young Clifford, his son

Lord Scales

Lord Say

Sir Humphrey Stafford and William Stafford, his
Brother

Sir John Stanley

Vaux

Alexander Iden, a Kentish gentleman

John Hume, and John Southwell, two priests

Roger Bolingbroke, a conjurer

Margery Jourdain, a witch

A Spirit

Thomas Horner, an armourer and Peter his man

Saunder Simpcox, an imposter

Mayor of Saint Albans

Jack Cade, a rebel

146

GEORGE BEVIS, JOHN HOLLAND, DICK, a butcher,
SMITH, a weaver, MICHAEL (followers of Jack Cade)
Two Murderers
A LIEUTENANT, A MASTER, A MASTER'S MATE,
WALTER WHITMORE, TWO GENTLEMEN, prisoners
with Suffolk

Lords, ladies, attendants, petitioners, aldermen, officers,
soldiers, messengers, guards, citizens, a sheriff, a herald

# Act I

## SCENE I
## Westminster. The palace.

*Flourish of trumpets. Enter the King, Gloucester, Salisbury,
Warwick, and Cardinal Beaufort on the one side;
the Queen, Suffolk, York, Somerset, and Buckingham
on the other*

SUFFOLK
As by your high imperial majesty
I had in charge at my depart for France,
As procurator to your excellence,
To marry Princess Margaret for your grace;
So, in the famous ancient city Tours,
In presence of the Kings of France and Sicily,
The Dukes of Orleans, Calaber, Brittany, and Alençon,
Seven earls, twelve barons, and twenty reverend bishops,
I have performed my task and was espoused;
And humbly now upon my bended knee,
In sight of England and her lordly peers,
Deliver up my title in the Queen
To your most gracious hands, that are the substance
Of that great shadow I did represent—
The happiest gift that ever marquess gave,
The fairest queen that ever king received.
KING
Suffolk, arise. Welcome, Queen Margaret.
I can express no kinder sign of love
Than this kind kiss. O Lord that lends me life,
Lend me a heart replete with thankfulness!

For you have given me in this beauteous face
A world of earthly blessings to my soul,
If sympathy of love unites our thoughts.

QUEEN
Great King of England and my gracious lord,
The mutual conference that my mind has had
By day, by night, waking and in my dreams,
In courtly company or at my beads,
With you, my most beloved sovereign,
Makes me the bolder to salute my king
With ruder terms, such as my wit affords,
And overjoy of heart does minister.

KING
Her sight did ravish, but her grace in speech,
Her words so clad with wisdom's majesty,
Make me from wondering fall to weeping joys,
Such is the fullness of my heart's content.
Lords, with one cheerful voice welcome my love.

*All kneel*

ALL
Long live Queen Margaret, England's happiness!

*Flourish*

QUEEN
We thank you all.

SUFFOLK
My Lord Protector, so it please your grace,
Here are the articles of contracted peace
Between our sovereign and the French King Charles,
For eighteen months concluded by consent.

GLOUCESTER (*reads*) *Imprimis, it is agreed between the French King Charles and William de la Pole, Marquess of Suffolk, ambassador for Henry King of England, that the said Henry shall espouse the Lady Margaret, daughter unto Reignier King of Naples, Sicily, and Jerusalem, and crown her Queen of England ere the thirtieth of May next ensuing. Item, it is further agreed between them that the duchy of Anjou and the county of Maine shall be released and delivered over to the King her father—*

*Gloucester lets the contract fall*

KING
  Uncle, how now?
GLOUCESTER       Pardon me, gracious lord.
  Some sudden qualm has struck me at the heart
  And dimmed my eyes, that I can read no further.
KING
  Uncle of Winchester, I pray read on.
CARDINAL (*reads*) *Item, it is further agreed between them that the duchy of Anjou and the county of Maine shall be released and delivered over to the King her father, and she sent over at the King of England's own proper cost and charges, without having any dowry.*
KING
  They please us well. Lord Marquess, kneel down.
  We here create you the first Duke of Suffolk
  And girt you with the sword. Cousin of York,
  We here discharge your grace from being Regent
  In the parts of France, till term of eighteen months
  Is full expired. Thanks, uncle Winchester,
  Gloucester, York, Buckingham, Somerset,
  Salisbury, and Warwick.
  We thank you all for this great favour done
  In entertainment to my princely Queen.

Come, let us in, and with all speed provide
To see her coronation be performed.
                    *Exeunt King, Queen, and Suffolk*

GLOUCESTER

Brave peers of England, pillars of the state,
To you Duke Humphrey must unload his grief,
Your grief, the common grief of all the land.
What? Did my brother Henry spend his youth,
His valour, coin, and people in the wars?
Did he so often lodge in open field,
In winter's cold and summer's parching heat,
To conquer France, his true inheritance?
And did my brother Bedford toil his wits
To keep by policy what Henry got?
Have you yourselves, Somerset, Buckingham,
Brave York, Salisbury, and victorious Warwick,
Received deep scars in France and Normandy?
Or have my uncle Beaufort and myself,
With all the learnèd Council of the realm,
Studied so long, sat in the Council House
Early and late, debating to and fro
How France and Frenchmen might be kept in awe?
And had his highness in his infancy
Crownèd in Paris in despite of foes?
And shall these labours and these honours die?
Shall Henry's conquest, Bedford's vigilance,
Your deeds of war, and all our counsel die?
O peers of England, shameful is this league,
Fatal this marriage, cancelling your fame,
Blotting your names from books of memory,
Razing the characters of your renown,
Defacing monuments of conquered France,
Undoing all, as all had never been!

CARDINAL

Nephew, what means this passionate discourse,
This peroration with such circumstance?

For France, 'tis ours; and we will keep it still.
GLOUCESTER
   Ay, uncle, we will keep it, if we can;
   But now it is impossible we should.
   Suffolk, the new-made duke that rules the roast,
   Has given the duchy of Anjou and Maine
   Unto the poor King Reignier, whose large style
   Agrees not with the leanness of his purse.
SALISBURY
   Now by the death of him that died for all,
   These counties were the keys of Normandy.
   But wherefore weeps Warwick, my valiant son?
WARWICK
   For grief that they are past recovery;
   For, were there hope to conquer them again,
   My sword should shed hot blood, my eyes no tears.
   Anjou and Maine? Myself did win them both;
   Those provinces these arms of mine did conquer;
   And are the cities that I got with wounds
   Delivered up again with peaceful words?
   *Mort Dieu!* [God's death!]
YORK
   For Suffolk's duke, may he be suffocated,
   That dims the honour of this warlike isle!
   France should have torn and rent my very heart
   Before I would have yielded to this league.
   I never read but England's kings have had
   Large sums of gold and dowries with their wives;
   And our King Henry gives away his own,
   To match with her that brings no vantages.
GLOUCESTER
   A proper jest, and never heard before,
   That Suffolk should demand a whole fifteenth
   For costs and charges in transporting her!
   She should have stayed in France, and starved in France,
   Before—

CARDINAL
  My lord of Gloucester, now you grow too hot;
  It was the pleasure of my lord the King.

GLOUCESTER
  My lord of Winchester, I know your mind;
  'Tis not my speeches that you do mislike,
  But 'tis my presence that does trouble you.
  Rancour will out; proud prelate, in your face
  I see your fury. If I longer stay,
  We shall begin our ancient bickerings.
  Lordings, farewell; and say, when I am gone,
  I prophesied France will be lost ere long.

                                      *Exit Gloucester*

CARDINAL
  So there goes our Protector in a rage.
  It is known to you he is my enemy;
  Nay more, an enemy unto you all,
  And no great friend, I fear me, to the King.
  Consider, lords, he is the next of blood
  And heir apparent to the English crown.
  Had Henry got an empire by his marriage,
  And all the wealthy kingdoms of the west,
  There's reason he should be displeased at it.
  Look to it, lords; let not his smoothing words
  Bewitch your hearts. Be wise and circumspect.
  What though the common people favour him,
  Calling him 'Humphrey, the good Duke of Gloucester',
  Clapping their hands and crying with loud voice
  'Jesu maintain your royal excellence!'
  With 'God preserve the good Duke Humphrey!',
  I fear me, lords, for all this flattering gloss,
  He will be found a dangerous Protector.

BUCKINGHAM
  Why should he then protect our sovereign,
  He being of age to govern of himself?
  Cousin of Somerset, join you with me,

And all together, with the Duke of Suffolk,
We'll quickly hoist Duke Humphrey from his seat.
CARDINAL
This weighty business will not brook delay;
I'll to the Duke of Suffolk now at once.                   *Exit*
SOMERSET
Cousin of Buckingham, though Humphrey's pride
And greatness of his place are grief to us,
Yet let us watch the haughty Cardinal;
His insolence is more intolerable
Than all the princes' in the land beside.
If Gloucester is displaced, he'll be Protector.
BUCKINGHAM
Or you or I, Somerset, will be Protector,
Despite Duke Humphrey or the Cardinal.
                              *Exeunt Buckingham and Somerset*
SALISBURY
Pride went before; Ambition follows him.
While these do labour for their own preferment,
Behoves it us to labour for the realm.
I never saw but Humphrey Duke of Gloucester
Did bear him like a noble gentleman.
Oft have I seen the haughty Cardinal,
More like a soldier than a man of the church,
As stout and proud as he were lord of all,
Swear like a ruffian, and demean himself
Unlike the ruler of a commonweal.
Warwick, my son, the comfort of my age,
Your deeds, your plainness, and your house-keeping
Have won the greatest favour of the commons,
Excepting none but good Duke Humphrey.
And, brother York, your acts in Ireland,
In bringing them to civil discipline,
Your late exploits done in the heart of France,
When you were Regent for our sovereign,
Have made you feared and honoured of the people.

Join we together for the public good,
In what we can to bridle and suppress
The pride of Suffolk and the Cardinal,
With Somerset's and Buckingham's ambition;
And, as we may, cherish Duke Humphrey's deeds
While they do tend the profit of the land.

WARWICK
So God help Warwick, as he loves the land
And common profit of his country!

YORK
And so says York—(*aside*) for he has greatest cause.

SALISBURY
Then let's make haste away, and look unto the main.

WARWICK
Unto the main! O father, Maine is lost!
That Maine which by main force Warwick did win,
And would have kept so long as breath did last!
Main chance, father, you meant; but I meant Maine,
Which I will win from France or else be slain.

                                      *Exeunt Warwick and Salisbury*

YORK
Anjou and Maine are given to the French;
Paris is lost; the state of Normandy
Stands on a ticklish point now they are gone.
Suffolk concluded on the articles,
The peers agreed, and Henry was well pleased
To change two dukedoms for a duke's fair daughter.
I cannot blame them all; what is it to them?
'Tis yours they give away, and not their own.
Pirates may make cheap pennyworths of their pillage
And purchase friends and give to courtesans,
Still revelling like lords till all be gone.
While then the silly owner of the goods
Weeps over them, and wrings his hapless hands,
And shakes his head, and trembling stands aloof,
While all is shared and all is borne away,

Ready to starve, and dares not touch his own.
So York must sit and fret and bite his tongue,
While his own lands are bargained for and sold.
It seems the realms of England, France, and Ireland
Bear that proportion to my flesh and blood
As did the fatal brand Althaea burnt
Unto the Prince's heart of Calydon.
Anjou and Maine both given unto the French!
Cold news for me; for I had hope of France,
Even as I have of fertile England's soil.
A day will come when York shall claim his own,
And therefore I will take the Nevils' parts
And make a show of love to proud Duke Humphrey;
And, when I spy advantage, claim the crown,
For that's the golden mark I seek to hit.
Nor shall proud Lancaster usurp my right,
Nor hold the sceptre in his childish fist,
Nor wear the diadem upon his head,
Whose church-like humours fit not for a crown.
Then, York, be still awhile till time does serve;
Watch you, and wake when others are asleep,
To pry into the secrets of the state—
Till Henry, surfeiting in joys of love
With his new bride and England's dear-bought queen,
And Humphrey with the peers are fallen at jars.
Then will I raise aloft the milk-white rose,
With whose sweet smell the air shall be perfumed,
And in my standard bear the arms of York,
To grapple with the house of Lancaster.
And force perforce I'll make him yield the crown,
Whose bookish rule has pulled fair England down.

*Exit*

## SCENE II
### Gloucester's house.

*Enter the Duke of Gloucester and the Duchess*

DUCHESS
  Why droops my lord like over-ripened corn,
  Hanging the head at Ceres' plenteous load?
  Why does the great Duke Humphrey knit his brows,
  As frowning at the favours of the world?
  Why are your eyes fixed to the sullen earth,
  Gazing on that which seems to dim your sight?
  What see you there? King Henry's diadem,
  Enchased with all the honours of the world?
  If so, gaze on, and grovel on your face,
  Until your head is circled with the same.
  Put forth your hand, reach at the glorious gold.
  What, is it too short? I'll lengthen it with mine;
  And having both together heaved it up,
  We'll both together lift our heads to heaven,
  And never more abase our sight so low
  As to allow one glance unto the ground.
GLOUCESTER
  O Nell, sweet Nell, if you do love your lord,
  Banish the canker of ambitious thoughts!
  And may that thought, when I imagine ill
  Against my king and nephew, virtuous Henry,
  Be my last breathing in this mortal world!
  My troublous dreams this night do make me sad.
DUCHESS
  What dreamed my lord? Tell me, and I'll requite it
  With sweet rehearsal of my morning's dream.
GLOUCESTER
  I thought this staff, my office-badge in court,
  Was broken in twain—by whom I have forgotten,
  But, as I think, it was by the Cardinal.

And on the pieces of the broken wand
Were placed the heads of Edmund Duke of Somerset
And William de la Pole, first Duke of Suffolk.
This was my dream; what it does bode, God knows.

DUCHESS

Tut, this was nothing but an argument
That he that breaks a stick of Gloucester's grove
Shall lose his head for his presumptiòn.
Listen to me, my Humphrey, my sweet Duke:
I thought I sat in seat of majesty
In the cathedral church of Westminster,
And in that chair where kings and queens were crowned,
Where Henry and Dame Margaret kneeled to me,
And on my head did set the diadem.

GLOUCESTER

Nay, Eleanor, then must I chide outright:
Presumptuous dame! Ill-nurtured Eleanor!
Are you not second woman in the realm,
And the Protector's wife, beloved of him?
Have you not worldly pleasure at command
Above the reach or compass of your thought?
And will you still be hammering treachery,
To tumble down your husband and yourself
From top of honour to disgrace's feet?
Away from me, and let me hear no more!

DUCHESS

What, what, my lord? Are you so choleric
With Eleanor, for telling but her dream?
Next time I'll keep my dreams unto myself,
And not be checked.

GLOUCESTER

Nay, be not angry; I am pleased again.

*Enter a Messenger*

MESSENGER
  My Lord Protector, it is his highness' pleasure
  You do prepare to ride unto Saint Albans,
  Whereat the King and Queen do mean to hawk.
GLOUCESTER
  I go. Come, Nell, you will ride with us?
DUCHESS
  Yes, my good lord, I'll follow presently.
                    *Exeunt Gloucester and Messenger*
  Follow I must; I cannot go before
  While Gloucester bears this base and humble mind.
  Were I a man, a duke, and next of blood,
  I would remove these tedious stumbling-blocks
  And smooth my way upon their headless necks;
  And, being a woman, I will not be slack
  To play my part in Fortune's pageant.
  Where are you there? Sir John! Nay, fear not, man.
  We are alone; here's none but you and I.

                    *Enter Hume*

HUME
  Jesus preserve your royal majesty!
DUCHESS
  What say you? 'Majesty'! I am but 'grace'.
HUME
  But, by the grace of God and Hume's advice,
  Your grace's title shall be multiplied.
DUCHESS
  What say you, man? Have you as yet conferred
  With Margery Jourdain, the cunning witch,
  With Roger Bolingbroke, the conjurer?
  And will they undertake to do me good?
HUME
  This they have promised: to show your highness
  A spirit raised from depth of under ground,

That shall make answer to such questions
As by your grace shall be propounded him.
DUCHESS
It is enough; I'll think upon the questions.
When from Saint Albans we do make return,
We'll see these things effected to the full.
Here, Hume, take this reward. Make merry, man,
With your confederates in this weighty cause.        *Exit*
HUME
Hume must make merry with the Duchess' gold;
Marry [Indeed], and shall. But how now, Sir John
    Hume?
Seal up your lips and give no words but mum;
The business asks for silent secrecy.
Dame Eleanor gives gold to bring the witch;
Gold cannot come amiss, were she a devil.
Yet have I gold flies from another coast—
I dare not say from the rich Cardinal
And from the great and new-made Duke of Suffolk.
Yet I do find it so; for, to be plain,
They, knowing Dame Eleanor's aspiring humour,
Have hired me to undermine the Duchess,
And buzz these conjurations in her brain.
They say 'A crafty knave does need no broker';
Yet am I Suffolk and the Cardinal's broker.
Hume, if you take not heed, you shall go near
To call them both a pair of crafty knaves.
Well, so it stands; and thus, I fear, at last
Hume's knavery will be the Duchess' wreck.
And her attainder[1] will be Humphrey's fall.
Sort how it will, I shall have gold for all.          *Exit*

---

[1]Condemnation for treason.

## SCENE III
### Westminster. The palace.

*Enter Peter and other Petitioners*

FIRST PETITIONER My masters, let's stand close. My Lord
Protector will come this way by and by, and then we
may deliver our supplications in the group.

SECOND PETITIONER Sure, the Lord protect him, for he's a
good man. Jesu bless him!

*Enter Suffolk and the Queen*

PETER Here he comes, I think, and the Queen with him.
I'll be the first, sure.

SECOND PETITIONER Come back, fool. This is the Duke of
Suffolk and not my Lord Protector.

SUFFOLK How now, fellow? Would you anything with me?

FIRST PETITIONER I pray, my lord, pardon me; I took you for
my Lord Protector.

QUEEN *(reads)* 'For my Lord Protector'? Are your supplications to his lordship? Let me see them. What is yours?

FIRST PETITIONER Mine is, please your grace, against John
Goodman, my lord Cardinal's man, for keeping my
house, and lands, and wife, and all, from me.

SUFFOLK Your wife too! That's some wrong indeed.—What's
yours? What's here? *(Reads)* 'Against the Duke of Suffolk,
for enclosing the commons of Melford.' How now, sir
knave!

SECOND PETITIONER Alas, sir, I am but a poor petitioner
of our whole township.

PETER *(offering his petition)* Against my master, Thomas
Horner, for saying that the Duke of York was rightful
heir to the crown.

QUEEN What say you? Did the Duke of York say he was
rightful heir to the crown?

PETER That my master was? No, for sure; my master said
    that he was, and that the King was an usurper.
SUFFOLK Who is there?

*Enter a servant*

Take this fellow in, and send for his master with a
messenger at once. We'll hear more of your matter before
the King.                                *Exit servant with Peter*
QUEEN
    And as for you that love to be protected
    Under the wings of our Protector's grace,
    Begin your suits anew and sue to him.

*She tears the petitions*

Away, base rascals! Suffolk, let them go.
ALL PETITIONERS Come, let's be gone.                *Exeunt*
QUEEN
    My lord of Suffolk, say, is this the guise,
    Is this the fashion in the court of England?
    Is this the government of Britain's isle,
    And this the royalty of Albion's king?
    What, shall King Henry be a pupil still
    Under the surly Gloucester's governance?
    Am I a queen in title and in style,
    And must be made a subject to a duke?
    I tell you, Pole, when in the city of Tours
    You ran a tilt in honour of my love
    And stole away the ladies' hearts of France,
    I thought King Henry had resembled you
    In courage, courtship, and proportiòn.
    But all his mind is bent to holiness,
    To number Ave-Maries on his beads;
    His champions are the prophets and apostles,
    His weapons holy words of sacred writ;

His study is his tilt-yard, and his loves
Are brazen images of canònized saints.
I would the College of the Cardinals
Would choose him Pope, and carry him to Rome,
And set the triple crown upon his head—
That were a state fit for his holiness.

SUFFOLK
Madam, be patient. As I was cause
Your highness came to England, so will I
In England work your grace's full content.

QUEEN
Beside the haughty Protector have we Beaufort
The imperious churchman, Somerset, Buckingham,
And grumbling York; and not the least of these
But can do more in England than the King.

SUFFOLK
And he of these that can do most of all
Cannot do more in England than the Nevils;
Salisbury and Warwick are no simple peers.

QUEEN
Not all these lords do vex me half so much
As that proud dame, the Lord Protector's wife;
She sweeps it through the court with troops of ladies,
More like an empress than Duke Humphrey's wife.
Strangers in court do take her for the queen.
She bears a duke's revenues on her back,
And in her heart she scorns our poverty.
Shall I not live to be avenged on her?
Contemptuous base-born strumpet as she is,
She vaunted among her minions the other day
The very train of her worst wearing gown
Was better worth than all my father's lands,
Till Suffolk gave two dukedoms for his daughter.

SUFFOLK
Madam, myself have limed a bush for her,
And placed a choir of such enticing birds

That she will alight to listen to their lays,
And never mount to trouble you again.
So let her rest; and, madam, listen to me,
For I am bold to counsel you in this:
Although we fancy not the Cardinal,
Yet must we join with him and with the lords
Till we have brought Duke Humphrey in disgrace.
As for the Duke of York, this late complaint
Will make but little for his benefit.
So one by one we'll weed them all at last,
And you yourself shall steer the happy helm.

*Sound a sennet. Enter the King, Gloucester, the Cardinal,*
*Buckingham, York, Salisbury, Warwick, Somerset, and the*
*Duchess of Gloucester*

KING
For my part, noble lords, I care not which;
Or Somerset or York, all's one to me.
YORK
If York has ill demeaned himself in France,
Then let him be denied the Regentship.
SOMERSET
If Somerset is unworthy of the place,
Let York be Regent. I will yield to him.
WARWICK
Whether your grace is worthy, yea or no,
Dispute not that; York is the worthier.
CARDINAL
Ambitious Warwick, let your betters speak.
WARWICK
The Cardinal's not my better in the field.
BUCKINGHAM
All in this presence are your betters, Warwick.
WARWICK
Warwick may live to be the best of all.

SALISBURY
  Peace, son; and show some reason, Buckingham,
  Why Somerset should be preferred in this.
QUEEN
  Because the King, in fact, will have it so.
GLOUCESTER
  Madam, the King is old enough himself
  To give his view. These are no women's matters.
QUEEN
  If he is old enough, what needs your grace
  To be Protector of his excellence?
GLOUCESTER
  Madam, I am Protector of the realm,
  And at his pleasure will resign my place.
SUFFOLK
  Resign it then, and leave your insolence.
  Since you were king—as who is king but you?—
  The commonwealth has daily run to wreck,
  The Dauphin has prevailed beyond the seas,
  And all the peers and nobles of the realm
  Have been as bondmen to your sovereignty.
CARDINAL
  The commons have you racked; the clergy's bags
  Are lank and lean with your extortions.
SOMERSET
  Your sumptuous buildings and your wife's attire
  Have cost a mass of public treasury too.
BUCKINGHAM
  Your cruelty in executiòn
  Upon offenders has exceeded law,
  And left you to the mercy of the law.
QUEEN
  Your sale of offices and towns in France,
  If they were known, as the suspèct is great,
  Would make you quickly hop without your head.
                                    *Exit Gloucester*

*The Queen lets fall her fan*

Give me my fan. What, minion, can ye not?

*She gives the Duchess of Gloucester a box on the ear*

I cry you mercy, madam; was it you?
DUCHESS
Was it I? Yes, I it was, proud Frenchwoman.
Could I come near your beauty with my nails,
I could set my ten commandments on your face.
KING
Sweet aunt, be quiet; it was against her will.
DUCHESS
Against her will, good King? Look to it in time.
She'll hamper you, and dandle you like a baby.
Though in this place most master wears no breeches,
She shall not strike Dame Eleanor unrevenged.    *Exit*
BUCKINGHAM
Lord Cardinal, I will follow Eleanor,
And listen after Humphrey, how he proceeds.
She's tickled now; her fury needs no spurs,
She'll gallop far enough to her destruction.    *Exit*

*Enter Gloucester*

GLOUCESTER
Now, lords, my choler being overblown
With walking once about the quadrangle,
I come to talk of commonwealth affairs.
As for your spiteful false objectìons,
Prove them, and I lie open to the law;
But God in mercy so deal with my soul
As I in duty love my king and country!
But to the matter that we have in hand:

I say, my sovereign, York is meetest man
To be your Regent in the realm of France.

SUFFOLK
Before we make election, give me leave
To show some reason of no little force
That York is most unmeet of any man.

YORK
I'll tell you, Suffolk, why I am unmeet:
First, that I cannot flatter you in pride;
Next, if I am appointed for the place,
My lord of Somerset will keep me here,
Without discharge, money, or furniture,
Till France is won into the Dauphin's hands.
Last time I danced attendance on his will
Till Paris was besieged, famished, and lost.

WARWICK
That can I witness, and a fouler fact
Did never traitor in the land commit.

SUFFOLK
Peace, headstrong Warwick!

WARWICK
Image of pride, why should I hold my peace?

*Enter Horner the armourer and Peter, guarded*

SUFFOLK
Because here is a man accused of treason.
Pray God the Duke of York excuses himself!

YORK
Does anyone accuse York for a traitor?

KING
What mean you, Suffolk? Tell me, what are these?

SUFFOLK
Please it your majesty, this is the man
That does accuse his master of high treason.
His words were these: that Richard Duke of York

Was rightful heir unto the English crown,
And that your majesty was an usurper.

KING Say, man, were these your words?

HORNER If it shall please your majesty, I never said nor
thought any such matter. God is my witness, I am
falsely accused by the villain.

PETER By these ten bones, my lords, he did speak them to
me in the garret one night as we were scouring my lord
of York's armour.

YORK
Base dunghill villain and mechanical,
I'll have your head for this your traitor's speech.
I do beseech your royal majesty,
Let him have all the rigour of the law.

HORNER Alas, my lord, hang me if ever I spoke the words.
My accuser is my apprentice, and when I did correct
him for his fault the other day, he did vow upon his
knees he would be even with me. I have good witness of
this; therefore I beseech your majesty, do not cast away
an honest man for a villain's accusation.

KING
Uncle, what shall we say to this in law?

GLOUCESTER
This sentence, my lord, if I may judge:
Let Somerset be Regent over the French,
Because in York this breeds suspiciòn.
And let these have a day appointed them
For single combat in convenient place,
For he has witness of his servant's malice.
This is the law, and this Duke Humphrey's judgement.

SOMERSET
I humbly thank your royal majesty.

HORNER
And I accept the combat willingly.

PETER Alas, my lord, I cannot fight; for God's sake, pity
   my case. The spite of man prevails against me. O Lord,
   have mercy upon me! I never shall be able to fight a
   blow. O Lord, my heart!
GLOUCESTER
   Boy, either you must fight or else be hanged.
KING Away with them to prison; and the day of combat
   shall be the last of the next month. Come, Somerset,
   we'll see you sent away!                    *Flourish. Exeunt*

# SCENE IV
## Gloucester's garden.

*Enter the witch, Margery Jourdain, the two priests, Hume
and Southwell, and Bolingbroke*

HUME Come, my masters, the Duchess, I tell you, expects
   performance of your promises.
BOLINGBROKE Master Hume, we are therefore provided.
   Will her ladyship behold and hear our exorcisms?
HUME Ay, what else? Fear you not her courage.
BOLINGBROKE I have heard her reported to be a woman of
   an invincible spirit; but it shall be convenient, Master
   Hume, that you be by her aloft, while we are busy
   below; and so I pray you go in God's name, and leave us.
                                          *Exit Hume*
   Mother Jourdain, be you prostrate and grovel on the
   earth. John Southwell, read you; and let us to our work.

*Enter the Duchess of Gloucester aloft, with Hume*

DUCHESS Well said, my masters, and welcome all. To this
   gear the sooner the better.
BOLINGBROKE
   Patience, good lady; wizards know their times.

Deep night, dark night, the silence of the night,
The time of night when Troy was set on fire,
The time when screech-owls cry and ban-dogs howl,
And spirits walk, and ghosts break up their graves,
That time best fits the work we have in hand.
Madam, sit you and fear not. Whom we raise
We will make fast within a hallowed verge.

*They do the ceremonies belonging, and make the magic
circle. Southwell reads 'Conjuro te' etc. It thunders and
lightens, then the Spirit rises*

SPIRIT
*Adsum.* [Here I am].
JOURDAIN
Asmath!
By the eternal God, whose name and power
You tremble at, answer what I shall ask;
For till you speak, you shall not pass from hence.
SPIRIT
Ask what you will. That I had said and done!
BOLINGBROKE (*reads*)
*First, of the King: what shall of him become?*
SPIRIT
The duke yet lives that Henry shall depose;
But him outlive, and die a violent death.

*Southwell writes the answer*

BOLINGBROKE (*reads*)
*What fates await the Duke of Suffolk?*
SPIRIT
By water shall he die, and take his end.
BOLINGBROKE (*reads*)
*What shall befall the Duke of Somerset?*

SPIRIT

Let him shun castles;
Safer shall he be upon the sandy plains
Than where castles mounted stand.
Have done, for more I hardly can endure.

BOLINGBROKE

Descend to darkness and the burning lake!
False fiend, be gone!

> *Thunder and lightning. Exit Spirit*

> *Enter York and Buckingham with their guard*

YORK

Lay hands upon these traitors and their trash.
Beldame, I think we watched you at an inch.
What, madam, are you there? The King and
    commonweal
Are deeply indebted for this piece of pains.
My Lord Protector will, I doubt it not,
See you well rewarded for these good deserts.

DUCHESS

Not half so bad as yours to England's king,
Injurious duke, that threat where is no cause.

BUCKINGHAM

True, madam, none at all. What call you this?
Away with them, let them be clapped up close,
And kept asunder. You, madam, shall with us.
Stafford, take her to you.

> *Exeunt above the Duchess and Hume, guarded*

We'll see your trinkets here all forthcoming.
All away!

> *Exeunt Jourdain, Southwell, Bolingbroke guarded*

YORK

Lord Buckingham, I think you watched her well.
A pretty plot, well chosen to build upon!
Now pray, my lord, let's see the devil's writ.

What have we here?
(*Reads*) *The duke yet lives that Henry shall depose;*
*But him outlive and die a violent death.*
Why, this is just
*Aio te, Aeacida, Romanos vincere posse.*[2]
Well, to the rest:
*Tell me what fate awaits the Duke of Suffolk?*
*By water shall he die, and take his end.*
*What shall befall the Duke of Somerset?*
*Let him shun castles;*
*Safer shall he be upon the sandy plains*
*Than where castles mounted stand.*
Come, come, my lords, these oracles
Are hardly attained and hardly understood.
The King is now in progress towards Saint Albans;
With him the husband of this lovely lady.
Thither go these news, as fast as horse can carry them—
A sorry breakfast for my Lord Protector.

BUCKINGHAM
Your grace shall give me leave, my lord of York,
To be the post, in hope of his reward.

YORK
At your pleasure, my good lord. Who's within there, ho?

*Enter a servingman*

Invite my lords of Salisbury and Warwick
To sup with me tomorrow night. Away!              *Exeunt*

---

[2]Deliberately ambiguous. I state that you, descendant of
Aeacus, can conquer the Romans. *Or,* that the Romans can
conquer you.

# Act II

## SCENE I
## St. Albans.

*Enter the King, Queen, Gloucester, Cardinal, and Suffolk,*
*with falconers hallooing*

QUEEN
Believe me, lords, for flying at the brook,
I saw not better sport these seven years' day;
Yet, by your leave, the wind was very high,
And, ten to one, old Joan had not gone out.

KING
But what a point, my lord, your falcon made,
And what a pitch she flew above the rest!
To see how God in all his creatures works!
Yea, man and birds are fond of climbing high.

SUFFOLK
No marvel, if it likes your majesty,
My Lord Protector's hawks do tower so well;
They know their master loves to be aloft,
And bears his thoughts above his falcon's pitch.

GLOUCESTER
My lord, it is but a base ignoble mind
That mounts no higher than a bird can soar.

CARDINAL
I thought as much; he would be above the clouds.

GLOUCESTER
Ay, my lord Cardinal, how think you by that?
Were it not good your grace could fly to heaven?

KING
  The treasury of everlasting joy.
CARDINAL
  Your heaven is on earth; your eyes and thoughts
  Beat on a crown, the treasure of your heart,
  Pernicious Protector, dangerous peer,
  That smooth it so with King and commonweal!
GLOUCESTER
  What, Cardinal? Is your priesthood grown peremptory?
  *Tantaene animis coelestibus irae?*[1]
  Churchmen so hot? Good uncle, hide such malice;
  With such holiness can you do it?
SUFFOLK
  No malice, sir; no more than well becomes
  So good a quarrel and so bad a peer.
GLOUCESTER
  As who, my lord?
SUFFOLK                  Why, as you, my lord,
  If it likes your lordly Lord's Protectorship.
GLOUCESTER
  Why, Suffolk, England knows your insolence.
QUEEN
  And your ambition, Gloucester.
KING                                    I pray you peace,
  Good Queen, and whet not on these furious peers;
  For blessèd are the peace-makers on earth.
CARDINAL
  Let me be blessèd for the peace I make
  Against this proud Protector with my sword!
GLOUCESTER (*aside to Cardinal*)
  Faith, holy uncle, would it were come to that!
CARDINAL (*aside to Gloucester*)
  Certainly, when you dare.

---

[1]Is there so much danger in heavenly minds?

GLOUCESTER (*aside to Cardinal*)
    Make up no factious numbers for the matter;
    In your own person answer your abuse.
CARDINAL (*aside to Gloucester*)
    Ay, where you dare not peep; or if you dare,
    This evening on the east side of the grove.
KING
    How now, my lords?
CARDINAL                    Believe me, cousin Gloucester,
    Had not your man put up the fowl so suddenly,
    We had had more sport. (*Aside to Gloucester*) Come with
        your two-hand sword.
GLOUCESTER
    True, uncle.
CARDINAL (*aside to Gloucester*)
    Are you advised? The east side of the grove.
GLOUCESTER (*aside to Cardinal*)
    Cardinal, I am with you.
KING                           Why, how now, uncle Gloucester?
GLOUCESTER
    Talking of hawking; nothing else, my lord.
    (*Aside to Cardinal*)
    Now, by God's mother, priest, I'll shave your crown for
        this,
    Or all my fence shall fail.
CARDINAL (*aside to Gloucester*) Medice, teipsum —[2]
    Protector, see to it well; protect yourself.
KING
    The winds grow high; so do your stomachs, lords.
    How irksome is this music to my heart!
    When such strings jar, what hope of harmony?
    I pray, my lords, let me compound this strife.

            Enter *a Man crying* 'A miracle!'

------

[2]Physician, heal yourself.

GLOUCESTER
What means this noise?
Fellow, what miracle do you proclaim?

MAN
A miracle! A miracle!

SUFFOLK
Come to the King and tell him what miracle.

MAN
In faith, a blind man at Saint Alban's shrine
Within this half-hour has received his sight,
A man that never saw in his life before.

KING
Now God be praised, that to believing souls
Gives light in darkness, comfort in despair!

*Enter the Mayor of Saint Albans and his brethren,
bearing the man Simpcox in a chair, his Wife
and others following*

CARDINAL
Here come the townsmen, in procession,
To present your highness with the man.

KING
Great is his comfort in this earthly vale,
Although by his sight his sin is multiplied.

GLOUCESTER
Stand by, my masters; bring him near the King.
His highness' pleasure is to talk with him.

KING
Good fellow, tell us here the circumstance,
That we for you may glorify the Lord.
What, have you been long blind and now restored?

SIMPCOX Born blind, if it please your grace.

WIFE Ay, indeed was he.

SUFFOLK What woman is this?

WIFE His wife, if it like your worship.

GLOUCESTER Had you been his mother, you could have
better told.

KING Where were you born?

SIMPCOX At Berwick in the north, if it like your grace.

KING
Poor soul, God's goodness has been great to you.
Let never day or night unhallowed pass,
But still remember what the Lord has done.

QUEEN
Tell me, good fellow, came you here by chance,
Or of devotion, to this holy shrine?

SIMPCOX
God knows, of pure devotion, being called
A hundred times and oftener, in my sleep,
By good Saint Alban, who said 'Simon, come;
Come, offer at my shrine, and I will help you.'

WIFE
Most true, for sure; and many time and oft
Myself have heard a voice to call him so.

CARDINAL
What, are you lame?

SIMPCOX                    Ay, God Almighty help me!

SUFFOLK
How came you so?

SIMPCOX                    A fall off of a tree.

WIFE
A plum-tree, master.

GLOUCESTER                How long have you been blind?

SIMPCOX
O, born so, master.

GLOUCESTER          What! And would climb a tree?

SIMPCOX

But that in all my life, when I was a youth.

WIFE

Too true; and bought his climbing very dear.

GLOUCESTER

Mass, you loved plums well, that would venture so.

SIMPCOX

Alas, good master, my wife desired some damsons,
And made me climb with danger of my life.

GLOUCESTER

A subtle knave! But yet it shall not serve.
Let me see your eyes; wink now; now open them.
In my opinion yet you see not well.

SIMPCOX Yes, master, clear as day, I thank God and Saint
Alban.

GLOUCESTER

Say you me so? What colour is this cloak of?

SIMPCOX Red, master, red as blood.

GLOUCESTER

Why, that's well said. What colour is my gown of?

SIMPCOX Black, forsooth, coal-black as jet.

KING

Why then, you know what colour jet is of?

SUFFOLK

And yet, I think, jet did he never see.

GLOUCESTER

But cloaks and gowns before this day a many.

WIFE

Never, before this day, in all his life.

GLOUCESTER Tell me, fellow, what's my name?

SIMPCOX Alas, master, I know not.

GLOUCESTER What's his name?

SIMPCOX I know not.

GLOUCESTER Nor his?

SIMPCOX No indeed, master.

GLOUCESTER What's your own name?

SIMPCOX Saunder Simpcox, if it please you, master.

GLOUCESTER Then, Saunder, sit there, the lyingest knave in Christendom. If you had been born blind, you might as well have known all our names as thus to name the several colours we do wear. Sight may distinguish of colours; but suddenly to nominate them all, it is impossible. My lords, Saint Alban here has done a miracle; and would you not think his cunning to be great, that could restore this cripple to his legs again?

SIMPCOX O master, that you could!

GLOUCESTER My masters of Saint Albans, have you not beadles in your town, and things called whips?

MAYOR Yes, my lord, if it please your grace.

GLOUCESTER Then send for one presently.

MAYOR Fellow, go fetch the beadle hither straight.

*Exit an attendant*

GLOUCESTER Now fetch me a stool hither by and by. Now, fellow, if you mean to save yourself from whipping, leap me over this stool and run away.

SIMPCOX Alas, master, I am not able to stand alone. You go about to torture me in vain.

*Enter a Beadle with whips*

GLOUCESTER Well, sir, we must have you find your legs. Beadle, whip him till he leaps over that same stool.

BEADLE I will, my lord. Come on, fellow, off with your doublet quickly.

SIMPCOX Alas, master, what shall I do? I am not able to stand.

*After the Beadle has hit him once, he leaps over the stool and runs away; they follow and cry 'A miracle!'*

KING
  O God, see you this, and bear so long?
QUEEN
  It made me laugh to see the villain run.
GLOUCESTER
  Follow the knave, and take this drab away.
WIFE Alas, sir, we did it for pure need.
GLOUCESTER
  Let them be whipped through every market-town
  Till they come to Berwick, from whence they came.
            *Exeunt Mayor and Beadle dragging Simpcox's Wife*
CARDINAL
  Duke Humphrey has done a miracle today.
SUFFOLK
  True; made the lame to leap and fly away.
GLOUCESTER
  But you have done more miracles than I;
  You made in a day, my lord, whole towns to fly.

            *Enter Buckingham*

KING
  What tidings with our cousin Buckingham?
BUCKINGHAM
  Such as my heart does tremble to unfold:
  A sort of naughty persons, lewdly bent,
  Under the countenance and confederacy
  Of Lady Eleanor, the Protector's wife.
  The ringleader and head of all this rout,
  Have practised dangerously against your state,
  Dealing with witches and with conjurers,
  Whom we have apprehended in the fact,
  Raising up wicked spirits from under ground,
  Demanding of King Henry's life and death,
  And others of your highness' Privy Council,
  As more at large your grace shall understand.

CARDINAL
  And so, my Lord Protector, by this means
  Your lady is forthcoming yet at London.
  (*Aside to Gloucester*)
  This news, I think, has turned your weapon's edge;
  'Tis likely, my lord, you will not keep your hour.

GLOUCESTER
  Ambitious churchman, leave to afflict my heart.
  Sorrow and grief have vanquished all my powers;
  And, vanquished as I am, I yield to you
  Or to the meanest groom.

KING
  O God, what mischiefs work the wicked ones,
  Heaping confusion on their own heads thereby!

QUEEN
  Gloucester, see here the tainting of your nest,
  And look yourself be faultless, you were best.

GLOUCESTER
  Madam, for myself, to heaven I do appeal,
  How I have loved my king and commonweal;
  And for my wife I know not how it stands.
  Sorry I am to hear what I have heard.
  Noble she is; but if she has forgotten
  Honour and virtue, and conversed with such
  As, like to pitch, defile nobility,
  I banish her my bed and company,
  And give her as a prey to law and shame
  That has dishonoured Gloucester's honest name.

KING
  Well, for this night we will repose us here;
  Tomorrow toward London back again,
  To look into this business thoroughly,
  And call these foul offenders to their answers,
  And poise the cause in Justice' equal scales,
  Whose beam stands sure, whose rightful cause prevails.
                                        *Flourish. Exeunt*

## SCENE II
### Duke of York's garden.

*Enter York, Salisbury, and Warwick*

YORK
  Now, my good lords of Salisbury and Warwick,
  Our simple supper ended, give me leave,
  In this close walk, to satisfy myself
  In craving your opinion of my title,
  Which is infallible, to the English crown.
SALISBURY
  My lord, I long to hear it at full.
WARWICK
  Sweet York, begin; and if your claim is good,
  The Nevils are your subjects to command.
YORK
  Then thus:
  Edward the Third, my lords, had seven sons:
  The first, Edward the Black Prince, Prince of Wales;
  The second, William of Hatfield; and the third,
  Lionel Duke of Clarence; next to whom
  Was John of Gaunt, the Duke of Lancaster;
  The fifth was Edmund Langley, Duke of York;
  The sixth was Thomas of Woodstock, Duke of
      Gloucester;
  William of Windsor was the seventh and last.
  Edward the Black Prince died before his father,
  And left behind him Richard, his only son,
  Who, after Edward the Third's death, reigned as king
  Till Henry Bolingbroke, Duke of Lancaster,
  The eldest son and heir of John of Gaunt,
  Crowned by the name of Henry the Fourth,
  Seized on the realm, deposed the rightful king,
  Sent his poor queen to France, from whence she came,
  And him to Pomfret; where, as all you know,

Harmless Richard was murdered traitorously.
WARWICK
    Father, the Duke has told the truth;
    Thus got the house of Lancaster the crown.
YORK
    Which now they hold by force and not by right;
    For Richard, the first son's heir, being dead,
    The issue of the next son should have reigned.
SALISBURY
    But William of Hatfield died without an heir.
YORK
    The third son, Duke of Clarence, from whose line
    I claim the crown, had issue Philippa, a daughter,
    Who married Edmund Mortimer, Earl of March;
    Edmund had issue, Roger Earl of March;
    Roger had issue, Edmund, Anne, and Eleanor.
SALISBURY
    This Edmund, in the reign of Bolingbroke,
    As I have read, laid claim unto the crown,
    And, but for Owen Glendower, had been king,
    Who kept him in captivity till he died.
    But to the rest.
YORK          His eldest sister, Anne,
    My mother, being heir unto the crown,
    Married Richard Earl of Cambridge, who was
    To Edmund Langley, Edward the Third's fifth son, son.
    By her I claim the kingdom.
    Roger third Earl of March was the son
    Of Edmund Mortimer, who married Philippa,
    Sole daughter unto Lionel Duke of Clarence.
    So, if the issue of the elder son
    Succeeds before the younger, I am king.
WARWICK
    What plain proceeding is more plain than this?
    Henry does claim the crown from John of Gaunt,
    The fourth son; York claims it from the third.

Till Lionel's issue fails, his should not reign;
It fails not yet, but flourishes in you,
And in your sons, fair slips of such a stock.
Then, father Salisbury, kneel we together,
And in this private plot be we the first
That shall salute our rightful sovereign
With honour of his birthright to the crown.

WARWICK *and* SALISBURY

Long live our sovereign Richard, England's king!

YORK

We thank you, lords; but I am not your king
Till I am crowned, and till my sword is stained
With heart-blood of the house of Lancaster;
And that's not suddenly to be performed
But with advice and silent secrecy.
Do you as I do in these dangerous days,
Wink at the Duke of Suffolk's insolence,
At Beaufort's pride, at Somerset's ambition,
At Buckingham, and all the crew of them,
Till they have snared the shepherd of the flock,
That virtuous prince, the good Duke Humphrey.
'Tis that they seek; and they, in seeking that,
Shall find their deaths, if York can prophesy.

SALISBURY

My lord, break we off; we know your mind at full.

WARWICK

My heart assures me that the Earl of Warwick
Shall one day make the Duke of York a king.

YORK

And, Nevil, this I do assure myself:
Richard shall live to make the Earl of Warwick
The greatest man in England but the king.          *Exeunt*

## SCENE III
### Law Courts.

*Sound trumpets. Enter the King, Queen, Gloucester, York,*
*Suffolk, and Salisbury; the Duchess of Gloucester, Margery*
*Jourdain, Southwell, Hume, and Bolingbroke, guarded*

KING
Stand forth, Dame Eleanor Cobham, Gloucester's wife.
In sight of God and us your guilt is great;
Receive the sentence of the law for sins
Such as by God's book are adjudged to death.
You four, from hence to prison back again;
From thence unto the place of execution.
The witch in Smithfield shall be burnt to ashes,
And you three shall be strangled on the gallows.
You, madam, for you are more nobly born,
Despoilèd of your honour in your life,
Shall, after three days' open penance done,
Live in your country here in banishment
With Sir John Stanley in the Isle of Man.
DUCHESS
Welcome is banishment; welcome were my death.
GLOUCESTER
Eleanor, the law, you see, has judged you;
I cannot justify whom the law condemns.
My eyes are full of tears, my heart of grief.
  *Exeunt the Duchess and the other prisoners, guarded*
Ah, Humphrey, this dishonour in your age
Will bring your head with sorrow to the ground!
I beseech your majesty give me leave to go;
Sorrow would solace, and my age would ease.
KING
Stay, Humphrey Duke of Gloucester. Ere you go,
Give up your staff. Henry will to himself
Protector be; and God shall be my hope,

My stay, my guide, and lantern to my feet.
And go in peace, Humphrey, no less beloved
Than when you were Protector to your King.

QUEEN

I see no reason why a king of years
Should be to be protected like a child.
God and King Henry govern England's realm!
Give up your staff, sir, and the King his realm.

GLOUCESTER

My staff? Here, noble Henry, is my staff;
As willingly do I the same resign
As ere your father Henry made it mine;
And even as willingly at your feet I leave it
As others would ambitiously receive it.
Farewell, good King. When I am dead and gone,
May honourable peace attend your throne.              *Exit*

QUEEN

Why, now are Henry King and Margaret Queen;
And Humphrey Duke of Gloucester scarce himself,
That bears so shrewd a maim; two pulls at once—
His lady banished and a limb lopped off.
This staff of honour seized, there let it stand
Where it best fits to be, in Henry's hand.

SUFFOLK

Thus droops this lofty pine and hangs its sprays;
Thus Eleanor's pride dies in her youngest days.

YORK

Lords, let him go. Please it your majesty,
This is the day appointed for the combat,
And ready are the appellant and defendant,
The armourer and his man, to enter the lists,
So please your highness to behold the fight.

QUEEN

Ay, good my lord; for purposely therefore
Left I the Court to see this quarrel tried.

KING
> In God's name, see the lists and all things fit;
> Here let them end it, and God defend the right!
YORK
> I never saw a fellow worse set up,
> Or more afraid to fight, than is the appellant,
> The servant of this armourer, my lords.

*Enter at one door Horner, drunk, and his Neighbours; he
enters with his staff with a sand-bag fastened to it; at the
other door Peter, with a drum and sand-bag, and Prentices.*

FIRST NEIGHBOUR Here, neighbour Horner, I drink to you
    in a cup of sack; and fear not, neighbour, you shall do
    well enough.
SECOND NEIGHBOUR And here, neighbour, here's a cup of
    malmsey.
THIRD NEIGHBOUR And here's a pot of good double beer,
    neighbour. Drink, and fear not your man.
HORNER Let it come, in faith, and I'll pledge you all; and a
    fig for Peter!
FIRST PRENTICE Here, Peter, I drink to you; and be not
    afraid.
SECOND PRENTICE Be merry, Peter, and fear not your
    master. Fight for the credit of apprentices.
PETER I thank you all. Drink and pray for me, I pray you,
    for I think I have taken my last draught in this world.
    Here, Robin, if I die, I give you my apron; and, Will,
    you shall have my hammer; and here, Tom, take all the
    money that I have. O Lord bless me, I pray God, for I am
    never able to deal with my master, he has learnt so
    much fence already.
SALISBURY Come, leave your drinking and fall to blows.
    Fellow, what's your name?
PETER Peter, for sure.
SALISBURY Peter? What more?

PETER Thump.

SALISBURY Thump? Then see you thump your master well.

HORNER Masters, I am come hither, as it were, upon my man's instigation, to prove him a knave and myself an honest man. Touching the Duke of York, I will take my death I never meant him any ill, nor the King, nor the Queen; and therefore, Peter, have at you with a downright blow.

YORK Dispatch; this knave's tongue begins to double. Sound, trumpets, alarum to the combatants.

*Alarum; they fight and Peter strikes Horner down*

HORNER Hold, Peter, hold! I confess, I confess treason.

*He dies*

YORK Take away his weapon. Fellow, thank God and the good wine in your master's way.

PETER O God, have I overcome my enemies in this presence? O Peter, you have prevailed in right!

KING
Go, take hence that traitor from our sight;
For by his death we do perceive his guilt,
And God in justice has revealed to us
The truth and innocence of this poor fellow,
Whom he had thought to have murdered wrongfully.
Come, fellow, follow us for your reward.

*Sound a flourish. Exeunt*

# SCENE IV
## A street.

*Enter Gloucester and his men in mourning cloaks*

GLOUCESTER
  Thus sometimes has the brightest day a cloud;
  And after summer evermore succeeds
  Barren winter, with its wrathful nipping cold;
  So cares and joys abound, as seasons fleet.
  Sirs, what's o'clock?
SERVANT                    Ten, my lord.
GLOUCESTER
  Ten is the hour that was appointed me
  To watch the coming of my punished duchess;
  Hardly may she endure the flinty streets,
  To tread them with her tender-feeling feet.
  Sweet Nell, ill can your noble mind now brook
  The abject people gazing on your face
  With envious looks, laughing at your shame,
  That once did follow your proud chariot wheels
  When you did ride in triumph through the streets.
  But soft, I think she comes; and I'll prepare
  My tear-stained eyes to see her miseries.

*Enter the Duchess of Gloucester barefoot, in a white sheet
and verses pinned on her back and a taper burning in her
  hand, with Sir John Stanley, the Sheriff, and officers*

SERVANT
  So please your grace, we'll take her from the Sheriff.
GLOUCESTER
  No, stir not for your lives; let her pass by.
DUCHESS
  Come you, my lord, to see my open shame?
  Now you do penance too. Look how they gaze!
  See how the giddy multitude do point
  And nod their heads and throw their eyes on you.
  Ah, Gloucester, hide you from their hateful looks,
  And, in your closet pent up, rue my shame,
  And ban your enemies, both mine and yours.

GLOUCESTER
  Be patient, gentle Nell; forget this grief.
DUCHESS
  Ah, Gloucester, teach me to forget myself;
  For while I think I am your married wife,
  And you a prince, Protector of this land,
  I think I should not thus be led along,
  Boxed up in shame, with papers on my back,
  And followed with a rabble that rejoice
  To see my tears and hear my deep-fetched groans.
  The ruthless flint does cut my tender feet,
  And when I start, the envious people laugh
  And bid me be advisèd how I tread.
  Ah, Humphrey, can I bear this shameful yoke?
  Think you that ever I'll look upon the world,
  Or count them happy that enjoy the sun?
  No, dark shall be my light, and night my day;
  To think upon my pomp shall be my hell.
  Sometime I'll say I am Duke Humphrey's wife,
  And he a prince and ruler of the land;
  Yet so he ruled and such a prince he was
  As he stood by while I, his forlorn duchess,
  Was made a wonder and a pointing-stock
  To every idle rascal follower.
  But be you mild and blush not at my shame,
  And stir at nothing till the axe of death
  Hangs over you, as sure it shortly will;
  For Suffolk, he that can do all in all
  With her that hates you and does hate us all,
  And York, and impious Beaufort, that false priest,
  Have all limed bushes to betray your wings;
  And fly you how you can, they'll tangle you.
  But fear not you until your foot is snared,
  Nor ever seek forestalling of your foes.
GLOUCESTER
  Ah, Nell, forbear! You aim now all awry;

I must offend before I am attainted;
And had I twenty times so many foes,
And each of them had twenty times their power,
All these could not procure me any harm
So long as I am loyal, true, and crimeless.
Would have me rescue you from this reproach?
Why, yet your scandal were not wiped away,
But I in danger for the breach of law.
Your greatest help is quiet, gentle Nell.
I pray you sort your heart to patiènce;
These few days' wonder will be quickly worn.

*Enter a Herald*

HERALD
I summon your grace to his majesty's parliament,
To be held at Bury the first of this next month.
GLOUCESTER
And my consent never asked herein before!
This is close dealing. Well, I will be there.

*Exit Herald*

My Nell, I take my leave; and, Master Sheriff,
Let not her penance exceed the King's commission.
SHERIFF
If it please your grace, here my commission stays,
And Sir John Stanley is appointed now
To take her with him to the Isle of Man.
GLOUCESTER
Must you, Sir John, protect my lady here?
STANLEY
So am I given in charge, may it please your grace.
GLOUCESTER
Entreat her not the worse in that I pray
You use her well. The world may laugh again;
And I may live to do you kindness if
You do it her. And so, Sir John, farewell.

DUCHESS
What, gone, my lord, and bid me not farewell?

GLOUCESTER
Witness my tears, I cannot stay to speak.

*Exit Gloucester with his men*

DUCHESS
Are you gone too? All comfort go with you!
For none abides with me; my joy is death—
Death, at whose name I oft have been afraid,
Because I wished this world's eternity.
Stanley, I pray you, go and take me hence;
I care not whither, for I beg no favour;
Only convey me where you are commanded.

STANLEY
Why, madam, that is to the Isle of Man,
There to be used according to your state.

DUCHESS
That's bad enough, for I am but reproach;
And shall I then be used reproachfully?

STANLEY
Like to a duchess and Duke Humphrey's lady,
According to that state you shall be used.

DUCHESS
Sheriff, farewell, and better than I fare,
Although you have been cònduct of my shame.

SHERIFF
It is my office; and, madam, pardon me.

DUCHESS
Ay, ay, farewell; your office is discharged.
Come, Stanley, shall we go?

STANLEY
Madam, your penance done, throw off this sheet,
And go we to attire you for our journey.

DUCHESS
My shame will not be shifted with my sheet.
No; it will hang upon my richest robes

And show itself, attire me how I can.
Go, lead the way; I long to see my prison.          *Exeunt*

# Act III

## SCENE I
## Bury St. Edmunds Abbey.

*Sound a sennet. Enter the King, Queen, Cardinal,*
*Suffolk, York, Buckingham, Salisbury, and Warwick*
*to the parliament*

KING
I muse my lord of Gloucester is not come;
'Tis not his wont to be the hindmost man,
Whatever occasion keeps him from us now.

QUEEN
Can you not see? Or will you not observe
The strangeness of his altered countenance?
With what a majesty he bears himself,
How insolent of late he is become,
How proud, how pèremptory, and unlike himself?
We know the time since he was mild and affable,
And if we did but glance a far-off look,
Immediately he was upon his knee,
That all the court admired him for submission.
But meet him now, and be it in the morn,
When everyone will give the time of day,
He knits his brow and shows an angry eye,
And passes by with stiff unbowèd knee,
Disdaining duty that to us belongs.
Small curs are not regarded when they grin,
But great men tremble when the lion roars;
And Humphrey is no little man in England.
First note that he is near you in descent,

197

And should you fall, he is the next will mount.
It seems to me it is no policy,
Respecting what a rancorous mind he bears
And his advantage following your decease,
That he should come about your royal person
Or be admitted to your highness' Council.
By flattery has he won the commons' hearts,
And when he pleases to make commotiòn,
It is to be feared they all will follow him.
Now it is spring, and weeds are shallow-rooted;
Suffer them now and they'll o'ergrow the garden,
And choke the herbs for want of husbandry.
The reverent care I bear unto my lord
Made me collect these dangers in the Duke.
If it is foolish call it a woman's fear;
Which fear if better reasons can supplant,
I will subscribe and say I wronged the Duke.
My lord of Suffolk, Buckingham, and York,
Reprove my allegation if you can;
Or else conclude my words effectual.

SUFFOLK
Well has your highness seen into this Duke;
And had I first been put to speak my mind,
I think I should have told your grace's tale.
The Duchess by his subornatiòn,
Upon my life, began her devilish practices;
Or if he was not privy to those faults,
Yet by reputing of his high descent,
As next the King he was successive heir,
And such high vaunts of his nobility,
Did instigate the bedlam brain-sick Duchess
By wicked means to frame our sovereign's fall.
Smooth runs the water where the brook is deep,
And in his simple show he harbours treason.
The fox barks not when he would steal the lamb.

No, no, my sovereign, Gloucester is a man
Unsounded yet and full of deep deceit.

CARDINAL
Did he not, contrary to form of law,
Devise strange deaths for small offences done?

YORK
And did he not, in his Protectorship,
Levy great sums of money through the realm
For soldiers' pay in France, and never sent it?
By means whereof the towns each day revolted.

BUCKINGHAM
Tut, these are petty faults to faults unknown,
Which time will bring to light in smooth Duke
    Humphrey.

KING
My lords, at once; the care you have of us,
To mow down thorns that would annoy our foot,
Is worthy praise; but, shall I speak my conscience,
Our kinsman Gloucester is as innocent
From meaning treason to our royal person
As is the sucking lamb or harmless dove.
The Duke is virtuous, mild, and too well given
To dream on evil or to work my downfall.

QUEEN
Ah, what's more dangerous than this foolish trust?
Seems he a dove? His feathers are but borrowed,
For he's disposèd as the hateful raven.
Is he a lamb? His skin is surely lent him,
For he's inclined as is the ravenous wolves.
Who cannot steal a shape that means deceit?
Take heed, my lord; the welfare of us all
Hangs on the cutting short that fraudful man.

*Enter Somerset*

SOMERSET
All health unto my gracious sovereign!

KING
Welcome, Lord Somerset. What news from France?
SOMERSET
That all your interest in those territories
Is utterly bereft you; all is lost.
KING
Cold news, Lord Somerset; but God's will be done!
YORK (*aside*)
Cold news for me; for I had hope of France
As firmly as I hope for fertile England.
Thus are my blossoms blasted in the bud,
And caterpillars eat my leaves away;
But I will remedy this affair ere long,
Or sell my title for a glorious grave.

*Enter Gloucester*

GLOUCESTER
All happiness unto my lord the King!
Pardon, my liege, that I have stayed so long.
SUFFOLK
Nay, Gloucester, know that you are come too soon,
Unless you were more loyal than you are.
I do arrest you of high treason here.
GLOUCESTER
Well, Suffolk, you shall not see me blush,
Nor change my countenance for this arrest;
A heart unspotted is not easily daunted.
The purest spring is not so free from mud
As I am clear from treason to my sovereign.
Who can accuse me? Wherein am I guilty?
YORK
'Tis thought, my lord, that you took bribes of France;
And, being Protector, stayed the soldiers' pay,
By means whereof his highness has lost France.

GLOUCESTER
   Is it but thought so? What are they that think it?
   I never robbed the soldiers of their pay,
   Nor ever had one penny bribe from France.
   So help me God, as I have watched the night,
   Ay, night by night, in studying good for England!
   That coin that ever I wrested from the King,
   Or any groat I hoarded to my use,
   Be brought against me at my trial day!
   No, many a pound of my own proper store,
   Because I would not tax the needy commons,
   Have I dispursèd to the garrisons,
   And never asked for restitutiòn.
CARDINAL
   It serves you well, my lord, to say so much.
GLOUCESTER
   I say no more than truth, so help me God!
YORK
   In your Protectorship you did devise
   Strange tortures for offenders, never heard of,
   That England was defamed by tyranny.
GLOUCESTER
   Why, 'tis well known that, while I was Protector,
   Pity was all the fault that was in me;
   For I should melt at an offender's tears,
   And lowly words were ransom for their fault.
   Unless it was a bloody murderer
   Or foul felonious thief that fleeced poor passengers,
   I never gave them condign punishment.
   Murder indeed, that bloody sin, I tortured
   Above the felon or what trespass else.
SUFFOLK
   My lord, these faults are easy, quickly answered;
   But mightier crimes are laid unto your charge,
   Whereof you cannot easily purge yourself.
   I do arrest you in his highness' name;

And here commit you to my lord Cardinal
To keep until your further time of trial.

KING

My lord of Gloucester, it is my special hope
That you will clear yourself from all suspense;
My conscience tells me you are innocent.

GLOUCESTER

Ah, gracious lord, these days are dangerous;
Virtue is choked with foul ambitiòn,
And charity chased hence by rancour's hand;
Foul subornation is predominant,
And equity exiled your highness' land.
I know their complot is to have my life;
And if my death might make this island happy,
And prove the period of their tyranny,
I would expend it with all willingness.
But mine is made the prologue to their play;
For thousands more, that yet suspect no peril,
Will not conclude their plotted tragedy.
Beaufort's red sparkling eyes blab his heart's malice,
And Suffolk's cloudy brow his stormy hate;
Sharp Buckingham unburdens with his tongue
The envious load that lies upon his heart;
And doggèd York, that reaches at the moon,
Whose overweening arm I have plucked back,
By false charges levels at my life.
And you, my sovereign lady, with the rest,
Causeless have laid disgraces on my head,
And with your best endeavour have stirred up
My dearest liege to be my enemy.
Ay, all of you have laid your heads together—
Myself had notice of your conventicles—
And all to make away my guiltless life.
I shall not want false witness to condemn me,
Nor store of treasons to augment my guilt;
The ancient proverb will be well effected:
'A staff is quickly found to beat a dog.'

CARDINAL
   My liege, his railing is intolerable.
   If those that care to keep your royal person
   From treason's secret knife and traitor's rage
   Are thus upbraided, chidden, rated at,
   And the offender granted scope of speech,
   It will make them cool in zeal unto your grace.
SUFFOLK
   Has he not twitted our sovereign lady here
   With ignominious words, though clerkly couched,
   As if she had subornèd some to swear
   False allegations to overthrow his state?
QUEEN
   But I can give the loser leave to chide.
GLOUCESTER
   Far truer spoken than meant. I lose indeed;
   Curse the winners, for they played me false!
   And well such losers may have leave to speak.
BUCKINGHAM
   He'll wrest the sense and hold us here all day.
   Lord Cardinal, he is your prisoner.
CARDINAL
   Sirs, take away the Duke and guard him sure.
GLOUCESTER
   Ah, thus King Henry throws away his crutch
   Before his legs are firm to bear his body.
   Thus is the shepherd beaten from your side,
   And wolves are gnarling who shall gnaw you first.
   Ah, that my fear were false; ah, that it were!
   For, good King Henry, your decay I fear.
           *Exit Gloucester, guarded by the Cardinal's men*
KING
   My lords, what to your wisdoms seems it best
   Do or undo, as if ourself were here.
QUEEN
   What, will your highness leave the parliament?

KING
>Ay, Margaret; my heart is drowned with grief,
>Whose flood begins to flow within my eyes,
>My body round engirt with misery;
>For what's more miserable than discontent?
>Ah, uncle Humphrey, in your face I see
>The map of honour, truth, and loyalty;
>And yet, good Humphrey, is the hour to come
>That ever I proved you false or feared your faith.
>What lowering star now envies your estate,
>That these great lords, and Margaret our Queen,
>Do seek subversion of your harmless life?
>You never did them wrong, nor any man wrong;
>And as the butcher takes away the calf,
>And binds the wretch, and beats it when it strays,
>Bearing it to the bloody slaughter-house,
>Even so remorseless have they borne him hence.
>And as the dam runs lowing up and down,
>Looking the way her harmless young one went,
>And can do naught but wail her darling's loss;
>Even so myself bewail good Gloucester's case
>With sad unhelpful tears, and with dimmed eyes
>Look after him, and cannot do him good,
>So mighty are his vowèd enemies.
>His fortunes I will weep, and between each groan
>Say 'Who's a traitor? Gloucester he is none.'
>>*Exit with Buckingham, Salisbury, and Warwick*

QUEEN
>Free lords, cold snow melts with the sun's hot beams:
>Henry my lord is cold in great affairs,
>Too full of foolish pity; and Gloucester's show
>Beguiles him as the mournful crocodile
>With sorrow snares relenting passengers;
>Or as the snake rolled in a flowering bank,
>With shining checkered slough, does sting a child

That for the beauty thinks it excellent.
Believe me, lords, were none more wise than I—
And yet herein I judge my own wit good—
This Gloucester should be quickly rid the world,
To rid us from the fear we have of him.

CARDINAL
That he should die is worthy policy;
But yet we want a colour for his death.
'Tis meet he be condemned by course of law.

SUFFOLK
But in my mind that is no policy.
The King will labour still to save his life,
The commons haply rise to save his life;
And yet we have but trivial argument,
More than mistrust, that shows him worthy death.

YORK
So that, by this, you would not have him die.

SUFFOLK
Ah, York, no man alive so glad as I.

YORK
'Tis York that has more reason for his death.
But, my lord Cardinal, and you, my lord of Suffolk,
Say as you think, and speak it from your souls:
Were it not all one, an empty eagle were set
To guard the chicken from a hungry kite,
As place Duke Humphrey for the King's Protector?

QUEEN
So the poor chicken should be sure of death.

SUFFOLK
Madam, 'tis true; and were it not madness then
To make the fox surveyor of the fold?
Who being accused a crafty murderer,
His guilt should be but idly posted over
Because his purpose is not executed.
No; let him die, in that he is a fox,

By nature proved an enemy to the flock,
Before his chaps be stained with crimson blood,
As Humphrey proved by reasons to my liege.
And do not stand on quibbles how to slay him;
Be it by gins, by snares, by subtlety,
Sleeping or waking, 'tis no matter how,
So he is dead; for that is good deceit
Which mates him first that first intends deceit.

QUEEN
Thrice-noble Suffolk, 'tis resolutely spoken.

SUFFOLK
Not resolute, unless so much were done;
For things are often spoken and seldom meant;
But that my heart accords well with my tongue,
Seeing the deed is meritorious,
And to preserve my sovereign from his foe,
Say but the word and I will be his priest.

CARDINAL
But I would have him dead, my lord of Suffolk,
Ere you can take due orders for a priest.
Say you consent and approve well the deed,
And I'll provide his executioner;
I tender so the safety of my liege.

SUFFOLK
Here is my hand; the deed is worthy doing.

QUEEN
And so say I.

YORK
And I; and now we three have spoken it,
It skills not greatly who impugns our judgement.

*Enter a Post*

POST
Great lords, from Ireland am I come full speed,
To signify that rebels there are up

And put the Englishmen unto the sword.
Send succours, lords, and stop the rage betime,
Before the wound does grow incurable;
For, being green, there is great hope of help.

CARDINAL

A breach that craves a quick and urgent stop!
What counsel give you in this weighty cause?

YORK

Somerset should be sent as Regent thither.
'Tis meet that lucky ruler be employed;
Witness the fortune he has had in France.

SOMERSET

If York, with all his far-fetched policy,
Had been the Regent there instead of me,
He never would have stayed in France so long.

YORK

No, not to lose it all, as you have done.
I rather would have lost my life betimes
Than bring a burden of dishonour home,
By staying there so long till all were lost.
Show me one scar charàctered on your skin;
Men's flesh preserved so whole do seldom win.

QUEEN

Nay then, this spark will prove a raging fire
If wind and fuel be brought to feed it with.
No more, good York; sweet Somerset, be still.
Your fortune, York, had you been Regent there,
Might happily have proved far worse than his.

YORK

What, worse than naught? Nay, then a shame take all!

SOMERSET

And, in the number, you that wish me shame!

CARDINAL

My lord of York, try what your fortune is.
The uncivil kerns of Ireland are in arms
And temper clay with blood of Englishmen;

To Ireland will you lead a band of men,
Collected choicely, from each county some,
And try your hap against the Irishmen?

YORK

I will, my lord, so please his majesty.

SUFFOLK

Why, our authority is his consent,
And what we do establish he confirms.
Then, noble York, take you this task in hand.

YORK

I am content. Provide me soldiers, lords,
While I take order for my own affairs.

SUFFOLK

A charge, Lord York, that I will see performed.
But now return we to the false Duke Humphrey.

CARDINAL

No more of him; for I will deal with him
That henceforth he shall trouble us no more.
And so break off, the day is almost spent.
Lord Suffolk, you and I must talk of that event.

YORK

My lord of Suffolk, within fourteen days
At Bristol I expect my soldiers;
For there I'll ship them all for Ireland.

SUFFOLK

I'll see it truly done, my lord of York.

*Exeunt all but York*

YORK

Now, York, or never, steel your fearsome thoughts,
And change misdoubt to resolutiòn;
Be that you hope to be, or what you are
Resign to death; it is not worth the enjoying.
Let pale-faced fear keep with the mean-born man,
And find no harbour in a royal heart.
Faster than spring-time showers come thought on
    thought,

And not a thought but thinks on dignity.
My brain, more busy than the labouring spider,
Weaves tedious snares to trap my enemies.
Well, nobles, well; 'tis politicly done,
To send me packing with a host of men.
I fear me you but warm the starvèd snake,
Which, cherished in your breasts, will sting your hearts.
'Twas men I lacked, and you will give them me;
I take it kindly; yet be well assured
You put sharp weapons in a madman's hands.
While I in Ireland nourish a mighty band,
I will stir up in England some black storm
Shall blow ten thousand souls to heaven or hell,
And this fierce tempest shall not cease to rage
Until the golden circuit on my head,
Like the glorious sun's transparent beams,
Does calm the fury of this mad-bred flaw.
And, for a minister of my intent,
I have seduced a headstrong Kentishman,
John Cade of Ashford,
To make commotion, as full well he can,
Under the title of John Mortimer.
In Ireland have I seen this stubborn Cade
Oppose himself against a troop of kerns,
And fought so long till his thighs with darts
Were almost like a sharp-quilled porcupine;
And, in the end being rescued, I have seen
Him caper upright like a wild Morisco,
Shaking the bloody darts as he his bells.
Full often, like a shag-haired crafty kern,
Has he conversèd with the enemy,
And undiscovered come to me again
And given me notice of their villainies.
This devil here shall be my substitute;
For that John Mortimer, who now is dead,
In face, in gait, in speech he does resemble,

By this I shall perceive the commons' mind,
How they affect the house and claim of York.
Say he is taken, racked, and torturèd,
I know no pain they can inflict upon him
Will make him say I moved him to those arms.
Say that he thrives, as 'tis most likely he will,
Why, then from Ireland come I with my strength,
And reap the harvest which that rascal sowed,
For Humphrey being dead, as he shall be,
And Henry put apart, the next for me.                    *Exit*

# SCENE 2
## State-room at Bury St. Edmunds.

*Enter two Murderers running from the murder of
the Duke of Gloucester*

FIRST MURDERER
Run to my lord of Suffolk; let him know
We have dispatched the Duke as he commanded.
SECOND MURDERER
O that it were to do! What have we done?
Did you ever hear a man so penitent?

*Enter Suffolk*

FIRST MURDERER Here comes my lord.
SUFFOLK Now, sirs, have you dispatched this thing?
FIRST MURDERER Ay, my good lord, he's dead.
SUFFOLK
Why, that's well said. Go, get you to my house;
I will reward you for this venturous deed.
The King and all the peers are here at hand.
Have you laid fair the bed? Are all things well,
According as I gave directiòns?

FIRST MURDERER It is, my good lord.
SUFFOLK Away, be gone!                          *Exeunt Murderers*

*Sound trumpets. Enter the King, Queen, Cardinal, and*
*Somerset, with attendants*

KING
  Go, call our uncle to our presence straight;
  Say we intend to try his grace today
  If he is guilty, as 'tis publishèd.
SUFFOLK
  I'll call him immediately, my noble lord.          *Exit*
KING
  Lords, take your places; and, I pray you all,
  Proceed no straiter against our uncle Gloucester
  Than from true evidence, of good esteem,
  He is approved in practice culpable.
QUEEN
  God forbid any malice should prevail
  That faultless may condemn a noble man!
  Pray God he may acquit him of suspicion!
KING
  I thank you, Meg; these words content me much.

*Enter Suffolk*

  How now? Why look you so pale? Why tremble you?
  Where is our uncle? What's the matter, Suffolk?
SUFFOLK
  Dead in his bed, my lord. Gloucester is dead.
QUEEN
  Heavens, God forfend!
CARDINAL
  God's secret judgement; I did dream tonight
  The Duke was dumb and could not speak a word.

*The King swoons*

QUEEN
  How fares my lord? Help, lords! The King is dead.
SOMERSET
  Rear up his body; wring him by the nose.
QUEEN
  Run, go, help, help! O Henry, open your eyes!
SUFFOLK
  He does revive again. Madam, be patient.
KING
  O heavenly God!
QUEEN                    How fares my gracious lord?
SUFFOLK
  Comfort, my sovereign! Gracious Henry, comfort!
KING
  What, does my lord of Suffolk comfort me?
  Came he right now to sing a raven's note,
  Whose dismal tune bereft my vital powers;
  And thinks he that the chirping of a wren,
  By crying comfort from a hollow breast,
  Can chase away the first-conceivèd sound?
  Hide not your poison with such sugared words;
  Lay not your hands on me; forbear, I say;
  Their touch affrights me as a serpent's sting.
  You baleful messenger, out of my sight!
  Upon your eyeballs murderous tyranny
  Sits in grim majesty to fright the world.
  Look not upon me, for your eyes are wounding;
  Yet do not go away; come, basilisk,[1]
  And kill the innocent gazer with your sight;
  For in the shade of death I shall find joy,
  In life but double death, now Gloucester's dead.

---

[1]Fabled creature whose look was supposed to kill.

QUEEN
 Why do you rate my lord of Suffolk thus?
 Although the Duke was enemy to him,
 Yet he, most Christian-like, laments his death,
 And for myself, foe as he was to me,
 Might liquid tears or heart-offending groans
 Or blood-consuming sighs recall his life,
 I would be blind with weeping, sick with groans,
 Look pale as primrose with blood-drinking sighs,
 And all to have the noble Duke alive.
 What know I how the world may deem of me?
 For it is known we were but hollow friends;
 It may be judged I made the Duke away;
 So shall my name with slander's tongue be wounded,
 And princes' Courts be filled with my reproach.
 This get I by his death. Ay me, unhappy,
 To be a queen and crowned with infamy!
KING
 Ah, woe is me for Gloucester, wretched man!
QUEEN
 Be woe for me, more wretched than he is.
 What, do you turn away and hide your face?
 I am no loathsome leper; look on me.
 What! Are you like the adder waxen deaf?
 Be poisonous too and kill your forlorn Queen.
 Is all your comfort shut in Gloucester's tomb?
 Why, then Dame Margaret was never your joy.
 Erect his statue and worship it,
 And make my image but an alehouse sign.
 Was I for this nigh wrecked upon the sea,
 And twice by awkward wind from England's bank
 Driven back again unto my native clime?
 What boded this, but well forewarning wind
 Did seem to say 'Seek not a scorpion's nest,
 Nor set your footing on this unkind shore'?
 What did I then, but cursed the gentle gusts

And he that loosed them forth their brazen caves;
And bid them blow towards England's blessèd shore,
Or turn our stern upon a dreadful rock.
Yet Aeolus would not be a murderer,
But left that dreadful office unto you;
The pretty vaulting sea refused to drown me,
Knowing that you would have me drowned on shore
With tears as salt as sea through your unkindness.
The splitting rocks cowered in the sinking sands,
And would not dash me with their ragged sides,
Because your flinty heart, more hard than they,
Might in your palace perish Margaret.
As far as I could ken your chalky cliffs,
When from your shore the tempest beat us back,
I stood upon the hatches in the storm,
And when the dusky sky began to rob
My earnest-gaping sight of your land's view,
I took a costly jewel from my neck—
A heart it was, bound in with diamonds—
And threw it towards your land. The sea received it,
And so I wished your body might my heart;
And even with this I lost fair England's view,
And bid my eyes be tracking with my heart,
And called them blind and dusky spectacles
For losing ken of Albion's wishèd coast.
How often have I tempted Suffolk's tongue—
The agent of your foul inconstancy—
To sit and witch me, as Ascanius did
When he to madding Dido would unfold
His father's acts, commenced in burning Troy!
Am I not bewitched like her? Or you not false like him?
Ay me! I can no more. Die, Margaret!
For Henry weeps that you do live so long.

*Noise within. Enter Warwick, Salisbury, and Commons*

WARWICK
  It is reported, mighty sovereign,
  That good Duke Humphrey traitorously is murdered
  By Suffolk and the Cardinal Beaufort's means.
  The commons, like an angry hive of bees
  That want their leader, scatter up and down
  And care not whom they sting in his revenge.
  Myself have calmed their angry mutiny,
  Until they hear the order of his death.
KING
  That he is dead, good Warwick, 'tis too true;
  But how he died God knows, not Henry.
  Enter his chamber, view his breathless corpse,
  And comment then upon his sudden death.
WARWICK
  That shall I do, my liege. Stay, Salisbury,
  With the rude multitude till I return.
        *Exeunt Warwick, then Salisbury and the commons*
KING
  O you that judge all things, stay my thoughts,
  My thoughts that labour to persuade my soul
  Some violent hands were laid on Humphrey's life.
  If my suspicion is false, forgive me, God,
  For judgement only does belong to you.
  Fain would I go to chafe his pallid lips
  With twenty thousand kisses, and to drain
  Upon his face an ocean of salt tears,
  To tell my love unto his dumb deaf trunk,
  And with my fingers feel his hand unfeeling.
  But all in vain are these mean obsequies,
  And to survey his dead and earthy image,
  What were it but to make my sorrow greater?

*Bed put forth with Gloucester's body. Enter Warwick*

WARWICK
    Come hither, gracious sovereign, view this body.
KING
    That is to see how deep my grave is made;
    For with his soul fled all my worldly solace,
    For, seeing him, I see my life in death.
WARWICK
    As surely as my soul intends to live
    With that dread King that took our state upon him
    To free us from his Father's wrathful curse,
    I do believe that violent hands were laid
    Upon the life of this thrice-faméd Duke.
SUFFOLK
    A dreadful oath, sworn with a solemn tongue!
    What instance gives Lord Warwick for his vow?
WARWICK
    See how the blood is settled in his face.
    Oft have I seen a timely-parted ghost
    Of ashy semblance, meagre, pale, and bloodless,
    Being all descended to the labouring heart;
    Which, in the conflict that it holds with death,
    Attracts the same for aidance against the enemy;
    Which with the heart there cools, and never returns
    To blush and beautify the cheek again.
    But see, his face is black and full of blood,
    His eyeballs further out than when he lived,
    Staring full ghastly like a strangled man;
    His hair upreared, his nostrils stretched with struggling;
    His hands abroad displayed, as one that grasped
    And tugged for life, and was by strength subdued.
    Look, on the sheets his hair, you see, is sticking;
    His well-proportioned beard made rough and rugged,
    Like the summer's corn by tempest lodged.
    It cannot be but he was murdered here;
    The least of all these signs is probable.

SUFFOLK
  Why, Warwick, who should do the Duke to death?
  Myself and Beaufort had him in protection;
  And we, I hope, sir, are no murderers.
WARWICK
  But both of you were vowed Duke Humphrey's foes,
  And you, in truth, had the good Duke to keep;
  Likely you would not feast him like a friend,
  And it is well seen he found an enemy.
QUEEN
  Then you perhaps suspect these noblemen
  As guilty of Duke Humphrey's untimely death.
WARWICK
  Who finds the heifer dead and bleeding fresh,
  And sees fast by a butcher with an axe,
  But will suspect 'twas he that made the slaughter?
  Who finds the partridge in the fierce kite's nest,
  But may imagine how the bird was dead,
  Although the kite soars with unbloodied beak?
  Even so suspicious is this tragedy.
QUEEN
  Are you the butcher, Suffolk? Where's your knife?
  Is Beaufort termed a kite? Where are his talons?
SUFFOLK
  I wear no knife to slaughter sleeping men;
  But here's a vengeful sword, rusted with ease,
  That shall be scourèd in his rancorous heart
  That slanders me with murder's crimson badge.
  Say, if you dare, proud Lord of Warwickshire,
  That I am faulty in Duke Humphrey's death.

                                        *Exit Cardinal*
WARWICK
  What dares not Warwick, if false Suffolk dares him?
QUEEN
  He dares not calm his contumelious spirit,

Nor cease to be an arrogant controller,
Though Suffolk dares him twenty thousand times.

WARWICK

Madam, be still, with reverence may I say,
For every word you speak in his behalf
Is slander to your royal dignity.

SUFFOLK

Blunt-witted lord, ignoble in demeanour!
If ever lady wronged her lord so much,
Your mother took into her blameful bed
Some stern untutored churl, and noble stock
Was grafted with crabtree slip, whose fruit you are,
And never of the Nevils' noble race.

WARWICK

But that the guilt of murder bucklers you
And I should rob the deathsman of his fee,
Quitting you thereby of ten thousand shames;
And that my sovereign's presence makes me mild,
I would, false murderous coward, on your knee
Make you beg pardon for your passèd speech,
And say it was your mother that you meant;
That you yourself were born in bastardy,
And, after all this fearful homage done,
Give you your hire and send your soul to hell,
Pernicious blood-sucker of sleeping men!

SUFFOLK

You shall be waking while I shed your blood,
If from this presence you dare go with me.

WARWICK

Away even now, or I will drag you hence.
Unworthy though you are, I'll cope with you,
And do some service to Duke Humphrey's ghost.

*Exeunt Suffolk and Warwick*

KING

What stronger breastplate than a heart untainted!
Thrice is he armed that has his quarrel just;

And he but naked, though locked up in steel,
Whose conscience with injustice is corrupted.

*A noise within*

QUEEN
What noise is this?

*Enter Suffolk and Warwick with their weapons drawn*

KING
Why, how now, lords! Your wrathful weapons drawn
Here in our presence? Dare you be so bold?
Why, what tumultuous clamour have we here?
SUFFOLK
The traitorous Warwick, with the men of Bury,
Set all upon me, mighty sovereign.

*Enter Salisbury*

SALISBURY (*to the Commons*)
Sirs, stand apart; the King shall know your mind.
Dread lord, the commons send you word by me,
Unless Lord Suffolk straight is done to death,
Or banishèd fair England's territories,
They will by violence tear him from your palace
And torture him with grievous lingering death.
They say by him the good Duke Humphrey died;
They say in him they fear your highness' death;
And mere instinct of love and loyalty,
Free from a stubborn opposite intent,
As being thought to contradict your liking,
Makes them thus forward in his banishment.
They say, in care of your most royal person,
That if your highness should intend to sleep,
And charge that no man should disturb your rest
In pain of your dislike, or pain of death,

Yet, notwithstanding such a strait edict,
Were there a serpent seen, with forkèd tongue,
That slily glided towards your majesty,
It were but necessary you were waked,
Lest, being suffered in that harmful slumber,
The mortal worm might make the sleep eternal.
And therefore do they cry, though you forbid,
That they will guard you, whether you will or no,
From such ill serpents as false Suffolk is;
With whose envenomèd and fatal sting,
Your loving uncle, twenty times his worth,
They say is shamefully bereft of life.

COMMONS (*within*)
An answer from the King, my lord of Salisbury!

SUFFOLK
'Tis like the commons, rude unpolished hinds,
Could send such message to their sovereign.
But you, my lord, were glad to be employed,
To show how happy an orator you are.
But all the honour Salisbury has won
Is that he was the lord ambassador
Sent from a sort of tinkers to the King.

COMMONS (*within*)
An answer from the King, or we will all break in!

KING
Go, Salisbury, and tell them all from me
I thank them for their tender loving care;
And had I not been cited so by them,
Yet did I purpose as they do entreat;
For sure my thoughts do hourly prophesy
Mischance unto my state by Suffolk's means.
And therefore by his majesty I swear
Whose far unworthy deputy I am,
He shall not breathe infection in this air
But three days longer, on the pain of death.

                                        *Exit Salisbury*

QUEEN

  O Henry, let me plead for gentle Suffolk!

KING

  Ungentle Queen, to call him gentle Suffolk!
  No more, I say; if you do plead for him,
  You will but add increase unto my wrath.
  Had I but said, I would have kept my word;
  But when I swear, it is irrevocable.
  (*To Suffolk*)
  If after three days' space you here are found
  On any ground that I am ruler of,
  The world shall not be ransom for your life.
  Come, Warwick, come, good Warwick, go with me;
  I have great matters to impart to thee.

                *Exeunt all but the Queen and Suffolk*

QUEEN

  Mischance and sorrow go along with you!
  Heart's discontent and sour affliction
  Be playfellows to keep you company!
  There's two of you, the devil make a third,
  And threefold vengeance tend upon your steps!

SUFFOLK

  Cease, gentle Queen, these execrations,
  And let your Suffolk take his heavy leave.

QUEEN

  Fie, coward woman and soft-hearted wretch!
  Have you not spirit to curse your enemy?

SUFFOLK

  A plague upon them! Wherefore should I curse them?
  Would curses kill, as does the mandrake's groan,
  I would invent as bitter searching terms,
  As curst, as harsh, and horrible to hear,
  Delivered strongly through my fixèd teeth,
  With full as many signs of deadly hate,
  As lean-faced Envy in her loathsome cave.
  My tongue should stumble in my earnest words,

My eyes should sparkle like the beaten flint,
My hair be fixed on end, as one distract;
Ay, every joint should seem to curse and ban;
And even now my burdened heart would break,
Should I not curse them. Poison be their drink!
Gall, worse than gall, the daintiest that they taste!
Their sweetest shade, a grove of cypress trees!
Their chiefest prospect, murdering basilisks!
Their softest touch as smart as lizards' stings!
Their music frightful as the serpent's hiss,
And boding screech-owls make the consort full!
And the foul terrors in dark-seated hell—

QUEEN
Enough, sweet Suffolk; you torment yourself,
And these dread curses, like the sun against glass,
Or like an overchargèd gun, recoil
And turns the force of them upon yourself.

SUFFOLK
You bade me curse, and will you bid me leave?
Now, by the ground that I am banished from,
Well could I curse away a winter's night,
Though standing naked on a mountain top,
Where biting cold would never let grass grow,
And think it but a minute spent in sport.

QUEEN
O, let me entreat you cease. Give me your hand
That I may dew it with my mournful tears;
Nor let the rain of heaven wet this place
To wash away my woeful monuments.
O, could this kiss be printed in your hand,
That you might think upon these by the seal,
Through whom a thousand sighs are breathed for you.
So get you gone, that I may know my grief;
'Tis but surmised while you are standing by,
As one that surfeits thinking on a want.
I will recall you, or, be well assured,

Adventure to be banishèd myself;
And banishèd I am, if but from you.
Go, speak not to me; even now be gone.
O, go not yet. Even thus two friends condemned
Embrace and kiss and take ten thousand leaves,
Lother a hundred times to part than die.
Yet now farewell, and farewell life with you.

SUFFOLK

Thus is poor Suffolk ten times banishèd,
Once by the King and three times thrice by you.
'Tis not the land I care for, were you thence;
A wilderness is populous enough,
So Suffolk had your heavenly company;
For where you are, there is the world itself,
With every single pleasure in the world;
And where you are not, desolatiòn.
I can no more. Live to enjoy your life;
Myself no joy in naught but that you live.

*Enter Vaux*

QUEEN

Whither goes Vaux so fast? What news, I pray?

VAUX

To signify unto his majesty
That Cardinal Beaufort is at point of death;
For suddenly a grievous sickness took him,
That makes him gasp, and stare, and catch the air,
Blaspheming God, and cursing men on earth.
Sometimes he talks as if Duke Humphrey's ghost
Were by his side; sometimes he calls the King,
And whispers to his pillow, as to him,
The secrets of his overchargèd soul.
And I am sent to tell his majesty
That even now he cries aloud for him.

QUEEN
  Go tell this heavy message to the King.
                                            *Exit Vaux*
  Ay me! What is this world! What news are these!
  But wherefore grieve I at an hour's poor loss,
  Omitting Suffolk's exile, my soul's treasure?
  Why only, Suffolk, mourn I not for you,
  And with the southern clouds contend in tears,
  Theirs for the earth's increase, mine for my sorrows?
  Now get you hence; the King, you know, is coming;
  If you are found by me you are but dead.
SUFFOLK
  If I depart from you I cannot live,
  And in your sight to die, what were it else
  But like a pleasant slumber in your lap?
  Here could I breathe my soul into the air,
  As mild and gentle as the cradle-babe
  Dying with mother's dug between its lips.
  Where, from your sight, I should be raging mad,
  And cry out for you to close up my eyes,
  To have you with your lips to stop my mouth.
  So should you either turn my flying soul,
  Or I should breathe it so into your body,
  And then it lived in sweet Elysium.
  To die by you were but to die in jest;
  From you to die were torture more than death.
  O, let me stay, befall what may befall!
QUEEN
  Away! Though parting is a fretful còrrosive,
  It is applièd to a deathful wound.
  To France, sweet Suffolk! Let me hear from you;
  For wheresoever you are in this world's globe,
  I'll have an Iris that shall find you out.
SUFFOLK
  I go.

QUEEN And take my heart with you.

*She kisses him*

SUFFOLK
A jewel, locked into the woefullest casket
That ever did contain a thing of worth.
Even as a splitted bark so sunder we;
This way fall I to death.
QUEEN                          This way for me.
*Exeunt in opposite directions*


# SCENE III
## Beaufort's bed-chamber.

*Enter the King, Salisbury, and Warwick,*
*to the Cardinal in bed*

KING
How fares my lord? Speak, Beaufort, to your sovereign.
CARDINAL
If you are Death, I'll give you England's treasure,
Enough to purchase such another island,
So you will let me live, and feel no pain.
KING
Ah, what a sign it is of evil life
Where death's approach is seen so terrible!
WARWICK
Beaufort, it is your sovereign speaks to you.
CARDINAL
Bring me unto my trial when you will.
Died he not in his bed? Where should he die?
Can I make men live whether they will or no?
O, torture me no more! I will confess.
Alive again? Then show me where he is;

I'll give a thousand pound to look upon him.
He has no eyes; the dust has blinded them.
Comb down his hair; look, look, it stands upright,
Like lime-twigs set to catch my wingèd soul.
Give me some drink; and bid the apothecary
Bring the strong poison that I bought of him.

KING

O you eternal mover of the heavens,
Look with a gentle eye upon this wretch;
O, beat away the busy meddling fiend
That lays strong siege unto this wretch's soul,
And from his bosom purge this black despair.

WARWICK

See how the pangs of death do make him grin!

SALISBURY

Disturb him not; let him pass peaceably.

KING

Peace to his soul, if God's good pleasure be!
Lord Cardinal, if you think on heaven's bliss,
Hold up your hand, make signal of your hope.

*The Cardinal dies*

He dies and makes no sign. O God, forgive him!

WARWICK

So bad a death argues a monstrous life.

KING

Forbear to judge, for we are sinners all.
Close up his eyes, and draw the curtain close;
And let us all to meditatìon.                    *Exeunt*

# Act IV

## SCENE I
### The Kent coast.

*Alarum. Ordnance goes off. Enter a Lieutenant, a Master,*
*a Master's Mate, Walter Whitmore, Suffolk, disguised, two*
*Gentlemen prisoners, and soldiers*

LIEUTENANT
  The gaudy, blabbing, and remorseful day
  Is crept into the bosom of the sea;
  And now loud howling wolves arouse the jades
  That drag the tragic melancholy night;
  Which with their drowsy, slow, and flagging wings
  Drape dead men's graves, and from their misty jaws
  Breathe foul contagious darkness in the air.
  Therefore bring forth the soldiers of our prize,
  For while our pinnace anchors in the Downs
  Here shall they make their ransom on the sand,
  Or with their blood stain this discoloured shore.
  Master, this prisoner freely give I; you;
  And you that are his mate make use of this;
  The other, Walter Whitmore, is your share.
FIRST GENTLEMAN
  What is my ransom, master? Let me know.
MASTER
  A thousand crowns, or else lay down your head.
MATE
  And so much shall you give, or off goes yours.
LIEUTENANT
  What, think you much to pay two thousand crowns,

227

And bear the name and carriage of gentleman?
Cut both the villains' throats; for die you shall.
The lives of those when we have lost in fight
Be counterpoised with such a petty sum!

FIRST GENTLEMAN
I'll give it, sir; and therefore spare my life.

SECOND GENTLEMAN
And so will I, and write home for it straight.

WHITMORE
I lost my eye in laying the prize aboard,
*(To Suffolk)* And therefore to revenge it shall you die;
And so should these, if I might have my will.

LIEUTENANT
Be not so rash. Take ransom; let him live.

SUFFOLK
Look on my George; I am a gentleman.
Rate me at what you will, you shall be paid.

WHITMORE
And so am I; my name is Walter Whitmore.
How now! Why start you? What, does death affright?

SUFFOLK
Your name affrights me, in whose sound is death.
A cunning man did calculate my birth,
And told me that by Water[1] I should die.
Yet let not this make you be bloody-minded;
Your name is Gualtier, being rightly sounded.

WHITMORE
Gualtier or Walter, which it is I care not.
Never yet did base dishonour blur our name
But with our sword we wiped away the blot.
Therefore, when merchant-like I sell revenge,
Broken be my sword, my arms torn and defaced,
And I proclaimed a coward through the world.

---

[1]Elizabethans pronounced Walter as Water.

SUFFOLK
  Stay, Whitmore, for your prisoner is a prince,
  The Duke of Suffolk, William de la Pole.
WHITMORE
  The Duke of Suffolk, muffled up in rags!
SUFFOLK
  Ay, but these rags are no part of the Duke;
  Jove sometimes went disguised, and why not I?
LIEUTENANT
  But Jove was never slain, as you shall be.
SUFFOLK
  Obscure and lousy swain, King Henry's blood,
  The honourable blood of Lancaster,
  Must not be shed by such a jaded groom.
  Have you not kissed your hand and held my stirrup?
  Bare-headed plodded by my foot-cloth mule,
  And thought you happy when I shook my head?
  How often have you waited at my cup,
  Fed from my trencher, kneeled down at the board,
  When I have feasted with Queen Margaret?
  Remember it and let it make you crest-fallen,
  Ay, and allay this your abortive pride,
  How in our voiding lobby have you stood
  And duly waited for my coming forth.
  This hand of mine has written in your behalf,
  And therefore shall it charm your riotous tongue.
WHITMORE
  Speak, captain, shall I stab the fòrlorn swain?
LIEUTENANT
  First let my words stab him, as he has me.
SUFFOLK
  Base slave, your words are blunt and so are you.
LIEUTENANT
  Convey him hence, and on our longboat's side
  Strike off his head.

SUFFOLK          You dare not, for your own.
LIEUTENANT
  Yes, Poole.
SUFFOLK Poole?
LIEUTENANT Poole! Sir Poole! Lord!
  Ay, kennel, puddle, sink, whose filth and dirt
  Trouble the silver spring where England drinks;
  Now will I dam up this your yawning mouth
  For swallowing the treasure of the realm.
  Your lips that kissed the Queen shall sweep the ground;
  And you that smiled at good Duke Humphrey's death
  Against the senseless winds shall grin in vain,
  Which in contempt shall hiss at you again.
  And wedded be you to the hags of hell,
  For daring to betrothe a mighty lord
  Unto the daughter of a worthless king,
  Having neither subject, wealth, nor diadem.
  By devilish policy are you grown great,
  And, like ambitious Sulla, overgorged
  With gobbets of your mother's bleeding heart.
  By you Anjou and Maine were sold to France,
  The false revolting Normans now through you
  Disdain to call us lord, and Picardy
  Has slain their governors, surprised our forts,
  And sent the ragged soldiers wounded home.
  The princely Warwick, and the Nevils all,
  Whose dreaded swords were never drawn in vain,
  As hating you, are rising up in arms,
  And now the house of York, thrust from the crown
  By shameful murder of a guiltless king
  And lofty, proud, encroaching tyranny,
  Burns with revenging fire; whose hopeful colours
  Advance our half-faced sun, striving to shine,
  Under which is written 'Invitis nubibus' [In spite of
    clouds]
  The commons here in Kent are up in arms;

And to conclude, reproach and beggary
Are crept into the palace of our King,
And all by you. Away! Convey him hence.

SUFFOLK
O that I were a god, to shoot forth thunder
Upon these paltry, servile, abject drudges.
Small things make base men proud. This villain here,
Being captain of a pinnace, threatens more
Than Bargulus, the strong Illyrian pirate.
Drones suck not eagles' blood, but rob beehives.
It is impossible that I should die
By such a lowly vassal as yourself.
Your words move rage and not remorse in me.

LIEUTENANT
Ay, but my deeds shall stay your fury soon.

SUFFOLK
I go on message from the Queen to France;
I charge you, waft me safely across the Channel.

LIEUTENANT
Walter!

WHITMORE
Come, Suffolk, I must waft you to your death.

SUFFOLK
*Pene gelidus timor occupat artus;*[2]
It is you I fear.

WHITMORE
You shall have cause to fear before I leave you.
What, are you daunted now? Now will you stoop?

FIRST GENTLEMAN
My gracious lord, entreat him, speak him fair.

SUFFOLK
Suffolk's imperial tongue is stern and rough,
Used to command, untaught to plead for favour.
Far be it we should honour such as these

---

[2]Cold fear almost paralyses the limbs.

With humble suit. No, rather let my head
Stoop to the block than these knees bow to any
Save to the God of heaven, and to my king;
And sooner dance upon a bloody pole
Than stand uncovered to the vulgar groom.
True nobility is exempt from fear;
More can I bear than you dare execute.

LIEUTENANT
Hale him away, and let him talk no more.

SUFFOLK
Come, soldiers, show what cruelty you can,
That this my death may never be forgot.
Great men often die by vile scoundrels:
A Roman sworder and banditto slave
Murdered sweet Tully; Brutus' bastard hand
Stabbed Julius Caesar; savage islanders
Pompey the Great; and Suffolk dies by pirates.
                    *Exeunt Whitmore and soldiers with Suffolk*

LIEUTENANT
And as for these whose ransom we have set,
It is our pleasure one of them should depart;
Therefore come you with us, and let him go.
                    *Exeunt all but the First Gentleman*


*Enter Walter Whitmore with the body of Suffolk*


WHITMORE
There let his head and lifeless body lie,
Until the Queen his mistress buries it.                *Exit*

FIRST GENTLEMAN
O, barbarous and bloody spectacle!
His body will I bear unto the King;
If he revenges it not, yet will his friends;
So will the Queen, that living held him dear.
                    *Exit with the body*

## SCENE II
## Blackheath.

*Enter George Bevis and John Holland*

BEVIS Come, and get you a sword, though made of a lath;
they have been up these two days.

HOLLAND They have the more need to sleep now then.

BEVIS I tell you, Jack Cade the clothier means to dress the
commonwealth, and turn it, and set a new nap upon it.

HOLLAND So he had need, for 'tis threadbare. Well, I say it
was never merry world in England since gentlemen
came up.

BEVIS O miserable age! Virtue is not regarded in
handicraftsmen.

HOLLAND The nobility think scorn to go in leather aprons.

BEVIS Nay, more; the King's Council are no good workmen.

HOLLAND True; and yet it is said 'Labour in your vocation';
which is as much to say as 'Let the magistrates be
labouring men'; and therefore should we be magistrates.

BEVIS You have hit it; for there's no better sign of a brave
mind than a hard hand.

HOLLAND I see them, I see them! There's Best's son, the
tanner of Wingham.

BEVIS He shall have the skins of our enemies to make dog's
leather of.

HOLLAND And Dick the butcher.

BEVIS Then is sin struck down like an ox, and iniquity's
throat cut like a calf.

HOLLAND And Smith the weaver.

BEVIS Ergo [therefore], their thread of life is spun.

HOLLAND Come, come, let's fall in with them.

*Drums. Enter Jack Cade, Dick the butcher, Smith the
weaver, and a sawyer, with others*

CADE  We John Cade, so termed of our supposed father—

DICK  (*aside*) Or rather of stealing a cade [cask] of herrings.

CADE  For our enemies shall fall before us, inspired with the spirit of putting down kings and princes. Command silence.

DICK  Silence!

CADE  My father was a Mortimer—

DICK  (*aside*) He was an honest man and a good bricklayer.

CADE  My mother a Plantagenet—

DICK  (*aside*) I knew her well; she was a midwife.

CADE  My wife descended of the Lacys—

DICK  (*aside*) She was indeed a pedlar's daughter, and sold many laces.

SMITH  (*aside*) But now of late, not able to travel with her furred pack, she washes bucks [dirty linen] here at home.

CADE  Therefore am I of an honourable house.

DICK  (*aside*) Ay, by my faith, the field is honourable, and there was he born, under a hedge; for his father had never a house but the cage.

CADE  Valiant I am.

SMITH  (*aside*) He must needs, for beggary is valiant.

CADE  I am able to endure much.

DICK  (*aside*) No question of that; for I have seen him whipped three market days together.

CADE  I fear neither sword nor fire.

SMITH  (*aside*) He need not fear the sword, for his coat is proof against it.

DICK  (*aside*) But I think he should stand in fear of fire, being burnt in the hand for stealing of sheep.

CADE  Be brave then; for your captain is brave, and vows reformation. There shall be in England seven halfpenny loaves sold for a penny; the three-hooped pot shall have ten hoops; and I will make it felony to drink small beer. All the realm shall be in common, and in Cheapside shall my palfrey go to grass. And when I am king, as king I will be—

ALL God save your majesty!

CADE I thank you, good people. There shall be no money; all shall eat and drink on my score; and I will apparel them all in one livery, that they may agree like brothers, and worship me their lord.

DICK The first thing we do, let's kill all the lawyers.

CADE Nay, that I mean to do. Is not this a lamentable thing, that the skin of an innocent lamb should be made parchment? That parchment, being scribbled over, should undo a man? Some say the bee stings, but I say 'tis the bee's wax, for I did but seal once to a thing, and I was never my own man since. How now? Who's there?

*Enter some rebels with the Clerk of Chartham*

SMITH The clerk of Chartham; he can write and read and cast accounts.

CADE O, monstrous!

SMITH We took him setting of boys' copies.

CADE Here's a villain!

SMITH He has a book in his pocket with red letters in it.

CADE Nay, then he is a conjurer.

DICK Nay, he can make obligations, and write court-hand.

CADE I am sorry for it. The man is a proper man, of my honour; unless I find him guilty, he shall not die. Come hither, man, I must examine you. What is your name?

CLERK Emmanuel.

DICK They use to write it on the top of letters. It will go hard with you.

CADE Let me alone. Do you use to write your name? Or have you a mark to yourself, like an honest plain-dealing man?

CLERK Sir, I thank God I have been so well brought up that I can write my name.

ALL He has confessed; away with him! He's a villain and a traitor.

CADE Away with him, I say; hang him with his pen and inkhorn about his neck.

*Exit Clerk guarded*

*Enter Michael*

MICHAEL Where's our general?

CADE Here I am, you particular fellow.

MICHAEL Fly, fly, fly! Sir Humphrey Stafford and his brother are hard by, with the King's forces.

CADE Stand, villain, stand, or I'll fell you down. He shall be encountered by a man as good as himself. He is but a knight, is he?

MICHAEL No.

CADE To equal him I will make myself a knight at once. (*He kneels*) Rise up, Sir John Mortimer. (*He rises*) Now have at him!

*Enter Sir Humphrey Stafford and his brother,*
*with drum and soldiers*

STAFFORD
Rebellious hinds, the filth and scum of Kent,
Marked for the gallows, lay your weapons down;
Home to your cottages, forsake this groom.
The King is merciful, if you return.

BROTHER
But angry, wrathful, and inclined to blood,
If you go forward; therefore yield, or die.

CADE
As for these silken-coated slaves, I care not;
It is to you, good people, that I speak,
Over whom, in time to come, I hope to reign;
For I am rightful heir unto the crown.

STAFFORD
Villain, your father was a plasterer;
And you yourself a shearman, are you not?

CADE
And Adam was a gardener.

BROTHER                                    And what of that?

CADE
Sure, this: Edmund Mortimer, Earl of March,
Married the Duke of Clarence' daughter, did he not?

STAFFORD
Ay, sir.

CADE
By her he had two children at one birth.

BROTHER
That's false.

CADE
Ay, there's the question; but I say 'tis true:
The elder of them, being put to nurse,
Was by a beggar-woman stolen away;
And, ignorant of his birth and parentage,
Became a bricklayer when he came to age.
His son am I; deny it if you can.

DICK
Nay, 'tis too true; therefore he shall be king.

SMITH Sir, he made a chimney in my father's house, and
the bricks are alive at this day to testify it; therefore
deny it not.

STAFFORD
And will you credit this base drudge's words,
That speaks he knows not what?

ALL
Ay, sure, will we; therefore get you gone.

BROTHER
Jack Cade, the Duke of York has taught you this.

CADE (aside) He lies, for I invented it myself. (To Stafford)
Go to, fellow, tell the King from me that for his father's
sake, Henry the Fifth, in whose time boys went to

spancounter for French crowns,[2] I am content he shall
reign. But I'll be Protector over him.

DICK And furthermore, we'll have the Lord Say's head for
selling the dukedom of Maine.

CADE And good reason; for thereby is England mained
and fain to go with a staff, but that my power holds it
up. Fellow kings, I tell you that that Lord Say has gelded
the commonwealth and made it an eunuch; and more
than that, he can speak French; and therefore he is a
traitor.

STAFFORD O gross and miserable ignorance!

CADE Nay, answer if you can; the Frenchmen are our
enemies; go to, then, I ask but this: can he that speaks
with the tongue of an enemy be a good counsellor, or
no?

ALL No, no; and therefore we'll have his head.

BROTHER
Well, seeing gentle words will not prevail,
Assail them with the army of the King.

STAFFORD
Herald, away! And throughout every town
Proclaim them traitors that are up with Cade;
That those who fly before the battle ends
May, even in their wives' and children's sight,
Be hanged up for example at their doors.
And you that are the King's friends, follow me.
                          *Exit with his brother and soldiers*

CADE
And you that love the commons, follow me.
Now show yourselves men; 'tis for liberty.
We will not leave one lord, one gentleman;
Spare none but such as go in clouted shoes,
For they are thrifty honest men, and such
As would, but that they dare not, take our parts.

---

[2]An Elizabethan game, with usual insinuation of venereal disease.

DICK They are all in order, and march toward us.

CADE But then are we in order when we are most out of
order. Come, march forward.                         *Exeunt*

## SCENE III
## The same.

*Alarums to the fight, wherein both the Staffords are slain.*
*Enter Cade and the rest*

CADE Where's Dick, the butcher of Ashford?

DICK Here, sir.

CADE They fell before you like sheep and oxen, and you
behaved yourself as if you had been in your own
slaughter-house. Therefore thus will I reward you: the
Lent shall be as long again as it is; and you shall have a
licence to kill for a hundred lacking one.

DICK I desire no more.

CADE And to speak truth, you deserve no less.

*He puts on Sir Humphrey Stafford's armour*

This monument of the victory will I bear; and the
bodies shall be dragged at my horse heels till I do come
to London, where we will have the Mayor's sword borne
before us.

DICK If we mean to thrive and do good, break open the
gaols and let out the prisoners.

CADE Doubt not that, I warrant you. Come, let's march
towards London.                                     *Exeunt*

## SCENE IV
## Westminster Palace.

*Enter the King with a petition and the Queen with Suffolk's
head, Buckingham, and Lord Say*

QUEEN *(aside)*
  Oft have I heard that grief softens the mind,
  And makes it fearful and degenerate;
  Think therefore on revenge and cease to weep.
  But who can cease to weep and look on this?
  Here may his head lie on my throbbing breast;
  But where's the body that I should embrace?
BUCKINGHAM What answer makes your grace to the rebels'
  supplication?
KING
  I'll send some holy bishop to entreat;
  For God forbid so many simple souls
  Should perish by the sword! And I myself,
  Rather than bloody war shall cut them short,
  Will parley with Jack Cade their general.
  But stay, I'll read it over once again.
QUEEN *(aside)*
  Ah, barbarous villains! Has this lovely face
  Ruled like a wandering planet over me,
  And could it not enforce them to relent,
  That were unworthy to behold the same?
KING
  Lord Say, Jack Cade has sworn to have your head.
SAY
  Ay, but I hope your highness shall have his.
KING
  How now, madam?
  Still lamenting and mourning for Suffolk's death?
  I fear me, love, if now I had been dead,
  You would not have mourned so much for me.

QUEEN
  No, my love; I should not mourn, but die for you.

*Enter First Messenger*

KING
  How now? What news? Why come you in such haste?
FIRST MESSENGER
  The rebels are in Southwark; fly, my lord!
  Jack Cade proclaims himself Lord Mortimer,
  Descended from the Duke of Clarence' house,
  And calls your grace usurper, openly,
  And vows to crown himself in Westminster.
  His army is a ragged multitude
  Of hinds and peasants, rude and merciless;
  Sir Humphrey Stafford and his brother's death
  Have given them heart and courage to proceed.
  All scholars, lawyers, courtiers, gentlemen,
  They call false caterpillars and intend their death.
KING
  O, graceless men, they know not what they do.
BUCKINGHAM
  My gracious lord, retire to Kenilworth,
  Until a force be raised to put them down.
QUEEN
  Ah, were the Duke of Suffolk now alive,
  These Kentish rebels would be soon appeased!
KING
  Lord Say, the traitors hate you well;
  Therefore away with us to Kenilworth.
SAY
  So might your grace's person be in danger.
  The sight of me is odious in their eyes;
  And therefore in this city will I stay,
  And live alone as secret as I may.

*Enter Second Messenger*

SECOND MESSENGER
  Jack Cade has gotten London Bridge;
  The citizens fly and forsake their houses;
  The rascal people, thirsting after prey,
  Join with the traitor; and they jointly swear
  To spoil the city and your royal Court.
BUCKINGHAM
  Then linger not, my lord. Away! Take horse!
KING
  Come, Margaret. God, our hope, will succour us.
QUEEN
  My hope is gone, now Suffolk is deceased.
KING (*to Lord Say*)
  Farewell, my lord. Trust not the Kentish rebels.
BUCKINGHAM
  Trust nobody, for fear you are betrayed.
SAY
  The trust I have is in my innocence,
  And therefore am I bold and resolute.                    *Exeunt*


# SCENE V
## The Tower of London.

*Enter Lord Scales above. Then enter three Citizens below*

SCALES How now? Is Jack Cade slain?
FIRST CITIZEN No, my lord, nor likely to be slain; for they
  have won the bridge, killing all those that withstand
  them. The Lord Mayor craves aid of your honour from
  the Tower to defend the city from the rebels.
SCALES
  Such aid as I can spare you shall command,
  But I am troubled here with them myself;

The rebels have assayed to win the Tower.
But get you to Smithfield and gather head,
And thither I will send you Matthew Gough.
Fight for your king, your country, and your lives;
And so farewell, for I must hence again.          *Exeunt*


# SCENE VI
## A London street.

*Enter Jack Cade and the rest, and strikes his
staff on London Stone*

CADE Now is Mortimer lord of this city. And here, sitting
upon London Stone, I charge and command that, at the
city's cost, the Pissing Conduit run nothing but claret
wine this first year of our reign. And now henceforward
it shall be treason for any that calls me other than Lord
Mortimer.

*Enter a Soldier, running*

SOLDIER Jack Cade! Jack Cade!
CADE Knock him down there.
                *They kill him*
SMITH If this fellow is wise, he'll never call you Jack Cade
more; I think he has a very fair warning.
DICK My lord, there's an army gathered together in
Smithfield.
CADE Come then, let's go fight with them. But first, go
and set London Bridge on fire and, if you can, burn
down the Tower too. Come, let's away.          *Exeunt*

## SCENE VII
Smithfield.

*Alarums. Matthew Gough is slain, and the rest. Then enter*
*Jack Cade with his followers*

CADE So, sirs. Now go some and pull down the Savoy;
others to the Inns of Court; down with them all.

DICK I have a suit unto your lordship.

CADE Be it a lordship, you shall have it for that word.

DICK Only that the laws of England may come out of your
mouth.

HOLLAND (*aside*) Mass, it will be sore law then, for he was
thrust in the mouth with a spear, and 'tis not whole yet.

SMITH (*aside to Holland*) Nay, John, it will be stinking
law, for his breath stinks with eating toasted cheese.

CADE I have thought upon it; it shall be so. Away! Burn
all the records of the realm; my mouth shall be the
parliament of England.

HOLLAND (*aside*) Then we are like to have biting statutes,
unless his teeth are pulled out.

CADE And henceforward all things shall be in common.

*Enter a Messenger*

MESSENGER My lord, a prize, a prize! Here's the Lord Say,
who sold the towns in France; he that made us pay
one-and-twenty fifteens, and one shilling to the pound,
the last subsidy.

*Enter Bevis with Lord Say*

CADE Well, he shall be beheaded for it ten times. Ah, you
say, you serge, nay, you buckram lord! Now are you
within point-blank of our jurisdiction regal. What can
you answer to my majesty for giving up of Normandy

unto Mounsieur Basimecu,[3] the Dolphin of France? Be
it known unto you by these presence, [presents] even the
presence of Lord Mortimer, that I am the broom that
must sweep the court clean of such filth as you are. You
have most traitorously corrupted the youth of the realm
in erecting a grammar school; and whereas before, our
forefathers had no other books but the score and the
tally, you have caused printing to be used; and, contrary
to the King's crown and dignity, you have built a paper-
mill. It will be proved to your face that you have men
about you that usually talk of a noun and a verb, and
such abominable words as no Christian ear can endure
to hear. You have appointed justices of the peace, to call
poor men before them about matters they were not able
to answer. Moreover, you have put them in prison; and
because they could not read, you have hanged them;
when, indeed, only for that cause they have been most
worthy to live. You do ride in a foot-cloth, do you not?

SAY What of that?

CADE Sure, you ought not to let your horse wear a cloak,
when honester men than you go in their hose and
doublets.

DICK And work in their shirt too; as myself, for example,
that am a butcher.

SAY You men of Kent—

DICK What say you of Kent?

SAY Nothing but this: 'tis *bona terra, mala gens.* [good
land, ill people].

CADE Away with him! Away with him! He speaks Latin.

SAY
Hear me but speak, and bear me where you will.
Kent, in the *Commentaries* Caesar wrote,
Is termed the civilest place of all this isle;
Sweet is the country, because full of riches,

---

[3]Vulgar French for Kiss-my-arse.

The people liberal, valiant, active, wealthy;
Which makes me hope you are not void of pity.
I sold not Maine, I lost not Normandy;
Yet to recover them would lose my life.
Justice with favour have I always done;
Prayers and tears have moved me, gifts could never.
When have I aught exacted at your hands,
But to maintain the King, the realm, and you?
Large gifts have I bestowed on learnèd clerks,
Because my book preferred me to the King;
And seeing ignorance is the curse of God,
Knowledge the wing wherewith we fly to heaven,
Unless you are possessed with devilish spirits,
You cannot but forbear to murder me.
This tongue has parleyed unto foreign kings
For your behoof—

CADE Tut, when struck you one blow in the field?

SAY
  Great men have reaching hands; oft have I struck
  Those that I never saw, and struck them dead.

BEVIS O monstrous coward! What, to come behind folks?

SAY
  These cheeks are pale for watching for your good.

CADE Give him a box on the ear, and that will make them
  red again.

SAY
  Long sitting to determine poor men's causes
  Has made me full of sickness and diseases.

CADE You shall have a hempen caudle [cordial] then, and
  the help of hatchet.

DICK Why do you quiver, man?

SAY
  The palsy and not fear provokes me.

CADE Nay, he nods at us as who should say 'I'll be even
  with you'. I'll see if his head will stand steadier on a
  pole or no. Take him away and behead him.

SAY
Tell me: wherein have I offended most?
Have I affected wealth or honour? Speak.
Are my chests filled up with extorted gold?
Is my apparel sumptuous to behold?
Whom have I injured, that you seek my death?
These hands are free from guiltless bloodshedding,
This breast from harbouring foul deceitful thoughts.
O, let me live!

CADE *(aside)* I feel remorse in myself with his words; but
I'll bridle it. He shall die, if it is but for pleading so well
for his life. Away with him! He has a familiar under his
tongue; he speaks not in God's name. Go, take him
away, I say; and strike off his head at once, and then
break into his son-in-law's house, Sir James Cromer,
and strike off his head, and bring them both upon two
poles hither.

ALL It shall be done.

SAY
Ah, countrymen, if, when you make your prayers,
God should be so obdùrate as yourselves,
How would it fare with your departed souls?
And therefore yet relent and save my life.

CADE Away with him! And do as I command you.

                    *Exeunt some rebels with Lord Say*
The proudest peer in the realm shall not wear a head on
his shoulders, unless he pays me tribute; there shall not
a maid be married, but she shall pay to me her maidenhead, ere they have it. Men shall hold of me *in capite*;[4]
and we charge and command that their wives be as free as
heart can wish or tongue can tell.

DICK My lord, when shall we go to Cheapside and take up
commodities upon our bills?

---

[4]By the head, i.e. in chief.

CADE Sure, at once.
ALL O, brave!

*Enter one with the heads of Say and Cromer upon two poles*

CADE But is not this braver? Let them kiss one another; for
they loved well when they were alive. Now part them
again, lest they consult about the giving up of some
more towns in France. Soldiers, defer the spoil of the
city until night; for with these borne before us, instead
of maces, will we ride through the streets, and at every
corner have them kiss. Away!                          *Exeunt*

# SCENE VIII
## Southwark.

*Alarum and retreat. Enter Cade and all his rabble*

CADE Up Fish Street! Down Saint Magnus' Corner!
Kill and knock down! Throw them into Thames!

*Sound a parley*

What noise is this I hear? Dare any be so bold to sound
retreat or parley, when I command them kill?

*Enter Buckingham and old Clifford, attended*

BUCKINGHAM
Ay, here they are that dare and will disturb you;
Know, Cade, we come ambassadors from the King
Unto the commons, whom you have misled;
And here pronounce free pardon to them all
That will forsake you and go home in peace.
CLIFFORD
What say you, countrymen, will you relent

And yield to mercy, while it is offered you,
Or let a rebel lead you to your deaths?
Who loves the King and will embrace his pardon,
Fling up his cap and say 'God save his majesty!'
Who does hate him, and honours not his father,
Henry the Fifth, that made all France to quake,
Shake he his weapon at us and pass by.

ALL God save the King! God save the King!

CADE What, Buckingham and Clifford, are you so brave?
And you, base peasants, do you believe him? Will you
needs be hanged with your pardons about your necks?
Has my sword therefore broken through London gates,
that you should leave me at the White Hart in Southwark? I thought you would never have given out these
arms till you had recovered your ancient freedom. But
you are all cowards and dastards, and delight to live in
slavery to the nobility. Let them break your backs with
burdens, take your houses over your heads, ravish your
wives and daughters before your faces. For me, I will
make shift for one, and so God's curse light upon you
all!

ALL We'll follow Cade! We'll follow Cade!

CLIFFORD
Is Cade the son of Henry the Fifth,
That thus you do exclaim you'll go with him?
Will he conduct you through the heart of France,
And make the meanest of you earls and dukes?
Alas, he has no home, no place to fly to;
Nor knows he how to live but by the spoil,
Unless by robbing of your friends and us.
Were it not a shame, that while you live at jar,
The fearful French, whom you late vanquishèd,
Should make a start over seas and vanquish you?
I think already in this civil broil
I see them lording it in London streets,
Crying 'Villain!' unto all they meet.

Better ten thousand base-born Cades miscarry
Than you should stoop unto a Frenchman's mercy.
To France! To France! And get what you have lost;
Spare England, for it is your native coast.
Henry has money; you are strong and manly;
God on our side, doubt not of victory.

ALL  A Clifford! A Clifford! We'll follow the King and
Clifford.

CADE (*aside*) Was ever feather so lightly blown to and fro
as this multitude? The name of Henry the Fifth hales
them to a hundred mischiefs and makes them leave me
desolate. I see them lay their heads together to surprise
me. My sword make way for me, for here is no staying. —
In despite of the devils and hell, have through the very
midst of you! And heavens and honour be witness that
no want of resolution in me, but only my followers' base
and ignominious treasons, make me betake to my heels.

*Exit*

BUCKINGHAM
What, is he fled? Go some and follow him;
And he that brings his head unto the King
Shall have a thousand crowns for his reward.

*Exeunt some of them*

Follow me, soldiers; we'll devise a means
To reconcile you all unto the King.        *Exeunt*


# SCENE IX
## Kenilworth Castle.

*Sound trumpets. Enter the King, Queen,
and Somerset, on the terrace*


KING
Was ever king that joyed an earthly throne,
And could command no more content than I?

No sooner was I crept out of my cradle
But I was made a king at nine months old;
Was never subject longed to be a king
As I do long and wish to be a subject.

*Enter Buckingham and Clifford*

BUCKINGHAM
Health and glad tidings to your majesty!
KING
Why, Buckingham, is the traitor Cade surprised?
Or is he but retired to make him strong?

*Enter many, with halters about their necks*

CLIFFORD
He is fled, my lord, and all his powers do yield,
And humbly thus with halters on their necks,
Expect your highness' sentence of life or death.
KING
Then, heaven, set open your everlasting gates
To entertain my vows of thanks and praise!
Soldiers, this day have you redeemed your lives,
And showed how well you love your prince and country;
Continue ever in this so good a mind,
And, Henry, though he may be unfortunate,
Assure yourselves, will never be unkind.
And so, with thanks and pardon to you all,
I do dismiss you to your several counties.
ALL God save the King! God save the King!

*Enter a Messenger*

MESSENGER
Please it your grace to be advertisèd
The Duke of York is newly come from Ireland,

And with a powerful and a mighty force
Of gallowglasses and stout kerns
Is marching hitherward in proud array;
And ever proclaims, as yet he comes along,
His arms are only to remove from you
The Duke of Somerset, whom he terms a traitor.

KING

Thus stands my state, between Cade and York distressed;
Like to a ship that, having escaped a tempest,
Is straightway calmed and boarded by a pirate.
But now is Cade driven back, his men dispersed,
And now is York in arms to second him.
I pray you, Buckingham, go and meet him,
And ask him what's the reason of these arms.
Tell him I'll send Duke Edmund to the Tower;
And, Somerset, we will commit you thither,
Until his army is dismissed from him.

SOMERSET

My lord,
I'll yield myself to prison willingly,
Or unto death, to do my country good.

KING

In any case, be not too rough in terms,
For he is fierce and cannot brook hard language.

BUCKINGHAM

I will, my lord, and doubt not so to deal
As all things shall redound unto your good.

KING

Come, wife, let's in and learn to govern better;
For yet may England curse my wretched reign.

                                    *Flourish. Exeunt*

## SCENE X
### Iden's garden in Kent.

*Enter Cade*

CADE Fie on ambitions! Fie on myself, that have a sword
and yet am ready to famish! These five days have I hid
me in these woods, and durst not peep out, for all the
country is watched for me. But now am I so hungry
that, if I might have a lease of my life for a thousand
years, I could stay no longer. Wherefore, on a brick wall
have I climbed into this garden, to see if I can eat grass
or pick a salad another while, which is not amiss to cool
a man's stomach this hot weather. And I think this
word 'sallet' [helmet] was born to do me good; for many
a time, but for a sallet, my brain-pan had been cleft by
a brown bill. And many a time, when I have been dry
and bravely marching, it has served me instead of a
quart pot to drink in; and now the word 'sallet' must
serve me to feed on.

*Enter Iden*

IDEN
Lord, who would live turmoilèd in the Court,
And may enjoy such quiet walks as these?
This small inheritance my father left me
Contents me, and is worth a monarchy.
I seek not to wax great by others' waning,
Or gather wealth I care not with what envy;
Suffices that I have maintains my state,
And sends the poor well pleasèd from my gate.
CADE *(aside)* Here's the lord of the soil come to seize me
for a stray, for entering his fee-simple without leave. *(To
Iden)* Ah, villain, you will betray me, and get a thou-
sand crowns of the King by carrying my head to him;

but I'll make you eat iron like an ostrich, and swallow
my sword like a great pin, ere you and I part.

IDEN

Why, rude companion, whatsoever you are,
I know you not; why then should I betray you?
Is it not enough to break into my garden,
And like a thief to come to rob my grounds,
Climbing my walls in spite of me the owner,
But you will brave me with these saucy terms?

CADE Brave you? Ay, by the best blood that ever was
broached, and beard you too. Look on me well; I have
eaten no meat these five days, yet come you and your
five men, and if I do not leave you all as dead as a
door-nail, I pray God I may never eat grass more.

IDEN

Nay, it shall never be said, while England stands,
That Alexander Iden, an esquire of Kent,
Took odds to combat a poor famished man.
Oppose your steadfast gazing eyes to mine,
See if you can outface me with your looks;
Set limb to limb, and you are far the lesser;
Your hand is but a finger to my fist;
Your leg a stick comparèd with this truncheon.
My foot shall fight with all the strength you have;
And if my arm is heavèd in the air,
Your grave is dug already in the earth.
As for words, whose greatness answers words,
Let this my sword report what speech forbears.

CADE By my valour, the most complete champion that
ever I heard! Steel, if you turn the edge, or cut not out
the burly-boned clown in chines of beef ere you sleep in
your sheath, I beseech God on my knees you may be
turned to hobnails.

*Here they fight and Cade falls*

O, I am slain! Famine and no other has slain me; let ten
thousand devils come against me, and give me but the
ten meals I have lost, and I'd defy them all. Wither,
garden, and be henceforth a burying-place to all that do
dwell in this house, because the unconquered soul of
Cade is fled.

IDEN
Is it Cade that I have slain, that monstrous traitor?
Sword, I will hallow you for this your deed,
And hang you over my tomb when I am dead;
Never shall this blood be wiped from your point,
But you shall wear it as a herald's coat,
To blazon the honour that your master got.

CADE Iden, farewell; and be proud of your victory. Tell
Kent from me she has lost her best man, and exhort all
the world to be cowards; for I, that never feared any, am
vanquished by famine, not by valour.                *He dies*

IDEN
How much you wrong me, heaven be my judge.
Die, damnèd wretch, the curse of her that bore you;
And as I thrust your body in with my sword,
So wish I I might thrust your soul to hell.
Hence will I drag you headlong by the heels
Unto a dunghill, which shall be your grave,
And there cut off your most ungracious head;
Which I will bear in triumph to the King,
Leaving your trunk for crows to feed upon.          *Exit*

# Act V

## SCENE I
### Between Blackheath and Dartford.

*Enter York and his Irish soldiers, with drum and colours*

YORK
From Ireland thus comes York to claim his right,
And pluck the crown from feeble Henry's head.
Ring, bells, aloud; burn bonfires clear and bright,
To entertain great England's lawful king.
Ah, *sancta majestas!* Who would not buy you dear?
Let them obey that know not how to rule;
This hand was made to handle naught but gold.
I cannot give due action to my words,
Unless a sword or sceptre balances it.
A sceptre shall it have, have I a soul,
On which I'll toss the flower-de-luce of France.

*Enter Buckingham*

Whom have we here? Buckingham to disturb me?
The King has sent him, sure; I must dissemble.
BUCKINGHAM
York, if you mean well, I greet you well.
YORK
Humphrey of Buckingham, I accept your greeting.
Are you a messenger, or come of pleasure?
BUCKINGHAM
A messenger from Henry, our dread liege,
To know the reason of these arms in peace;

Or why you, being a subject as I am,
Against your oath and true allegiance sworn,
Should raise so great a force without his leave,
Or dare to bring your force so near the Court?

YORK *(aside)*

Scarce can I speak, my choler is so great.
O, I could hew up rocks and fight with flint,
I am so angry at these abject terms;
And now, like Ajax Telamonius,
On sheep or oxen could I spend my fury.
I am far better born than is the King,
More like a king, more kingly in my thoughts;
But I must make fair weather yet awhile,
Till Henry is more weak, and I more strong. —
Buckingham, I pray you pardon me,
That I have given no answer all this while;
My mind was troubled with deep melancholy.
The cause why I have brought this army hither
Is to remove proud Somerset from the King,
Seditious to his grace and to the state.

BUCKINGHAM

That is too much presumption on your part;
But if your arms are to no other end,
The King has yielded unto your demand:
The Duke of Somerset is in the Tower.

YORK

Upon your honour, is he prisoner?

BUCKINGHAM

Upon my honour, he is prisoner.

YORK

Then, Buckingham, I do dismiss my troops.
Soldiers, I thank you all; disperse yourselves;
Meet me tomorrow in Saint George's Field,
You shall have pay and everything you wish.

*Exeunt soldiers*

And let my sovereign, virtuous Henry,

Command my eldest son—nay, all my sons—
As pledges of my fealty and love;
I'll send them all as willing as I live.
Lands, goods, horse, armour, anything I have,
Is his to use, so Somerset may die.

BUCKINGHAM
York, I commend this kind submissiòn;
We twain will go into his highness' tent.

*Enter the King and attendants*

KING
Buckingham, does York intend no harm to us,
That thus he marches with you arm in arm?

YORK
In all submission and humility
York does present himself unto your highness.

KING
Then what intend these forces you do bring?

YORK
To heave the traitor Somerset from hence,
And fight against that monstrous rebel Cade,
Who since I heard to be discomfited.

*Enter Iden, with Cade's head*

IDEN
If one so rude and of so mean condition
May pass into the presence of a king,
Lo, I present your grace a traitor's head,
The head of Cade, whom I in combat slew.

KING
The head of Cade? Great God, how just are you!
O, let me view his visage, being dead,
That living wrought me such exceeding trouble.
Tell me, my friend, are you the man that slew him?

IDEN
  I was, if it likes your majesty.
KING
  How are you called? And what is your degree?
IDEN
  Alexander Iden, that is my name,
  A poor esquire of Kent, that loves his king.
BUCKINGHAM
  So please it you, my lord, it were not amiss
  He were created knight for his good service.
KING
  Iden, kneel down.

                    *Iden kneels*

          Rise up a knight.
  We give you for reward a thousand marks,
  And will that you henceforth attend on us.
IDEN
  May Iden live to merit such a bounty,
  And never live but true unto his liege.

          *Enter the Queen and Somerset*

KING
  See, Buckingham, Somerset comes with the Queen;
  Go, bid her hide him quickly from the Duke.
QUEEN
  For thousand Yorks he shall not hide his head,
  But boldly stand and front him to his face.
YORK
  How now? Is Somerset at liberty?
  Then, York, unloose your long-imprisoned thoughts
  And let your tongue be equal with your heart.
  Shall I endure the sight of Somerset?
  False King! Why have you broken faith with me,

Knowing how hardly I can brook abuse?
'King' did I call you? No, you are not king;
Not fit to govern and rule multitudes,
Who dare not—no, nor can not—rule a traitor.
That head of yours does not become a crown;
Your hand is made to grasp a palmer's staff,
And not to grace an awful princely sceptre.
That gold must round engirt these brows of mine,
Whose smile and frown, like to Achilles' spear,
Is able with the change to kill and cure.
Here is a hand to hold a sceptre up,
And with the same to act controlling laws.
Give place; by heaven, you shall rule no more
Over him whom heaven created for your ruler.

SOMERSET
O monstrous traitor! I arrest you, York,
Of capital treason against the King and crown.
Obey, audacious traitor; kneel for grace.

YORK
Would have me kneel? First let me ask of these
If they can brook I bow a knee to man.
Fellow, call in my sons to be my bail;

*Exit an attendant*

I know, ere they will have me go to ward,
They'll pawn their swords for my enfranchisement.

QUEEN
Call hither Clifford; bid him come at once,
To say if now the bastard boys of York
Shall be the surety for their traitor father.

*Exit an attendant*

YORK
O blood-bespotted Neapolitan,
Outcast of Naples, England's bloody scourge!
The sons of York, your betters in their birth,
Shall be their father's bail, and bane to those
That for my surety will refuse the boys.

*Enter at one door Edward and Richard with their troops*

See where they come; I'll warrant they'll make it good.

*Enter at another door Clifford and*
*Young Clifford with troops.*

QUEEN
And here comes Clifford to deny their bail.

CLIFFORD
Health and all happiness to my lord the King!

*He kneels*

YORK
I thank you, Clifford; say, what news with you?
Nay, do not fright us with an angry look.
We are your sovereign, Clifford; kneel again.
For your mistaking so, we pardon you.

CLIFFORD
This is my king, York; I do not mistake;
But you mistake me much to think I do.
To Bedlam with him! Is the man grown mad?

KING
Ay, Clifford; a bedlam and ambitious humour
Makes him oppose himself against his king.

CLIFFORD
He is a traitor; let him to the Tower,
And chop away that factious pate of his.

QUEEN
He is arrested, but will not obey;
His sons, he says, shall give their words for him.

YORK
Will you not, sons?

EDWARD
Ay, noble father, if our words will serve.

RICHARD
  And if words will not, then our weapons shall.
CLIFFORD
  Why, what a brood of traitors have we here!
YORK
  Look in a glass and call your image so;
  I am your king, and you a false-heart traitor.
  Call hither to the stake my two brave bears,
  That with the very shaking of their chains
  They may astonish these ill-lurking curs;
  Bid Salisbury and Warwick come to me.

*Enter the Earls of Warwick and Salisbury with troops.*

CLIFFORD
  Are these your bears? We'll bait your bears to death,
  And manacle the bearward in their chains,
  If you dare bring them to the baiting-place.
RICHARD
  Oft have I seen a hot o'erweening cur
  Run back and bite, because he was withheld;
  Which, being suffered with the bear's fierce paw,
  Has clapped his tail between his legs and cried.
  And such a piece of service will you do,
  If you oppose yourselves to match Lord Warwick.
CLIFFORD
  Hence, heap of wrath, foul ill-formed lump,
  As crookèd in your manners as your shape!
YORK
  Nay, we shall heat you thoroughly anon.
CLIFFORD
  Take heed, lest by your heat you burn yourselves.
KING
  Why, Warwick, has your knee forgotten to bow?
  Old Salisbury, shame to your silver hair,
  You mad misleader of your brain-sick son!

What, will you on your deathbed play the ruffian,
And seek for sorrow with your spectacles?
O, where is faith? O, where is loyalty?
If it is banished from the frosty head,
Where shall it find a harbour in the earth?
Will you go dig a grave to find out war,
And shame your honourable age with blood?
Why are you old and want experience?
Or wherefore do abuse it, if you have it?
For shame! In duty bend your knee to me,
That bows unto the grave with your great age.

SALISBURY
My lord, I have considered with myself
The title of this most renownèd Duke;
And in my conscience do repute his grace
The rightful heir to England's royal seat.

KING
Have you not sworn allegiance unto me?

SALISBURY
I have.

KING
Can you dispense with heaven for such an oath?

SALISBURY
It is great sin to swear unto a sin,
But greater sin to keep a sinful oath.
Who can be bound by any solemn vow
To do a murderous deed, to rob a man,
To force a spotless virgin's chastitẏ,
To rob the orphan of his patrimony,
To wring the widow from her customed right—
And have no other reason for this wrong
But that he was bound by a solemn oath?

QUEEN
A subtle traitor needs no sophister.

KING
Call Buckingham, and bid him arm himself.

YORK

Call Buckingham and all the friends you have,
I am resolved for death or dignity.

CLIFFORD

The first I warrant you, if dreams prove true.

WARWICK

You were best to go to bed and dream again,
To keep you from the tempest of the field.

CLIFFORD

I am resolved to bear a greater storm
Than any you can conjure up today;
And that I'll write upon your very helmet,
Might I but know you by your house's badge.

WARWICK

Now by my father's badge, old Nevil's crest,
The rampant bear chained to the ragged staff,
This day I'll wear aloft my very helmet,
As on a mountain top the cedar shows,
That keeps its leaves in spite of any storm,
Even to affright you with the view thereof.

CLIFFORD

And from your helmet I will rend your bear
And tread it under foot with all contempt,
Despite the bearward that protects the bear.

YOUNG CLIFFORD

And so to arms, victorious father,
To quell the rebels and their accomplices.

RICHARD

Fie, charity, for shame! Speak not in spite,
For you shall sup with Jesu Christ tonight.

YOUNG CLIFFORD

Deformity, that's more than you can tell.

RICHARD

If not in heaven, you'll surely sup in hell.          *Exeunt*

# SCENE II
## St. Albans.

*Alarums. Enter Warwick*

WARWICK
  Clifford of Cumberland, 'tis Warwick calls;
  And if you do not hide you from the bear,
  Now when the angry trumpet sounds alarum,
  And dead men's cries do fill the empty air,
  Clifford, I say, come forth and fight with me.
  Proud northern lord, Clifford of Cumberland,
  Warwick is hoarse with calling you to arms.

*Enter York*

  How now, my noble lord? What, all afoot?
YORK
  The deadly-handed Clifford slew my steed;
  But match to match I have encountered him,
  And made a prey for carrion kites and crows
  Even of the bonny beast he loved so well.

*Enter Clifford*

WARWICK
  Of one or both of us the time is come.
YORK
  Hold, Warwick! Seek you out some other chase,
  For I myself must hunt this deer to death.
WARWICK
  Then nobly, York; 'tis for a crown you fight.
  As I intend, Clifford, to thrive today,
  It grieves my soul to leave you unassailed.     *Exit*
CLIFFORD
  What see you in me, York? Why do you pause?

YORK

With your brave bearing should I be in love,
But that you are so fast my enemy.

CLIFFORD

Nor should your prowess want praise and esteem,
But that 'tis shown ignobly and in treason.

YORK

So let it help me now against your sword,
As I in justice and true right express it.

CLIFFORD

My soul and body on the action both!

YORK

A dreadful wager! Address you instantly!

*They fight and York kills Clifford*

CLIFFORD

*La fin couronne les oeuvres.*[1]                    *He dies*

YORK

Thus war has given you peace, for you are still.
Peace with his soul, heaven, if it is your will!    *Exit*

*Enter Young Clifford*

YOUNG CLIFFORD

Shame and confusion! All is on the rout;
Fear frames disorder, and disorder wounds
Where it should guard. O war, you son of hell,
Whom angry heavens do make their minister,
Throw in the frozen bosoms of our part
Hot coals of vengeance! Let no soldier fly.
He that is truly dedicated to war
Has no self-love; nor he that loves himself

---

[1]The end crowns the deeds.

Has not essentially, but by circumstance,
The name of valour.

*He sees his dead father*

                    O, let the vile world end,
And the ordainèd flames of the last day
Knit earth and heaven together.
Now let the general trumpet blow his blast,
Particularities and petty sounds
To cease! Were you ordained, dear father,
To lose your youth in peace, and to achieve
The silver livery of advisèd age,
And, in your reverence and your chair-days, thus
To die in ruffian battle? Even at this sight
My heart is turned to stone, and while 'tis mine
It shall be stony. York not our old men spares;
No more will I their babes; tears virginal
Shall be to me even as the dew to fire;
And beauty, that the tyrant oft reclaims,
Shall to my flaming wrath be oil and flax.
Henceforth, I will not have to do with pity:
Meet I an infant of the house of York,
Into as many gobbets will I cut it
As wild Medea young Absyrtus did.
In cruelty will I seek out my fame.
Come, you new ruin of old Clifford's house;
As did Aeneas old Anchises bear,
So bear I you upon my manly shoulders.
But then Aeneas bore a living load,
Nothing so heavy as these woes of mine.
                    *Exit with his father on his back*

*Enter Richard and Somerset to fight. Somerset is killed*

RICHARD
So, lie you there;

For underneath an alehouse' paltry sign,
The Castle in Saint Albans, Somerset
Has made the wizard famous in his death.
Sword, hold your temper; heart, be wrathful still;
Priests pray for enemies, but princes kill.                    *Exit*

*Fight. Enter the King, Queen, and soldiers*

QUEEN
Away, my lord! You are slow. For shame, away!
KING
Can we outrun the heavens? Good Margaret, stay.
QUEEN
What are you made of? You'll nor fight nor fly.
Now is it manhood, wisdom, and defence,
To give the enemy way, and to secure us
By what we can, which can no more but fly.

*Alarum afar off*

If you are taken, we then should see the bottom
Of all our fortunes; but if we haply escape—
As well we may if not through your neglect—
We shall to London get, where you are loved,
And where this breach now in our fortunes made
May readily be stopped.

*Enter Young Clifford*

YOUNG CLIFFORD
But that my heart's on future mischief set,
I would speak blasphemy ere bid you fly;
But fly you must; incurable despair
Reigns in the hearts of all our present forces.
Away, for your relief! And we will live
To see their day and them our fortune give.
Away, my lord, away!                              *Exeunt*

# SCENE III
## Near St. Albans.

*Alarum. Retreat. Enter York, Richard, Warwick, and soldiers with drum and colours*

YORK
    Old Salisbury, who can report of him,
    That winter lion, who in rage forgets
    Agèd contusions and all brush of time;
    And, like a gallant in the brow of youth,
    Repairs him with occasion? This happy day
    Is not itself, nor have we won one foot,
    If Salisbury is lost.
RICHARD          My noble father,
    Three times today I helped him to his horse,
    Three times bestrode him; thrice I led him off,
    Persuaded him from any further act.
    But ever where danger was, there I met him,
    And like rich hangings in a homely house,
    So was his will in his old feeble body.
    But, noble as he is, look where he comes.

*Enter Salisbury*

SALISBURY
    Now, by my sword, well have you fought today;
    By the mass, so did we all. I thank you, Richard.
    God knows how long it is I have to live,
    And it has pleased him that three times today
    You have defended me from imminent death.
    Well, lords, we have not got that which we have;
    'Tis not enough our foes are this time fled,
    Being opposites of such repairing nature.
YORK
    I know our safety is to follow them;

For, as I hear, the King is fled to London,
To call a present court of parliament.
Let us pursue him ere the writs go forth.
What says Lord Warwick? Shall we after them?
WARWICK
After them! Nay, before them, if we can.
Now by my hand, lords, 'twas a glorious day.
Saint Albans battle, won by famous York,
Shall be eternized in all age to come.
Sound drum and trumpets, and to London all,
And more such days as these to us befall!        *Exeunt*

# King Henry
# The Sixth,
# Part Three

# INTRODUCTION

The *Third Part of King Henry VI* has even more intractable and confusing material to deal with, if anything, than the first two parts of the trilogy, but we may notice that it is well organised with increased power of construction and better written, with fewer bathetic and casual lines. The whole confused story of the Wars of the Roses is the subject, with battles, marches, killings, ups and downs, quick changes of fortune—Fortune's wheel to the Elizabethans. We may tire of the constant taunts exchanged between parties in the inveterate feud between Lancaster and York, with bloody-minded characters on both sides—Queen Margaret and Richard of York matched against each other. But we must remember that this is a Revenge play, of the type that won immense popularity with Kyd's *The Spanish Tragedy.* The actor-dramatist sought to out-do it with his *Titus Andronicus,* which has many analogies with this *Third Part.* More, the revenge *motif,* in addition to its audience-appeal, serves to integrate this play better, with its mutual taunts and reminders, forebodings and prophecies, with some use of dramatic irony, to knit things together.

The character of Richard III is foreshadowed—to make Shakespeare's first inspired play. The trilogy is not inspired; on the other hand, it is not hack-work like most Elizabethan drama. It is prentice work of high competence and

great promise: firm, if crude, characterisation; marked
constructive power, with some strong scenes, if sometimes
the poet takes over and we have descriptive passages which
are non-dramatic and may well be cut in production. The
most appealing of these is the King's long soliloquy, longing for peace and a quiet country life amid the insatiable
conflicts for power among his lords. Henry is, by contrast,
and for all his weakness, the one appealing character.

Queen Margaret is courageous and stout-hearted in
adversity, but blood-thirsty, cruel in victory: the killing of
York's boy, Rutland, and dipping a napkin in his blood to
hand the father to dry his tears, is an unforgettable horror.
For all the mutual killings of grown men, it was not the
thing to kill children—and this barbarity is made to point
forward to what Richard III will eventually do with his
brother's children, the Princes in the Tower. It was York's
taunting reproach to Margaret,

O tiger's heart wrapped in a woman's hide—

the line must have made a strong impression—which
Greene cited, substituting 'player's hide', in his attack on
Shakespeare in 1592. So the trilogy belongs to 1590–2.
Everything substantiates this. The passage,

Like one that stands upon a promontory
And spies a far-off shore where he would tread,

is shortly to be echoed in a Sonnet. Clarence's word,

I will not *ruinate* my father's house,

recurs in one of the earliest Sonnets of just this date.
Actually, this rare word occurs in all Shakespeare only
here and in *Titus Andronicus*. No difficulty in dating

these works—we need only notice the speed with which Shakespeare worked once he got going.

The classics in his background are more to the fore than ever: I have counted a dozen passages where classical instances are cited—no point in specifying them all; they provided mental furniture ready to hand for comparisons and images, and came readily to mind. Or he cites a line from Ovid's *Heroides*, just to show that he can do it as well as any university wit:

Di faciant laudis summa sit ista tuae.

He was at this time in close association with Marlowe, and we notice that the lines,

How sweet a thing it is to wear a crown,
Within whose circuit is Elysium,
And all that poets feign of bliss and joy,

are echoes from him. So too the citation of Machiavelli, when Richard declares himself a conscious pupil of that school—indeed the whole conception of Richard as a Machiavellian villain owes much to Marlowe, Shakespeare's immediate senior and prime influence upon him—though such contrasting personalities.

The theatre is present, as always, in images and citations:

as if the tragedy
Were played in jest by counterfeiting actors.

Or again,

What scene of death has Roscius now to act?—

Roscius, most famous of Roman actors. Bear-baiting, a familiar spectacle in every Elizabethan town, is visually evoked:

Or as a bear encompassed round with dogs,
Which having pinched a few and made them cry,
The rest stand all aloof and bark at him.

Deer-hunting provides an oasis amid all the killings,
though even here it is the keepers of a deer-park who
discover the poor wandering King and surrender him to
prison in the Tower, where he was eventually murdered by
Richard.

Under this thick-grown brake we'll shroud ourselves;
For through this laund [glade] anon the deer will
    come,
And in this covert will we make our stand,
Culling the principal of all the deer.

And so on. Hare-coursing occurs too, the subject of the
long inset into *Venus and Adonis* of this time, which
gives the impression of a separate poem, perhaps written
earlier, inserted into the work. Edward IV's wooing of
Elizabeth Woodville, the widowed young Lady Grey, provides another agreeable oasis, in which the amorous
Edward—handsomest man in Europe, and an able commander or he would never have won Henry VI's throne—is
persuaded from his predatory intentions to an honourable
proposal of marriage. This makes as agreeable reading as
viewing—though it was bad politics, for it brought about
the breach with Warwick and King Louis of France.
What follows is the 'strongest' scene in the play, in
which Warwick reverses his Yorkist allegiance and goes
over to Margaret to restore Henry VI. This leads to the
fatal defeats of Barnet and Tewkesbury, where the young
Edward, Prince of Wales, was hacked down by the Yorkist
leaders.

Henry was hopeless as a king, though he can sum up
the course of events justly enough:

Now one the better, then another best;
Both tugging to be victors, breast to breast,
Yet neither conqueror nor conquerèd:
Such is the equal poise of this fell war.

A more able ruler would have knocked sense into the heads of both sides, or, rather, by exerting his authority, would have prevented the dissolution of order into civil war. This is indeed the constant political message of all Shakespeare's plays—the necessity of order, authority, obedience, if society is to hold together.

Henry would have immeasurably preferred the quiet life of a 'homely swain', rather than the strain of kingship he inherited, with the fatal neurotic malady of the Valois, through his mother, Henry V's Catherine of France. And we have the long and famous soliloquy of Act II Scene V, celebrating the virtues and charms of country life—as they certainly appealed to William Shakespeare:

Gives not the hawthorn bush a sweeter shade
To shepherds looking on their silly [innocent] sheep?
O yes, it does; a thousand-fold it does.
And to conclude, the shepherd's homely curds,
His cold thin drink out of his leather bottle,
His wonted sleep under a fresh tree's shade—

all very nostalgic to a hard-pressed actor working in London to keep the family at Stratford going.

Warwickshire is indeed more to the front than ever, not only scenes at well known places like Coventry and Warwick, but he knows the smaller places, as a War-wickshireman would—Dunsmore, Southam, Daventry, besides citing leading county families in these plays, Somervilles and Lucys.

We notice a peculiarity in his usage, the constant use of the subordinate 'is' for has with such verbs as become.

Sometimes it reads quite awkwardly: 'where our right father is become', I have modernised to 'is at large.' Or, 'where is Warwick then become?' I have substituted 'to be found.' But it is a curious feature of Shakespeare's grammar—as if it were French—to say 'is' come, or 'is' become, where we should say has come, or has become. There is no point in retaining archaic spellings for familiar words, like 'mought' for might, 'recompt' for recount, 'moe' for more, as many editions do. Sometimes the Elizabethan use of a preposition leads to confusion: for example 'of' for to, in 'Now here a period *of* tumultuous broils', when it means putting a period *to* them. Sometimes it is clearer to say 'by' where Shakespeare says 'with'. Elizabethans used the word 'doubt' where we should say fear, and 'still' for ever. These have been modernised, as plural subjects with singular verbs, double negatives and archaic subjunctives have been regularised. Shortenings like 'ha'' for have, ''t' for it, and in some cases 'o'er' has been filled out; and accents supplied to make scansion clear.

# CHARACTERS

KING HENRY THE SIXTH
Margaret of Anjou, his wife, QUEEN
Edward, PRINCE OF WALES, their son
DUKE OF EXETER
DUKE OF SOMERSET
EARL OF NORTHUMBERLAND } supporters of the house
EARL OF WESTMORLAND of Lancaster
EARL OF OXFORD
LORD CLIFFORD
SIR JOHN SOMERVILLE
DUKE OF YORK, Richard Plantagenet
EDWARD, Earl of March, later Duke }
   of York and King Edward IV
RICHARD, Duke of Gloucester } sons of the Duke
GEORGE, Duke of Clarence of York
Edmund, EARL OF RUTLAND
SIR JOHN MORTIMER }
SIR HUGH MORTIMER } uncles of the Duke of York
DUKE OF NORFOLK
MARQUESS OF MONTAGUE }
EARL OF WARWICK
EARL OF PEMBROKE } supporters of the house
LORD HASTINGS of York
LORD STAFFORD
SIR WILLIAM STANLEY }
SIR JOHN MONTGOMERY
ELIZABETH, LADY GREY, later wife of Edward IV, Queen
Prince Edward, her infant son
EARL RIVERS, brother of Lady Grey
Henry, Earl of Richmond

LEWIS THE ELEVENTH, King of France
LADY BONA, his sister

MESSENGERS, TUTOR, A SON that has killed his father, A
FATHER that has killed his son, TWO KEEPERS, A NOBLE-
MAN, POSTS, WATCHMEN, A HUNTSMAN, LIEUTENANT
of the Tower of London, MAYOR of York
Soldiers, attendants, Admiral Bourbon, aldermen, Mayor
of Coventry, nurse

# Act I

## SCENE I
### Westminster. The Parliament House.

*Alarum. Enter York, Edward, Richard, Norfolk, Montague,*
*Warwick, and soldiers, with white roses in their hats*

WARWICK
  I wonder how the King escaped our hands?
YORK
  While we pursued the horsemen of the north,
  He slily stole away and left his men.
  Whereat the great Lord of Northumberland,
  Whose warlike ears could never brook retreat,
  Cheered up the drooping army; and himself,
  Lord Clifford, and Lord Stafford, all abreast,
  Charged our main army's front and, breaking in,
  Were by the swords of common soldiers slain.
EDWARD
  Lord Stafford's father, Duke of Buckingham,
  Is either slain or wounded dangerously;
  I cleft his helmet with a downright blow.
  That this is true, father, behold his blood.
MONTAGUE
  And, brother, here's the Earl of Wiltshire's blood,
  Whom I encountered as the armies joined.
RICHARD
  Speak you for me and tell them what I did.

  *He throws down Somerset's head*

YORK
  Richard has best deserved of all my sons.
  But is your grace dead, my lord of Somerset?
NORFOLK
  Such hope have all the line of John of Gaunt!
RICHARD
  Thus do I hope to shake King Henry's head.
WARWICK
  And so do I. Victorious Prince of York,
  Before I see you seated in that throne
  Which now the house of Lancaster usurps,
  I vow by heaven these eyes shall never close.
  This is the palace of the fearful King,
  And this the regal seat; possess it, York;
  For this is yours and not King Henry's heirs'.
YORK
  Assist me then, sweet Warwick, and I will;
  For hither we have broken in by force.
NORFOLK
  We will all assist you; he that flies shall die.
YORK
  Thanks, gentle Norfolk; stay by me, my lords.
  And, soldiers, stay and lodge by me this night.

                    *They go up*

WARWICK
  And when the King comes, offer him no violence,
  Unless he seek to thrust you out perforce.
YORK
  The Queen this day here holds her parliament,
  But little thinks we shall be of her council;
  By words or blows here let us win our right.
RICHARD
  Armed as we are, let's stay within this house.

WARWICK

The bloody parliament shall this be called
Unless Plantagenet, Duke of York, is king,
And bashful Henry deposed, whose cowardice
Has made us by-words to our enemies.

YORK

Then leave me not; my lords, be resolute;
I mean to take possession of my right.

WARWICK

Neither the King nor he that loves him best,
The proudest he that holds up Lancaster,
Dares stir a wing if Warwick shakes his bells.
I'll plant Plantagenet, root him up who dares.
Resolve you, Richard; claim the English crown.

*Flourish. Enter King Henry, Clifford, Northumberland,*
*Westmorland, Exeter, and soldiers, with*
*red roses in their hats*

KING

My lords, look where the sturdy rebel sits,
Even in the chair of state! Perhaps he means,
Backed by the power of Warwick, that false peer,
To aspire unto the crown and reign as king.
Earl of Northumberland, he slew your father,
And yours, Lord Clifford; and you both have vowed
    revenge
On him, his sons, his favourites, and his friends.

NORTHUMBERLAND

If I am not, heavens be revenged on me!

CLIFFORD

The hope thereof makes Clifford mourn in steel.

WESTMORLAND

What! Shall we suffer this? Let's pluck him down.
My heart for anger burns; I cannot brook it.

KING

Be patient, gentle Earl of Westmorland.

CLIFFORD

    Patience is for poltroons, such as he;

    He durst not sit there had your father lived.

    My gracious lord, here in the parliament

    Let us assail the family of York.

NORTHUMBERLAND

    Well have you spoken, cousin; be it so.

KING

    Ah, know you not the city favours them,

    And they have troops of soldiers at their beck?

EXETER

    But when the Duke is slain they'll quickly fly.

KING

    Far be the thought of this from Henry's heart,

    To make a shambles of the Parliament House!

    Cousin of Exeter, frowns, words, and threats

    Shall be the war that Henry means to use.

    You factious Duke of York, descend from my throne,

    And kneel for grace and mercy at my feet;

    I am your sovereign.

YORK                                    I am yours.

EXETER

    For shame, come down; he made you Duke of York.

YORK

    It was my inheritance, as the earldom was.

EXETER

    Your father was a traitor to the crown.

WARWICK

    Exeter, you are a traitor to the crown

    In following this usurping Henry.

CLIFFORD

    Whom should he follow but his natural king?

WARWICK

    True, Clifford; that is Richard Duke of York.

KING

    And shall I stand, and you sit in my throne?

YORK
  It must and shall be so; content yourself.
WARWICK
  Be Duke of Lancaster; let him be king.
WESTMORLAND
  He is both king and Duke of Lancaster;
  And that the Lord of Westmorland shall maintain.
WARWICK
  And Warwick shall disprove it. You forget
  That we are those who chased you from the field
  And slew your fathers, and with colours spread
  Marched through the city to the palace gates.
NORTHUMBERLAND
  Yes, Warwick, I remember it to my grief;
  And, by his soul, you and your house shall rue it.
WESTMORLAND
  Plantagenet, of you and these your sons,
  Your kinsmen, and your friends, I'll have more lives
  Than drops of blood were in my father's veins.
CLIFFORD
  Urge it no more; lest now, instead of words,
  I send you, Warwick, such a messenger
  As shall revenge his death before I stir.
WARWICK
  Poor Clifford, how I scorn his worthless threats!
YORK
  Will you we show our title to the crown?
  If not, our swords shall plead it in the field.
KING
  What title have you, traitor, to the crown?
  Your uncle was, as you are, Duke of York;
  Your grandfather, Roger Mortimer, Earl of March.
  I am the son of Henry the Fifth,
  Who made the Dauphin and the French to stoop
  And seized upon their towns and provinces.

WARWICK

Talk not of France, since you have lost it all.

KING

The Lord Protector lost it, and not I.

When I was crowned I was but nine months old.

RICHARD

You are old enough now and yet, I think, you lose.

Father, tear the crown from the usurper's head.

EDWARD

Sweet father, do so; set it on your head.

MONTAGUE

Good brother, as you love and honour arms,

Let's fight it out and not stand cavilling thus.

RICHARD

Sound drums and trumpets, and the King will fly.

YORK

Sons, peace!

KING

Peace, you! And give King Henry leave to speak.

WARWICK

Plantagenet shall speak first. Hear him, lords;

And be you silent and attentive too,

For he that interrupts him shall not live.

KING

Think you that I will leave my kingly throne,

Wherein my grandsire and my father sat?

No; first shall war unpeople this my realm;

Ay, and their colours, often borne in France,

And now in England to our hearts' great sorrow,

Shall be my winding-sheet. Why faint you, lords?

My title's good, and better far than his.

WARWICK

Prove it, Henry, and you shall be king.

KING

Henry the Fourth by conquest got the crown.

YORK

It was by rebellion against his king.

KING *(aside)*
    I know not what to say; my title's weak. —
    Tell me, may not a king adopt an heir?
YORK
    What then?
KING
    For if he may, then am I lawful king;
    For Richard, in the view of many lords,
    Resigned the crown to Henry the Fourth,
    Whose heir my father was, and I am his.
YORK
    He rose against him, being his sovereign,
    And made him to resign his crown perforce.
WARWICK
    Suppose, my lords, he did it unconstrained,
    Think you it prejudicial to his crown?
EXETER
    No; for he could not so resign his crown
    But that the next heir should succeed and reign.
KING
    Are you against us, Duke of Exeter?
EXETER
    His is the right, and therefore pardon me.
YORK
    Why whisper you, my lords, and answer not?
EXETER
    My conscience tells me he is lawful king.
KING *(aside)*
    All will revolt from me and turn to him.
NORTHUMBERLAND
    Plantagenet, for all the claim you lay,
    Think not that Henry shall be so deposed.
WARWICK
    Deposed he shall be, in despite of all.
NORTHUMBERLAND
    You are deceived; 'tis not your southern power

Of Essex, Norfolk, Suffolk, nor of Kent,
Which makes you thus presumptuous and proud,
Can set the Duke up in despite of me.

CLIFFORD

King Henry, be your title right or wrong,
Lord Clifford vows to fight in your defence;
May that ground gape and swallow me alive,
Where I shall kneel to him that slew my father!

KING

O Clifford, how your words revive my heart!

YORK

Henry of Lancaster, resign your crown.
What mutter you, or what conspire you, lords?

WARWICK

Do right unto this princely Duke of York,
Or I will fill the house with armèd men,
And over the chair of state, where now he sits,
Write up his title with usurping blood.

*He stamps with his foot, and the soldiers show themselves*

KING

My lord of Warwick, hear but one word;
Let me for this my lifetime reign as king.

YORK

Confirm the crown to me and to my heirs,
And you shall reign in quiet while you live.

KING

I am content; Richard Plantagenet,
Enjoy the kingdom after my decease.

CLIFFORD

What wrong is this unto the Prince your son!

WARWICK

What good is this to England and himself!

WESTMORLAND

Base, fearful, and despairing Henry!

CLIFFORD
How have you injured both yourself and us!
WESTMORLAND
I cannot stay to hear these articles.
NORTHUMBERLAND
Nor I.
CLIFFORD
Come, cousin, let us tell the Queen these news.
WESTMORLAND
Farewell, faint-hearted and degenerate King,
In whose cold blood no spark of honour bides.     *Exit*
NORTHUMBERLAND
Be you a prey unto the house of York,
And die in bonds for this unmanly deed!     *Exit*
CLIFFORD
In dreadful war may you be overcome,
Or live in peace abandoned and despised!     *Exit*
WARWICK
Turn this way, Henry, and regard them not.
EXETER
They seek revenge and therefore will not yield.
KING
Ah, Exeter!
WARWICK     Why should you sigh, my lord?
KING
Not for myself, Lord Warwick, but my son,
Whom I unnaturally shall disinherit.
But be it as it may. (*To York*) I here entail
The crown to you and to your heirs for ever;
Conditionally that here you take an oath
To cease this civil war; and, while I live,
To honour me as your king and sovereign;
And neither by treason nor hostility
To seek to put me down and reign yourself.
YORK
This oath I willingly take and will perform.

WARWICK
Long live King Henry! Plantagenet, embrace him.
KING
And long live you and these your forward sons!
YORK
Now York and Lancaster are reconciled.
EXETER
Accursed be he that seeks to make them foes!

*Sennet. Here they come down*

YORK
Farewell, my gracious lord; I'll to my castle.
                                        *Exeunt York and his sons*
WARWICK
And I'll keep London with my soldiers.                    *Exit*
NORFOLK
And I to Norfolk with my followers.                       *Exit*
MONTAGUE
And I unto the sea from whence I came.                    *Exit*
KING
And I with grief and sorrow to the Court.

*Enter the Queen and the Prince of Wales*

EXETER
Here comes the Queen, whose looks betray her anger;
I'll steal away.
KING                          Exeter, so will I.
QUEEN
Nay, go not from me, I will follow you.
KING
Be patient, gentle Queen, and I will stay.
QUEEN
Who can be patient in such extremes?
Ah, wretched man! Would I had died a maid,

And never seen you, never borne you son,
Seeing you have proved so unnatural a father!
Has he deserved to lose his birthright thus?
Had you but loved him half so well as I,
Or felt that pain which I did for him once,
Or nourished him as I did with my blood,
You would have left your dearest heart-blood there,
Rather than have made that savage Duke your heir
And disinherited your only son.

PRINCE
Father, you cannot disinherit me;
If you are king, why should not I succeed?

KING
Pardon me, Margaret; pardon me, sweet son;
The Earl of Warwick and the Duke enforced me.

QUEEN
Enforced you! Are you king, and will be forced?
I shame to hear you speak. Ah, timorous wretch!
You have undone yourself, your son, and me;
And given unto the house of York such head
As you shall reign but by their sufferance.
To entail him and his heirs unto the crown,
What is it but to make your sepulchre,
And creep into it far before your time?
Warwick is Chancellor and the Lord of Calais;
Stern Falconbridge commands the narrow seas;
The Duke is made Protector of the realm;
And yet shall you be safe? Such safety finds
The trembling lamb environèd with wolves.
Had I been there, which am a simple woman,
The soldiers should have tossed me on their pikes
Before I would have granted to that act.
But you prefer your life before your honour;
And, seeing you do, I here divorce myself
Both from your table, Henry, and your bed,
Until that act of parliament is repealed

Whereby my son is disinherited.
The northern lords that have forsworn your colours
Will follow mine, if once they see them spread;
And spread they shall be, to your foul disgrace
And utter ruin of the house of York.
Thus do I leave you. Come, son, let's away.
Our army is ready; come, we'll after them.

KING

Stay, gentle Margaret, and hear me speak.

QUEEN

You have spoken too much already; get you gone.

KING

Gentle son Edward, you will stay with me?

QUEEN

Ay, to be murdered by his enemies.

PRINCE

When I return with victory from the field,
I'll see your grace; till then I'll follow her.

QUEEN

Come, son, away; we may not linger thus.

*Exeunt Queen and Prince*

KING

Poor Queen! How love to me and to her son
Has made her break out into terms of rage!
Revenged may she be on that hateful Duke,
Whose haughty spirit, wingèd with desire,
Will cost my crown, and like an empty eagle
Feed on the flesh of me and my son!
The loss of those three lords torments my heart;
I'll write unto them and entreat them fair.
Come, cousin, you shall be the messenger.

EXETER

And I, I hope, shall reconcile them all.

*Flourish. Exeunt*

## SCENE II
## Near Wakefield.

*Enter Richard, Edward, and Montague*

RICHARD
  Brother, though I am youngest, give me leave.
EDWARD
  No, I can better play the orator.
MONTAGUE
  But I have reasons strong and forcible.

*Enter the Duke of York*

YORK
  Why, how now, sons and brother! At a strife?
  What is your quarrel? How began it first?
EDWARD
  No quarrel, but a slight contention.
YORK
  About what?
RICHARD
  About that which concerns your grace and us—
  The crown of England, father, which is yours.
YORK
  Mine, boy? Not till King Henry is dead.
RICHARD
  Your right depends not on his life or death.
EDWARD
  Now you are heir; therefore enjoy it now.
  By giving the house of Lancaster leave to breathe,
  It will outrun you, father, in the end.
YORK
  I took an oath that he should quietly reign.
EDWARD
  But for a kingdom any oath may be broken;
  I would break a thousand oaths to reign one year.

RICHARD
  No; God forbid your grace should be forsworn.
YORK
  I shall be, if I claim by open war.
RICHARD
  I'll prove the contrary, if you'll hear me speak.
YORK
  You can not, son; it is impossible.
RICHARD
  An oath is of no moment, being not taken
  Before a true and lawful magistrate
  That has authority over him that swears;
  Henry had none, but did usurp the place.
  Then, seeing 'twas he that made you to depose,
  Your oath, my lord, is vain and frivolous.
  Therefore to arms! And, father, do but think
  How sweet a thing it is to wear a crown,
  Within whose circuit is Elysium
  And all that poets feign of bliss and joy.
  Why do we linger thus? I cannot rest
  Until the white rose that I wear is dyed
  Even in the lukewarm blood of Henry's heart.
YORK
  Richard, enough! I will be king or die.
  Brother, you shall to London immediately
  And whet on Warwick to this enterprise.
  You, Richard, shall to the Duke of Norfolk
  And tell him privily of our intent.
  You, Edward, shall unto my Lord Cobham,
  With whom the Kentishmen will willingly rise;
  In them I trust, for they are soldiers,
  Witty, courteous, liberal, full of spirit.
  While you are thus employed, what rests more
  But that I seek occasion how to rise,
  And yet the King not privy to my drift,
  Nor any of the house of Lancaster?

*Enter a Messenger*

But stay; what news? Why come you in such post?
MESSENGER
The Queen with all the northern earls and lords
Intend here to besiege you in your castle.
She is hard by with twenty thousand men;
And therefore fortify your hold, my lord.
YORK
Ay, with my sword. What! Think you that we fear them?
Edward and Richard, you shall stay with me;
My brother Montague shall post to London.
Let noble Warwick, Cobham, and the rest,
Whom we have left protectors of the King,
With powerful policy strengthen themselves,
And trust not simple Henry nor his oaths.
MONTAGUE
Brother, I go; I'll win them, fear it not;
And thus most humbly I do take my leave. *Exit*

*Enter Sir John Mortimer and Sir Hugh
Mortimer, his brother*

YORK
Sir John and Sir Hugh Mortimer, my uncles,
You are come to Sandal in a happy hour;
The army of the Queen mean to besiege us.
SIR JOHN
She shall not need; we'll meet her in the field.
YORK
What, with five thousand men?
RICHARD
Ay, with five hundred, father, for a need.
A woman's general; what should we fear?

*A march afar off*

EDWARD
   I hear their drums; let's set our men in order,
   And issue forth and bid them battle straight.
YORK
   Five men to twenty! Though the odds are great,
   I doubt not, uncle, of our victory.
   Many a battle have I won in France
   When the enemy have been ten to one;
   Why should I not now have the like success?     *Exeunt*


# SCENE III
## The same.

*Alarum. Enter Rutland and his Tutor*


RUTLAND
   Ah, whither shall I fly to escape their hands?
   Ah, tutor, look where bloody Clifford comes!

*Enter Clifford and soldiers*


CLIFFORD
   Chaplain, away! Your priesthood saves your life.
   As for the brat of this accursèd duke,
   Whose father slew my father, he shall die.
TUTOR
   And I, my lord, will bear him company.
CLIFFORD
   Soldiers, away with him!
TUTOR
   Ah, Clifford, murder not this innocent child,
   Lest you are hated both of God and man.
                           *Exit, dragged off by soldiers*

CLIFFORD
> How now? Is he dead already? Or is it fear
> That makes him close his eyes? I'll open them.

RUTLAND
> So looks the pent-up lion over the wretch
> That trembles under his devouring paws;
> And so he walks, insulting over his prey,
> And so he comes, to rend his limbs asunder.
> Ah, gentle Clifford, kill me with your sword,
> And not with such a cruel threatening look!
> Sweet Clifford, hear me speak before I die.
> I am too mean a subject for your wrath;
> Be you revenged on men, and let me live.

CLIFFORD
> In vain you speak, poor boy; my father's blood
> Has stopped the passage where your words should enter.

RUTLAND
> Then let my father's blood open it again;
> He is a man and, Clifford, cope with him.

CLIFFORD
> Had I your brethren here, their lives and yours
> Were not revenge sufficient for me;
> No, if I dug up your forefathers' graves
> And hung their rotten coffins up in chains,
> It could not slake my ire nor ease my heart.
> The sight of any of the house of York
> Is as a fury to torment my soul;
> And till I root out their accursèd line
> And leave not one alive, I live in hell.
> Therefore—

*He lifts his sword*

RUTLAND
> O, let me pray before I take my death!
> To you I pray; sweet Clifford, pity me!

CLIFFORD
  Such pity as my rapier's point affords.
RUTLAND
  I never did you harm; why will you slay me?
CLIFFORD
  Your father has.
RUTLAND            It was ere I was born.
  You have one son; for his sake pity me,
  Lest in revenge thereof, since God is just,
  He is as miserably slain as I.
  Ah, let me live in prison all my days;
  And when I give occasion of offence,
  Then let me die, for now you have no cause.
CLIFFORD
  No cause?
  Your father slew my father; therefore die.

                   *He stabs Rutland*

RUTLAND
  *Di faciant laudis summa sit ista tuae.*[1]            *He dies*
CLIFFORD
  Plantagenet! I come, Plantagenet!
  And this your son's blood cleaving to my blade
  Shall rust upon my weapon, till your blood
  Congealed with this, does make me wipe off both.  *Exit*


                   SCENE IV
                   The same.


         *Alarum. Enter Richard Duke of York*


YORK
  The army of the Queen has got the field;

_____
[1]May the gods make this be the pinnacle of your fame!

My uncles both are slain in rescuing me;
And all my followers to the eager foe
Turn back and fly, like ships before the wind
Or lambs pursued by hunger-starvèd wolves.
My sons, God knows what has bechancèd them;
But this I know, they have demeaned themselves
Like men born to renown by life or death.
Three times did Richard make a lane to me,
And thrice cried 'Courage, father! Fight it out!'
And full as oft came Edward to my side,
With purple longsword, painted to the hilt
In blood of those that had encountered him.
And when the hardiest warriors did retire,
Richard cried 'Charge! And give no foot of ground!'
And cried 'A crown, or else a glorious tomb!
A sceptre or an earthly sepulchre!'
With this we charged again; but, out, alas!
We budged again; as I have seen a swan
With useless labour swim against the tide
And spend its strength with overmatching waves.

*A short alarum within*

Ah, hark! The fatal followers do pursue,
And I am faint and cannot fly their fury;
And were I strong, I would not shun their fury.
The sands are numbered that make up my life;
Here must I stay, and here my life must end.

*Enter the Queen, Clifford, Northumberland, the young
Prince, and soldiers*

Come, bloody Clifford, rough Northumberland,
I dare your quenchless fury to more rage;
I am your butt, and I abide your shot.

NORTHUMBERLAND
  Yield to our mercy, proud Plantagenet.
CLIFFORD
  Ay, to such mercy as his ruthless arm
  With downright payment showed unto my father.
  Now Phaëthon has tumbled from his car,
  And made an evening at the noontide mark.
YORK
  My ashes, as the phoenix, may bring forth
  A bird that will revenge upon you all;
  And in that hope I throw my eyes to heaven,
  Scorning whatever you can afflict me with.
  Why come you not? What! Multitudes, and fear?
CLIFFORD
  So cowards fight when they can fly no further;
  So doves do peck the falcon's piercing talons;
  So desperate thieves, all hopeless of their lives,
  Breathe out invectives against the officers.
YORK
  O Clifford, but bethink you once again,
  And in your thought o'errun my former time;
  And, if you can for blushing, view this face,
  And bite your tongue that slanders him with cowardice
  Whose frown has made you faint and fly ere this!
CLIFFORD
  I will not bandy with you word for word,
  But buckler with you blows, twice two for one.

               *He draws his sword*

QUEEN
  Hold, valiant Clifford! For a thousand causes
  I would prolong awhile the traitor's life.
  Wrath makes him deaf; speak you, Northumberland.
NORTHUMBERLAND
  Hold, Clifford! Do not honour him so much

To prick your finger, though to wound his heart.
What valour were it, when a cur does grin,
For one to thrust his hand between his teeth,
When he might spurn him with his foot away?
It is war's prize to take all vantages;
And ten to one is no impeach of valour.

*They fight and York is taken*

CLIFFORD
Ay, ay, so strives the woodcock with the gin.
NORTHUMBERLAND
So does the cony struggle in the net.
YORK
So triumph thieves upon their conquered booty;
So true men yield, with robbers so o'ermatched.
NORTHUMBERLAND
What would your grace have done unto him now?
QUEEN
Brave warriors, Clifford and Northumberland,
Come, make him stand upon this molehill here
That reached at mountains with outstretchèd arms,
Yet parted but the shadow with his hand.
What! Was it you that would be England's king?
Was it you that revelled in our parliament
And made a preachment of your high descent?
Where are your mess of sons to back you now?
The wanton Edward, and the lusty George?
And where's that valiant crook-back prodigy,
Dicky your boy, that with his grumbling voice
Was wont to cheer his dad in mutinies?
Or, with the rest, where is your darling Rutland?
Look, York, I stained this napkin with the blood
That valiant Clifford, with his rapier's point,
Made issue from the bosom of the boy;
And if your eyes can water for his death,

I give you this to dry your cheeks with now.
Alas, poor York! But that I hate you deadly,
I should lament your miserable state.
I pray you grieve, to make me merry, York.
What! Has your fiery heart so parched your entrails
That not a tear can fall for Rutland's death?
Why are you patient, man? You should be mad;
And I, to make you mad, do mock you thus.
Stamp, rave, and fret, that I may sing and dance.
You would be fee'd, I see, to make me sport;
York cannot speak, unless he wears a crown.
A crown for York! And, lords, bow low to him;
Hold you his hands while I do set it on.

*She puts a paper crown on York's head*

Ay, certain, sir, now looks he like a king!
Ay, this is he that took King Henry's chair;
And this is he was his adopted heir.
But how is it that great Plantagenet
Is crowned so soon, and broke his solemn oath?
As I consider, you should not be king
Till our King Henry had shaken hands with Death.
And will you pale your head in Henry's glory,
And rob his temples of the diadem,
Now in his life, against your holy oath?
O, 'tis a fault too too unpardonable!
Off with the crown; and, with the crown, his head;
And, while we breathe, take time to do him dead.

CLIFFORD
That is my office, for my father's sake.
QUEEN
Nay, stay; let's hear the orisons he makes.
YORK
She-wolf of France, but worse than wolves of France,
Whose tongue more poisons than the adder's tooth!

How ill-beseeming is it in your sex
To triumph, like an Amazonian trull,
Upon their woes whom Fortune makes capture of!
But that your face is mask-like, and unchanging,
Made impudent with use of evil deeds,
I would assay, proud Queen, to make you blush.
To tell you whence you came, of whom derived,
Were shame enough to shame you, were you not
    shameless.
Your father bears the style of King of Naples,
Of both Sicily and Jerusalem,
Yet not so wealthy as an English yeoman.
Has that poor monarch taught you to insult?
It needs not, nor it profits you, proud Queen;
Unless the adage must be verified,
That beggars mounted run their horse to death.
'Tis beauty that does oft make women proud,
But, God does know, your share thereof is small.
'Tis virtue that does make them most admired;
The contrary does make you wondered at.
'Tis government that makes them seem divine;
The want thereof makes you abominable.
You are as opposite to every good
As the Antipodes are unto us,
Or as the south to the Septentrion.
O tiger's heart wrapped in a woman's hide!
How could you drain the lifeblood of the child,
To bid the father wipe his eyes with it,
And yet be seen to bear a woman's face?
Women are soft, mild, pitiful, and flexible;
You stern, obdùrate, flinty, rough, remorseless.
Bid you me rage? Why, now you have your wish;
Would have me weep? Why, now you have your will;
For raging wind blows up incessant showers,
And when the rage allays, the rain begins.
These tears are my sweet Rutland's obsequies,

And every drop cries vengeance for his death
Against you, fierce Clifford, and you, false
   Frenchwoman.

NORTHUMBERLAND

Bless me, but his passion moves me so
That hardly can I check my eyes from tears.

YORK

That face of his the hungry cannibals
Would not have touched, would not have stained with
   blood;
But you are more inhuman, more inexorable,
O, ten times more, than tigers of Hyrcania.
See, ruthless Queen, a hapless father's tears;
This cloth you dipped in blood of my sweet boy,
And I with tears do wash the blood away.
Keep you the napkin, and go boast of this;
And if you tell the heavy story right,
Upon my soul, the hearers will shed tears;
Yea, even my foes will shed fast-falling tears,
And say 'Alas, it was a piteous deed!'
There, take the crown, and with the crown my curse;
And in your need such comfort come to you
As now I reap at your too cruel hand!
Hard-hearted Clifford, take me from the world;
My soul to heaven, my blood upon your heads!

NORTHUMBERLAND

Had he been slaughter-man to all my kin,
I should not for my life but weep with him,
To see how inly sorrow grieves his soul.

QUEEN

What, weeping-ripe, my Lord Northumberland?
Think but upon the wrong he did us all,
And that will quickly dry your melting tears.

CLIFFORD

Here's for my oath, here's for my father's death.

*He stabs York*

QUEEN
   And here's to right our gentle-hearted King.

*She stabs York*

YORK
   Open your gate of mercy, gracious God!
   My soul flies through these wounds to seek out Thee.
                                              *He dies*
QUEEN
   Off with his head, and set it on York gates;
   So York may overlook the town of York.
                                    *Flourish. Exeunt*

# Act II

## SCENE I
### Near Mortimer's Cross.

*A march. Enter Edward, Richard, and their troops*

EDWARD
  I wonder how our princely father escaped,
  Or whether he escaped away or no
  From Clifford's and Northumberland's pursuit.
  Had he been taken, we should have heard the news;
  Had he been slain, we should have heard the news;
  Or had he escaped, I think we should have heard
  The happy tidings of his good escape.
  How fares my brother? Why is he so sad?

RICHARD
  I cannot joy, until I am resolved
  Where our right valiant father is at large.
  I saw him in the battle range about,
  And watched him how he singled Clifford forth.
  I thought he bore him in the thickest troop
  As does a lion in a herd of cattle;
  Or as a bear encompassed round with dogs,
  Which having pinched a few and made them cry,
  The rest stand all aloof and bark at him.
  So fared our father with his enemies;
  So fled his enemies my warlike father.
  I think it prize enough to be his son.
  See how the morning opens her golden gates,
  And takes her farewell of the glorious sun!

How well resembles it the prime of youth,
Trimmed like a youngster prancing to his love!

EDWARD

Dazzle my eyes, or do I see three suns?

RICHARD

Three glorious suns, each one a perfect sun;
Not separated with the racking clouds,
But severed in a pale clear-shining sky.
See, see! They join, embrace, and seem to kiss,
As if they vowed some league inviolable;
Now are they but one lamp, one light, one sun.
In this the heaven figures some event.

EDWARD

'Tis wondrous strange, the like yet never heard of.
I think it cites us, brother, to the field,
That we, the sons of brave Plantagenet,
Each one already blazing by our deeds,
Should notwithstanding join our lights together
And over-shine the earth as this the world.
Whatever it bodes, henceforward will I bear
Upon my buckler three fair-shining suns.

RICHARD

Nay, bear three daughters; by your leave I speak it,
You love the breeder better than the male.

*Enter a Messenger, blowing a horn*

But what are you, whose heavy looks foretell
Some dreadful story hanging on your tongue?

MESSENGER

Ah, one that was a woeful looker-on
What time the noble Duke of York was slain,
Your princely father and my loving lord.

EDWARD

O, speak no more, for I have heard too much.

RICHARD

Say how he died, for I will hear it all.

MESSENGER
   Environèd he was with many foes,
   And stood against them, as the hope of Troy
   Against the Greeks that would have entered Troy.
   But Hercules himself must yield to odds;
   And many strokes, though with a little axe,
   Hews down and fells the hardest-timbered oak.
   By many hands your father was subdued;
   But only slaughtered by the ireful arm
   Of unrelenting Clifford and the Queen,
   Who crowned the gracious Duke in high despite,
   Laughed in his face. And when with grief he wept,
   The ruthless Queen gave him to dry his cheeks
   A napkin steepèd in the harmless blood
   Of sweet young Rutland, by rough Clifford slain.
   And after many scorns, many foul taunts,
   They took his head, and on the gates of York
   They set the same; and there it does remain,
   The saddest spectacle that ever I viewed.
EDWARD
   Sweet Duke of York, our prop to lean upon,
   Now you are gone, we have no staff, no stay.
   O Clifford, boisterous Clifford! You have slain
   The flower of Europe for his chivalry;
   And treacherously have you vanquished him,
   For hand to hand he would have vanquished you.
   Now my soul's palace is become a prison;
   Ah, would it break from hence, that this my body
   Might in the ground be closèd up in rest!
   For never henceforth shall I joy again;
   Never, O never, shall I see more joy!
RICHARD
   I cannot weep, for all my body's moisture
   Scarce serves to quench my furnace-burning heart;
   Nor can my tongue unload my heart's great burden;
   For self-same wind that I should speak with now

Is kindling coals that fires all my breast,
And burns me up with flames that tears would quench.
To weep is to make less the depth of grief;
Tears then for babes, blows and revenge for me!
Richard, I bear your name; I'll venge your death,
Or die renownèd by attempting it.

EDWARD
His name that valiant Duke has left with you;
His dukedom and his chair with me are left.

RICHARD
Nay, if you are that princely eagle's bird,
Show your descent by gazing against the sun:
For 'chair and dukedom', 'throne and kingdom' say;
Either that is yours, or else you were not his.

*March. Enter Warwick, the Marquess of Montague,*
*and their troops*

WARWICK
How now, fair lords! What fare? What news abroad?

RICHARD
Great Lord of Warwick, if we should recount
Our baleful news, and at each word's deliverance
Stab poniards in our flesh till all were told,
The words would add more anguish than the wounds.
O valiant lord, the Duke of York is slain!

EDWARD
O Warwick, Warwick! That Plantagenet,
Which held you dearly as his soul's redemption,
Is by the stern Lord Clifford done to death.

WARWICK
Ten days ago I drowned these news in tears;
And now, to add more measure to your woes,
I come to tell you things since then befallen.
After the bloody fray at Wakefield fought,
Where your brave father breathed his latest gasp,

Tidings, as swiftly as the posts could run,
Were brought me of your loss and his departure.
I, then in London, keeper of the King,
Mustered my soldiers, gathered flocks of friends,
Marched toward Saint Albans to intercept the Queen,
Bearing the King in my behalf along.
For by my scouts I was advèrtisèd
That she was coming with a full intent
To dash our late decree in parliament
Touching King Henry's oath and your succession.
Short tale to make, we at Saint Albans met,
Our armies joined, and both sides fiercely fought;
But whether 'twas the coldness of the King,
Who looked full gently on his warlike Queen,
That robbed my soldiers of their heated spirit;
Or whether 'twas report of her success,
Or more than common fear of Clifford's rigour,
Who thunders to his captives blood and death,
I cannot judge. But, to conclude with truth,
Their weapons there like lightning came and went;
Our soldiers', like the night-owl's lazy flight,
Or like a lazy thresher with a flail,
Fell gently down, as if they struck their friends.
I cheered them up with justice of our cause,
With promise of high pay and great rewards;
But all in vain; they had no heart to fight,
And we in them no hope to win the day.
So that we fled; the King unto the Queen;
Lord George your brother, Norfolk, and myself
In haste, post-haste, are come to join with you;
For in the Marches here we heard you were,
Making another army to fight again.

EDWARD
Where is the Duke of Norfolk, gentle Warwick?
And when came George from Burgundy to England?

WARWICK

    Some six miles off the Duke is with the soldiers;
    And for your brother, he was lately sent
    From your kind aunt, Duchess of Burgundy,
    With aid of soldiers to this needful war.

RICHARD

    'Twas odds, perhaps, when valiant Warwick fled;
    Oft have I heard his praises in pursuit,
    But never till now his scandal of retreat.

WARWICK

    Nor now my scandal, Richard, do you hear;
    For you shall know this strong right hand of mine
    Can pluck the diadem from faint Henry's head,
    And wring the awful sceptre from his fist,
    Were he as famous and as bold in war
    As he is famed for mildness, peace, and prayer.

RICHARD

    I know it well, Lord Warwick; blame me not:
    'Tis love I bear your glories makes me speak.
    But in this troublous time what's to be done?
    Shall we go throw away our coats of steel,
    And wrap our bodies in black mourning gowns,
    Numbering our Ave-Maries with our beads?
    Or shall we on the helmets of our foes
    Tell our devotion with revengeful arms?
    If for the last, say ay, and to it, lords.

WARWICK

    Why, therefore Warwick came to seek you out,
    And therefore comes my brother Montague.
    Attend me, lords. The proud insulting Queen,
    With Clifford and the haughty Northumberland,
    And of their feather many more proud birds,
    Have wrought the easy-melting King like wax.
    He swore consent to your successiòn,
    His oath enrollèd in the parliament;
    And now to London all the crew are gone,
    To frustrate both his oath and what besides

May make against the house of Lancaster.
Their army, I think, is thirty thousand strong.
Now, if the help of Norfolk and myself,
With all the friends that you, brave Earl of March,
Among the loving Welshmen can procure,
Will but amount to five and twenty thousand,
Why, come! To London will we march at once,
And once again bestride our foaming steeds,
And once again cry 'Charge!' upon our foes;
But never once again turn back and fly.

RICHARD

Ay, now I think I hear great Warwick speak.
Never may he live to see a sunshine day
That cries 'Retreat!' if Warwick bids him stay.

EDWARD

Lord Warwick, on your shoulder will I lean;
And when you fail—as God forbid the hour!—
Must Edward fall, which peril heaven forfend!

WARWICK

No longer Earl of March, but Duke of York;
The next degree is England's royal throne;
For King of England shall you be proclaimed
In every borough as we pass along;
And he that throws not up his cap for joy
Shall for the fault make forfeit of his head.
King Edward, valiant Richard, Montague,
Stay we no longer, dreaming of renown,
But sound the trumpets, and about our task.

RICHARD

Then Clifford, were your heart as hard as steel,
As you have shown it flinty by your deeds,
I come to pierce it, or to give you mine.

EDWARD

Then strike up drums; God and Saint George for us!

*Enter a Messenger*

WARWICK
  How now! What news?
MESSENGER
  The Duke of Norfolk sends you word by me
  The Queen is coming with a powerful host,
  And craves your company for speedy counsel.
WARWICK
  Why then it sorts, brave warriors; let's away.

                                              *Exeunt*


# SCENE II
## Before York.

*Flourish. Enter the King, Queen, Clifford, Northumberland,
   and the young Prince, with drum and trumpets*

QUEEN
  Welcome, my lord, to this brave town of York.
  Yonder's the head of that arch-enemy
  That sought to be encompassed with your crown.
  Does not the object cheer your heart, my lord?
KING
  Ay, as the rocks cheer them that fear their wreck;
  To see this sight, it irks my very soul.
  Withhold revenge, dear God! 'Tis not my fault,
  Nor wittingly have I infringed my vow.
CLIFFORD
  My gracious liege, this too much lenity
  And harmful pity must be laid aside.
  To whom do lions cast their gentle looks?
  Not to the beast that would usurp their den.
  Whose hand is that the forest bear does lick?
  Not his that spoils her young before her face.
  Who escapes the lurking serpent's mortal sting?
  Not he that sets his foot upon her back.

The smallest worm will turn, being trodden on.
And doves will peck in safeguard of their brood.
Ambitious York did level at your crown,
You smiling while he knitted his angry brows;
He, but a duke, would have his son a king,
And raise his issue like a loving sire;
You, being a king, blessed with a goodly son,
Did yield consent to disinherit him,
Which argued you a most unloving father.
Unreasonable creatures feed their young;
And though man's face be fearful to their eyes,
Yet, in protection of their tender ones,
Who has not seen them, even with those wings
Which sometimes they have used with fearful flight,
Make war with him that climbed unto their nest,
Offering their own lives in their young's defence?
For shame, my liege, make them your precedent!
Were it not pity that this goodly boy
Should lose his birthright by his father's fault,
And long hereafter say unto his child
'What my great-grandfather and grandsire got
My careless father fondly gave away'?
Ah, what a shame were this! Look on the boy;
And let his manly face, which promises
Successful fortune, steel your melting heart
To hold your own and leave your own with him.

KING

Full well has Clifford played the orator,
Inferring arguments of mighty force.
But, Clifford, tell me, did you never hear
That things ill got had ever got ill luck?
And happy always was it for that son
Whose father for his hoarding went to hell?
I'll leave my son my virtuous deeds behind;
And would my father had left me no more!
For all the rest is held at such a rate

As brings a thousand-fold more care to keep
Than in possession any jot of pleasure.
Ah, cousin York! Would your best friends did know
How it does grieve me that your head is here!

QUEEN

My lord, cheer up your spirits; our foes are nigh,
And this soft courage makes your followers faint.
You promised knighthood to our forward son;
Unsheathe your sword and dub him immediately.
Edward, kneel down.

KING

Edward Plantagenet, arise a knight;
And learn this lesson: draw your sword in right.

PRINCE

My gracious father, by your kingly leave,
I'll draw it as apparent to the crown,
And in that quarrel use it to the death.

CLIFFORD

Why, that is spoken like a tòward prince.

*Enter a Messenger*

MESSENGER

Royal commanders, be in readiness;
For with a band of thirty thousand men
Comes Warwick, backing up the Duke of York.
And in the towns, as they do march along,
Proclaims him king, and many fly to him.
Arraign your army, for they are at hand.

CLIFFORD

I would your highness would depart the field;
The Queen has best success when you are absent.

QUEEN

Ay, good my lord, and leave us to our fortune.

KING

Why, that's my fortune too; therefore I'll stay.

NORTHUMBERLAND
  Be it with resolution then to fight.
PRINCE
  My royal father, cheer these noble lords,
  And hearten those that fight in your defence;
  Unsheathe your sword, good father; cry 'Saint George!'

  *March. Enter Edward, Warwick, Richard, Clarence,*
          *Norfolk, Montague, and soldiers*

EDWARD
  Now, perjured Henry, will you kneel for grace,
  And set your diadem upon my head;
  Or bide the mortal fortune of the field?
QUEEN
  Go, rate your minions, proud insulting boy!
  Becomes it you to be thus bold in terms
  Before your sovereign and your lawful king?
EDWARD
  I am his king, and he should bow his knee.
  I was adopted heir by his consent;
  Since when, his oath is broken; for, as I hear,
  You, that are king, though he does wear the crown,
  Have caused him by new act of parliament
  To blot out me, and put his own son in.
CLIFFORD
  And reason too;
  Who should succeed the father but the son?
RICHARD
  Are you there, butcher? O, I cannot speak!
CLIFFORD
  Ay, crook-back, here I stand to answer you,
  Or any he the proudest of your sort.
RICHARD
  'Twas you that killed young Rutland, was it not?
CLIFFORD
  Ay, and old York, and yet not satisfied.

RICHARD
For God's sake, lords, give signal to the fight.

WARWICK
What say you, Henry? Will you yield the crown?

QUEEN
Why, how now, long-tongued Warwick! Dare you speak?
When you and I met at Saint Albans last,
Your legs did better service than your hands.

WARWICK
Then 'twas my turn to fly, and now it is yours.

CLIFFORD
You said so much before, and yet you fled.

WARWICK
'Twas not your valour, Clifford, drove me thence.

NORTHUMBERLAND
No, nor your manhood that durst make you stay.

RICHARD
Northumberland, I hold you reverently.
Break off the parley; for scarce I can refrain
The execution of my big-swollen heart
Upon that Clifford, that cruel child-killer.

CLIFFORD
I slew your father; call you him a child?

RICHARD
Ay, like a dastard and a treacherous coward,
As you did kill our tender brother Rutland;
But ere sun set I'll make you curse the deed.

KING
Have done with words, my lords, and hear me speak.

QUEEN
Defy them then, or else hold close your lips.

KING
I pray you give no limits to my tongue;
I am a king and privileged to speak.

CLIFFORD
My liege, the wound that bred this meeting here

Cannot be cured by words; therefore be still.

RICHARD

Then, executioner, unsheathe your sword.
By him that made us all, I am resolved
That Clifford's manhood lies upon his tongue.

EDWARD

Say, Henry, shall I have my right or no?
A thousand men have broken their fasts today,
That never shall dine unless you yield the crown.

WARWICK

If you deny, their blood upon your head;
For York in justice puts his armour on.

PRINCE

If that is right which Warwick says is right,
There is no wrong, but everything is right.

RICHARD

Whoever got you, there your mother stands;
For, well I know, you have your mother's tongue.

QUEEN

But you are neither like your sire nor dam;
But like a foul misshapen deformity,
Marked by the destinies to be avoided,
As venom toads or lizards' dreadful stings.

RICHARD

Iron of Naples hidden with English gilt,
Whose father bears the title of a king—
As if a channel should be called the sea—
Shame you not, knowing whence you derive,
To let your tongue detect your base-born heart?

EDWARD

A wisp of straw were worth a thousand crowns
To make this shameless strumpet know herself.
Helen of Greece was fairer far than you,
Although your husband may be Menelaus;
And never was Agamemnon's brother wronged
By that false woman, as this king by you.

His father revelled in the heart of France,
And tamed the King, and made the Dauphin stoop;
And had he matched according to his state,
He might have kept that glory to this day.
But when he took a beggar to his bed
And graced your poor sire with his bridal day,
Even then that sunshine brewed a shower for him
That washed his father's fortunes forth of France,
And heaped sedition on his crown at home.
For what has broached this tumult but your pride?
Had you been meek, our title still had slept;
And we, in pity for the gentle King,
Had slipped our claim until another age.

CLARENCE
But when we saw our sunshine made your spring,
And that your summer bred us no increase,
We set the axe to your usurping root.
And though the edge has somewhat hit ourselves,
Yet know you, since we have begun to strike,
We'll never leave till we have hewn you down,
Or bathed your growing with our heated bloods.

EDWARD
And in this resolution I defy you;
Not willing any longer conference,
Since you deny the gentle King to speak.
Sound trumpets! Let our bloody colours wave!
And either victory, or else a grave!

QUEEN
Stay, Edward.

EDWARD
No, wrangling woman, we'll no longer stay;
These words will cost ten thousand lives this day.

                                                    *Exeunt*

## SCENE III
### Near Towton.

*Alarum. Enter Warwick*

WARWICK
  Forspent with toil, as runners with a race,
  I lay me down a little while to breathe;
  For strokes received, and many blows repaid,
  Have robbed my strong-knit sinews of their strength,
  And, spite of spite, needs must I rest a while.

*Enter Edward, running*

EDWARD
  Smile, gentle heaven, or strike, ungentle death!
  For this world frowns, and Edward's sun is clouded.
WARWICK
  How now, my lord! What hap? What hope of good?

*Enter Clarence*

CLARENCE
  Our hap is loss, our hope but sad despair;
  Our ranks are broken, and ruin follows us.
  What counsel give you? Whither shall we fly?
EDWARD
  Useless is flight; they follow us with wings,
  And weak we are and cannot shun pursuit.

*Enter Richard*

RICHARD
  Ah, Warwick, why have you withdrawn yourself?
  Your brother's blood the thirsty earth has drunk,
  Broached with the steely point of Clifford's lance;

And in the very pangs of death he cried,
Like then a dismal clangour heard from far,
'Warwick, revenge! Brother, revenge my death!'
So, underneath the belly of their steeds,
That stained their fetlocks in his smoking blood,
The noble gentleman gave up the ghost.

WARWICK
Then let the earth be drunk now with our blood;
I'll kill my horse, because I will not fly.
Why stand we like soft-hearted women here,
Wailing our losses, while the foe does rage;
And look upon, as if the tragedy
Were played in jest by counterfeiting actors?
Here on my knee I vow to God above
I'll never pause again, never stand still,
Till either death has closed these eyes of mine
Or fortune given me measure of revenge.

EDWARD
O Warwick, I do bend my knee with yours;
And in this vow do chain my soul to yours!
And, ere my knee rises from the earth's cold face,
I throw my hands, my eyes, my heart to Thee,
You setter-up and plucker-down of kings;
Beseeching you, if with your will it stands
That to my foes this body must be prey,
Yet that your brazen gates of heaven may open
And give sweet passage to my sinful soul!
Now, lords, take leave until we meet again,
Wherever it be, in heaven or in earth.

RICHARD
Brother, give me your hand; and, gentle Warwick,
Let me embrace you in my weary arms.
I, that did never weep, now melt with woe
That winter should cut off our spring-time so.

WARWICK
Away, away! Once more, sweet lords, farewell.

CLARENCE
    Yet let us all together to our troops,
    And give them leave to fly that will not stay;
    And call them pillars that will stand to us;
    And, if we thrive, promise them such rewards
    As victors wear at the Olympian games.
    This may plant courage in their quailing breasts;
    For yet is hope of life and victory.
    Dally no longer; make we hence at once.            *Exeunt*

## SCENE IV
## The same.

*Excursions. Enter Richard and Clifford*

RICHARD
    Now, Clifford, I have singled you alone.
    Suppose this arm is for the Duke of York,
    And this for Rutland, both bound to revenge,
    Were you environed with a brazen wall.
CLIFFORD
    Now, Richard, I am with you here alone.
    This is the hand that stabbed your father York,
    And this the hand that slew your brother Rutland,
    And here's the heart that triumphs in their death
    And cheers these hands that slew your sire and brother
    To execute the like upon yourself;
    And so, have at you!

*They fight. Warwick comes. Clifford flies*

RICHARD
    Nay, Warwick, single out some other chase;
    For I myself will hunt this wolf to death.

                                                       *Exeunt*

## SCENE V
## The same.

*Alarum. Enter King Henry alone*

KING
> This battle fares like to the morning's war,
> When dying clouds contend with growing light,
> What time the shepherd, blowing of his nails,
> Can neither call it perfect day nor night.
> Now sways it this way, like a mighty sea
> Forced by the tide to combat with the wind;
> Now sways it that way, like the self-same sea
> Forced to retire by fury of the wind.
> Sometimes the flood prevails, and then the wind;
> Now one the better, then another best;
> Both tugging to be victors, breast to breast,
> Yet neither conqueror nor conquerèd;
> So is the equal poise of this fierce war.
> Here on this molehill will I sit me down.
> To whom God will, there be the victory!
> For Margaret my Queen, and Clifford too,
> Have chidden me from the battle, swearing both
> They prosper best of all when I am thence.
> Would I were dead, if God's good will were so!
> For what is in this world but grief and woe?
> O God! I think it were a happy life
> To be no better than a homely swain;
> To sit upon a hill, as I do now;
> To carve out dials carefully, point by point,
> Thereby to see the minutes how they run:
> How many make the hour full complete,
> How many hours bring about the day,
> How many days will finish up the year,
> How many years a mortal man may live.
> When this is known, then to divide the times:

So many hours must I tend my flock,
So many hours must I take my rest,
So many hours must I contemplate,
So many hours must I sport myself,
So many days my ewes have been with young,
So many weeks ere the poor fools will breed,
So many years ere I shall shear the fleece.
So minutes, hours, days, months, and years,
Passed over to the end they were created,
Would bring white hairs unto a quiet grave.
Ah, what a life were this! How sweet! How lovely!
Gives not the hawthorn bush a sweeter shade
To shepherds looking on their silly sheep
Than does a rich embroidered canopy
To kings that fear their subjects' treachery?
O yes, it does; a thousand-fold it does.
And to conclude, the shepherd's homely curds,
His cold thin drink out of his leather bottle,
His wonted sleep under a fresh tree's shade,
All which secure and sweetly he enjoys,
Are far beyond a prince's delicates,
His viands sparkling in a golden cup,
His body couched in an elaborate bed,
When care, mistrust, and treason wait on him.

*Alarum. Enter at one door a Son that has killed his father,*
*with the body in his arms*

SON
Ill blows the wind that profits nobody.
This man whom hand to hand I slew in fight
May be possessèd with some store of crowns;
And I, that haply take them from him now,
May yet ere night yield both my life and them
To some man else, as this dead man does me. —
Who's this? O God! It is my father's face,

Whom in this conflict I, unaware, have killed.
O, heavy times, begetting such events!
From London by the King was I pressed forth;
My father, being the Earl of Warwick's man,
Came on the part of York, pressed by his master;
And I, who at his hands received my life,
Have by my hands of life bereavèd him.
Pardon me, God, I knew not what I did!
And pardon, father, for I knew not you!
My tears shall wipe away these bloody marks;
And no more words till they have flowed their fill.

KING

O, piteous spectacle! O, bloody times!
While lions war and battle for their dens,
Poor harmless lambs abide their enmity.
Weep, wretched man; I'll aid you tear for tear;
And let our hearts and eyes, like civil war,
Be blind with tears, and break o'ercharged with grief.

*Enter at another door a Father that has killed his son, with
the body in his arms*

FATHER

You that so stoutly have resisted me,
Give me your gold, if you have any gold;
For I have bought it with a hundred blows.
But let me see: is this our foeman's face?
Ah, no, no, no, it is my only son!
Ah, boy, if any life is left in you,
Throw up your eye! See, see what showers arise,
Blown with the windy tempest of my heart,
Upon your wounds, that kill my eye and heart!
O, pity, God, this miserable age!
What stratagems, how savage, butcherly,
Erroneous, mutinous, and unnatural,
This deadly quarrel daily does beget!

O boy, your father gave you life too soon,
And has bereft you of your life too late!

KING

Woe above woe! Grief more than common grief!
O that my death would stay these ruthful deeds!
O, pity, pity, gentle heaven, pity!
The red rose and the white are on his face,
The fatal colours of our striving houses;
The one his purple blood right well resembles;
The other his pale cheeks, it seems, presents.
Wither one rose, and let the other flourish;
If you contend, a thousand lives must wither.

SON

How will my mother for a father's death
Take on with me and never be satisfied!

FATHER

How will my wife for slaughter of my son
Shed seas of tears and never be satisfied!

KING

How will the country for these woeful chances
Misthink the King and not be satisfied!

SON

Was ever son so rued a father's death?

FATHER

Did ever father so bemoan his son?

KING

Did ever king so grieve for subjects' woe?
Much is your sorrow; mine ten times so much.

SON

I'll bear you hence, where I may weep my fill.
                    *Exit with the body of his father*

FATHER

These arms of mine shall be your winding-sheet;
My heart, sweet boy, shall be your sepulchre,
For from my heart your image never shall go;
My sighing breast shall be your funeral bell.

And so punctilious will your father be,
Even for the loss of you, having no more,
As Priam was for all his valiant sons.
I'll bear you hence; and let them fight that will,
For I have murdered where I should not kill.

*Exit with the body of his son*

KING

Sad-hearted men, much overgone with care,
Here sits a king more woeful than you are.

*Alarums. Enter the Queen, Prince, and Exeter*

PRINCE

Fly, father, fly! For all your friends are fled,
And Warwick rages like a chafèd bull.
Away! For death does hold us in pursuit.

QUEEN

Mount you, my lord; towards Berwick post at once.
Edward and Richard, like a brace of greyhounds
Having the fearful flying hare in sight,
With fiery eyes sparkling for very wrath,
And bloody steel grasped in their ireful hands,
Are at our backs; and therefore hence at once.

EXETER

Away! For vengeance comes along with them;
Nay, stay not to expostulate, make speed;
Or else come after; I'll away before.

KING

Nay, take me with you, good sweet Exeter;
Not that I fear to stay, but love to go
Whither the Queen intends. Forward! Away!

*Exeunt*

## SCENE VI
## The same.

*A loud alarum. Enter Clifford, wounded*

CLIFFORD
Here burns my candle out; ay, here it dies,
Which, while it lasted, gave King Henry light.
O Lancaster, I fear your overthrow
More than my body's parting with my soul!
My love and fear glued many friends to you;
And, now I fall, your tough commixture melts,
Impairing Henry, strengthening misproud York.
The common people swarm like summer flies;
And whither fly the gnats but to the sun?
And who shines now but Henry's enemies?
O Phoebus, had you never given consent
That Phaëthon should check your fiery steeds,
Your burning car never had scorched the earth!
And, Henry, had you swayed as kings should do,
Or as your father and his father did,
Giving no ground unto the house of York,
They never then had sprung like summer flies;
I and ten thousand in this luckless realm
Had left no mourning widows for our death;
And you this day had kept your chair in peace.
For what does cherish weeds but gentle air?
And what makes robbers bold but too much lenity?
Useless are plaints, and cureless are my wounds;
No way to fly, nor strength to hold out flight;
The foe is merciless and will not pity,
For at their hands I have deserved no pity.
The air has got into my deadly wounds,
And much loss of blood does make me faint.
Come, York and Richard, Warwick and the rest;
I stabbed your fathers' bosoms; split my breast.

*He faints*

*Alarum and retreat. Enter Edward, Richard, Clarence,*
*Warwick, Montague, and soldiers*

EDWARD
  Now breathe we, lords; good fortune bids us pause,
  And smooth the frowns of war with peaceful looks.
  Some troops pursue the bloody-minded Queen,
  That led calm Henry, though he was a king,
  As does a sail, filled with a fretting gust,
  Command an argosy to stem the waves.
  But think you, lords, that Clifford fled with them?
WARWICK
  No, 'tis impossible he should escape;
  For, though before his face I speak the words,
  Your brother Richard marked him for the grave;
  And wheresoever he is, he's surely dead.
                    *Clifford groans and then dies*
EDWARD Whose soul is that which takes her heavy leave?
RICHARD A deadly groan, like life and death's departing.
EDWARD
  See who it is; and, now the battle's ended,
  If friend or foe, let him be gently used.
RICHARD
  Revoke that word of mercy, for 'tis Clifford;
  Who not contented that he lopped the branch
  In hewing Rutland when his leaves put forth,
  But set his murdering knife unto the root
  From whence that tender spray did sweetly spring:
  I mean our princely father, Duke of York.
WARWICK
  From off the gates of York fetch down the head,
  Your father's head, which Clifford placèd there;
  Instead whereof let this supply the room:
  Measure for measure must be answerèd.

EDWARD

Bring forth that fatal screech-owl to our house,
That nothing sung but death to us and ours;
Now death shall stop his dismal threatening sound
And his ill-boding tongue no more shall speak.

WARWICK

I think his understanding is bereft.
Speak, Clifford, do you know who speaks to you?
Dark cloudy death o'ershades his beams of life,
He neither sees nor hears us what we say.

RICHARD

O, would he did! And so perhaps he does;
'Tis but his policy to counterfeit,
Because he would avoid such bitter taunts
Which in the time of death he gave our father.

CLARENCE

If so you think thus, vex him with sharp words.

RICHARD

Clifford, ask mercy and obtain no grace.

EDWARD

Clifford, repent in useless penitence.

WARWICK

Clifford, devise excuses for your faults.

CLARENCE

While we devise sharp tortures for your faults.

RICHARD

You did love York, and I am son to York.

EDWARD

You pitied Rutland; I will pity you.

CLARENCE

Where's Captain Margaret to fence you now?

WARWICK

They mock you, Clifford; swear as you were wont.

RICHARD

What! Not an oath? Nay, then the world goes hard
When Clifford cannot spare his friends an oath.
I know by that he's dead; and, by my soul,

If this right hand would buy two höurs' life,
That I in all despite might rail at him,
This hand should chop it off, and with the issuing blood
Stifle the villain whose unstanchèd thirst
York and young Rutland could not satisfy.

WARWICK
Ay, but he's dead. Off with the traitor's head,
And rear it in the place your father's stands.
And now to London with triumphant march,
There to be crownèd England's royal king;
From whence shall Warwick cut the sea to France,
And ask the Lady Bona for your queen.
So shall you sinew both these lands together;
And, having France your friend, you shall not dread
The scattered foe that hopes to rise again;
For though they cannot greatly sting to hurt,
Yet look to have them buzz to offend your ears.
First will I see the coronatiòn,
And then to Brittany I'll cross the sea
To effect this marriage, so it please my lord.

EDWARD
Even as you will, sweet Warwick, let it be;
For in your shoulder do I build my seat,
And never will I undertake the thing
Wherein your counsel and consent are wanting.
Richard, I will create you Duke of Gloucester,
And George, of Clarence; Warwick, as ourself,
Shall do and undo as him pleases best.

RICHARD
Let me be Duke of Clarence, George of Gloucester;
For Gloucester's dukedom is too ominous.

WARWICK
Tut, that's a foolish observatiòn;
Richard, be Duke of Gloucester. Now to London,
To see these honours in possessiòn.                    *Exeunt*

# Act III

## SCENE I
## A forest in the North.

*Enter two Keepers, with cross-bows in their hands*

FIRST KEEPER
Under this thick-grown brake we'll shroud ourselves;
For through this glade anon the deer will come,
And in this covert will we make our stand,
Culling the principal of all the deer.

SECOND KEEPER
I'll stay above the hill, so both may shoot.

FIRST KEEPER
That cannot be; the noise of your cross-bow
Will scare the herd, and so my shot is lost.
Here stand we both, and aim we at the best;
And so the time shall not seem tedious,
I'll tell you what befell me on a day
In this self place where now we mean to stand.

SECOND KEEPER
Here comes a man; let's stay till he is past.

*Enter King Henry, disguised, with a prayer-book*

KING
From Scotland am I stolen, even of pure love,
To greet my own land with my wishful sight.
No, Harry, Harry, it is no land of yours;
Your place is filled, your sceptre wrung from you,
Your balm washed off wherewith you were anointed.

No bending knee will call you Caesar now,
No humble suitors press to speak for right,
No, not a man comes for redress from you;
For how can I help them and not myself?

FIRST KEEPER

Ay, here's a deer whose skin's a keeper's fee:
This is the former king; let's seize upon him.

KING

Let me embrace you, sour adversity,
For wise men say it is the wisest course.

SECOND KEEPER

Why linger we? Let us lay hands upon him.

FIRST KEEPER

Forbear awhile; we'll hear a little more.

KING

My Queen and son are gone to France for aid;
And, as I hear, the great commanding Warwick
Is thither gone to crave the French King's sister
To wife for Edward. If this news is true,
Poor Queen and son, your labour is but lost;
For Warwick is a subtle orator,
And Lewis a prince soon won with moving words.
By this account then Margaret may win him;
For she's a woman to be pitied much.
Her sighs will make a battery in his breast;
Her tears will pierce into a marble heart;
The tiger will be mild while she does mourn;
And Nero will be tainted with remorse,
To hear and see her plaints, her brinish tears.
Ay, but she's come to beg, Warwick to give;
She, on his left side, craving aid for Henry,
He, on his right, asking a wife for Edward.
She weeps, and says her Henry is deposed;
He smiles, and says his Edward is installed;
That she, poor wretch, for grief can speak no more;
While Warwick tells his title, smooths the wrong,

Infers new arguments of mighty strength,
And in conclusion wins the King from her,
With promise of his sister, and what else,
To strengthen and support King Edward's place.
O Margaret, thus it will be; and you, poor soul,
Are then forsaken, as you went forlorn!

SECOND KEEPER
Say, what are you that talk of kings and queens?

KING
More than I seem, and less than I was born to:
A man at least, for less I should not be;
And men may talk of kings, and why not I?

SECOND KEEPER
Ay, but you talk as if you were a king.

KING
Why, so I am, in mind, and that's enough.

SECOND KEEPER
But if you are a king, where is your crown?

KING
My crown is in my heart, not on my head;
Not decked with diamonds and Indian stones,
Nor to be seen; my crown is called content;
A crown it is that seldom kings enjoy.

SECOND KEEPER
Well, if you are a king crowned with content,
Your crown content and you must be contented
To go along with us; for, as we think,
You are the king King Edward has deposed;
And we his subjects, sworn in all allegiance,
Will apprehend you as his enemy.

KING
But did you never swear, and break an oath?

SECOND KEEPER
No, never such an oath, and will not now.

KING
Where did you dwell when I was King of England?

SECOND KEEPER
    Here in this country, where we now remain.
KING
    I was anointed king at nine months old;
    My father and my grandfather were kings,
    And you were sworn true subjects unto me;
    And tell me, then, have you not broken your oaths?
FIRST KEEPER
    No, for we were subjects but while you were king.
KING
    Why, am I dead? Do I not breathe a man?
    Ah, simple men, you know not what you swear!
    Look, as I blow this feather from my face,
    And as the air blows it to me again,
    Obeying with my wind when I do blow,
    And yielding to another when it blows,
    Commanded always by the greater gust;
    Such is the lightness of you common men.
    But do not break your oaths; for of that sin
    My mild entreaty shall not make you guilty.
    Go where you will, the King shall be commanded;
    And be you kings, command, and I'll obey.
FIRST KEEPER
    We are true subjects to the King, King Edward.
KING
    So would you be again to Henry,
    If he were seated as King Edward is.
FIRST KEEPER
    We charge you in God's name, and the King's,
    To go with us unto the officers.
KING
    In God's name, lead; your king's name be obeyed;
    And what God will, that let your king perform;
    And what he wills, I humbly yield unto.

                                              *Exeunt*

## SCENE II
### Westminster. The royal palace.

*Enter King Edward, Richard Duke of Gloucester, George
Duke of Clarence, and Lady Grey*

EDWARD
  Brother of Gloucester, at Saint Albans field
  This lady's husband, Sir Richard Grey, was slain,
  His lands then seized on by the conqueror.
  Her suit is now to repossess those lands;
  Which we in justice cannot well deny,
  Because in quarrel of the house of York
  The worthy gentleman did lose his life.
RICHARD
  Your highness shall do well to grant her suit;
  It is dishonour to deny it her.
EDWARD
  It is no less; but yet I'll make a pause.
RICHARD *(aside to Clarence)*
  Yes, is it so?
  I see the lady has a thing to grant
  Before the King will grant her humble suit.
CLARENCE *(aside to Richard)*
  He knows the game; how true he keeps the wind!
RICHARD *(aside to Clarence)*
  Silence!
EDWARD
  Widow, we will consider of your suit;
  And come some other time to know our mind.
LADY GREY
  Right gracious lord, I cannot brook delay;
  May it please your highness to resolve me now,
  And what your pleasure is shall satisfy me.
RICHARD *(aside to Clarence)*
  Ay, widow? Then I'll warrant you all your lands,

If what then pleases him shall pleasure you.
Fight closer, or, good faith, you'll catch a blow.

CLARENCE (*aside to Richard*)
I fear her not unless she chances to fall.

RICHARD (*aside to Clarence*)
God forbid that! For he'll take advantage.

EDWARD
How many children have you, widow? Tell me.

CLARENCE (*aside to Richard*)
I think he means to beg a child of her.

RICHARD (*aside to Clarence*)
Nay then, whip me; he'll rather give her two.

LADY GREY
Three, my most gracious lord.

RICHARD (*aside to Clarence*)
You shall have four, if you'll be ruled by him.

EDWARD
Pity they should lose their father's lands.

LADY GREY
Be pitiful, dread lord, and grant it then.

EDWARD
Lords, give us leave; I'll try this widow's wit.

RICHARD (*aside to Clarence*)
Ay, good leave have you; for you will have leave,
Till youth takes leave and leave you to the crutch.

*Richard and Clarence go out of earshot*

EDWARD
Now tell me, madam, do you love your children?

LADY GREY
Ay, full as dearly as I love myself.

EDWARD
And would you not do much to do them good?

LADY GREY
To do them good I would sustain some harm.

EDWARD
  Then get your husband's lands, to do them good.
LADY GREY
  Therefore I came unto your majesty.
EDWARD
  I'll tell you how these lands are to be got.
LADY GREY
  So shall you bind me to your highness' service.
EDWARD
  What service will you do me, if I give them?
LADY GREY
  What you command, that rests in me to do.
EDWARD
  But you will take exception to my boon.
LADY GREY
  No, gracious lord, except I cannot do it.
EDWARD
  Ay, but you can do what I mean to ask.
LADY GREY
  Why, then I will do what your grace commands.
RICHARD (*aside to Clarence*)
  He plies her hard; and much rain wears the marble.
CLARENCE (*aside to Richard*)
  As red as fire! Nay, then her wax must melt.
LADY GREY
  Why stops my lord? Shall I not hear my task?
EDWARD
  An easy task; 'tis but to love a king.
LADY GREY
  That's soon performed, because I am a subject.
EDWARD
  Why, then, your husband's lands I freely give you.
LADY GREY
  I take my leave with many thousand thanks.
RICHARD (*aside to Clarence*)
  The match is made; she seals it with a curtsy.

EDWARD
  But stay you; 'tis the fruits of love I mean.
LADY GREY
  The fruits of love I mean, my loving liege.
EDWARD
  Ay, but I fear me in another sense.
  What love, think you, I sue so much to get?
LADY GREY
  My love till death, my humble thanks, my prayers;
  That love which virtue begs and virtue grants.
EDWARD
  No, by my word, I did not mean such love.
LADY GREY
  Why, then you mean not as I thought you did.
EDWARD
  But now you partly may perceive my mind.
LADY GREY
  My mind will never grant what I perceive
  Your highness aims at, if I aim aright.
EDWARD
  To tell you plain, I aim to lie with you.
LADY GREY
  To tell you plain, I had rather lie in prison.
EDWARD
  Why, then you shall not have your husband's lands.
LADY GREY
  Why, then my honesty shall be my dower;
  For by that loss I will not purchase them.
EDWARD
  Therein you wrong your children mightily.
LADY GREY
  Herein your highness wrongs both them and me.
  But, mighty lord, this merry inclination
  Accords not with the sadness of my suit:
  Please you dismiss me, either with ay or no.

EDWARD
    Ay, if you will say 'ay' to my request;
    No, if you do say 'no' to my demand.
LADY GREY
    Then, no, my lord. My suit is at an end.
RICHARD (*aside to Clarence*)
    The widow likes him not; she knits her brows.
CLARENCE (*aside to Richard*)
    He is the bluntest wooer in Christendom.
EDWARD (*aside*)
    Her looks do argue her replete with modesty;
    Her words do show her wit incomparable;
    All her perfections challenge sovereignty.
    One way or other, she is for a king;
    And she shall be my love or else my queen.
    (*To Lady Grey*)
    Say that King Edward take you for his queen?
LADY GREY
    'Tis better said than done, my gracious lord.
    I am a subject fit to jest with, now,
    But far unfit to be a sovereign.
EDWARD
    Sweet widow, by my state I swear to you
    I speak no more than what my soul intends;
    And that is, to enjoy you for my love.
LADY GREY
    And that is more than I will yield unto.
    I know I am too mean to be your queen,
    And yet too good to be your concubine.
EDWARD
    You cavil, widow; I did mean my queen.
LADY GREY
    'Twill grieve your grace my sons should call you father.
EDWARD
    No more than when my daughters call you mother.
    You are a widow and you have some children;
    And, by God's mother, I, being but a bachelor,

Have some others. Why, 'tis a happy thing
To be the father unto many sons.
Answer no more, for you shall be my queen.

RICHARD (*aside to Clarence*)
The ghostly father now has done his shrift.

CLARENCE (*aside to Richard*)
When he was made a shriver, 'twas for shift.

EDWARD
Brothers, you muse what chat we two have had.

RICHARD
The widow likes it not, for she looks very sad.

EDWARD
You'd think it strange if I should marry her.

CLARENCE
To whom, my lord?

EDWARD                        Why, Clarence, to myself.

RICHARD
That would be ten days' wonder at the least.

CLARENCE
That's a day longer than a wonder lasts.

RICHARD
By so much is the wonder in extremes.

EDWARD
Well, jest on, brothers; I can tell you both
Her suit is granted for her husband's lands.

*Enter a Nobleman*

NOBLEMAN
My gracious lord, Henry your foe is taken,
And brought your prisoner to your palace gate.

EDWARD
See that he is conveyed unto the Tower;
And go we, brothers, to the man that took him,
To question of his apprehensiòn.
Widow, go you along. Lords, use her honourably.

*Exeunt all but Richard*

RICHARD

    Ay, Edward will use women honourably.

    Would he were wasted, marrow, bones, and all,

    That from his loins no hopeful branch may spring,

    To cross me from the golden time I look for!

    And yet, between my soul's desire and me—

    The lustful Edward's title burièd—

    Is Clarence, Henry, and his son young Edward,

    And all the unlooked-for issue of their bodies,

    To take their rooms, ere I can place myself:

    A cold premeditation for my purpose!

    Why then, I do but dream on sovereignty;

    Like one that stands upon a promontory

    And spies a far-off shore where he would tread,

    Wishing his foot were equal with his eye,

    And chides the sea that sunders him from thence,

    Saying he'll drain it dry to have his way;

    So do I wish the crown, being so far off;

    And so I chide the means that keep me from it;

    And so I say I'll cut the causes off,

    Flattering me with impossibilities.

    My eye's too quick, my heart o'erweens too much,

    Unless my hand and strength could equal them.

    Well, say there is no kingdom then for Richard,

    What other pleasure can the world afford?

    I'll make my heaven in a lady's lap,

    And deck my body in gay ornaments,

    Bewitch sweet ladies with my words and looks.

    O, miserable thought! And more unlikely

    Than to accomplish twenty golden crowns!

    Why, love forswore me in my mother's womb;

    Because I should not deal in her soft laws,

    She did corrupt frail nature with some bribe

    To shrink my arm up like a withered shrub;

    To make an envious mountain on my back,

Where sits deformity to mock my body;
To shape my legs of an unequal size;
To disproportion me in every part,
Like to a chaos, or an unlicked bear-whelp
That carries no impression like the dam.
And am I then a man to be beloved?
O, monstrous fault, to harbour such a thought!
Then, since this earth affords no joy to me
But to command, to check, to overbear such
As are of better person than myself,
I'll make my heaven to dream upon the crown,
And, while I live, to account this world but hell,
Until my misshaped trunk that bears this head
Be round impalèd with a glorious crown.
And yet I know not how to get the crown,
For many lives stand between me and home;
And I—like one lost in a thorny wood,
That rends the thorns and is rent by the thorns,
Seeking a way and straying from the way,
Not knowing how to find the open air,
But toiling desperately to find it out—
Torment myself to catch the English crown.
And from that torment I will free myself,
Or hew my way out with a bloody axe.
Why, I can smile, and murder while I smile,
And cry 'Content!' to that which grieves my heart,
And wet my cheeks with artificial tears,
And frame my face to all occasiòns.
I'll drown more sailors than the mermaid shall;
I'll slay more gazers than the basilisk;
I'll play the orator as well as Nestor,
Deceive more slily than Ulysses could,
And, like a Sinon, take another Troy.
I can add colours to the chameleon,
Change shapes with Proteus for advantages,
And set the murderous Machiavel to school.

Can I do this, and cannot get a crown?
Tut, were it farther off, I'll pluck it down.          *Exit*

## SCENE III
## France. The royal palace.

*Flourish. Enter Lewis the French King, his sister Bona,
admiral Bourbon; Prince Edward, Queen Margaret, and
the Earl of Oxford. Lewis sits and rises up again*

LEWIS
Fair Queen of England, worthy Margaret,
Sit down with us; it ill befits your state
And birth that you should stand while Lewis sits.
QUEEN
No, mighty King of France; now Margaret
Must strike her sail and learn awhile to serve
Where kings command. I was, I must confess,
Great Albion's Queen in former golden days;
But now mischance has trodden my title down,
And with dishonour laid me on the ground.
Where I must take like seat unto my fortune
And to my humble seat conform myself.
LEWIS
Why, say, fair Queen, whence springs this deep despair?
QUEEN
From such a cause as fills my eyes with tears
And stops my tongue, while heart is drowned in cares.
LEWIS
Whatever it be, be you ever like yourself,
And sit you by our side.

*He seats her by him*

Yield not your neck

To Fortune's yoke, but let your dauntless mind
Still ride in triumph over all mischance.
Be plain, Queen Margaret, and tell your grief;
It shall be eased, if France can yield relief.

QUEEN
Those gracious words revive my drooping thoughts
And give my tongue-tied sorrows leave to speak.
Now, therefore, be it known to noble Lewis
That Henry, sole possessor of my love,
Is from a king become a banished man,
And forced to live in Scotland a forlorn.
While proud ambitious Edward Duke of York
Usurps the regal title and the seat
Of England's true-anointed lawful King.
This is the cause that I, poor Margaret,
With this my son, Prince Edward, Henry's heir,
Am come to crave your just and lawful aid.
And if you fail us, all our hope is done.
Scotland has will to help, but cannot help;
Our people and our peers are both misled,
Our treasure seized, our soldiers put to flight,
And, as you see, ourselves in heavy plight.

LEWIS
Renownèd Queen, with patience calm the storm,
While we do think a means to break it off.

QUEEN
The more we stay, the stronger grows our foe.

LEWIS
The more I stay, the more I'll succour you.

QUEEN
O, but impatience waits on true sorrow.
And see where comes the breeder of my sorrow!

*Enter Warwick*

LEWIS
What's he approaches boldly to our presence?

QUEEN
  Our Earl of Warwick, Edward's greatest friend.
LEWIS
  Welcome, brave Warwick. What brings you to France?

                    *He descends. She rises*

QUEEN
  Ay, now begins a second storm to rise,
  For this is he that moves both wind and tide.
WARWICK
  From worthy Edward, King of Albion,
  My lord and sovereign, and your vowèd friend,
  I come, in kindness and unfeignèd love,
  First, to do greetings to your royal person;
  And then to crave a league of amity.
  And lastly to confirm that amity
  With nuptial knot, if you agree to grant
  That virtuous Lady Bona, your fair sister,
  To England's King in lawful marriage.
QUEEN (*aside*)
  If that goes forward, Henry's hope is done.
WARWICK (*to Bona*)
  And, gracious madam, in our king's behalf,
  I am commanded, with your leave and favour,
  Humbly to kiss your hand, and with my tongue
  To tell the passion of my sovereign's heart;
  Where fame, late entering at his heedful ears,
  Has placed your beauty's image and your virtue.
QUEEN
  King Lewis and Lady Bona, hear me speak,
  Before you answer Warwick. His demand
  Springs not from Edward's well-meant honest love,
  But from deceit bred by necessity;
  For how can tyrants safely govern home,

Unless abroad they purchase great alliance?
To prove him tyrant this reason may suffice,
That Henry the King lives still; but were he dead,
Yet here Prince Edward stands, King Henry's son.
Look, therefore, Lewis, that by this league and marriage
You draw not on your danger and dishonour;
For though usurpers sway the rule awhile,
Yet heavens are just, and time suppresses wrongs.

WARWICK
Injurious Margaret!

PRINCE                    And why not 'Queen'?

WARWICK
Because your father Henry did usurp;
And you no more are prince than she is queen.

OXFORD
Then Warwick disannuls great John of Gaunt,
Who did subdue the greatest part of Spain;
And, after John of Gaunt, Henry the Fourth,
Whose wisdom was a mirror to the wisest;
And, after that wise prince, Henry the Fifth,
Who by his prowess conquerèd all France—
From these our Henry lineally descends.

WARWICK
Oxford, how haps it in this smooth discourse
You told not how Henry the Sixth has lost
All that which Henry the Fifth had gotten?
I think these peers of France should smile at that.
But for the rest, you tell a pedigree
Of threescore and two years—a silly time
To make prescription for a kingdom's worth.

OXFORD
Why, Warwick, can you speak against your liege,
Whom you obeyèd thirty and six years,
And not betray your treason with a blush?

WARWICK
Can Oxford, that did ever fence the right,

Now buckler falsehood with a pedigree?
For shame! Leave Henry, and call Edward king.

OXFORD

Call him my king by whose injurious doom
My elder brother, the Lord Aubrey Vere,
Was done to death? And more than so, my father,
Even in the downfall of his mellowed years,
When nature brought him to the door of death?
No, Warwick, no; while life upholds this arm,
This arm upholds the house of Lancaster.

WARWICK

And I the house of York.

LEWIS

Queen Margaret, Prince Edward, and Oxford,
Vouchsafe, at our request, to stand aside
While I use further conference with Warwick.

*They stand aloof*

QUEEN (*aside*)

Heavens grant that Warwick's words bewitch him not!

LEWIS

Now, Warwick, tell me even upon your conscience,
Is Edward your true king? For I were loth
To link with him that were not lawfully chosen.

WARWICK

Thereon I pawn my credit and my honour.

LEWIS

But is he gracious in the people's eye?

WARWICK

The more that Henry was unfortunate.

LEWIS

Then further, all dissembling set aside,
Tell me for truth the measure of his love
Unto our sister Bona.

WARWICK                    Such it seems

As may beseem a monarch like himself.
Myself have often heard him say and swear
That this his love was an eternal plant,
Whereof the root was fixed in virtue's ground,
The leaves and fruit maintained with beauty's sun,
Exempt from envy, but not from disdain—
Unless the Lady Bona quits his pain.

LEWIS
Now, sister, let us hear your firm resolve.

BONA
Your grant, or your denial, shall be mine;
(*To Warwick*) Yet I confess that often ere this day,
When I have heard your king's desert recounted,
My ear has tempted judgement to desire.

LEWIS
Then, Warwick, thus: our sister shall be Edward's;
And now forthwith shall articles be drawn
Touching the jointure that your king must make,
Which with her dowry shall be counterpoised.
Draw near, Queen Margaret, and be a witness
That Bona shall be wife to the English king.

PRINCE
To Edward, but not to the English king.

QUEEN
Deceitful Warwick! It was your device
By this alliance to make void my suit;
Before your coming Lewis was Henry's friend.

LEWIS
And still is friend to him and Margaret;
But if your title to the crown is weak,
As may appear by Edward's good success,
Then 'tis but reason I should be released
From giving aid which late I promisèd.
Yet shall you have all kindness at my hand
That your estate requires and mine can yield.

WARWICK
  Henry now lives in Scotland at his ease,
  Where having nothing, nothing can he lose.
  And as for you yourself, our former queen,
  You have a father able to maintain you,
  And better it is you troubled him than France.
QUEEN
  Peace, impudent and shameless Warwick, peace,
  Proud setter-up and puller-down of kings!
  I will not hence till, with my talk and tears,
  Both full of truth, I make King Lewis behold
  Your sly trickery and your lord's false love;
  For both of you are birds of self-same feather.

                *Post blowing a horn within*

LEWIS
  Warwick, this is some post to us or you.

                *Enter the Post*

POST (*to Warwick*)
  My lord ambassador, these letters are for you,
  Sent from your brother, Marquess Montague;
  (*To Lewis*)
  These from our King unto your majesty;
  (*To Queen*)
  And, madam, these for you, from whom I know not.

                *They all read their letters*

OXFORD
  I like it well that our fair Queen and mistress
  Smiles at her news, while Warwick frowns at his.
PRINCE
  Nay, mark how Lewis stamps as he were nettled;
  I hope all is for the best.

LEWIS

Warwick, what are your news? And yours, fair Queen?

QUEEN

Mine, such as fill my heart with unhoped joys.

WARWICK

Mine, full of sorrow and heart's discontent.

LEWIS

What! Has your king married the Lady Grey?
And now, to soothe your forgery and his,
Sends me a paper to persuade me patience?
Is this the alliance that he seeks with France?
Dares he presume to scorn us in this manner?

QUEEN

I told your majesty as much before:
This proves Edward's love and Warwick's honesty!

WARWICK

King Lewis, I here protest in sight of heaven,
And by the hope I have of heavenly bliss,
That I am clear from this misdeed of Edward's,
No more my king, for he dishonours me,
But most himself, if he could see his shame.
Did I forget that by the house of York
My father came untimely to his death?
Did I let pass the abuse done to my niece?
Did I impale him with the regal crown?
Did I put Henry from his native right?
Am I rewarded at the last with shame?
Shame on himself! For my desert is honour;
And to repair my honour lost for him,
I here renounce him and return to Henry.
My noble Queen, let former grudges pass,
And henceforth I am your true servitor.
I will revenge his wrong to Lady Bona
And replant Henry in his former state.

QUEEN

Warwick, these words have turned my hate to love;

And I forgive and quite forget old faults,
And joy that you become King Henry's friend.
WARWICK
So much his friend, ay, his unfeignèd friend,
That if King Lewis deigns to furnish us
With some few bands of chosen soldiers,
I'll undertake to land them on our coast
And force the tyrant from his seat by war.
'Tis not his new-made bride shall succour him;
And as for Clarence, as my letters tell me,
He's very likely now to fall from him
For matching more for wanton lust than honour,
Or than for strength and safety of our country.
BONA
Dear brother, how shall Bona be revenged
But by your help to this distressèd Queen?
QUEEN
Renownèd Prince, how shall poor Henry live
Unless you rescue him from foul despair?
BONA
My quarrel and this English Queen's are one.
WARWICK
And mine, fair-Lady Bona, joins with yours.
LEWIS
And mine with hers, and yours, and Margaret's.
Therefore at last I firmly am resolved:
You shall have aid.
QUEEN
Let me give humble thanks for all at once.
LEWIS
Then, England's messenger, return in post
And tell false Edward, your supposèd king,
That Lewis of France is sending over masquers
To revel it with him and his new bride;
You see what's passed, go fright your king with it.

BONA
Tell him, in hope he'll prove a widower shortly,
I'll wear the willow garland for his sake.

QUEEN
Tell him my mourning weeds are laid aside,
And I am ready to put armour on.

WARWICK
Tell him from me that he has done me wrong,
And therefore I'll uncrown him ere it be long.
There's your reward; be gone.                    *Exit Post*

LEWIS                          But, Warwick,
You and Oxford, with five thousand men,
Shall cross the seas and bid false Edward battle;
And, as occasion serves, this noble Queen
And Prince shall follow with a fresh supply.
Yet, ere you go, but answer me one doubt:
What pledge have we of your firm loyalty?

WARWICK
This shall assure my constant loyalty:
That if our Queen and this young Prince agree,
I'll join my eldest daughter and my joy
To him forthwith in holy wedlock bonds.

QUEEN
Yes, I agree, and thank you for your motion.
Son Edward, she is fair and virtuous;
Therefore delay not, give your hand to Warwick;
And, with your hand, your faith irrevocable
That only Warwick's daughter shall be yours.

PRINCE
Yes, I accept her, for she well deserves it;
And here, to pledge my vow, I give my hand.

*He gives his hand to Warwick*

LEWIS
Why stay we now? These soldiers shall be levied,
And you, Lord Bourbon, our High Admiral,

Shalt waft them over with our royal fleet.
I long till Edward falls by war's mischance,
For mocking marriage with a dame of France.

*Exeunt all but Warwick*

WARWICK
I came from Edward as ambassador,
But I return his sworn and mortal foe;
Matter of marriage was the charge he gave me,
But dreadful war shall answer his demand.
Had he none else to make a fool but me?
Then none but I shall turn his jest to sorrow.
I was the chief that raised him to the crown,
And I'll be chief to bring him down again;
Not that I pity Henry's misery,
But seek revenge on Edward's mockery.              *Exit*

# Act IV

## SCENE 1
### Westminster. The royal palace.

*Enter Richard, Clarence, Somerset, and Montague*

RICHARD
  Now tell me, brother Clarence, what think you
  Of this new marriage with the Lady Grey?
  Has not our brother made a worthy choice?
CLARENCE
  Alas, you know, 'tis far from hence to France;
  How could he stay till Warwick made return?
SOMERSET
  My lords, forbear this talk; here comes the King.

*Flourish. Enter Edward, attended; Lady Grey, as queen;*
  *Pembroke, Stafford, Hastings, and other courtiers*

RICHARD
  And his well-chosen bride.
CLARENCE
  I mind to tell him plainly what I think.
EDWARD
  Now, brother of Clarence, how like you our choice,
  That you stand pensive, as half-malcontent?
CLARENCE
  As well as Lewis of France, or the Earl of Warwick,
  Who are so weak of courage and in judgement
  That they'll take no offence at our abuse.

EDWARD
    Suppose they take offence without a cause,
    They are but Lewis and Warwick; I am Edward,
    Your king and Warwick's, and must have my will.

RICHARD
    And shall have your will, because our king;
    Yet hasty marriage seldom proves so well.

EDWARD
    Yea, brother Richard, are you offended too?

RICHARD
    Not I;
    No, God forbid that I should wish them severed
    Whom God has joined together; it is pity
    To sunder them that yoke so well together.

EDWARD
    Setting your scorns and your mislike aside,
    Tell me some reason why the Lady Grey
    Should not become my wife and England's queen.
    And you too, Somerset and Montague,
    Speak freely what you think.

CLARENCE
    Then this is my opinion: that King Lewis
    Becomes your enemy, for mocking him
    About the marriage of the Lady Bona.

RICHARD
    And Warwick, doing what you gave in charge,
    Is now dishonourèd by this new marriage.

EDWARD
    What if both Lewis and Warwick are appeased
    By such invention as I can devise?

MONTAGUE
    Yet, to have joined with France in such alliance
    Would more have strengthened this our commonwealth
    Against foreign storms than any home-bred marriage.

HASTINGS
    Why, knows not Montague that of itself
    England is safe, if true within itself?

MONTAGUE

But the safer when it is backed with France.

HASTINGS

'Tis better using France than trusting France;
Let us be backed with God and with the seas
Which he has given for fence impregnable,
And with their helps only defend ourselves;
In them and in ourselves our safety lies.

CLARENCE

For this one speech Lord Hastings well deserves
To have the heir of the Lord Hungerford.

EDWARD

Ay, what of that? It was my will and grant;
And for this once my will shall stand for law.

RICHARD

And yet I think your grace has not done well
To give the heir and daughter of Lord Scales
Unto the brother of your loving bride.
She better would have fitted me or Clarence;
But in your bride you bury brotherhood.

CLARENCE

Or else you would not have bestowed the heir
Of the Lord Bonville on your new wife's son,
And leave your brothers to go speed elsewhere.

EDWARD

Alas, poor Clarence! Is it for a wife
That you are malcontent? I will provide you.

CLARENCE

In choosing for yourself, you showed your judgement;
Which being shallow, you shall give me leave
To play the broker in my own behalf;
And to that end I shortly mind to leave you.

EDWARD

Leave me, or tarry. Edward will be king,
And not be tied unto his brother's will.

LADY GREY

    My lords, before it pleased his majesty
    To raise my state to title of a queen,
    Do me but right, and you must all confess
    That I was not ignoble of descent;
    And meaner than myself have had like fortune.
    But as this title honours me and mine,
    So your dislikes, to whom I would be pleasing,
    Do cloud my joys with danger and with sorrow.

EDWARD

    My love, forbear to fawn upon their frowns;
    What danger or what sorrow can befall you,
    So long as Edward is your constant friend,
    And their true sovereign, whom they must obey?
    Nay, whom they shall obey, and love you too,
    Unless they seek for hatred at my hands;
    Which if they do, yet will I keep you safe,
    And they shall feel the vengeance of my wrath.

RICHARD (*aside*)

    I hear, yet say not much, but think the more.

*Enter a Post*

EDWARD

    Now, messenger, what letters or what news
    From France?

POST

    My sovereign liege, no letters; and few words,
    But such as I, without your special pardon,
    Dare not relate.

EDWARD

    Go to, we pardon you; therefore, in brief,
    Tell me their words as near as you can guess them.
    What answer makes King Lewis unto our letters?

POST

    At my depart, these were his very words:
    'Go tell false Edward, your supposèd king,

That Lewis of France is sending over masquers
To revel it with him and his new bride.'
EDWARD

Is Lewis so brave? Perhaps he thinks me Henry.
But what said Lady Bona to my marriage?
POST

These were her words, uttered with mild disdain:
'Tell him, in hope he'll prove a widower shortly,
I'll wear the willow garland for his sake.'
EDWARD

I blame not her, she could say little less;
She had the wrong. But what said Henry's queen?
For I have heard that she was there in place.
POST

'Tell him,' quoth she, 'my mourning weeds are done,
And I am ready to put armour on.'
EDWARD

Perhaps she minds to play the Amazon.
But what said Warwick to these injuries?
POST

He, more incensed against your majesty
Than all the rest, discharged me with these words:
'Tell him from me that he has done me wrong,
And therefore I'll uncrown him ere it be long.'
EDWARD

Ha! Dare the traitor breathe out so proud words?
Well, I will arm me, being thus forewarned;
They shall have wars and pay for their presumption.
But say, is Warwick friends with Margaret?
POST

Ay, gracious sovereign; they are so linked in friendship,
That young Prince Edward marries Warwick's daughter.
CLARENCE

Perhaps the elder; Clarence will have the younger.
Now, brother King, farewell, and sit you fast,
For I will hence to Warwick's other daughter;

That, though I want a kingdom, yet in marriage
I may not prove inferior to yourself.
You that love me and Warwick, follow me.
                    *Exit Clarence, and Somerset follows*

RICHARD (*aside*)
    Not I; my thoughts aim at a further matter.
    I stay not for the love of Edward, but the crown.

EDWARD
    Clarence and Somerset both gone to Warwick!
    Yet am I armed against the worst can happen;
    And haste is needful in this desperate case.
    Pembroke and Stafford, you in our behalf
    Go levy men, and make prepare for war;
    They are already, or quickly will be, landed;
    Myself in person will straight follow you.
                    *Exeunt Pembroke and Stafford*
    But, ere I go, Hastings and Montague,
    Resolve my doubt. You twain, of all the rest,
    Are near to Warwick by blood and by alliance;
    Tell me if you love Warwick more than me.
    If it is so, then both depart to him;
    I rather wish you foes than hollow friends.
    But if you mind to hold your true obedience,
    Give me assurance with some friendly vow,
    That I may never have you in suspect.

MONTAGUE
    So God help Montague as he proves true!

HASTINGS
    And Hastings as he favours Edward's cause!

EDWARD
    Now, brother Richard, will you stand by us?

RICHARD
    Ay, in despite of all that shall withstand you.

EDWARD
    Why, so. Then I am sure of victory.
    Now therefore let us hence, and lose no hour

Till we meet Warwick with his foreign power.

*Exeunt*


## SCENE II
## Warwickshire. A plain.

*Enter Warwick and Oxford in England,*
*with French soldiers*

WARWICK
Trust me, my lord, all hitherto goes well;
The common people by numbers swarm to us.

*Enter George and Somerset*

But see where Somerset and Clarence come!
Speak suddenly, my lords, are we all friends?
CLARENCE
Fear not that, my lord.
WARWICK
Then, gentle Clarence, welcome unto Warwick;
And welcome, Somerset. I hold it cowardice
To rest mistrustful where a noble heart
Has pawned an open hand in sign of love.
Else might I think that Clarence, Edward's brother,
Were but a feignèd friend to our proceedings;
But welcome, sweet Clarence; my daughter shall be
    yours.
And now what rests but, in night's coverture,
Your brother being carelessly encamped,
His soldiers lurking in the towns about,
And but attended by a simple guard,
We may surprise and take him at our pleasure?
Our scouts have found the adventure very easy;
That, as Ulysses and stout Diomede

With sleight and manhood stole to Rhesus' tents,
And brought from thence the Thracian fatal steeds,
So we, well covered with the night's black mantle,
At unawares may beat down Edward's guard
And seize himself. I say not 'slaughter him',
For I intend but only to surprise him.
You that will follow me to this attempt,
Applaud the name of Henry with your leader.

*They all cry* 'Henry!'

Why, then, let's on our way in silent sort;
For Warwick and his friends, God and Saint George!

*Exeunt*


# SCENE III
## Near Warwick.

*Enter three Watchmen, to guard King Edward's tent*

FIRST WATCHMAN
  Come on, my masters; each man take his stand.
  The King by this is set him down to sleep.
SECOND WATCHMAN What, will he not to bed?
FIRST WATCHMAN
  Why, no; for he has made a solemn vow
  Never to lie and take his natural rest
  Till Warwick or himself be quite suppressed.
SECOND WATCHMAN
  Tomorrow then perhaps shall be the day,
  If Warwick is so near as men report.
THIRD WATCHMAN
  But say, I pray, what nobleman is that
  That with the King here rests now in his tent?

FIRST WATCHMAN
   'Tis the Lord Hastings, the King's chiefest friend.
THIRD WATCHMAN
   O, is it so? But why commands the King
   That his chief followers lodge in towns about him,
   While he himself keeps in the cold field?
SECOND WATCHMAN
   'Tis the more honour, because more dangerous.
THIRD WATCHMAN
   Ay, but give me worship and quietness;
   I like it better than a dangerous honour.
   If Warwick knew in what estate he stands,
   'Tis to be feared that he would waken him.
FIRST WATCHMAN
   Unless our halberds did shut up his passage.
SECOND WATCHMAN
   Ay, wherefore else guard we his royal tent,
   But to defend his person from night-foes?

*Enter Warwick, Clarence, Oxford, Somerset,*
*and French soldiers, silently*

WARWICK
   This is his tent; and see where stand his guard.
   Courage, my masters! Honour now or never!
   But follow me, and Edward shall be ours.
FIRST WATCHMAN Who goes there?
SECOND WATCHMAN Stay, or you die!

*Warwick and the rest cry 'Warwick! Warwick!' and set*
*upon the guard, who fly, crying 'Arm! Arm!'. The drum*
*playing and trumpet sounding, enter Warwick, Somerset,*
*and the rest, bringing King Edward out in his gown,*
*sitting in a chair. Richard and Hastings fly*

SOMERSET What are they that fly there?

WARWICK Richard and Hastings; let them go. Here is the
  Duke.

EDWARD
  'The Duke'! Why, Warwick, when we parted,
  You called me king.

WARWICK                   Ay, but the case is altered:
  When you disgraced me in my embassy,
  Then I degraded you from being king,
  And come now to create you Duke of York.
  Alas! How should you govern any kingdom,
  That know not how to use ambassadors,
  Nor how to be contented with one wife,
  Nor how to use your brothers brotherly,
  Nor how to study for the people's welfare,
  Nor how to shroud yourself from enemies?

EDWARD
  Yea, brother of Clarence, are you here too?
  Nay, then I see that Edward needs must down.
  Yet, Warwick, in despite of all mischance,
  Of you yourself and all your accomplices,
  Edward will always bear himself as king.
  Though Fortune's malice overthrows my state,
  My mind exceeds the compass of her wheel.

WARWICK
  Then, for his mind, be Edward England's king.

*He takes off Edward's crown*

  But Henry now shall wear the English crown,
  And be true king indeed, you but the shadow.
  My lord of Somerset, at my request,
  See that forthwith Duke Edward be conveyed
  Unto my brother, Archbishop of York.
  When I have fought with Pembroke and his fellows,
  I'll follow you, and tell what answer
  Lewis and the Lady Bona send to him.
  Now for a while farewell, good Duke of York.

EDWARD

What fates impose, that men must needs abide;
It helps not to resist both wind and tide.

*They lead him out forcibly*

OXFORD

What now remains, my lords, for us to do
But march to London with our soldiers?

WARWICK

Ay, that's the first thing that we have to do;
To free King Henry from imprisonment
And see him seated in the regal throne.          *Exeunt*


# SCENE IV
## Westminster. The royal palace.

*Enter Rivers and Lady Grey*


RIVERS

Madam, what make you in this sudden change?

LADY GREY

Why, brother Rivers, are you yet to learn
What late misfortune is befallen King Edward?

RIVERS

What! Loss of some pitched battle against Warwick?

LADY GREY

No, but the loss of his own royal person.

RIVERS

Then is my sovereign slain?

LADY GREY

Ay, almost slain, for he is taken prisoner,
Either betrayed by falsehood of his guard
Or by his foe surprised at unawares,
And, as I further have to understand,
Is new committed to the Bishop of York,
Fierce Warwick's brother and by that our foe.

RIVERS
　　These news, I must confess, are full of grief;
　　Yet, gracious madam, bear it as you may;
　　Warwick may lose, that now has won the day.

LADY GREY
　　Till then fair hope must hinder life's decay;
　　And I the rather wean me from despair
　　For love of Edward's offspring in my womb.
　　This is it that makes me bridle passion
　　And bear with mildness my misfortune's cross;
　　Ay, ay, for this I draw in many a tear
　　And stop the rising of blood-sucking sighs,
　　Lest with my sighs or tears I blast or drown
　　King Edward's fruit, true heir to the English crown.

RIVERS
　　But, madam, where is Warwick to be found?

LADY GREY
　　I am informèd that he comes towards London,
　　To set the crown once more on Henry's head.
　　Guess you the rest: King Edward's friends must down.
　　But to prevent the tyrant's violence—
　　For trust not him that has once broken faith—
　　I'll hence forthwith unto the sanctuary,
　　To save at least the heir of Edward's right.
　　There shall I rest secure from force and fraud.
　　Come, therefore, let us fly while we may fly;
　　If Warwick takes us, we are sure to die.

　　　　　　　　　　　　　　　　　　　　　　　*Exeunt*


# SCENE V
## Near Middleham Castle.

*Enter Richard, Hastings, and Sir William Stanley*

RICHARD
　　Now, my Lord Hastings and Sir William Stanley,

Leave off to wonder why I drew you hither
Into this chiefest thicket of the park.
Thus stands the case: you know our King, my brother,
Is prisoner to the Bishop here, at whose hands
He has good usage and great liberty,
And, often but attended with weak guard,
Comes hunting this way to disport himself.
I have advèrtised him by secret means
That if about this hour he makes this way
Under the colour of his usual game,
He shall here find his friends with horse and men
To set him free from his captivity.

*Enter King Edward and a Huntsman with him*

HUNTSMAN
This way, my lord; for this way lies the game.
EDWARD
Nay, this way, man; see where the huntsmen stand.
Now, brother of Gloucester, Lord Hastings, and the rest,
Stand you thus close to steal the Bishop's deer?
RICHARD
Brother, the time and case require all haste;
Your horse stands ready at the park corner.
EDWARD
But whither shall we then?
HASTINGS                               To Lynn, my lord.
And ship from thence to Flanders?
RICHARD
Well guessed, believe me; for that was my meaning.
EDWARD
Stanley, I will requite your forwardness.
RICHARD
But wherefore stay we? 'Tis no time to talk.

EDWARD
Huntsman, what say you? Will you go along?
HUNTSMAN
Better do so than tarry and be hanged.
RICHARD
Come then, away; let's have no more ado.
EDWARD
Bishop, farewell; shield you from Warwick's frown;
And pray that I may repossess the crown.

*Exeunt*


# SCENE VI
## The Tower of London.

*Flourish. Enter King Henry the Sixth, Clarence, Warwick,
Somerset, young Henry Richmond, Oxford, Montague, and
the Lieutenant of the Tower*


KING
Master Lieutenant, now that God and friends
Have shaken Edward from the regal seat,
And turned my captive state to liberty,
My fear to hope, my sorrows unto joys,
At our enlargement what are your due fees?
LIEUTENANT
Subjects may challenge nothing of their sovereigns;
But if an humble prayèr may prevail,
I then crave pardon of your majesty.
KING
For what, Lieutenant? For well using me?
Nay, be you sure I'll well requite your kindness,
Because it made my imprisonment a pleasure.
Ay, such a pleasure as incagèd birds
Conceive when, after many moody thoughts,
At last by notes of household harmony
They quite forget their loss of liberty.

But, Warwick, after God, you set me free,
And chiefly therefore I thank God and you;
He was the author, you the instrument.
Therefore, that I may conquer Fortune's spite
By living low, where Fortune cannot hurt me,
And that the people of this blessèd land
May not be punished with my thwarting stars,
Warwick, although my head still wears the crown,
I here resign my government to you,
For you are fortunate in all your deeds.

WARWICK
Your grace has ever been famed for virtuous;
And now may seem as wise as virtuous
By spying and avoiding Fortune's malice,
For few men rightly temper with the stars.
Yet in this one thing let me blame your grace,
For choosing me when Clarence is in place.

CLARENCE
No, Warwick, you are worthy of the sway,
To whom the heavens in your nativity
Adjudged an olive branch and laurel crown,
As likely to be blessed in peace and war;
And therefore I yield you my free consent.

WARWICK
And I choose Clarence only for Protector.

KING
Warwick and Clarence, give me both your hands.
Now join your hands, and with your hands your hearts,
That no dissension hinder government.
I make you both Protectors of this land,
While I myself will lead a private life
And in devotion spend my latter days,
To sin's rebuke and my Creator's praise.

WARWICK
What answers Clarence to his sovereign's will?

CLARENCE
> That he consents, if Warwick yields consent;
> For on your fortune I repose myself.

WARWICK
> Why then, though loth, yet must I be content;
> We'll yoke together, like a double shadow
> To Henry's body, and supply his place;
> I mean, in bearing weight of government,
> While he enjoys the honour and his ease.
> And, Clarence, now then it is more than needful
> Forthwith that Edward be pronounced a traitor,
> And all his lands and goods be confiscate.

CLARENCE
> What else? And that succession be determined.

WARWICK
> Ay, therein Clarence shall not want his part.

KING
> But with the first of all your chief affairs,
> Let me entreat—for I command no more—
> That Margaret your Queen and my son Edward
> Be sent for, to return from France with speed.
> For, till I see them here, by doubtful fear
> My joy of liberty is half eclipsed.

CLARENCE
> It shall be done, my sovereign, with all speed.

KING
> My lord of Somerset, what youth is that,
> Of whom you seem to have so tender care?

SOMERSET
> My liege, it is young Henry Earl of Richmond.

KING
> Come hither, England's hope.

*He lays his hand on his head*

> If secret powers
> Suggest but truth to my divining thoughts,

This pretty lad will prove our country's bliss.
His looks are full of peaceful majesty,
His head by nature framed to wear a crown,
His hand to wield a sceptre, and himself
Likely in time to bless a regal throne.
Make much of him, my lords, for this is he
Must help you more than you are hurt by me.

*Enter a Post*

WARWICK
What news, my friend?
POST
That Edward is escapèd from your brother
And fled, as he hears since, to Burgundy.
WARWICK
Unsavoury news! But how made he escape?
POST
He was conveyed by Richard Duke of Gloucester
And the Lord Hastings, who attended him
In secret ambush on the forest side
And from the Bishop's huntsmen rescued him;
For hunting was his daily exercise.
WARWICK
My brother was too careless of his charge;
But let us hence, my sovereign, to provide
A salve for any sore that may betide.
*Exeunt all but Somerset, Richmond, and Oxford*
SOMERSET
My lord, I like not of this flight of Edward's;
For doubtless Burgundy will yield him help,
And we shall have more wars before it be long.
As Henry's late presaging prophecy
Did gladden my heart with hope of this young
    Richmond,
So does my heart misgive me, in these conflicts,

What may befall him, to his harm and ours.
Therefore, Lord Oxford, to prevent the worst,
Forthwith we'll send him hence to Brittany,
Till storms are past of civil enmity.

OXFORD

Ay, for if Edward repossesses the crown,
'Tis like that Richmond with the rest shall down.

SOMERSET

It shall be so; he shall to Brittany.
Come, therefore, let's about it speedily.

*Exeunt*


# SCENE VII
# Before York.

*Flourish. Enter Edward, Richard, Hastings, and soldiers*

EDWARD

Now, brother Richard, Lord Hastings, and the rest,
Yet thus far Fortune makes us now amends,
And says that once more I shall interchange
My wanèd state for Henry's regal crown.
Well have we passed and now repassed the seas
And brought desirèd help from Burgundy.
What then remains, we being thus arrived
From Ravenspurgh haven before the gates of York,
But that we enter, as into our dukedom?

RICHARD

The gates made fast! Brother, I like not this;
For many men that stumble at the threshold
Are well foretold that danger lurks within.

EDWARD

Tush, man, forebodings must not now affright us;
By fair or foul means we must enter in,
For hither will our friends repair to us.

HASTINGS
  My liege, I'll knock once more to summon them.

*Enter, on the walls, the Mayor of York and his brethren*

MAYOR
  My lords, we were forewarnèd of your coming,
  And shut the gates for safety of ourselves;
  For now we owe allegiance unto Henry.
EDWARD
  But, master Mayor, if Henry is your king,
  Yet Edward at the least is Duke of York.
MAYOR
  True, my good lord, I know you for no less.
EDWARD
  Why, and I challenge nothing but my dukedom,
  As being well content with that alone.
RICHARD *(aside)*
  But when the fox has once got in his nose,
  He'll soon find means to make the body follow.
HASTINGS
  Why, master Mayor, why stand you in a doubt?
  Open the gates; we are King Henry's friends.
MAYOR
  Ay, say you so? The gates shall then be opened.

*He descends*

RICHARD
  A wise stout captain, and soon persuaded!
HASTINGS
  The good old man would fain that all is well,
  So 'tis not due to him; but being entered,
  I doubt not, I, but we shall soon persuade
  Both him and all his brothers unto reason.

*Enter the Mayor and two aldermen, below*

EDWARD

So, master Mayor: these gates must not be shut
But in the night or in the time of war.
What! Fear not, man, but yield me up the keys;

*He takes his keys*

For Edward will defend the town and you,
And all those friends that deign to follow me.

*March. Enter Sir John Montgomery with drum and soldiers*

RICHARD

Brother, this is Sir John Montgomery,
Our trusty friend, unless I am deceived.

EDWARD

Welcome, Sir John! But why come you in arms?

MONTGOMERY

To help King Edward in his time of storm,
As every loyal subject ought to do.

EDWARD

Thanks, good Montgomery; but we now forget
Our title to the crown, and only claim
Our dukedom till God pleases to send the rest.

MONTGOMERY

Then fare you well, for I will hence again;
I came to serve a king and not a duke.
Drummer, strike up, and let us march away.

*The drum begins to march*

EDWARD

Nay, stay, Sir John, a while, and we'll debate
By what safe means the crown may be recovered.

MONTGOMERY
    What talk you of debating? In few words,
    If you'll not here proclaim yourself our king,
    I'll leave you to your fortune and be gone
    To keep them back that come to succour you.
    Why shall we fight, if you pretend no title?
RICHARD
    Why, brother, wherefore stand you on nice points?
EDWARD
    When we grow stronger, then we'll make our claim;
    Till then, 'tis wisdom to conceal our meaning.
HASTINGS
    Away with scrupulous wit! Now arms must rule.
RICHARD
    And fearless minds climb soonest unto crowns.
    Brother, we will proclaim you out of hand;
    The bruit thereof will bring you many friends.
EDWARD
    Then be it as you will; it is my right,
    And Henry but usurps the diadem.
MONTGOMERY
    Ay, now my sovereign speaks more like himself;
    And now will I be Edward's champion.
HASTINGS
    Sound trumpet; Edward shall be here proclaimed.
    Come, fellow soldier, make you proclamation.

*Flourish. Sound*

SOLDIER Edward the Fourth, by the grace of God, King of
    England and France, and Lord of Ireland, *etc.*
MONTGOMERY
    And whosoever gainsays King Edward's right,
    By this I challenge him to single fight.

*He throws down his gauntlet*

ALL
   Long live Edward the Fourth!
EDWARD
   Thanks, brave Montgomery, and thanks unto you all;
   If fortune serves me, I'll requite this kindness.
   Now, for this night, let's harbour here in York;
   And when the morning sun shall raise his car
   Above the border of this horizon,
   We'll forward towards Warwick and his mates;
   For well I know that Henry is no soldier.
   Ah, froward Clarence! How evil it beseems you
   To flatter Henry and forsake your brother!
   Yet, as we may, we'll meet both you and Warwick.
   Come on, brave soldiers; doubt not of the day,
   And, that once gotten, doubt not of large pay.   *Exeunt*

# SCENE VIII
## Westminster. The royal palace.

*Flourish. Enter King Henry, Warwick, Montague,*
*Clarence, and Oxford*

WARWICK
   What counsel, lords? Edward from Belgium,
   With hasty Germans and blunt Hollanders,
   Has passed in safety through the narrow seas,
   And with his troops does march swiftly to London;
   And many giddy people flock to him.
KING
   Let's levy men and beat him back again.
CLARENCE
   A little fire is quickly trodden out;
   Which, being suffered, rivers cannot quench.
WARWICK
   In Warwickshire I have true-hearted friends,

Not mutinous in peace, yet bold in war;
Those will I muster up; and you, son Clarence,
Shall stir up in Suffolk, Norfolk, and in Kent,
The knights and gentlemen to come with you.
You, brother Montague, in Buckingham,
Northampton, and in Leicestershire, shall find
Men well inclined to hear what you command.
And you, brave Oxford, wondrous well-beloved
In Oxfordshire, shall muster up your friends.
My sovereign, with the loving citizens,
Like to his island girt in with the ocean,
Or modest Dian circled with her nymphs,
Shall rest in London till we come to him.
Fair lords, take leave and stand not to reply.
Farewell, my sovereign.

KING
Farewell, my Hector and my Troy's true hope.

CLARENCE
In sign of truth, I kiss your highness' hand.

KING
Well-minded Clarence, be you fortunate!

MONTAGUE
Comfort, my lord; and so I take my leave.

OXFORD
And thus I seal my truth and bid adieu.

KING
Sweet Oxford, and my loving Montague,
And all at once, once more a happy farewell.

WARWICK
Farewell, sweet lords; let's meet at Coventry.

*Exeunt*


*Enter King Henry and Exeter*


KING
Here at the palace will I rest a while.

Cousin of Exeter, what thinks your lordship?
It seems the forces Edward has in field
Should not be able to encounter mine.

EXETER
The fear is that he will seduce the rest.

KING
That's not my fear. My worth has got me fame;
I have not stopped my ears to their demands,
Nor posted off their suits with slow delays.
My pity has been balm to heal their wounds,
My mildness has allayed their swelling griefs,
My mercy dried their water-flowing tears.
I have not been desirous of their wealth,
Nor much oppressed them with great subsidies,
Nor forward of revenge, though they much erred.
Then why should they love Edward more than me?
No, Exeter, these graces challenge grace;
And when the lion fawns upon the lamb,
The lamb will never cease to follow him.

*Shout within* 'A York! A York!'

EXETER
Hark, hark, my lord! What shouts are these?

*Enter Edward, Richard, and their soldiers*

EDWARD
Seize on the shame-faced Henry, bear him hence;
And once again proclaim us King of England.
You are the fount that makes small brooks to flow;
Now stops your spring; my sea shall suck them dry,
And swell so much the higher by their ebb.
Hence with him to the Tower; let him not speak.

*Exeunt some soldiers with King Henry*
And, lords, towards Coventry bend we our course,

Where pèremptory Warwick now remains.
The sun shines hot; and, if we use delay,
Cold biting winter mars our hoped-for hay.
RICHARD
Away betimes, before his forces join,
And take the great-grown traitor unawares.
Brave warriors, march at once towards Coventry.

*Exeunt*

# Act V

## SCENE I
### Coventry.

*Enter Warwick, the Mayor of Coventry, two Messengers,*
*and others upon the walls*

WARWICK
Where is the post that came from valiant Oxford?—
How far hence is your lord, my honest fellow?
FIRST MESSENGER
By this at Dunsmore, marching hitherward.
WARWICK
How far off is our brother Montague?
Where is the post that came from Montague?
SECOND MESSENGER
By this at Daintry, with a powerful troop.

*Enter Sir John Somerville*

WARWICK
Say, Somerville, what says my loving son?
And, by your guess, how nigh is Clarence now?
SOMERVILLE
At Southam I did leave him with his forces,
And do expect him here some two hours hence.

*A drum is heard*

WARWICK
Then Clarence is at hand; I hear his drum.

SOMERVILLE
It is not his, my lord. Here Southam lies;
The drum your honour hears marches from Warwick.
WARWICK
Who should that be? Perhaps, unlooked-for friends.
SOMERVILLE
They are at hand, and you shall quickly know.

*March. Flourish. Enter Edward, Richard, and soldiers*

EDWARD
Go, trumpet, to the walls and sound a parley.
RICHARD
See how the surly Warwick mans the wall!
WARWICK
O, unbidden spite! Is sportful Edward come?
Where slept our scouts, or how are they seduced,
That we could hear no news of his repair?
EDWARD
Now, Warwick, will you open the city gates,
Speak gentle words, and humbly bend your knee,
Call Edward king, and at his hands beg mercy?
And he shall pardon you these outrages.
WARWICK
Nay, rather, will you draw your forces hence,
Confess who set you up and plucked you down,
Call Warwick patron, and be penitent?
And you shall still remain the Duke of York.
RICHARD
I thought at least he would have said 'the King'.
Or did he make the jest against his will?
WARWICK
Is not a dukedom, sir, a goodly gift?
RICHARD
Ay, by my faith, for a poor earl to give;
I'll do you service for so good a gift.

WARWICK
  'Twas I that gave the kingdom to your brother.
EDWARD
  Why then, 'tis mine, if but by Warwick's gift.
WARWICK
  You are no Atlas for so great a weight;
  And, weakling, Warwick takes his gift again;
  And Henry is my king, Warwick his subject.
EDWARD
  But Warwick's king is Edward's prisoner;
  And, gallant Warwick, do but answer this:
  What is the body when the head is off?
RICHARD
  Alas, that Warwick had no more forecast,
  But while he thought to steal the single ten,
  The king was slily fingered from the deck!
  You left poor Henry at the Bishop's palace,
  And ten to one you'll meet him in the Tower.
EDWARD
  'Tis even so, yet you are Warwick still.
RICHARD
  Come, Warwick, take the time; kneel down, kneel down.
  Nay, when? Strike now, or else the iron cools.
WARWICK
  I had rather chop this hand off at a blow,
  And with the other fling it at your face,
  Than bear so low a sail to strike to you.
EDWARD
  Sail how you can, have wind and tide your friend,
  This hand, fast wound about your coal-black hair,
  Shall, while your head is warm and new cut off,
  Write in the dust this sentence with your blood:
  'Wind-changing Warwick now can change no more.'

*Enter Oxford, with drum and colours*

WARWICK
O, cheerful colours! See where Oxford comes!

OXFORD
Oxford, Oxford, for Lancaster!

*He leads his forces into the city*

RICHARD
The gates are open; let us enter too.

EDWARD
So other foes may set upon our backs.
Stand we in good array, for they no doubt
Will issue out again and bid us battle;
If not, the city being but of small defence,
We'll quickly rouse the traitors in the same.

WARWICK
O, welcome, Oxford, for we want your help.

*Enter Montague, with drum and colours*

MONTAGUE
Montague, Montague, for Lancaster!

*He leads his forces into the city*

RICHARD
You and your brother both shall buy this treason
Even with the dearest blood your bodies bear.

EDWARD
The harder matched, the greater victory;
My mind presages happy gain and conquest.

*Enter Somerset, with drum and colours*

SOMERSET
Somerset, Somerset, for Lancaster!

*He leads his forces into the city*

RICHARD
Two of your name, both Dukes of Somerset,
Have sold their lives unto the house of York,
And you shall be the third, if this sword holds.

*Enter George, with drum and colours*

WARWICK
And lo, where George of Clarence sweeps along,
Of force enough to bid his brother battle;
With whom an upright zeal to right prevails
More than the nature of a brother's love!
Come, Clarence, come; you will, if Warwick calls.
CLARENCE
Father of Warwick, know you what this means?

*He takes his red rose out of his hat and*
*throws it at Warwick*

Look here, I throw my infamy at you.
I will not ruinate my father's house,
Who gave his blood to lime the stones together,
And set up Lancaster. Why, think you, Warwick,
That Clarence is so harsh, so blunt, unnatural,
To bend the fatal instruments of war
Against his brother and his lawful king?
Perhaps you will object my holy oath;
To keep that oath were more impiety
Than Jephthah, when he sacrificed his daughter.
I am so sorry for my trespass made
That, to deserve well at my brother's hands,
I here proclaim myself your mortal foe,
With resolution, wheresoever I meet you—
As I will meet you, if you stir abroad—

To plague you for your foul misleading me.
And so, proud-hearted Warwick, I defy you,
And to my brother turn my blushing cheeks.
Pardon me, Edward, I will make amends;
And, Richard, do not frown upon my faults,
For I will henceforth be no more inconstant.

EDWARD
Now welcome more, and ten times more beloved,
Than if you never had deserved our hate.

RICHARD
Welcome, good Clarence; this is brother-like.

WARWICK
O passing traitor, perjured and unjust!

EDWARD
What, Warwick, will you leave the town and fight?
Or shall we beat the stones about your ears?

WARWICK
Alas, I am not cooped here for defence!
I will away towards Barnet presently,
And bid you battle, Edward, if you dare.

EDWARD
Yes, Warwick, Edward dares, and leads the way.
Lords, to the field; Saint George and victory!
                    *Exeunt Edward and his company March.*
                    *Warwick and his company follow*


# SCENE II
## Near Barnet.

*Alarum. Enter Edward, bringing forth Warwick wounded*

EDWARD
So, lie you there; die you, and die our fear;
For Warwick was a threat unto us all.
Now, Montague, sit fast; I seek for you,
That Warwick's bones may keep yours company.    *Exit*

WARWICK
   Ah, who is nigh? Come to me, friend or foe,
   And tell me who is victor, York or Warwick?
   Why ask I that? My mangled body shows,
   My blood, my want of strength, my sick heart shows,
   That I must yield my body to the earth,
   And, by my fall, the conquest to my foe.
   Thus yields the cedar to the axe's edge,
   Whose arms gave shelter to the princely eagle,
   Under whose shade the ramping lion slept,
   Whose top branch over-peered Jove's spreading tree
   And kept low shrubs from winter's powerful wind.
   These eyes, that now are dimmed with death's black veil,
   Have been as piercing as the midday sun,
   To search the secret treasons of the world;
   The wrinkles in my brows, now filled with blood,
   Were likened oft to kingly sepulchres;
   For who lived king, but I could dig his grave?
   And who dared smile when Warwick bent his brow?
   Lo, now my glory smeared in dust and blood!
   My parks, my walks, my manors that I had,
   Even now forsake me, and of all my lands
   Is nothing left me but my body's length.
   Why, what is pomp, rule, reign, but earth and dust?
   And, live we how we can, yet die we must.

*Enter Oxford and Somerset*

SOMERSET
   Ah, Warwick, Warwick! Were you as we are,
   We might recover all our loss again.
   The Queen from France has brought a powerful army;
   Even now we heard the news. Ah, could you fly!
WARWICK
   Why, then I would not fly. Ah, Montague,

If you are there, sweet brother, take my hand,
And with your lips keep in my soul a while!
You love me not; for, brother, if you did,
Your tears would wash this cold congealèd blood
That glues my lips and will not let me speak.
Come quickly, Montague, or I am dead.

SOMERSET
Ah, Warwick! Montague has breathed his last;
And to the latest gasp cried out for Warwick,
And said 'Commend me to my valiant brother.'
And more he would have said, and more he spoke,
Which sounded like a cannon in a vault,
That might not be distinguished; but at last
I well might hear, delivered with a groan,
'O, farewell, Warwick!'

WARWICK
Sweet rest his soul! Fly, lords, and save yourselves;
For Warwick bids you all farewell, to meet in heaven.

*He dies*

OXFORD
Away, away, to meet the Queen's great power.

*Here they bear away his body. Exeunt*

# SCENE III
## The same.

*Flourish. Enter King Edward in triumph, with Richard,
Clarence, and the rest*

EDWARD
Thus far our fortune keeps an upward course,
And we are graced with wreaths of victory.
But, in the midst of this bright-shining day,
I spy a black, suspicious, threatening cloud,
That will encounter with our glorious sun

Ere he attains his easeful western bed.
I mean, my lords, those forces that the Queen
Has raised in France have arrived upon our coast,
And, as we hear, march on to fight with us.

CLARENCE
A little gale will soon disperse that cloud
And blow it to the source from whence it came;
Your very beams will dry those vapours up,
For every cloud engenders not a storm.

RICHARD
The Queen is valued thirty thousand strong,
And Somerset, with Oxford, fled to her;
If she has time to breathe, be well assured
Her faction will be full as strong as ours.

EDWARD
We are advèrtised by our loving friends
That they do hold their course toward Tewkesbury.
We, having now the best at Barnet field,
Will thither straight, for willingness rids way;
And, as we march, our strength will be augmented
In every county as we go along.
Strike up the drum; cry 'Courage!' and away!

*Exeunt*


# SCENE IV
## Near Tewkesbury.

*Flourish. March. Enter the Queen, Prince Edward,*
*Somerset, Oxford, and soldiers*


QUEEN
Great lords, wise men never sit and wail their loss,
But cheerfully seek how to redress their harms.
What though the mast is now blown overboard,
The cable broken, the holding-anchor lost,

And half our sailors swallowed in the flood?
Yet lives our pilot still. Is it meet that he
Should leave the helm and, like a fearful lad,
With tearful eyes add water to the sea,
And give more strength to that which has too much;
While, in his moan, the ship splits on the rock,
Which industry and courage might have saved?
Ah, what a shame! Ah, what a fault were this!
Say Warwick was our anchor; what of that?
And Montague our topmast; what of him?
Our slaughtered friends the tackles; what of these?
Why, is not Oxford here another anchor?
And Somerset another goodly mast?
The friends of France our shrouds and tacklings?
And, though unskilful, why not Ned and I
For once allowed the skilful pilot's charge?
We will not from the helm to sit and weep,
But keep our course, though the rough wind says no,
From shelves and rocks that threaten us with wreck.
As good to chide the waves as speak them fair.
And what is Edward but a ruthless sea?
What Clarence but a quicksand of deceit?
And Richard but a ragged fatal rock?
All these the enemies to our poor bark.
Say you can swim; alas, it is but a while!
Tread on the sand; why, there you quickly sink.
Bestride the rock; the tide will wash you off,
Or else you famish; that's a threefold death.
This speak I, lords, to let you understand,
In case some one of you would fly from us,
That there's no hoped-for mercy with the brothers
More than with ruthless waves, with sands and rocks.
Why, courage then! What cannot be avoided
Is childish weakness to lament or fear.

PRINCE
I think a woman of this valiant spirit

Should, if a coward heard her speak these words,
Infuse his breast with magnanimity,
And make him, naked, foil a man at arms.
I speak not this as doubting any here;
For did I but suspect a fearful man,
He should have leave to go away betimes,
Lest in our need he might infect another
And make him of like spirit to himself.
If any such is here—as God forbid!—
Let him depart before we need his help.

OXFORD
Women and children of so high a courage,
And warriors faint! Why, it's perpetual shame.
O brave young Prince! Your famous grandfather
Does live again in you; long may you live
To bear his image and renew his glories!

SOMERSET
And he that will not fight for such a hope,
Go home to bed, and like the owl by day,
If he rises, be mocked and wondered at.

QUEEN
Thanks, gentle Somerset; sweet Oxford, thanks.

PRINCE
And take his thanks that yet has nothing else.

*Enter a Messenger*

MESSENGER
Prepare you, lords, for Edward is at hand,
Ready to fight; therefore be resolute.

OXFORD
I thought no less; it is his policy
To haste thus fast to find us unprovided.

SOMERSET
He is deceived; we are in readiness.

QUEEN
  This cheers my heart, to see your forwardness.
OXFORD
  Here pitch our troops; hence we will not budge.

*Flourish and march. Enter Edward, Richard,*
*Clarence, and soldiers*

EDWARD
  Brave followers, yonder stands the thorny wood,
  Which, by the heavens' assistance and your strength,
  Must by the roots be hewn up yet ere night.
  I need not add more fuel to your fire,
  For well I know you blaze to burn them out.
  Give signal to the fight, and to it, lords!
QUEEN
  Lords, knights, and gentlemen, what I should say
  My tears gainsay; for every word I speak,
  You see I drink the water of my eye.
  Therefore, no more but this: Henry, your sovereign,
  Is prisoner to the foe; his state usurped,
  His realm a slaughter-house, his subjects slain,
  His statutes cancelled, and his treasure spent;
  And yonder is the wolf that makes this spoil.
  You fight in justice; then in God's name, lords,
  Be valiant, and give signal to the fight.
                    *Alarums, retreat, excursions. Exeunt*


# SCENE V
## The same.

*Flourish. Enter Edward, Richard, Clarence, and their army,*
*with the Queen, Oxford, and Somerset, prisoners*


EDWARD
  Now here a period to tumultuous broils.

Away with Oxford to Hammes Castle straight;
For Somerset, off with his guilty head.
Go, bear them hence; I will not hear them speak.

OXFORD

For my part I'll not trouble you with words.

SOMERSET

Nor I, but stoop with patience to my fortune.

*Exeunt Oxford and Somerset, guarded*

QUEEN

So part we sadly in this troublous world,
To meet with joy in sweet Jerusalem.

EDWARD

Is proclamation made that who finds Edward
Shall have a high reward, and he his life?

RICHARD

It is; and lo, where youthful Edward comes!

*Enter the Prince, guarded*

EDWARD

Bring forth the gallant; let us hear him speak.
What! Can so young a thorn begin to prick?
Edward, what satisfaction can you make
For bearing arms, for stirring up my subjects,
And all the trouble you have turned me to?

PRINCE

Speak like a subject, proud ambitious York!
Suppose that I am now my father's mouth;
Resign your chair, and where I stand kneel you,
While I propose the self-same words to you,
Which, traitor, you would have me answer to.

QUEEN

Ah, that your father had been so resolved!

RICHARD

That you might still have worn the petticoat
And never have stolen the breech from Lancaster.

PRINCE
> Let Aesop fable in a winter's night;
> His currish riddles sort not with this place.

RICHARD
> By heaven, brat, I'll plague you for that word.

QUEEN
> Ay, you were born to be a plague to men.

RICHARD
> For God's sake, take away this captive scold.

PRINCE
> Nay, take away this scolding crook-back rather.

EDWARD
> Peace, wilful boy, or I will charm your tongue.

CLARENCE
> Untutored lad, you are too malapert.

PRINCE
> I know my duty; you are all undutiful.
> Lascivious Edward, and you perjured George,
> And you misshapen Dick, I tell you all
> I am your better, traitors as you are;
> And you usurp my father's right and mine.

EDWARD
> Take that, the likeness of this railer here.

*He stabs him*

RICHARD
> Sprawl you? Take that, to end your agony.

*He stabs him*

CLARENCE
> And there's for twitting me with perjury.

*He stabs him*

QUEEN
  O, kill me too!
RICHARD
  Indeed, and shall.

             *He offers to kill her*

EDWARD
  Hold, Richard, hold; for we have done too much.
RICHARD
  Why should she live to fill the world with words?
EDWARD
  What! Does she swoon? Use means for her recovery.
RICHARD
  Clarence, excuse me to the King my brother;
  I'll hence to London on a serious matter.
  Ere you come there, be sure to hear some news.
CLARENCE
  What? What?
RICHARD
  The Tower, the Tower.                          *Exit*
QUEEN
  O Ned, sweet Ned, speak to your mother, boy!
  Can you not speak? O traitors! Murderers!
  They that stabbed Caesar shed no blood at all,
  Did not offend, and were not worthy blame,
  If this foul deed were by to equal it.
  He was a man; this, in respect, a child;
  And men never spend their fury on a child.
  What's worse than murderer, that I may name it?
  No, no, my heart will burst then if I speak;
  And I will speak that so my heart may burst.
  Butchers and villains! Bloody cannibals!
  How sweet a plant have you untimely cropped!
  You have no children, butchers; if you had,
  The thought of them would have stirred up remorse.

But if you ever chance to have a child,
Look in his youth to have him so cut off
As, deathsmen, you have rid this sweet young Prince!

EDWARD

Away with her; go, bear her hence perforce.

QUEEN

Nay, never bear me hence, dispatch me here;
Here sheathe your sword; I'll pardon you my death.
What! Will you not? Then, Clarence, do it you.

CLARENCE

By heaven, I will not do you so much ease.

QUEEN

Good Clarence, do; sweet Clarence, do you do it.

CLARENCE

Did you not hear me swear I would not do it?

QUEEN

Ay, but you are used to forswear yourself,
'Twas sin before, but now it is charity.
What! Will you not? Where is that devil's butcher,
    Richard?
Ill-looking Richard; Richard, where are you?
You are not here; murder is your alms-deed;
Petitioners for blood you never put back.

EDWARD

Away, I say; I charge you, bear her hence.

QUEEN

So come to you and yours as to this Prince!

                                    *Exit, guarded*

EDWARD

Where's Richard gone?

CLARENCE

To London all in post; and, as I guess,
To make a bloody supper in the Tower.

EDWARD

He's sudden if a thing comes in his head.
Now march we hence; discharge the common sort

With pay and thanks, and let's away to London,
And see our gentle Queen how well she fares.
By this, I hope, she has a son for me.            *Exeunt*


# SCENE VI
## The Tower of London.

*Enter King Henry the Sixth and Richard below, with the
Lieutenant of the Tower on the walls*

RICHARD
Good day, my lord. What! At your book so hard?
KING
Ay, my good lord—'my lord', I should say rather.
'Tis sin to flatter; 'good' was little better.
'Good Gloucester' and 'good devil' were alike,
And both preposterous; therefore, not 'good lord'.
RICHARD
Fellow, leave us to ourselves; we must confer.
                                        *Exit Lieutenant*
KING
So flies the reckless shepherd from the wolf;
So first the harmless sheep does yield its fleece,
And next its throat unto the butcher's knife.
What scene of death has Roscius now to act?
RICHARD
Suspicion always haunts the guilty mind;
The thief does fear in each bush an officer.
KING
The bird that has been limèd in a bush,
With trembling wings misdoubts every bush;
And I, the hapless male to one sweet bird,
Have now the fatal object in my eye
Where my poor young was limed, was caught and
   killed.

RICHARD

    Why, what a peevish fool was that of Crete,

    That taught his son the office of a fowl!

    And yet, for all his wings, the fool was drowned.

KING

    I, Daedalus; my poor boy, Icarus;

    Your father, Minos, that denied our course;

    The sun that seared the wings of my sweet boy,

    Your brother Edward, and yourself, the sea

    Whose envious gulf did swallow up his life.

    Ah, kill me with your weapon, not with words!

    My breast can better brook your dagger's point

    Than can my ears that tragic history.

    But wherefore do you come? Is it for my life?

RICHARD

    Think you I am an executioner?

KING

    A persecutor I am sure you are;

    If murdering innocents is executing,

    Why, then you are an executioner.

RICHARD

    Your son I killed for his presumptiòn.

KING

    Had you been killed when first you did presume,

    You had not lived to kill a son of mine.

    And thus I prophesy, that many a thousand,

    Who now mistrust no parcel of my fear,

    And many an old man's sigh, and many a widow's,

    And many an orphan's water-standing eye—

    Men for their sons', wives for their husbands',

    And orphans for their parents' timeless death—

    Shall rue the hour that ever you were born.

    The owl shrieked at your birth, an evil sign;

    The night-crow cried, aboding luckless time;

    Dogs howled, and hideous tempests shook down trees;

    The raven rooked her on the chimney's top,

    And chattering magpies in dismal discords sang.

Your mother felt more than a mother's pain,
And yet brought forth less than a mother's hope,
To wit, an indigested and deformèd lump,
Not like the fruit of such a goodly tree.
Teeth had you in your head when you were born,
To signify you came to bite the world;
And if the rest is true which I have heard,     .
You came—

RICHARD
I'll hear no more; die, prophet, in your speech!

*He stabs him*

For this, among the rest, was I ordained.

KING
Ay, and for much more slaughter after this.
O, God forgive my sins, and pardon you!          *He dies*

RICHARD
What! Will the aspiring blood of Lancaster
Sink in the ground? I thought it would have mounted.
See how my sword weeps for the poor King's death!
O, may such purple tears be always shed
From those that wish the downfall of our house!
If any spark of life is yet remaining,
Down, down to hell; and say I sent you thither,

*He stabs him again*

I that have neither pity, love, nor fear.
Indeed, 'tis true that Henry told me of;
For I have often heard my mother say
I came into the world with my legs forward.
Had I not reason, think you, to make haste,
And seek their ruin that usurped our right?
The midwife wondered and the women cried
'O, Jesus bless us, he is born with teeth!'

And so I was, which plainly signified
That I should snarl and bite and play the dog.
Then, since the heavens have shaped my body so,
Let hell make crooked my mind to answer it.
I have no brother, I am like no brother;
And this word 'love', which greybeards call divine,
Be resident in men like one another
And not in me; I am myself alone.
Clarence, beware; you keep me from the light.
But I will sort a pitchy day for you;
For I will buzz abroad such prophecies
That Edward shall be fearful of his life,
And then, to purge his fear, I'll be your death.
King Henry and the Prince his son are gone;
Clarence, your turn is next, and then the rest,
Counting myself but bad till I am best.
I'll throw your body in another room
And triumph, Henry, in your day of doom.

*Exit with the body*

## SCENE VII
## Westminster. The royal palace.

*Flourish. Enter Edward and Lady Grey, as king and queen,
Clarence, Richard, Hastings, a nurse carrying the infant
prince, and attendants*

EDWARD
Once more we sit in England's royal throne,
Repurchased with the blood of enemies.
What valiant foemen, like to autumn's corn,
Have we mowed down in tops of all their pride!
Three Dukes of Somerset, threefold renowned
For hardy and undoubted champions;
Two Cliffords, as the father and the son;

And two Northumberlands—two braver men
Never spurred their coursers at the trumpet's sound;
With them, the two brave bears, Warwick and
  Montague,
That in their chains fettered the kingly lion
And made the forest tremble when they roared.
Thus have we swept suspicion from our seat
And made our footstool of security.
Come hither, Bess, and let me kiss my boy.
Young Ned, for you, your uncles and myself
Have in our armours watched the winter's night,
Went all afoot in summer's scalding heat,
That you might repossess the crown in peace;
And of our labours you shall reap the gain.

RICHARD *(aside)*
I'll blast his harvest, if your head were laid;
For yet I am not looked on in the world.
This shoulder was ordained so thick to heave;
And heave it shall some weight or break my back.
Work you the way, and that shall execute.

EDWARD
Clarence and Gloucester, love my lovely Queen;
And kiss your princely nephew, brothers both.

CLARENCE
The duty that I owe unto your majesty
I seal upon the lips of this sweet babe.

LADY GREY
Thanks, noble Clarence; worthy brother, thanks.

RICHARD
And that I love the tree from whence you sprang,
Witness the loving kiss I give the fruit.
*(Aside)* To say the truth, so Judas kissed his master,
And cried 'All hail!' when he did mean all harm.

EDWARD
Now am I seated as my soul delights,
Having my country's peace and brothers' loves.

CLARENCE
>What will your grace have done with Margaret?
>Reignier, her father, to the King of France
>Has pawned Sicily and Jerusalem,
>And hither have they sent it for her ransom.

EDWARD
>Away with her and waft her hence to France.
>And now what rests but that we spend the time
>With stately triumphs, mirthful comic shows,
>Such as befit the pleasure of the Court?
>Sound drums and trumpets! Farewell, sour annoy!
>For here, I hope, begins our lasting joy.            *Exeunt*

# Titus
# Andronicus

# INTRODUCTION

**T**itus Andronicus is a horrible play—I mean full of horrors, like Grand Guignol of earlier this century. It only shows how necessary it is to see the play in its proper historical perspective, instead of merely looking at the text, taking it literally in the manner of obtuse literary criticism. For one thing, it is not only a prentice-piece, Shakespeare's first attempt at classical tragedy, but also a school play, full of the Latin lore he had picked up—and recently taught—at school. It is noticeably, and somewhat incongruously, marked by country images, a countryman writing. Finally, he set himself to out-do Kyd's popular *Spanish Tragedy*, in the way Ben Jonson summed up in his biographical poem prefixed to the First Folio. The tyro succeeded in outdoing Kyd in horrors, if not in popularity— though we know, again from Jonson, that *Titus Andronicus* was popular.

And not only from Jonson: three quartos were printed before the First Folio, a unique copy of the first (1594) turning up in Sweden in only this century. It indicates not only what has been lost in the course of centuries but also what may be recovered—like the full story of the Sonnets and the identity of the Dark Lady only recently in ours.

The horrors come from classical sources: the story of Tereus and Philomela raped, her tongue pulled out; the

**411**

fearful banquet of human flesh served up, from Seneca's *Thyestes*. The first story came from Ovid, favourite poet in Elizabethan schools, as of both Marlowe and Shakespeare (the 'English Ovid'); while Seneca is cited in the play. We also have tags quoted from school-books, like the hackneyed lines of Horace's ode, 'Integer vitae, scelerisque purus.'

The play *reads* as if Shakespeare distanced himself from the horrors, remained unmoved by them. They are repellent to modern taste, though they appealed to Elizabethans, who went to the theatre for thrilling sensations (least of all for critical abstractions, or ethical disquisitions). But we may be abashed to remember that our own time has witnessed equal horrors on a much larger scale. Then, too, the play touches on another searching issue of our time, the racial one. The Empress Tamora, a Goth, is in love with Aaron the Moor, and has a base black child by him. Shakespeare is indeed 'for all time.'

The affinities and foreshadowings of Shakespeare's later work offer us great interest. Tamora is a well-realised character, clever, insinuating, scheming and ruthless: a precursor of Lady Macbeth, or of the Queen in *Cymbeline*. The villainous Aaron looks forward to Iago, the racial theme to *The Merchant of Venice;* Titus is a kind of Coriolanus, who has served Rome well, to be disdained and ill treated for it. Coriolanus is cited, when Titus threatens to do as he did by way of revenge. The play is a revenge-play, of the genre that was so popular from *The Spanish Tragedy* onwards—and Titus's feigned madness, always effective theatre, is imitated by the prentice dramatist from that play.

Shakespeare's Aaron has something in common with Marlowe's Barabas, and the two were in touch in these years, until Marlowe's miserable, inconsequent death in

May 1593. The two were writing for at least one company in common, the early Pembroke's—which performed
this play; so also did Strange's, and Sussex's. Shakespeare
was able to take it with other early work in his baggage to the Lord Chamberlain's on its formation in 1594
(perhaps this accounts for its first appearance in print
in that year). As Sisson points out, 'the play links up
closely with Shakespeare's other early work, with his
poems, *Venus and Adonis,* and *Lucrece* above all.' It also
chimes with 2 and 3 *Henry VI,* which had been performed by Pembroke's, while the latter of these is a revenge-
play too. In *Titus* the Empress Tamora appears disguised
as Revenge, her two sons, Rape and Murder, on either
side.

The story is not authentically Roman; it derives from
medieval folklore through some chap-book. But the actor,
commencing author, garnished it naively with his school
text-book learning.

> Titus: Lucius, what book is that she tosses so?
> Boy: Grandsire, 'tis Ovid's *Metamorphoses*—

the chief source, by the way, in both the original and in
Golding's translation, of Shakespeare's classical myths,
tales and images. Tamora's son knew Horace's verse from
school: 'I read it in the Grammar long ago', i.e. Lily's,
which was used in most Elizabethan schools. Titus quotes
a couple of lines from Seneca.

All this reads rather naively—the prentice author is out
to impress—and some of the lines are quite pedestrian, if
not positively bathetic. The same is true of the contemporary *Henry VI* plays. It is this that has led so many 'critics'
to doubt the authorship of these plays, at least in part.
This shows no historical sense, and not much sense of how
writers really write and develop. By the same token it

proves the absolute necessity of establishing chronological sequence—as this edition does—to show the development of Shakespeare's writing and art with time and experience. The play is of his earliest workmanship, say 1591, along with the *Henry VI* trilogy.

Actually it bears many recognisable signs of his authorship, not only parallels with his own work, but of his personality, taste and tricks of style even thus early. The couplet—

She is a woman, therefore may be wooed;
She is a woman, therefore may be won—

may be a commonplace, but it shortly is taken up again in the Sonnets. We have the countryman's regular fixation on hunting in all his early work:

The hunt is up, the morn is bright and grey,
The fields are fragrant and the woods are green.
Uncouple here and let us make a bay. (baying, hallooing)

We have a suspiciously familiar turn with

What, have you not full often struck a doe,
And borne her cleanly by the keeper's nose?

We need have no doubt whatever about the early and tenacious *contretemps* about the deer at Stratford—no disgrace involved: just the kind of sport spirited young men went in for, university men as well as not.[1]

The contemporary world breaks in, anachronistically, with the phrase 'twenty Popish tricks and ceremonies' —Elizabethan England, not classical Rome. We note too

---

[1] cf my *Simon Forman,* 282.

Shakespeare's constant observation, recorded in sonnets as
well as plays, of monuments and ruined monasteries, which
impressed the sensitive eye as he toured about the post-
Dissolution countryside. A Goth strayed from his troop—as
Shakespeare might have done from his troupe—

To gaze upon a ruinous monastery;

there 'within the wasted building' Tamora's child was
found.

The tricks of phrase and style bespeak Shakespeare no
less. The earliest malapropisms and puns based on them
appear with the Clown, as with Jack Cade in *Henry VI.*
This early descent into the realism of lower-class prose
comes as a relief after the tightly constricted early blank
verse. We recognise the author's addiction to rare words,
'fere' for spouse, and impressive words of his own invention,
'successantly' for successively; and his curious addiction
all his life to using the subordinate verb to be for the verb
to have. Here he says 'is leaped' for has leaped; and this
usage (as in French) occurs throughout his work. We note
also his regular confusion of 'which' for who—common
enough in Elizabethan English, but conspicuously frequent with him; as well as his regular preference for 'ta'en'
for taken, and such favourite words as 'spurn', 'power' (a
disyllable, which I have accented as such) for army, or
force; or 'exclaims' as a noun for exclamations. Along
with favourite phrases, like 'usurp on', 'insult upon'. These
things are virtually signatures to those who can recognise
them.

The text of the play is generally clear enough, though it
offers some difficulties here and there. Professor C.J. Sisson
reproves Professor Dover Wilson for interfering with it too
much in his *Cambridge* edition. Paradoxically, a modern

edition—along with the need to modernise to clarify obscurities and replace archaic forms—can keep more conservatively to the original Elizabethan *sense* and often finds editorial emendations unnecessary.

# CHARACTERS

SATURNINUS, son of the late Emperor of Rome, afterwards
  Emperor
BASSIANUS, brother of Saturninus
TITUS ANDRONICUS, a Roman general against the Goths
MARCUS ANDRONICUS, tribune of the people, brother of
  Titus

LUCIUS
QUINTUS
MARTIUS } sons of Titus Andronicus
MUTIUS

YOUNG LUCIUS, a boy, son of Lucius
PUBLIUS, son of Marcus Andronicus

SEMPTRONIUS
CAIUS } kinsmen of Titus Andronicus
VALENTINE

AEMILIUS, a noble Roman

ALARBUS
DEMETRIUS } sons of Tamora
CHIRON

AARON, a Moor, beloved by Tamora
A Captain, A Messenger, A Clown
TAMORA, Queen of the Goths
LAVINIA, daughter of Titus Andronicus
A Nurse, and a black Child
Romans and Goths, Senators, Tribunes, Officers, Soldiers,
  Attendants

**418**

# Act I

## SCENE I
## Rome. Before the Capitol; a tomb below.

*Flourish. Enter the Tribunes and Senators aloft.*
*And then enter below Saturninus and his Followers*
*at one door; and Bassianus and his Followers at the other,*
*with Drums and Trumpets*

SATURNINUS Noble patricians, patrons of my right,
    Defend the justice of my cause with arms.
    And, countrymen, my loving followers,
    Plead my successive title with your swords.
    I am his first-born son that was the last
    That wore the imperial diadem of Rome.
    Then let my father's honours live in me,
    Nor wrong my age with this indignity.
BASSIANUS Romans, friends, followers, favourers of my
    right,
    If ever Bassianus, Caesar's son,
    Was gracious in the eyes of royal Rome,
    Keep then this passage to the Capitol;
    And suffer not dishonour to approach
    The imperial seat, to virtue consecrate,
    To justice, continence, and nobility;
    But let desert in pure election shine;
    And, Romans, fight for freedom in your choice.

*Enter Marcus Andronicus, aloft, with the crown*

MARCUS Princes that strive by factions and by friends

Ambitiously for rule and empery,
Know that the people of Rome, for whom we stand
A special party, have by common voice
In election for the Roman empery
Chosen Andronicus surnamèd Pius
For many good and great deserts to Rome.
A nobler man, a braver warrior,
Lives not this day within the city walls.
He by the Senate is invited home
From weary wars against the barbarous Goths,
That with his sons, a terror to our foes,
Has yoked a nation strong, trained up in arms.
Ten years are spent since first he undertook
This cause of Rome, and chàstisèd with arms
Our enemies' pride. Five times he has returned
Bleeding to Rome, bearing his valiant sons
In coffins from the field.
And now at last, laden with honour's spoils,
Returns the good Andronicus to Rome,
Renownèd Titus, flourishing in arms.
Let us entreat by honour of his name
Whom worthily you would have now succeed,
And in the Capitol and Senate's right,
Whom you pretend to honour and adore,
That you withdraw you and abate your strength,
Dismiss your followers and, as suitors should,
Plead your deserts in peace and humbleness.
SATURNINUS How fair the tribune speaks to calm my
     thoughts.
BASSIANUS Marcus Andronicus, so I do confide
In your uprightness and integrity,
And so I love and honour you and yours,
Your noble brother Titus and his sons,
And her to whom my thoughts are humbled all,
Gracious Lavinia, Rome's rich ornament,
That I will here dismiss my loving friends:

And to my fortunes and the people's favour
Commit my cause in balance to be weighed.
                              *Exeunt Soldiers of Bassianus*
SATURNINUS Friends that have been thus forward in my
    right,
    I thank you all and here dismiss you all,
    And to the love and favour of my country
    Commit myself, my person, and the cause.
                              *Exeunt Soldiers of Saturninus.*
    Rome, be as just and gracious unto me
    As I am confident and kind to thee.
    Open the gates and let me in.
BASSIANUS Tribunes, and me, a poor competitor.

*Flourish. They go up into the Senate House.*
*Enter a Captain*

CAPTAIN Romans, make way. The good Andronicus,
    Patron of virtue, Rome's best champion,
    Successful in the battles that he fights,
    With honour and with fortune is returned
    From where he circumscribèd with his sword
    And brought to yoke the enemies of Rome.

*Sound drums and trumpets, enter two of Titus' sons,*
*Martius and Mutius; and then two men bearing a coffin*
*covered with black; then Lucius and Quintus, two other*
*sons; then Titus Andronicus. And then Tamora, Queen of*
*Goths, and her two sons, Chiron and Demetrius, with*
*Aaron the Moor, and others, including Tamora's son*
*Alarbus and other Goths, prisoners. Then set down the*
*coffin, and Titus speaks*

TITUS Hail, Rome, victorious in your mourning weeds!
    Lo, as the bark that has discharged her freight
    Returns with precious lading to the bay

From whence at first she weighed her anchorage,
Comes Andronicus, bound with laurel boughs,
To re-salute his country with his tears,
Tears of true joy for his return to Rome.
You great defender of this Capitol,
Stand gracious to the rites that we intend.
Romans, of five and twenty valiant sons,
Half of the number that King Priam had,
Behold the poor remains, alive and dead.
These that survive let Rome reward with love;
These that I bring unto their latest home,
With burial among their ancestors.
Here Goths have given me leave to sheathe my sword.
Titus unkind, and careless of your own,
Why suffer you your sons, unburied yet,
To hover on the dreadful shore of Styx?
Make way to lay them by their brethren then.

*They open the tomb*

There greet in silence, as the dead are wont,
And sleep in peace, slain in your country's wars.
O sacred receptacle of my joys,
Sweet cell of virtue and nobility,
How many sons have you of mine in store
That you will never render to me more!
LUCIUS Give us the proudest prisoner of the Goths,
That we may hew his limbs and on a pile
*Ad manes fratrum*[1] sacrifice his flesh
Before this earthy prison of their bones,
That so the shadows be not unappeased,
Nor we disturbed with omens on the earth.
TITUS I give him you, the noblest that survives,
The eldest son of this distressèd queen.

---

[1] To the spirits of our brothers.

TAMORA Stay, Roman brethren! Gracious conqueror,
    Victorious Titus, rue the tears I shed,
    A mother's tears in passion for her son:
    And if your sons were ever dear to you,
    O, think my son to be as dear to me.
    Suffice it not that we are brought to Rome
    To beautify your triumph and return,
    Captive to you and to your Roman yoke;
    But must my sons be slaughtered in the streets
    For valiant doings in their country's cause?
    O, if to fight for king and commonweal
    Were piety in yours, it is in these.
    Andronicus, stain not your tomb with blood.
    Will you draw near the nature of the gods?
    Draw near them then in being merciful.
    Sweet mercy is nobility's true badge:
    Thrice-noble Titus, spare my first-born son.
TITUS Patient yourself, madam, and pardon me.
    These are their brethren whom your Goths beheld
    Alive and dead, and for their brethren slain
    Religiously they ask a sacrifice:
    To this your son is marked, and die he must,
    To appease their groaning shadows that are gone.
LUCIUS Away with him, and make a fire straight,
    And with our swords, upon a pile of wood,
    Let's hew his limbs till they be clean consumed.
                 *Exeunt Titus' sons with Alarbus*
TAMORA O cruel irreligious piety!
CHIRON Was never Scythia half so barbarous.
DEMETRIUS Oppose not Scythia to ambitious Rome.
    Alarbus goes to rest, and we survive
    To tremble under Titus' threatening look.
    Then, madam, stand resolved, but hope as well
    The selfsame gods that armed the Queen of Troy
    With opportunity of sharp revenge
    Upon the Thracian tyrant in her tent

May favor Tamora, the Queen of Goths
(When Goths were Goths, and Tamora was queen),
To quit the bloody wrongs upon her foes.

*Enter the sons of Andronicus again*

LUCIUS See, lord and father, how we have performed
   Our Roman rites. Alarbus' limbs are lopped
   And entrails feed the sacrificing fire,
   Whose smoke like incense does perfume the sky.
   Remains naught but to inter our brethren
   And with loud alarums welcome them to Rome.
TITUS Let it be so, and let Andronicus
   Make this his latest farewell to their souls.

*Sound trumpets, and lay the coffin in the tomb*

In peace and honour rest you here, my sons;
Rome's readiest champions, repose you here in rest,
Secure from worldly chances and mishaps.
Here lurks no treason, here no envy swells,
Here grow no damnèd drugs, here are no storms,
No noise, but silence and eternal sleep.
In peace and honour rest you here, my sons.

*Enter Lavinia*

LAVINIA In peace and honour live Lord Titus long;
   My noble lord and father, live in fame.
   Lo, at this tomb my tributary tears
   I render for my brethren's obsequies,
   And at your feet I kneel, with tears of joy
   Shed on this earth for your return to Rome.
   O, bless me here with your victorious hand,
   Whose fortunes Rome's best citizens applaud.
TITUS Kind Rome, that have thus lovingly reserved

The cordial of my age to glad my heart.
Lavinia, live; outlive your father's days,
And fame's eternal date, for virtue's praise.
MARCUS (*aloft*) Long live Lord Titus, my belovèd brother,
　　Gracious triumpher in the eyes of Rome!
TITUS Thanks, gentle tribune, noble brother Marcus.
MARCUS And welcome, nephews, from successful wars,
　　You that survive, and you that sleep in fame.
　　Fair lords, your fortunes are alike in all
　　That in your country's service drew your swords;
　　But safer triumph is this funeral pomp
　　That has aspired to Solon's happiness
　　And triumphs over chance in honour's bed.
　　Titus Andronicus, the people of Rome,
　　Whose friend in justice you have ever been,
　　Send you by me, their tribune and their trust,
　　This royal robe of white and spotless hue,
　　And name you in election for the empire,
　　With these our late-deceasèd emperor's sons.
　　Be candidatus then, and put it on,
　　And help to set a head on headless Rome.
TITUS A better head her glorious body fits
　　Than his that shakes for age and feebleness.
　　What should I don this robe, and trouble you?
　　Be chosen with proclamatiòns to-day,
　　To-morrow yield up rule, resign my life,
　　And set abroad new business for you all?
　　Rome, I have been your soldier forty years,
　　And led my country's strength successfully,
　　And buried one and twenty valiant sons,
　　Knighted in field, slain manfully in arms,
　　In right and service of their noble country.
　　Give me a staff of honour for my age,
　　But not a sceptre to control the world.
　　Upright he held it, lords, that held it last.
MARCUS Titus, you shall obtain and ask the empery.

SATURNINUS Proud and ambitious tribune, can you tell?
TITUS Patience, Prince Saturninus.
SATURNINUS                                 Romans, do me right.
   Patricians, draw your swords, and sheathe them not
   Till Saturninus be Rome's emperor.
   Andronicus, would you were shipped to hell
   Rather than rob me of the people's hearts!
LUCIUS Proud Saturnine, interrupter of the good
   That noble-minded Titus means to you!
TITUS Content you, prince, I will restore to you
   The people's hearts, and wean them from themselves.
BASSIANUS Andronicus, I do not flatter you,
   But honour you, and will do till I die.
   My faction if you strengthen with your friends,
   I will most thankful be, and thanks to men
   Of noble minds is honorable reward.
TITUS People of Rome, and people's tribunes here,
   I ask your voices and your suffrages.
   Will you bestow them friendly on Andronicus?
TRIBUNES To gratify the good Andronicus,
   And gratulate his safe return to Rome,
   The people will accept whom he admits.
TITUS Tribunes, I thank you, and this suit I make,
   That you create our emperor's eldest son,
   Lord Saturnine; whose virtues will, I hope,
   Reflect on Rome as Titan's rays on earth,
   And ripen justice in this commonweal.
   Then, if you will elect by my advice,
   Crown him and say 'Long live our emperor!'
MARCUS With voices and applause of every sort,
   Patricians and plebeians, we create
   Lord Saturninus Rome's great emperor
   And say 'Long live our emperor Saturnine!'

                    *A long flourish*

SATURNINUS Titus Andronicus, for your favours done
   To us in our election this day
   I give you thanks in part of your deserts,
   And will with deeds requite your gentleness.
   And for an onset, Titus, to advance
   Your name and honorable family,
   Lavinia will I make my emperess,
   Rome's royal mistress, mistress of my heart,
   And in the sacred Pantheon her espouse.
   Tell me, Andronicus, does this motion please you?
TITUS It does, my worthy lord, and in this match
   I hold me highly honoured of your grace;
   And here in sight of Rome, to Saturnine,
   King and commander of our commonweal,
   The wide world's emperor, do I consecrate
   My sword, my chariot, and my prisoners,
   Presents well worthy Rome's imperious lord.
   Receive them then, the tribute that I owe,
   My honour's ensigns humbled at your feet.
SATURNINUS Thanks, noble Titus, father of my life.
   How proud I am of you and of your gifts
   Rome shall record, and when I do forget
   The least of these unspeakable deserts,
   Romans, forget your fealty to me.
TITUS *(to Tamora)* Now, madam, are you prisoner to an
   emperor,
   To him that for your honour and your state
   Will use you nobly and your followers.
SATURNINUS *(aside)* A goodly lady, trust me, of the hue
   That I would choose, were I to choose anew.—
   Clear up, fair queen, that cloudy countenance.
   Though chance of war has wrought this change of cheer,
   You come not to be made a scorn in Rome.
   Princely shall be your usage every way.
   Rest on my word, and let not discontent
   Daunt all your hopes. Madam, he comforts you

Can make you greater than the Queen of Goths.
Lavinia, you are not displeased with this?
LAVINIA Not I, my lord, since true nobility
  Warrants these words in princely courtesy.
SATURNINUS Thanks, sweet Lavinia. Romans, let us go.
  Ransomless here we set our prisoners free.
  Proclaim our honours, lords, with trump and drum.
                    *Flourish. Exeunt Saturninus, Tamora,*
                        *Demetrius, Chiron, and Aaron*
BASSIANUS Lord Titus, by your leave, this maid is mine.

                    *Seizes Lavinia*

TITUS How, sir! Are you in earnest then, my lord?
BASSIANUS Ay, noble Titus, and resolved as well
  To do myself this reason and this right.
MARCUS *'Suum cuique'* [to each his own] is our Roman
    justice:
  This prince in justice seizes but his own.
LUCIUS And that he will, and shall if Lucius lives
TITUS Traitors, away! Where is the emperor's guard?
  Treason, my lord! Lavinia is surprised!
SATURNINUS (*re-entering*) Surprised? By whom?
BASSIANUS                              By him that justly may
  Bear his betrothed from all the world away.
                    *Exeunt Bassianus and Marcus with Lavinia.*
MUTIUS Brothers, help to convey her hence away,
  And with my sword I'll keep this door safe.
                    *Exeunt Lucius, Quintus, and Martius*
TITUS Follow, my lord, and I'll soon bring her back.
                                        *Exit Saturninus*
MUTIUS My lord, you pass not here.
TITUS                              What, villain boy?
  Bar you me my way in Rome?
MUTIUS                              Help, Lucius, help!
                                        *Titus kills him*

*Enter Lucius*

LUCIUS My lord, you are unjust, and more than so,
  In wrongful quarrel you have slain your son.
TITUS Nor you, nor he, are any sons of mine;
  My sons would never so dishonour me.

*Enter aloft the Emperor with Tamora
and her two Sons, and Aaron*

  Traitor, restore Lavinia to the emperor.
LUCIUS Dead, if you will; but not to be his wife,
  That is another's lawful promised love.                    *Exit*
SATURNINUS No, Titus, no. The emperor needs her not,
  Nor her, nor you, nor any of your stock.
  I'll trust by leisure him that mocks me once;
  You never, nor your traitorous haughty sons,
  Confederates all thus to dishonour me.
  Was none in Rome to make a laughing stock
  But Saturnine? Full well, Andronicus,
  Agree these deeds with that proud brag of yours
  That said I begged the empire at your hands.
TITUS O monstrous! What reproachful words are these?
SATURNINUS But go your ways, go, give that changing
    piece
  To him that flourished for her with his sword.
  A valiant son-in-law you shall enjoy;
  One fit to bandy with your lawless sons,
  To ruffle in the commonwealth of Rome.
TITUS These words are razors to my wounded heart.
SATURNINUS And therefore, lovely Tamora, Queen of Goths,
  That like the stately Phoebe among her nymphs
  Do overshine the gallantest dames of Rome,
  If you be pleased with this my sudden choice,
  Behold, I choose you, Tamora, for my bride
  And will create you Emperess of Rome.

Speak, Queen of Goths, do you applaud my choice?
And here I swear by all the Roman gods—
Since priest and holy water are so near,
And tapers burn so bright, and everything
In readiness for Hymenaeus stands—
I will not re-salute the streets of Rome
Or climb my palace till from forth this place
I lead espoused my bride along with me.

TAMORA And here in sight of heaven to Rome I swear,
If Saturnine advances the Queen of Goths,
She will a handmaid be to his desires,
A loving nurse, a mother to his youth.

SATURNINUS Ascend, fair queen, Pantheon. Lords,
  accompany
Your noble emperor and his lovely bride,
Sent by the heavens for Prince Saturnine,
Whose wisdom has her fortune conquerèd.
There shall we consummate our spousal rites.

                                        *Exeunt. Titus remains*

TITUS I am not bid to wait upon this bride.
Titus, when were you wont to walk alone,
Dishonored thus and challengèd of wrongs?

*Enter Marcus and Titus' Sons, Lucius,
Quintus, and Martius*

MARCUS O Titus, see, O see what you have done,
In a bad quarrel slain a virtuous son.

TITUS No, foolish tribune, no: no son of mine,
Nor you, nor these, confederates in the deed
That has dishonoured all our family,
Unworthy brother, and unworthy sons!

LUCIUS But let us give him burial as becomes;
Give Mutius burial with our brethren then.

TITUS Traitors, away! He rests not in this tomb:
This monument five hundred years has stood,

Which I have sumptuously re-edified.
Here none but soldiers and Rome's servitors
Repose in fame; none basely slain in brawls.
Bury him where you can, he comes not here.
MARCUS My lord, this is impiety in you.
My nephew Mutius' deeds do plead for him;
He must be buried with his brethren now.

*Titus' two Sons speak*

QUINTUS, MARTIUS And shall, or him we will accompany.
TITUS And shall? What villain was it spoke that word?

*Titus' Son speaks*

QUINTUS He that would vouch it in any place but here.
TITUS What, would you bury him in my despite?
MARCUS No, noble Titus, but entreat of you
   To pardon Mutius and to bury him.
TITUS Marcus, even you have struck upon my crest,
   And with these boys my honour you have wounded.
   My foes I do repute you every one,
   So trouble me no more, but get you gone.
MARTIUS He is not with himself, let us withdraw.
QUINTUS Not I, till Mutius' bones be burièd.

*The Brother and the Sons kneel*

MARCUS Brother, for in that name does nature plead—
QUINTUS Father, and in that name does nature speak—
TITUS Speak you no more, if all the rest will speed.
MARCUS Renownèd Titus, more than half my soul—
LUCIUS Dear father, soul and substance of us all—
MARCUS Suffer your brother Marcus to inter
   His noble nephew here in virtue's nest,
   That died in honour and Lavinia's cause.

You art a Roman, be not barbarous:
The Greeks upon advice did bury Ajax,
That slew himself; and wise Laertes' son
Did graciously plead for his funeral.
Let not young Mutius then, that was your joy,
Be barred his entrance here.
TITUS                                        Rise, Marcus, rise.
The dismallest day is this that ever I saw,
To be dishonored by my sons in Rome.
Well, bury him, and bury me the next.

*They put him in the tomb*

LUCIUS There lie your bones, sweet Mutius, with your
    friends,
Till we with trophies do adorn your tomb.
ALL No man shed tears for noble Mutius;
    He lives in fame that died in virtue's cause.
                        *Exeunt all but Marcus and Titus*
MARCUS My lord, to step out of these dreary dumps,
    How comes it that the subtle Queen of Goths
    Is of a sudden thus advanced in Rome?
TITUS I know not, Marcus, but I know it is:
    Whether by device or no, the heavens can tell.
    Is she not then beholding to the man
    That brought her for this high good turn so far?
MARCUS Yes, and will nobly him remunerate.

*Flourish. Enter the Emperor, Tamora and her two Sons,*
*with Aaron, at one door. Enter at the other door Bassianus*
*and Lavinia, with others*

SATURNINUS So, Bassianus, you have played your prize.
    God give you joy, sir, of your gallant bride.
BASSIANUS And you of yours, my lord. I say no more
    Nor wish no less, and so I take my leave.
SATURNINUS Traitor, if Rome has law or we have power,
    You and your faction shall repent this rape.

BASSIANUS Rape call you it, my lord, to seize my own,
My true betrothèd love, and now my wife?
But let the laws of Rome determine all;
Meanwhile am I possessed of that is mine.
SATURNINUS It is good, sir. You are very short with us;
But if we live, we'll be as sharp with you.
BASSIANUS My lord, what I have done, as best I may
Answer I must, and shall do with my life.
Only thus much I give your grace to know:
By all the duties that I owe to Rome,
This noble gentleman, Lord Titus here,
Is in opinion and in honour wronged,
That in the rescue of Lavinia
With his own hand did slay his youngest son,
In zeal to you, and highly moved to wrath
To be controlled in that he frankly gave.
Receive him then to favour, Saturnine,
That has expressed himself in all his deeds
A father and a friend to you and Rome.
TITUS Prince Bassianus, cease to plead my deeds.
'Tis you, and those, that have dishonored me.
Rome and the righteous heavens be my judge
How I have loved and honoured Saturnine.
TAMORA My worthy lord, if ever Tamora
Were gracious in those princely eyes of yours,
Then hear me speak impartially for all;
And at my suit, sweet, pardon what is past.
SATURNINUS What, madam, be dishonored openly
And basely put it up without revenge?
TAMORA Not so, my lord; the gods of Rome forfend
I should be author to dishonour you!
But on my honour dare I undertake
For good Lord Titus' innocence in all,
Whose fury not dissembled speaks his griefs:
Then at my suit look graciously on him.

Lose not so noble a friend on vain suppose,
Nor with sour looks afflict his gentle heart.
(*Aside to Saturninus*) My lord, be ruled by me, be won
   at last;
Dissemble all your griefs and discontents:
You are but newly planted in your throne;
Lest, then, the people, and patricians too,
Upon a just survey take Titus' part,
And so supplant you for ingratitude,
Which Rome reputes to be a heinous sin.
Yield to entreats: and then let me alone,
I'll find a day to massacre them all
And raze their faction and their family,
The cruel father, and his traitorous sons,
To whom I suèd for my dear son's life;
And make them know what 'tis to let a queen
Kneel in the streets and beg for grace in vain.
(*Aloud*) Come, come, sweet emperor—come,
   Andronicus—
Take up this good old man, and cheer the heart
That dies in tempest of your angry frown.
SATURNINUS Rise, Titus, rise, my empress has prevailed.
TITUS I thank your majesty, and her, my lord.
These words, these looks, infuse new life in me.
TAMORA Titus, I am incorporate in Rome,
A Roman now adopted happily,
And must advise the emperor for his good.
This day all quarrels die, Andronicus.
And let it be my honour, good my lord,
That I have reconciled your friends and you.
For you, Prince Bassianus, I have passed
My word and promise to the emperor
That you will be more mild and tractable.
And fear not, lords, and you, Lavinia;
By my advice, all humbled on your knees
You shall ask pardon of his majesty.    *They kneel*

LUCIUS We do, and vow to heaven and to his highness
   That what we did was mildly as we might,
   Tendering our sister's honour and our own.
MARCUS That on my honour here do I protest.
SATURNINUS Away, and talk not, trouble us no more.
TAMORA Nay, nay, sweet emperor, we must all be friends.
   The tribune and his nephews kneel for grace.
   I will not be denied. Sweet heart, look back.
SATURNINUS Marcus, for your sake and your brother's
     here,
   And at my lovely Tamora's entreats,
   I do remit these young men's heinous faults.
   Stand up.                                        *They rise*
   Lavinia, though you left me like a churl,
   I found a friend; and sure as death I swore
   I would not part a bachelor from the priest.
   Come, if the emperor's court can feast two brides,
   You are my guest, Lavinia, and your friends.
   This day shall be a love-day, Tamora.
TITUS To-morrow, if it please your majesty
   To hunt the panther and the hart with me,
   With horn and hound we'll give your grace good-day.
SATURNINUS Be it so, Titus, and many thanks, too.
                                 *Exeunt*

# Act II

## SCENE I
The same.

*Sound trumpets. Aaron enters*

AARON Now climbs yet Tamora Olympus' top,
  Safe out of fortune's shot, and sits aloft,
  Secure of thunder's crack or lightning flash,
  Advanced above pale envy's threatening reach.
  As when the golden sun salutes the morn,
  And having gilt the ocean with its beams,
  Gallops the zodiac in its glistering coach
  And overlooks the highest-peering hills,
  So Tamora.
  Upon her wit does earthly honour wait,
  And virtue stoops and trembles at her frown.
  Then, Aaron, arm your heart and fit your thoughts
  To mount aloft with your imperial mistress,
  And mount her pitch whom you in triumph long
  Have prisoner held, fettered in amorous chains,
  And faster bound to Aaron's charming eyes
  Than is Prometheus tied to Caucasus.
  Away with slavish weeds and servile thoughts!
  I will be bright and shine in pearl and gold,
  To wait upon this new-made empress.
  To wait, said I? to wanton with this queen,
  This goddess, this Semiramis, this nymph,
  This siren that will charm Rome's Saturnine
  And see his shipwreck and his commonweal's.
  Holla! what storm is this?

*Enter Chiron and Demetrius, braving*

DEMETRIUS Chiron, your years want wit, your wits want
    edge
    And manners, to intrude where I am graced
    And may, for aught you know, affected be.
CHIRON Demetrius, you do overween in all,
    And so in this, to bear me down with threats.
    'Tis not the difference of a year or two
    Makes me less gracious, or you more fortunate:
    I am as able and as fit as you
    To serve, and to deserve my mistress' grace;
    And that my sword upon you shall approve,
    And plead my passions for Lavinia's love.
AARON Clubs, clubs! These lovers will not keep the peace.
DEMETRIUS Why, boy, although our mother, unadvised,
    Gave you a dancing rapier by your side,
    Are you so desperate grown to threaten your friends?
    Go to! Have your lath glued within your sheath
    Till you know better how to handle it.
CHIRON Meanwhile, sir, with the little skill I have,
    Full well shall you perceive how much I dare.
DEMETRIUS Ay, boy, grow you so brave?

*They draw*

AARON              Why, how now, lords?
    So near the emperor's palace dare ye draw
    And maintain such a quarrel openly?
    Full well I know the ground of all this grudge:
    I would not for a million of gold
    The cause were known to them it most concerns;
    Nor would your noble mother for much more
    Be so dishonored in the court of Rome.
    For shame, put up.
DEMETRIUS          Not I, till I have sheathed

My rapier in his bosom, and with that
Thrust those reproachful speeches down his throat
That he has breathed in my dishonour here.

CHIRON For that I am prepared and full resolved,
Foul-spoken coward, that thunder with your tongue
And with your weapon nothing dare perform.

AARON Away, I say!
Now, by the gods that warlike Goths adore,
This petty brawl will now undo us all.
Why, lords, and think you not how dangerous
It is to trespass on a prince's right?
What, is Lavinia then become so loose,
Or Bassianus so degenerate,
That for her love such quarrels may be broached
Without controlment, justice, or revenge?
Young lords, beware! and should the empress know
This discord's ground, the music would not please.

CHIRON I care not, I, knew she and all the world
I love Lavinia more than all the world.

DEMETRIUS Youngster, learn you to make some meaner
choice.
Lavinia is your elder brother's hope.

AARON Why, are you mad? or know you not in Rome
How furious and impatiènt they are,
And cannot brook competitors in love?
I tell you, lords, you do but plot your deaths
By this device.

CHIRON            Aaron, a thousand deaths
Would I propose to achieve her whom I love.

AARON To achieve her! How?

DEMETRIUS                     Why make you it so strange?
She is a woman, therefore may be wooed;
She is a woman, therefore may be won;
She is Lavinia, therefore must be loved.
What, man! more water glides beside the mill
Than knows the miller of; and easy it is

Of a cut loaf to steal a slice, we know:
Though Bassianus is the emperor's brother,
Better than he have worn Vulcan's badge.
AARON (*aside*) Ay, and as good as Saturninus may.
DEMETRIUS Then why should he despair that knows to
    court it
With words, fair looks, and liberality?
What, have not you full often struck a doe,
And borne her cleanly by the keeper's nose?
AARON Why, then, it seems some certain snatch or so
Would serve your turns.
CHIRON              Ay, so the turn were served.
DEMETRIUS Aaron, you have hit it.
AARON            Would you had hit it too!
Then should not we be tired with this ado.
Why, hark you, hark you, and are you such fools
To square for this? Would it offend you then
That both should speed?
CHIRON Faith, not me.
DEMETRIUS        Nor me, if I were one.
AARON For shame, be friends, and join for that you fight.
'Tis policy and stratagem must do
That you affect; and so must you resolve,
That what you cannot as you would achieve,
You must perforce accomplish as you may.
Take this of me: Lucrece was not more chaste
Than this Lavinia, Bassianus' love.
A speedier course than lingering languishment
Must we pursue, and I have found the path.
My lords, a solemn hunting is in hand;
There will the lovely Roman ladies troop:
The forest walks are wide and spaciòus,
And many unfrequented plots there are,
Fitted by kind for rape and villainy.
Single you thither then this dainty doe,
And strike her home by force, if not by words.

This way, or not at all, stand you in hope.
Come, come, our empress, with her sacred wit
To villainy and vengeance consecrate,
Will we acquaint as well what we intend;
And she shall file our engines with advice,
That will not suffer you to square yourselves,
But to your wishes' height advance you both.
The emperor's Court is like the house of fame,
The palace full of tongues, of eyes and ears:
The woods are ruthless, dreadful, deaf, and dull.
There speak and strike, brave boys, and take your turns,
There serve your lust, shadowed from heaven's eye,
And revel in Lavinia's treasury.
CHIRON Your counsel, lad, smells of no cowardice.
DEMETRIUS '*Sit fas aut nefas,*'[1] till I find the stream
  To cool this heat, a charm to calm these fits,
  '*Per Stygia, per manes vehor.*'[2]                   *Exeunt*


# SCENE II
## A forest near Rome.

*Enter Titus Andronicus and his three Sons, making a noise
     with hounds and horns; and Marcus*

TITUS The hunt is up, the morn is bright and grey,
  The fields are fragrant and the woods are green.
  Uncouple here and let us make a bay,
  And wake the emperor and his lovely bride,
  And rouse the prince, and ring a hunter's peal,
  That all the Court may echo with the noise.
  Sons, let it be your charge, as it is ours,
  To attend the emperor's person carefully;

---

[1]Be it right or wrong.
[2]Through infernal regions by ghosts I am driven.

I have been troubled in my sleep this night,
But dawning day new comfort has inspired.

*Here a cry of hounds, and wind horns in a peal, then enter*
*Saturninus, Tamora, Bassianus, Lavinia, Chiron,*
*Demetrius, and their Attendants*

Many good morrows to your majesty!
Madam, to you as many and as good!
I promisèd your grace a hunter's peal.
SATURNINUS And you have rung it lustily, my lords,
Somewhat too early for new-married ladies.
BASSIANUS Lavinia, how say you?
LAVINIA                              I say, no:
I have been broad awake two hours and more.
SATURNINUS Come on then, horse and chariots let us
    have,
And to our sport. Madam, now shall you see
Our Roman hunting.
MARCUS                    I have dogs, my lord,
Will rouse the proudest panther in the chase,
And climb the highest promontory top.
TITUS And I have horse will follow where the game
Makes way, and runs like swallows o'er the plain.
DEMETRIUS Chiron, we hunt not, we, with horse nor
    hound,
But hope to pluck a dainty doe to ground.        *Exeunt*


# SCENE III
## The same.

*Enter Aaron alone, with a bag of gold.*

AARON He that had wit would think that I had none,
To bury so much gold under a tree,

And never after to inherit it.
Let him that thinks of me so abjectly
Know that this gold must coin a stratagem,
Which, cunningly effected, will beget
A very excellent piece of villainy.
And so repose, sweet gold, for their unrest

*Hides the gold*

That have their alms out of the empress' chest.

*Enter Tamora*

TAMORA My lovely Aaron, wherefore look you sad
When everything does make a gleeful boast?
The birds chant melody on every bush,
The snake lies rollèd in the cheerful sun,
The green leaves quiver with the cooling wind,
And make a checkered shadow on the ground;
Under their sweet shade, Aaron, let us sit,
And while the babbling echo mocks the hounds,
Replying shrilly to the well-tuned horns,
As if a double hunt were heard at once,
Let us sit down and mark their bellowing noise.
And after conflict such as was supposed
The wandering prince and Dido once enjoyed,
When with a happy storm they were surprised,
And curtained with a counsel-keeping cave,
We may, each wreathèd in the other's arms,
Our pastimes done, possess a golden slumber;
While hounds and horns and sweet melodious birds
Be unto us as is a nurse's song
Of lullaby to bring her babe asleep.
AARON Madam, though Venus governs your desires,
Saturn is dominator over mine.
What signifies my deadly-standing eye,

My silence, and my cloudy melancholy,
My fleece of woolly hair that now uncurls
Even as an adder when she does unroll
To do some fatal execution?
No, madam, these are no venereal signs.
Vengeance is in my heart, death in my hand,
Blood and revenge are hammering in my head.
Hark, Tamora, the empress of my soul,
Which never hopes more heaven than rests in you,
This is the day of doom for Bassianus;
His Philomel must lose her tongue to-day,
Your sons make pillage of her chastity
And wash their hands in Bassianus' blood.
See you this letter? take it up, I pray you,
And give the king this fatal-plotted scroll.
Now question me no more; we are espied;
Here comes a parcel of our hopeful booty,
Which dreads not yet their lives' destruction.

*Enter Bassianus and Lavinia*

TAMORA Ah, my sweet Moor, sweeter to me than life.
AARON No more, great empress; Bassianus comes.
  Be cross with him, and I'll go fetch your sons
  To back your quarrels, whatsoever they be.          *Exit*
BASSIANUS Who have we here? Rome's royal emperess,
  Unfurnished of her well-beseeming troop?
  Or is it Dian, habited like her,
  Who has abandonèd her holy groves
  To see the general hunting in this forest?
TAMORA Saucy controller of my private steps!
  Had I the power that some say Dian had,
  Your temples should be planted instantly
  With horns, as was Actaeon's, and the hounds
  Should drive upon your new-transformèd limbs,
  Unmannerly intruder as you are!

LAVINIA Under your patience, gentle emperess,
  'Tis thought you have a goodly gift in horning,
  And to be suspect that your Moor and you
  Are singled forth to try experiments.
  Jove shield your husband from his hounds to-day!
  'Tis pity they should take him for a stag.
BASSIANUS Believe me, queen, your swart Cimmerian
  Does make your honour of his body's hue,
  Spotted, detested, and abominable.
  Why are you sequestered from all your train,
  Dismounted from your snow-white goodly steed,
  And wandered hither to an òbscure plot,
  Accompanied but with a barbarous Moor,
  If foul desire had not conducted you?
LAVINIA And being intercepted in your sport,
  Great reason that my noble lord is scolded
  For sauciness. I pray you let us hence,
  And let her joy her raven-colored love;
  This valley fits the purpose passing well.
BASSIANUS The king my brother shall have notice of this.
LAVINIA Ay, for these slips have made him noted long.
  Good king, to be so mightily abused!
TAMORA Why I have patience to endure all this!

*Enter Chiron and Demetrius*

DEMETRIUS How now, dear sovereign and our gracious
  mother,
  Why does your highness look so pale and wan?
TAMORA Have I not reason, think you, to look pale?
  These two enticed me hither to this place,
  A barren detested vale you see it is;
  The trees, though summer, yet forlorn and lean,
  O'ercome with moss and baleful mistletoe.
  Here never shines the sun; here nothing breeds,
  Unless the nightly owl or fatal raven:

And when they showed me this abhorrèd pit,
They told me, here, at dead time of the night,
A thousand fiends, a thousand hissing snakes,
Ten thousand swelling toads, as many hedgehogs,
Would make such fearful and confusèd cries
As any mortal body hearing it
Should straight fall mad, or else die suddenly.
No sooner had they told this hellish tale
But straight they told me they would bind me here
Unto the body of a dismal yew,
And leave me to this miserable death.
And then they called me foul adulteress,
Lascivious Goth, and all the bitterest terms
That ever ear did hear to such effect;
And had you not by wondrous fortune come,
This vengeance on me had they executed.
Revenge it, as you love your mother's life,
Or be you not henceforth called my children.
DEMETRIUS This is a witness that I am your son.

*Stabs Bassianus*

CHIRON And this for me, struck home to show my strength.
LAVINIA Ay, come, Semìramis, nay, barbarous Tamora,
    For no name fits your nature but your own.
TAMORA Give me the poniard; you shall know, my boys,
    Your mother's hand shall right your mother's wrong.
DEMETRIUS Stay, madam, here is more belongs to her:
    First thrash the corn, then after burn the straw.
    This minion stood upon her chastity,
    Upon her nuptial vow, her loyalty,
    And with that painted hope braves your mightiness;
    And shall she carry this unto her grave?
CHIRON For if she does, I would I were an eunuch.
    Drag hence her husband to some secret hole,
    And make his dead trunk pillow to our lust.

TAMORA But when you have the honey we desire,
   Let not this wasp outlive, us both to sting.
CHIRON I warrant you, madam, we will make that sure.
   Come, mistress, now perforce we will enjoy
   That nice-preservèd honesty of yours.
LAVINIA O Tamora, you bear a woman's face—
TAMORA I will not hear her speak, away with her!
LAVINIA Sweet lords, entreat her hear me but a word.
DEMETRIUS Listen, fair madam: let it be your glory
   To see her tears; but be your heart to them
   As unrelenting flint to drops of rain.
LAVINIA When did the tiger's young ones teach the dam?
   O, do not teach her wrath; she taught it you;
   The milk you sucked from her did turn to marble;
   Even at your teat you had your tyranny.
   Yet every mother breeds not sons alike.
   (*To Chiron*) Do you entreat her show a woman's pity.
CHIRON What, would you have me prove myself a bastard?
LAVINIA 'Tis true the raven does not hatch a lark:
   Yet have I heard—O, could I find it now!—
   The lion, moved with pity, did endure
   To have his princely paws pared all away.
   Some say that ravens foster forlorn children
   The while their own birds famish in their nests:
   O, be to me, though your hard heart say no,
   Nothing so kind, but something pitiful.
TAMORA I know not what it means, away with her!
LAVINIA O, let me teach you for my father's sake,
   That gave you life when well he might have slain you,
   Be not obdùrate, open your deaf ears.
TAMORA Had you in person never offended me,
   Even for his sake am I pitiless.
   Remember, boys, I poured forth tears in vain
   To save your brother from the sacrifice,
   But fierce Andronicus would not relent.
   Therefore away with her, and use her as you will;

The worse to her, the better loved by me.

LAVINIA O Tamora, be called a gentle queen
And with your own hands kill me in this place,
It is not life that I have begged so long.
Poor I was slain when Bassianus died.

TAMORA What beg you? foolish woman, let me go.

LAVINIA 'Tis present death I beg; and one thing more
That womanhood denies my tongue to tell.
O, keep me from their worse than killing lust,
And tumble me into some loathsome pit,
Where never man's eye may behold my body.
Do this, and be a charitable murderer.

TAMORA So should I rob my sweet sons of their fee.
No, let them satisfy their lust on you.

DEMETRIUS Away! for you have stayed us here too long.

LAVINIA No grace? no womanhood? Ah, beastly creature,
The blot and enemy to our general name!
Confusion fall—

CHIRON Nay then, I'll stop your mouth. Bring you her
husband.
This is the hole where Aaron bid us hide him.

*Demetrius throws the body of Bassianus into the pit; then
exeunt Demetrius and Chiron, dragging off Lavinia*

TAMORA Farewell, my sons: see that you make her sure.
Never let my heart know merry cheer indeed
Till all the Andronici be made away.
Now will I hence to seek my lovely Moor
And let my spleenful sons this trull deflower.       *Exit*

*Enter Aaron, with Quintus and Martius*

AARON Come on, my lords, the better foot before.
Straight will I bring you to the loathsome pit
Where I espied the panther fast asleep.

QUINTUS My sight is very dull, whatever it bodes.
MARTIUS And mine, I promise you: were it not for shame,
    Well could I leave our sport to sleep awhile.

              *Falls into the pit*

QUINTUS What, are you fallen? What subtle hole is this,
    Whose mouth is covered with rude-growing briers,
    Upon whose leaves are drops of new-shed blood
    As fresh as morning dew distilled on flowers?
    A very fatal place it seems to me.
    Speak, brother, have you hurt yourself with the fall?
MARTIUS O brother, with the dismallest object hurt
    That ever eye with sight made heart lament.
AARON Now will I fetch the king to find them here,
    That he thereby may have a likely guess
    How these were they that made away his brother.   *Exit*
MARTIUS Why do you not comfort me and help me out
    From this unhallowed and bloodstainèd hole?
QUINTUS I am surprisèd with an uncouth fear;
    A chilling sweat o'erruns my trembling joints;
    My heart suspects more than my eye can see.
MARTIUS To prove you have a true-divining heart,
    Aaron and you look down into this den
    And see a fearful sight of blood and death.
QUINTUS Aaron is gone, and my compassionate heart
    Will not permit my eyes once to behold
    The thing whereat it trembles by surmise.
    O, tell me who it is, for never till now
    Was I a child to fear I know not what.
MARTIUS Lord Bassianus lies befouled in blood,
    All on a heap, like to a slaughtered lamb,
    In this detested, dark, blood-drinking pit.
QUINTUS If it is dark, how do you know it is he?
MARTIUS Upon his bloody finger he does wear
    A precious ring that lightens all this hole,

Which, like a taper in some monument,
Does shine upon the dead man's earthy cheeks,
And shows the ragged entrails of this pit.
So pale did shine the moon on Pyramus
When he by night lay bathed in maiden blood.
O brother, help me with your fainting hand,
If fear has made you faint, as me it has,
Out of this fell devouring receptacle,
As hateful as Cocytus' misty mouth.

QUINTUS Reach me your hand, that I may help you out,
Or, wanting strength to do you so much good,
I may be plucked into the swallowing womb
Of this deep pit, poor Bassianus' grave.
I have no strength to pluck you to the brink.

MARTIUS Nor I the strength to climb without your help.

QUINTUS Your hand once more; I will not loose again
Till you are here aloft, or I below.
You can not come to me: I come to you.                *Falls in*

*Enter Saturninus and Aaron*

SATURNINUS Along with me: I'll see what hole is here,
And what he is that now is leaped into it.
Say, who are you that lately did descend
Into this gaping hollow of the earth?

MARTIUS The unhappy sons of old Andronicus,
Brought hither in a most unlucky hour
To find your brother Bassianus dead.

SATURNINUS My brother dead? I know you do but jest.
He and his lady both are at the lodge
Upon the north side of this pleasant chase;
'Tis not an hoùr since I left them there.

MARTIUS We know not where you left them all alive;
But, out alas! here have we found him dead.

*Enter Tamora, Andronicus, and Lucius*

TAMORA Where is my lord the king?

SATURNINUS Here, Tamora; though grieved with killing
    grief.

TAMORA Where is your brother Bassianus?

SATURNINUS Now to the bottom do you search my wound:
    Poor Bassianus here lies murderèd.

TAMORA Then all too late I bring this fatal writ,
    The complot of this untimely tragedy;
    And wonder greatly that man's face can fold
    In pleasing smiles such murderous tyranny.

*She gives Saturnine a letter*

SATURNINUS (*reads the letter*) 'For if we miss to meet him
    handsomely,
    Sweet huntsman, Bassianus it is we mean,
    Do you so much as dig the grave for him.
    You know our meaning: look for your reward
    Among the nettles at the elder tree
    Which overshades the mouth of that same pit
    Where we decreed to bury Bassianus.
    Do this, and purchase us your lasting friends.'
    O Tamora, was ever heard the like?
    This is the pit, and this the elder tree.
    Look, sirs, if you can find the huntsman out
    That should have murdered Bassianus here.

AARON My gracious lord, here is the bag of gold.

SATURNINUS (*to Titus*) Two of your whelps, fell curs of
    bloody kind,
    Have here bereft my brother of his life.
    Sirs, drag them from the pit unto the prison.
    There let them bide until we have devised
    Some never-heard-of torturing pain for them.

TAMORA What, are they in this pit? O wondrous thing!
    How easily murder is discoverèd!

TITUS High emperor, upon my feeble knee

I beg this boon, with tears not lightly shed,
That this fell fault of my accursèd sons,
Accursèd if the fault is proved in them—
SATURNINUS If it is proved? You see it is apparent.
Who found this letter? Tamora, was it you?
TAMORA Andronicus himself did take it up.
TITUS I did, my lord, yet let me be their bail;
For by my father's reverent tomb I vow
They shall be ready at your highness' will
To answer their suspicion with their lives.
SATURNINUS You shall not bail them: see you follow me.
Some bring the murdered body, some the murderers.
Let them not speak a word; the guilt is plain;
For, by my soul, were there worse end than death,
That end upon them should be executed.
TAMORA Andronicus, I will entreat the king;
Fear not for your sons, they shall do well enough.
TITUS Come, Lucius, come; stay not to talk with them.
                                                          *Exeunt*


# SCENE IV
## The same.

*Enter Demetrius and Chiron, with Lavinia, her hands cut
off, her tongue cut out, ravished*

DEMETRIUS So, now go tell, if now your tongue can speak,
Who 'twas that cut your tongue and ravished you.
CHIRON Write down your mind, betray your meaning so,
See if your stumps will let you play the scribe.
DEMETRIUS See how with signs and tokens she can scrawl.
CHIRON Go home, call for sweet water, wash your hands.
DEMETRIUS She has no tongue to call, nor hands to wash;
And so let's leave her to her silent walks.
CHIRON If 'twere my cause, I should go hang myself.

DEMETRIUS If you had hands to help you knit the cord.
                              *Exeunt Demetrius and Chiron*

                    *Enter Marcus, from hunting*

MARCUS Who is this? my niece, that flies away so fast!
  My niece, a word: where is your husband?
  If I do dream, would all my wealth would wake me!
  If I do wake, some planet strike me down,
  That I may slumber an eternal sleep!
  Speak, gentle niece, what stern ungentle hand
  Has lopped and hewed and made your body bare
  Of her two branches, those sweet ornaments
  Whose circling shadows kings have sought to sleep in,
  And might not gain so great a happiness
  As half your love? Why do you not speak to me?
  Alas, a crimson river of warm blood,
  Like to a bubbling fountain stirred with wind,
  Does rise and fall between your rosèd lips,
  Coming and going with your honey breath.
  But sure some Tereus has deflowerèd you,
  And, lest you should detect him, cut your tongue.
  Ah, now you turn away your face for shame,
  And, notwithstanding all this loss of blood,
  As from a conduit with three issuing spouts,
  Yet do your cheeks look red as Titan's face
  Blushing to be encountered with a cloud.
  Shall I speak for you? Shall I say 'tis so?
  O that I knew your heart, and knew the beast,
  That I might rail at him to ease my mind!
  Sorrow concealèd, like an oven stopped,
  Does burn the heart to cinders where it is.
  Fair Philomel, why she but lost her tongue,
  And in a tedious sampler sewed her mind:
  But, lovely niece, that mean is cut from you;
  A craftier Tereus, Lavinia, have you met,

And he has cut those pretty fingers off
That could have better sewed than Philomel.
O, had the monster seen those lily hands
Tremble like aspen leaves upon a lute
And make the silken strings delight to kiss them,
He would not then have touched them for his life.
Or had he heard the heavenly harmony
Which that sweet tongue has made,
He would have dropped his knife, and fallen asleep,
As Cerberus at the Thracian poet's feet.
Come, let us go and make your father blind,
For such a sight will blind a father's eye.
One hour's storm will drown the fragrant meads;
What will whole months of tears your father's eyes?
Do not draw back, for we will mourn with thee:
O, could our mourning ease your misery!          *Exeunt*

# Act III

## SCENE I
### Rome. A street.

*Enter Judges and Senators, with Martius and
Quintus, bound, passing to the place of execution,
Titus going before, pleading*

TITUS Hear me, grave fathers! noble tribunes, stay,
For pity of my age, whose youth was spent
In dangerous wars while you securely slept;
For all my blood in Rome's great quarrel shed,
For all the frosty nights that I have watched,
And for these bitter tears which now you see
Filling the agèd wrinkles in my cheeks—
Be pitiful to my condemnèd sons,
Whose souls are not corrupted as is thought.
For two and twenty sons I never wept,
Because they died in honour's lofty bed.

*Andronicus lies down, the Judges pass by*

For these, tribunes, in the dust I write
My heart's deep languor and my soul's sad tears.
Let my tears staunch the earth's dry appetite;
My sons' sweet blood will make it shame and blush.
O earth, I will befriend you more with rain
That shall distill from these two ancient eyes
Than youthful April shall with all its showers.
In summer's drought I'll drop upon you still,
In winter with warm tears I'll melt the snow,

And keep eternal spring-time on your face,
So you refuse to drink my dear sons' blood.

*Enter Lucius, with his weapon drawn*

O reverent tribunes! O gentle agèd men!
Unbind my sons, reverse the doom of death;
And let me say, that never wept before,
My tears are now prevailing orators!
LUCIUS O noble father, you lament in vain,
   The tribunes hear you not; no man is by,
   And you recount your sorrows to a stone.
TITUS Ah, Lucius, for your brothers let me plead.
   Grave tribunes, once more I entreat of you—
LUCIUS My gracious lord, no tribune hears you speak.
TITUS It is no matter, man: if they did hear,
   They would not mark me; or if they did mark,
   They would not pity me; yet plead I must,
   And useless unto them.
   Therefore I tell my sorrows to the stones,
   Who, though they cannot answer my distress,
   Yet in some sort they are better than the tribunes,
   Because they will not intercept my tale.
   When I do weep, they humbly at my feet
   Receive my tears and seem to weep with me;
   And were they but attirèd in grave dress,
   Rome could afford no tribunes like to these.
   A stone is soft as wax, tribunes more hard than stones:
   A stone is silent and offends us not,
   And tribunes with their tongues doom men to death.

*Rises*

But wherefore stand you with your weapon drawn?
LUCIUS To rescue my two brothers from their death;
   For which attempt the judges have pronounced

My everlasting doom of banishment.
TITUS O happy man! they have befriended you.
　Why, foolish Lucius, do you not perceive
　That Rome is but a wilderness of tigers?
　Tigers must prey, and Rome affords no prey
　But me and mine: how happy are you then
　From these devourers to be banishèd!
　But who comes with our brother Marcus here?

*Enter Marcus with Lavinia*

MARCUS Titus, prepare your agèd eyes to weep,
　Or if not so, your noble heart to break!
　I bring consuming sorrow to your age.
TITUS Will it consume me? let me see it then.
MARCUS This was your daughter.
TITUS 　　　　　　　　　　Why, Marcus, so she is.
LUCIUS Ay me, this object kills me!
TITUS Faint-hearted boy, arise and look upon her.
　Speak, Lavinia, what accursèd hand
　Has made you handless in your father's sight?
　What fool has added water to the sea
　Or brought a fagot to bright-burning Troy?
　My grief was at the height before you came,
　And now like Nilus it disdains its bounds.
　Give me a sword: I'll chop off my hands too;
　For they have fought for Rome, and all in vain;
　And they have nursed this woe in feeding life;
　In fruitless prayer have they been held up,
　And they have served me to effectless use.
　Now all the service I require of them
　Is that the one will help to cut the other.
　'Tis well, Lavinia, that you have no hands;
　For hands to do Rome service is but vain.
LUCIUS Speak, gentle sister, who has martyred you?
MARCUS O, that delightful engine of her thoughts

That blabbed them with such pleasing eloquence
Is torn from forth that pretty hollow cage,
Where like a sweet melodious bird it sang
Sweet varied notes, enchanting every ear!
LUCIUS O, say you for her, who has done this deed?
MARCUS O, thus I found her straying in the park,
Seeking to hide herself, as does the deer
That has received some incurable wound.
TITUS It was my deer, and he that wounded her
Has hurt me more than had he killed me dead;
For now I stand as one upon a rock,
Environed with a wilderness of sea,
Who marks the waxing tide grow wave by wave,
Expecting ever when some envious surge
Will in his brinish bowels swallow him.
This way to death my wretched sons are gone;
Here stands my other son, a banished man,
And here my brother, weeping at my woes:
But that which gives my soul the greatest blow
Is dear Lavinia, dearer than my soul.
Had I but seen your picture in this plight,
It would have maddened me: what shall I do
Now I behold your lively body so?
You have no hands to wipe away your tears,
Nor tongue to tell me who has martyred you.
Your husband he is dead, and for his death
Your brothers are condemned, and dead by this.
Look, Marcus! ah, son Lucius, look on her!
When I did name her brothers, then fresh tears
Stood on her cheeks, as does the honeydew
Upon a gathered lily almost withered.
MARCUS Perchance she weeps because they killed her
husband;
Perchance because she knows them innocent.
TITUS If they did kill your husband, then be joyful,
Because the law has taken revenge on them.

No, no, they would not do so foul a deed;
Witness the sorrow that their sister makes.
Gentle Lavinia, let me kiss your lips,
Or make some sign how I may do you ease.
Shall your good uncle and your brother Lucius
And you and I sit round about some fountain,
Looking all downwards to behold our cheeks
How they are stained, like meadows yet not dry
With miry slime left on them by a flood?
And in the fountain shall we gaze so long
Till the fresh taste be taken from that clearness,
And made a brine-pit with our bitter tears?
Or shall we cut away our hands like yours?
Or shall we bite our tongues, and in dumb shows
Pass the remainder of our hateful days?
What shall we do? let us that have our tongues
Plot some device of further misery,
To make us wondered at in time to come.

LUCIUS Sweet father, cease your tears; for at your grief
See how my wretched sister sobs and weeps.

MARCUS Patience, dear niece. Good Titus, dry your eyes.

TITUS Ah, Marcus, Marcus! brother, well I know
Your napkin cannot drink a tear of mine,
For you, poor man, have drowned it with your own.

LUCIUS Ah, my Lavinia, I will wipe your cheeks.

TITUS Mark, Marcus, mark! I understand her signs:
Had she a tongue to speak, now would she say
That to her brother which I said to you.
His napkin, with his true tears all bewet,
Can do no service on her sorrowful cheeks.
O, what a sympathy of woe is this:
As far from help as Limbo is from bliss!

*Enter Aaron*

AARON Titus Andronicus, my lord the emperor

Sends you this word, that, if you love your sons,
Let Marcus, Lucius, or yourself, old Titus,
Or any one of you, chop off your hand
And send it to the king: he for the same
Will send you hither both your sons alive;
And that shall be the ransom for their fault.
TITUS O gracious emperor! O gentle Aaron!
Did ever raven sing so like a lark
That gives sweet tidings of the sun's uprise?
With all my heart I'll send the emperor my hand.
Good Aaron, will you help to chop it off?
LUCIUS Stay, father, for that noble hand of yours
That has thrown down so many enemies,
Shall not be sent: my hand will serve the turn,
My youth can better spare my blood than you,
And therefore mine shall save my brothers' lives.
MARCUS Which of your hands has not defended Rome
And reared aloft the bloody battle-axe,
Writing destruction on the enemy's castle?
O, none of both but is of high desert:
My hand has been but idle; let it serve
To ransom my two nephews from their death;
Then have I kept it to a worthy end.
AARON Nay, come, agree whose hand shall go along,
For fear they die before their pardon comes.
MARCUS My hand shall go.
LUCIUS                          By heaven, it shall not go!
TITUS Sirs, strive no more. Such withered herbs as these
Are meet for plucking up, and therefore mine.
LUCIUS Sweet father, if I shall be thought your son,
Let me redeem my brothers both from death.
MARCUS And for our father's sake and mother's care,
Now let me show a brother's love to you.
TITUS Agree between you; I will spare my hand.
LUCIUS Then I'll go fetch an axe.
MARCUS But I will use the axe.

                     *Exeunt Lucius and Marcus*

TITUS Come hither, Aaron. I'll deceive them both:
   Lend me your hand, and I will give you mine.
AARON (*aside*) If that is called deceit, I will be honest,
   And never while I live deceive men so:
   But I'll deceive you in another sort,
   And that you'll say ere half an hour shall pass.

            *He cuts off Titus' hand.*
        *Enter Lucius and Marcus again*

TITUS Now stay your strife; what shall be is dispatched.
   Good Aaron, give his majesty my hand:
   Tell him it was a hand that warded him
   From thousand dangers; bid him bury it;
   More has it merited, that let it have.
   As for my sons, say I account of them
   As jewels purchased at an easy price;
   And yet dear too, because I bought my own.
AARON I go, Andronicus; and for your hand
   Look by and by to have your sons with you.
   (*Aside*) Their heads, I mean. O, how this villainy
   Does fat me with the very thought of it!
   Let fools do good, and fair men call for grace,
   Aaron will have his soul black like his face.     *Exit*
TITUS O, here I lift this one hand up to heaven,
   And bow this feeble ruin to the earth.
   If any powër pities wretched tears,
   To that I call! (*To Lavinia*) What, would you kneel with
     me?
   Do then, dear heart; for heaven shall hear our prayers,
   Or with our sighs we'll breathe the heavens dim
   And stain the sun with fog, as sometimes clouds
   When they do hug it in their melting bosoms.
MARCUS O brother, speak with possibility,
   And do not break into these deep extremes.

TITUS Is not my sorrow deep, having no bottom?
    Then be my passions bottomless with them!
MARCUS But yet let reason govern your lament.
TITUS If there were reason for these miseries,
    Then into limits could I bind my woes:
    When heaven does weep, does not the earth o'erflow?
    If the winds rage, does not the sea wax mad,
    Threatening the heavens with its swollen face?
    And will you have a reason for this trouble?
    I am the sea; hark how her sighs do flow!
    She is the weeping heaven, I the earth:
    Then must my sea be movèd with her sighs;
    Then must my earth with her continual tears
    Become a deluge, overflowed and drowned,
    For this my bowels cannot hide her woes,
    But like a drunkard must I vomit them.
    Then give me leave; for losers will have leave
    To ease their stomachs with their bitter tongues.

*Enter a Messenger, with two heads and a hand*

MESSENGER Worthy Andronicus, ill are you repaid
    For that good hand you sent the emperor.
    Here are the heads of your two noble sons,
    And here's your hand, in scorn to you sent back,
    Your grief their sports, your resolution mocked,
    That woe is me to think upon your woes
    More than remembrance of my father's death.        *Exit*
MARCUS Now let hot Etna cool in Sicily,
    And be my heart an ever-burning hell!
    These miseries are more than may be borne.
    To weep with them that weep does ease somewhat;
    But sorrow flouted at is double death.
LUCIUS Ah, that this sight should make so deep a wound,
    And yet detested life not shrink thereat;

That ever death should let life bear his name
Where life has no more interest but to breathe!

*Lavinia kisses Titus*

MARCUS Alas, poor heart, that kiss is comfortless
  As frozen water to a starvèd snake.
TITUS When will this fearful slumber have an end?
MARCUS Now farewell, flattery; die, Andronicus;
  You do not slumber: see your two sons' heads,
  Your warlike hand, your mangled daughter here,
  Your other banished son with this dear sight
  Struck pale and bloodless, and your brother, I,
  Even like a stony image, cold and numb.
  Ah, now no more will I control your griefs:
  Rend off your silver hair, your other hand
  Gnawing with your teeth; and be this dismal sight
  The closing up of our most wretched eyes.
  Now is a time to storm; why are you still?
TITUS Ha, ha, ha!
MARCUS Why do you laugh? it fits not with this hour.
TITUS Why, I have not another tear to shed;
  Besides, this sorrow is an enemy,
  And would usurp upon my watery eyes
  And make them blind with tributary tears.
  Then which way shall I find Revenge's cave?
  For these two heads do seem to speak to me,
  And threaten me I shall never come to bliss
  Till all these mischiefs be returned again
  Even in their throats that have committed them.
  Come, let me see what task I have to do.
  You heavy people, circle me about,
  That I may turn me to each one of you
  And swear unto my soul to right your wrongs.
  The vow is made. Come, brother, take a head;
  And in this hand the other will I bear.
  Lavinia, you shall be employed in this:

Bear you my hand, sweet wench, between your teeth.
As for you, boy, go get you from my sight,
You are an exile, and you must not stay.
Hie to the Goths and raise an army there;
And if you love me, as I think you do,
Let's kiss and part, for we have much to do.

*Exeunt all except Lucius*

LUCIUS Farewell, Andronicus, my noble father,
The woefullest man that ever lived in Rome.
Farewell, proud Rome, till Lucius comes again!
He loves his pledges dearer than his life.
Farewell, Lavinia, my noble sister.
O, would you were as you tofore have been!
But now not Lucius nor Lavinia lives
But in oblivion and hateful griefs.
If Lucius lives he will requite your wrongs
And make proud Saturnine and his empress
Beg at the gates like Tarquin and his queen.
Now will I to the Goths and raise a force,
To be revenged on Rome and Saturnine.     *Exit Lucius*


# SCENE II
## Rome. A room in Titus' house.

*A banquet. Enter Andronicus, Marcus, Lavinia,*
*and the Boy Lucius*

TITUS So, so, now sit; and look you eat no more
Than will preserve just so much strength in us
As will revenge these bitter woes of ours.
Marcus, unknit that sorrow-wreathen knot:
Your niece and I, poor creatures, want our hands,
And cannot passionate our tenfold grief
With folded arms. This poor right hand of mine
Is left to tyrannize upon my breath;

Which, when my heart, all mad with misery,
Beats in this hollow prison of my flesh,
Then thus I thump it down.
(*To Lavinia*) You map of woe, that thus do talk in signs,
When your poor heart beats with outrageous beating,
You can not strike it thus to make it still.
Wound it with sighing, girl, kill it with groans;
Or get some little knife between your teeth
And just against your heart make you a hole,
That all the tears that your poor eyes let fall
May run into that sink, and soaking in,
Drown the lamenting fool in sea-salt tears.

MARCUS Fie, brother, fie! teach her not thus to lay
Such violent hands upon her tender life.

TITUS How now! has sorrow made you dote already?
Why, Marcus, no man should be mad but I.
What violent hands can she lay on her life?
Ah, wherefore do you urge the name of hands,
To bid Aeneas tell the tale twice over,
How Troy was burnt and he made miserable?
O, handle not the theme, to talk of hands,
Lest we remember still that we have none.
Fie, fie, how franticly I square my talk,
As if we should forget we had no hands
If Marcus did not name the word of hands!
Come, let's fall to; and, gentle girl, eat this.
Here is no drink! hark, Marcus, what she says.
I can interpret all her martyred signs:
She says she drinks no other drink but tears,
Brewed with her sorrow, meshed upon her cheeks.
Speechless complainer, I will learn your thought.
In your dumb action will I be as perfect
As begging hermits in their holy prayers.
You shall not sigh, nor hold your stumps to heaven,
Nor wink, nor nod, nor kneel, nor make a sign,
But I of these will wrest an alphabet
And by still practice learn to know your meaning.

BOY Good grandsire, leave these bitter deep laments.
　Make my aunt merry with some pleasing tale.
MARCUS Alas, the tender boy, in passion moved,
　Does weep to see his grandsire's heaviness.
TITUS Peace, tender sapling, you are made of tears,
　And tears will quickly melt your life away.

*Marcus strikes the dish with a knife*

What do you strike at, Marcus, with your knife?
MARCUS At that that I have killed, my lord—a fly.
TITUS Out on you, murderer! You kill my heart;
　My eyes are cloyed with view of tyranny.
　A deed of death done on the innocent
　Becomes not Titus' brother. Get you gone!
　I see you are not for my company.
MARCUS Alas, my lord, I have but killed a fly.
TITUS But? How if that fly had a father and mother?
　How would he hang his slender gilded wings
　And buzz lamenting doings in the air!
　Poor harmless fly,
　That, with his pretty buzzing melody,
　Came here to make us merry, and you have killed him.
MARCUS Pardon me, sir; it was a black ill-looking fly,
　Like to the empress' Moor; therefore I killed him.
TITUS O, O, O!
　Then pardon me for reprehending you,
　For you have done a charitable deed.
　Give me your knife, I will insult on him,
　Flattering myself as if it were the Moor
　Come hither purposely to poison me.
　There's for yourself, and that's for Tamora.
　Ah, villain!
　Yet, I think, we are not brought so low
　But that between us we can kill a fly
　That comes in likeness of a coal-black Moor.

MARCUS Alas, poor man! Grief has so wrought on him
  He takes false shadows for true substances.
TITUS Come, clear away. Lavinia, go with me.
  I'll to your closet and go read with you
  Sad stories chancèd in the times of old.
  Come, boy, and go with me. Your sight is young,
  And you shall read when mine begins to dazzle.

                                               *Exeunt*

# Act IV

## SCENE I
### Before Titus' house.

*Enter Lucius' Son and Lavinia running after him;*
*the Boy flies from her with his books under his arm.*
*Enter Titus and Marcus*

BOY Help, grandsire, help! My aunt Lavinia
  Follows me everywhere, I know not why.
  Good uncle Marcus, see how swift she comes:
  Alas, sweet aunt, I know not what you mean.
MARCUS Stand by me, Lucius; do not fear your aunt.
TITUS She loves you, boy, too well to do you harm.
BOY Ay, when my father was in Rome she did.
MARCUS What means my niece Lavinia by these signs?
TITUS Fear her not, Lucius. Somewhat does she mean.
  See, Lucius, see, how much she makes of you:
  Somewhither would she have you go with her.
  Ah, boy, Cornelia never with more care
  Read to her sons than she has read to you
  Sweet poetry and Tully's Orator.
MARCUS Can you not guess wherefore she plies you thus?
BOY My lord, I know not, I, nor can I guess,
  Unless some fit or frenzy does possess her.
  For I have heard my grandsire say full oft,
  Extremity of griefs would make men mad;
  And I have read that Hecuba of Troy
  Ran mad for sorrow. That made me to fear,
  Although, my lord, I know my noble aunt
  Loves me as dear as ever my mother did,

And would not, but in fury, fright my youth;
Which made me down to throw my books, and fly,
Causeless, perhaps, but pardon me, sweet aunt.
And, madam, if my uncle Marcus goes,
I will most willingly attend your ladyship.
MARCUS Lucius, I will.

*Lavinia turns over with her stumps the books*
*which Lucius has let fall*

TITUS How now, Lavinia? Marcus, what means this?
Some book there is that she desires to see.
Which is it, girl, of these? Open them, boy.
But you are deeper read and better skilled:
Come and take choice of all my library,
And so beguile your sorrow, till the heavens
Reveal the damned contriver of this deed.
Why lifts she up her arms in sequence thus?
MARCUS I think she means that there were more than one
Confederate in the fact. Ay, more there were;
Or else to heaven she heaves them for revenge.
TITUS Lucius, what book is that she tosses so?
BOY Grandsire, 'tis Ovid's Metamorphoses.
My mother gave it me.
MARCUS                          For love of her that's gone
Perhaps she culled it from among the rest.
TITUS Soft; so busily she turns the leaves!
Help her: what would she find? Lavinia, shall I read?
This is the tragic tale of Philomel
And treats of Tereus' treason and his rape;
And rape, I fear, was root of your annoy.
MARCUS See, brother, see, note how she notes the leaves.
TITUS Lavinia, were you thus surprised, sweet girl,
Ravished and wronged as Philomèla was,
Forced in the ruthless, vast, and gloomy woods?
See, see!

Ay, such a place there is where we did hunt
(O had we never, never hunted there!)
Patterned by that the poet here describes,
By nature made for murders and for rapes.
MARCUS O, why should nature build so foul a den,
    Unless the gods delight in tragedies?
TITUS Give signs, sweet girl, for here are none but friends,
    What Roman lord it was durst do the deed.
    Or slunk not Saturnine, as Tarquin once,
    That left the camp to sin in Lucrece' bed?
MARCUS Sit down, sweet niece: brother, sit down by me.
    Apollo, Pallas, Jove, or Mercury,
    Inspire me, that I may this treason find.
    My lord, look here: look here, Lavinia!

*He writes his name with his staff, and guides it*
*with feet and mouth*

This sandy plot is plain; guide, if you can,
This after me. I have writ my name
Without the help of any hand at all.
Cursed be that heart that forced us to this shift!
Write you, good niece, and here display at last
What God will have discovered for revenge.
Heaven guide your pen to print your sorrows plain,
That we may know the traitors and the truth.

*She takes the staff in her mouth, guides it*
*with her stumps and writes*

TITUS O, do you read, my lord, what she has written?
    'Stuprum.[1] Chiron. Demetrius.'
MARCUS What, what! the lustful sons of Tamora
    Performers of this heinous bloody deed?

---

[1]Rape.

TITUS 'Magni dominator poli,
　　Tam lentus audis scelera? tam lentus vides?'2
MARCUS O, calm you, gentle lord! although I know
　　There is enough written upon this earth
　　To stir a mutiny in the mildest thoughts
　　And arm the minds of infants to exclaim.
　　My lord, kneel down with me; Lavinia, kneel;
　　And kneel, sweet boy, the Roman Hector's hope;
　　And swear with me, as with the woeful spouse
　　And father of that chaste dishonored dame,
　　Lord Junius Brutus swore for Lucrece' rape—
　　That we will prosecute by good advice
　　Mortal revenge upon these traitorous Goths,
　　And see their blood or die with this reproach.
TITUS 'Tis sure enough, if you knew how,
　　But if you hunt these bear-whelps, then beware:
　　The dam will wake, if she does wind you once;
　　She's with the lion deeply still in league,
　　And lulls him while she plays upon her back,
　　And when he sleeps will she do what she likes.
　　You are a young huntsman, Marcus; let alone;
　　And come, I will go get a leaf of brass,
　　And with a gad of steel will write these words,
　　And lay it by: the angry northern wind
　　Will blow these sands like Sibyl's leaves abroad,
　　And where's our lesson then? Boy, what say you?
BOY I say, my lord, that if I were a man,
　　Their mother's bedchamber should not be safe
　　For these base bondmen to the yoke of Rome.
MARCUS Ay, that's my boy! your father has full oft
　　For his ungrateful country done the like.
BOY And, uncle, so will I, if I do live.
TITUS Come, go with me into my armoury:

---

2Ruler of the great Pole, are you so slow to hear and see
crimes?

Lucius, I'll fit you; and with that my boy
Shall carry from me to the empress' sons
Presents that I intend to send them both.
Come, come; you'll do my message, will you not?
BOY Ay, with my dagger in their bosoms, grandsire.
TITUS No, boy, not so. I'll teach you another course.
Lavinia, come. Marcus, look to my house.
Lucius and I'll go brave it at the Court.
Ay, indeed, will we, sir; and we'll be waited on.
                    *Exeunt Titus, Lavinia, and Young Lucius*
MARCUS O heavens, can you hear a good man groan
And not relent, or not compassion him?
Marcus, attend him in his frenzied mood,
That has more scars of sorrow in his heart
Than foemen's marks upon his battered shield,
But yet so just that he will not revenge.
Revenge the heavens for old Andronicus!            *Exit*


# SCENE II
## The palace.

*Enter Aaron, Chiron, and Demetrius at one door, and at
the other door Young Lucius and another, with a bundle
of weapons, and verses written upon them*

CHIRON Demetrius, here's the son of Lucius;
He has some message to deliver us.
AARON Ay, some mad message from his mad grandfather.
BOY My lords, with all the humbleness I may,
I greet your honours from Andronicus—
(*Aside*) And pray the Roman gods confound you both.
DEMETRIUS Thank you, lovely Lucius, what's the news?
BOY (*aside*) That you are both deciphered, that's the news,
For villains marked with rape. (*Aloud*) May it please
you,

My grandsire, well-advised, has sent by me
The goodliest weapons of his armoury
To gratify your honourable youth,
The hope of Rome, for so he bid me say,
And so I do, and with his gifts present
Your lordships, that, whenever you have need,
You may be armèd and appointed well.
And so I leave you both — (*aside*) like bloody villains.
*Exit with Attendant*

DEMETRIUS What's here? a scroll, and written round about?
Let's see.
'Integer vitae scelerisque purus
Non eget Mauri iaculis nec arcu.'[3]

CHIRON O, 'tis a verse in Horace; I know it well.
I read it in the grammar long ago.

AARON Ay, just; a verse in Horace; right, you have it.
(*Aside*) Now what a thing it is to be an ass!
Here's no sound jest! the old man has found their guilt,
And sends them weapons wrapped about with lines
That wound, beyond their feeling, to the quick.
But were our witty empress well afoot,
She would applaud Andronicus' device.
But let her rest in her unrest awhile.
And now, young lords, was it not a happy star
Led us to Rome, strangers, and more than so,
Captives, to be advancèd to this height?
It did me good before the palace gate
To brave the tribune in his brother's hearing.

DEMETRIUS But me more good to see so great a lord
Basely propitiate and send us gifts.

AARON Had he not reason, Lord Demetrius?
Did you not use his daughter very friendly?

DEMETRIUS I would we had a thousand Roman dames

---

[3]He who is of upright life and free from crime needs not
the Moor's javelins or his bow.

At such a pass, by turn to serve our lust.
CHIRON A charitable wish and full of love!
AARON Here lacks but your mother then to say amen.
CHIRON And that would she for twenty thousand more.
DEMETRIUS Come, let us go and pray to all the gods
    For our belovèd mother in her pains.
AARON (*aside*) Pray to the devils; the gods have given us
    over.

*Trumpets sound*

DEMETRIUS Why do the emperor's trumpets flourish thus?
CHIRON Perhaps for joy the emperor has a son.
DEMETRIUS Soft, who comes here?

*Enter Nurse, with a blackamoor Child*

NURSE                        Good morrow, lords.
    O, tell me, did you see Aaron the Moor?
AARON Well, more or less, or never a whit at all,
    Here Aaron is; and what with Aaron now?
NURSE O gentle Aaron, we are all undone!
    Now help, or woe betide you evermore!
AARON Why, what a caterwauling do you keep!
    What do you wrap and fumble in your arms?
NURSE O, that which I would hide from heaven's eye—
    Our empress' shame and stately Rome's disgrace!
    She is delivered, lords, she is delivered.
AARON To whom?
NURSE          I mean she is brought a-bed.
AARON Well, God give her good rest! What has he sent
    her?
NURSE A devil.
AARON        Why, then she is the devil's dam:
    A joyful issue!
NURSE A joyless, dismal, black, and sorrowful issue!

Here is the babe, as loathsome as a toad
Among the fair-faced breeders of our clime.
The empress sends it you, your stamp, your seal,
And bids you christen it with your dagger's point.
AARON Curse! you whore! is black so base a hue?
Sweet wench, you are a beauteous blossom sure.
DEMETRIUS Villain, what have you done?
AARON That which you can not undo.
CHIRON You have undone our mother.
AARON Villain, I have done your mother.
DEMETRIUS And therein, hellish dog, you have undone
   her.
Woe to her chance, and damned her loathèd choice!
Accursed the offspring of so foul a fiend!
CHIRON It shall not live.
AARON It shall not die.
NURSE Aaron, it must; the mother wills it so.
AARON What, must it, nurse? then let no man but I
Do execution on my flesh and blood.
DEMETRIUS I'll broach the tadpole on my rapier's point.
Nurse, give it me; my sword shall soon dispatch it.
AARON Sooner this sword shall plough your bowels up.
Stay, murderous villains! will you kill your brother?
Now by the burning tapers of the sky,
That shone so brightly when this boy was got,
He dies upon my scimitar's sharp point
That touches this my first-born son and heir!
I tell you, young, not Encèladus,
With all his threatening band of Typhon's brood,
Nor great Alcìdes, nor the god of war,
Shall seize this prey out of his father's hands.
What, what, you ruddy, shallow-hearted boys!
You white-limed walls! you alehouse painted signs!
Coal-black is better than another hue
In that it scorns to bear another hue;
For all the water in the oceàn

Can never turn the swan's black legs to white,
Although she laves them hourly in the flood.
Tell the empress from me I am of age
To keep my own, excuse it how she can.
DEMETRIUS Will you betray your noble mistress thus?
AARON My mistress is my mistress; this myself,
    The vigor and the picture of my youth.
    This before all the world do I prefer.
    This despite the world will I keep safe,
    Or some of you shall smoke for it in Rome!
DEMETRIUS By this our mother is for ever shamed.
CHIRON Rome will despise her for this foul escape.
NURSE The emperor in his rage will doom her death.
CHIRON I blush to think upon this ignominy.
AARON Why, there's the privilege your beauty bears.
    Fie, treacherous hue, that will betray with blushing
    The closest acts and counsels of your heart!
    Here's a young lad framed of another look,
    Look how the black slave smiles upon the father,
    As who should say 'Old lad, I am your own.'
    He is your brother, lords, sensibly fed
    Of that self blood that first gave life to you;
    And from that womb where you imprisoned were
    He is enfranchisèd and come to light.
    Nay, he is your brother by the surer side,
    Although my seal be stampèd in his face.
NURSE Aaron, what shall I say unto the empress?
DEMETRIUS Advise you? Aaron, what is to be done,
    And we will all subscribe to your advice:
    Save you the child, if we may all be safe.
AARON Then sit we down and let us all consult.
    My son and I will have the wind of you:
    Keep there; now talk at pleasure of your safety.
DEMETRIUS How many women saw this child of his?
AARON Why, so, brave lords! when we join in league,
    I am a lamb; but if you brave the Moor,

The angry boar, the mountain lioness,
The ocean swells not so as Aaron storms.
But say again, how many saw the child?
NURSE Cornelia the midwife and myself,
And no one else but the delivered empress.
AARON The emperess, the midwife, and yourself:
Two may keep counsel when the third's away.
Go to the empress, tell her this I said.        *He kills her*
Week, week!
So cries a pig preparèd to the spit.
DEMETRIUS What mean you, Aaron? wherefore did you
    this?
AARON O Lord, sir, 'tis a deed of policy!
Shall she live to betray this guilt of ours,
A long-tongued babbling gossip? no, lords, no.
And now be it known to you my full intent.
Not far, one Mùliteus my countryman
His wife but yesternight was brought to bed;
His child is like to her, fair as you are.
Go fix with him, and give the mother gold,
And tell them both the circumstance of all;
And how by this their child shall be advanced,
And be receivèd for the emperor's heir
And substituted in the place of mine,
To calm this tempest whirling in the Court;
And let the emperor dandle him for his own.
Hark you, lords: you see I have given her physic,
And you must needs bestow her funeral.
The fields are near, and you are gallant grooms.
This done, see that you take no longer days,
But send the midwife presently to me.
The midwife and the nurse well made away,
Then let the ladies tattle what they please.
CHIRON Aaron, I see you will not trust the air
With secrets.
DEMETRIUS        For this care of Tamora,

Herself and hers are highly bound to you.
    *Exeunt Demetrius and Chiron, bearing off the body*
AARON Now to the Goths, as swift as swallow flies,
  There to dispose this treasure in my arms
  And secretly to greet the empress' friends.
  Come on, you thick-lipped slave, I'll bear you hence;
  For it is you that puts us to our shifts.
  I'll make you feed on berries and on roots,
  And feed on curds and whey, and suck the goat,
  And cabin in a cave, and bring you up
  To be a warrior and command a camp.        *Exit*


## SCENE III
### Before the palace.

*Enter Titus, Old Marcus, Young Lucius, and
others, with bows; Titus bears the arrows with letters
on the ends of them*

TITUS Come, Marcus, come; kinsmen, this is the way.
  Sir boy, let me see your archery:
  Look you draw home enough, and 'tis there straight.
  'Terras Astraea reliquit.'[4]
  Be you remembered, Marcus. She's gone, she's fled.
  Sirs, take you to your tools. You, cousins, shall
  Go sound the oceàn, and cast your nets;
  Happily you may catch her in the sea.
  Yet there's as little justice as at land.
  No, Publius and Sempronius, you must do it.
  'Tis you must dig with mattock and with spade
  And pierce the inmost centre of the earth;
  Then, when you come to Pluto's regiòn,
  I pray you deliver him this petition.

---

[4]Astraea, goddess of justice has left the earth.

Tell him it is for justice and for aid,
And that it comes from old Andronicus,
Shaken with sorrows in ungrateful Rome.
Ah, Rome! Well, well, I made you miserable
What time I threw the people's suffrages
On him that thus does tyrannize o'er me.
Go, get you gone, and pray be careful all,
And leave you not a man-of-war unsearched:
This wicked emperor may have shipped her hence;
And, kinsmen, then we may go pipe for justice.
MARCUS O Publius, is not this a heavy case,
  To see your noble uncle thus distract?
PUBLIUS Therefore, my lords, it highly us concerns
  By day and night to attend him carefully,
  And feed his humor kindly as we may,
  Till time begets some careful remedy.
MARCUS Kinsmen, his sorrows are past remedy.
  Join with the Goths, and with revengeful war
  Wreak it on Rome for this ingratitude,
  And vengeance on the traitor Saturnine.
TITUS Publius, how now? how now, my masters?
  What, have you met with her?
PUBLIUS No, my good lord; but Pluto sends you word,
  If you will have Revenge from hell, you shall.
  Sure, for Justice, she is so employed,
  He thinks, with Jove in heaven, or somewhere else,
  So that perforce you must needs stay a time.
TITUS He does me wrong to feed me with delays.
  I'll dive into the burning lake below,
  And pull her out of Acheron by the heels.
  Marcus, we are but shrubs, no cedars we,
  No big-boned men framed of the Cyclops' size;
  But metal, Marcus, steel to the very back,
  Yet wrung with wrongs more than our backs can bear;
  And, since there's no justice in earth nor hell,
  We will solicit heaven, and move the gods

To send down Justice to avenge our wrongs.
Come, to this task. You are a good archer, Marcus.

*He gives them the arrows*

'Ad Jovem,'[5] that's for you: here, 'ad Apollinem.'
'Ad Martem,' that's for myself.
Here, boy, 'to Pallas': here, 'to Mercury.'
'To Saturn,' Caius, not to Saturnine;
You were as good to shoot against the wind.
To it, boy! Marcus, loose when I bid.
Of my word, I have written to effect;
There's not a god left unsolicited.
MARCUS Kinsmen, shoot all your shafts into the Court:
We will afflict the emperor in his pride.
TITUS Now, masters, draw. O, well said, Lucius!
Good boy, in Virgo's lap; give it Pallas.
MARCUS My lord, I aim a mile beyond the moon.
Your letter is with Jupiter by this.
TITUS Ha, ha!
Publius, Publius, what have you done?
See, see, you have shot off one of Taurus' horns!
MARCUS This was the sport, my lord: when Publius shot,
The Bull, being galled, gave Aries such a knock
That down fell both the Ram's horns in the Court;
And who should find them but the empress' villain?
She laughed, and told the Moor he should not choose
But give them to his master for a present.
TITUS Why, there it goes! God give his lordship joy!

*Enter the Clown, with a basket, and two pigeons in it*

News, news from heaven! Marcus, the post is come.
Fellow, what tidings? Have you any letters?
Shall I have justice? what says Jupiter?

---

[5]To Jove, to Apollo, to Mars.

CLOWN Who? the gibbet-maker? He says that he has taken them down again, for the man must not be hanged till the next week.

TITUS But what says Jupiter I ask you?

CLOWN Alas, sir, I know not Jubiter; I never drank with him in all my life.

TITUS Why, villain, are not you the carrier?

CLOWN Ay, of my pigeons, sir; nothing else.

TITUS Why, did you not come from heaven?

CLOWN From heaven? alas, sir, I never came there. God forbid I should be so bold to press to heaven in my young days. Why, I am going with my pigeons to the tribunal plebs, to take up a matter of brawl betwixt my uncle and one of the emperal's men.

MARCUS Why, sir, that is as fit as can be to serve for your oration; and let him deliver the pigeons to the emperor from you.

TITUS Tell me, can you deliver an oration to the emperor with a grace?

CLOWN Nay, truly, sir, I could never say grace in all my life.

TITUS Fellow, come hither: make no more ado,
But give your pigeons to the emperor:
By me you shall have justice at his hands.
Hold, hold, meanwhile here's money for your charges.
Give me pen and ink.
Clown, can you with a grace deliver a supplication?

CLOWN Ay, sir.

TITUS Then here is a supplication for you. And when you come to him, at the first approach you must kneel; then kiss his foot; then deliver up your pigeons; and then look for your reward. I'll be at hand, sir: see you do it bravely.

CLOWN I warrant you, sir, let me alone.

TITUS Fellow, have you a knife? Come, let me see it.

Here, Marcus, fold it in the oratiòn;
For you have made it like an humble suppliant.
And when you have given it to the emperor,
Knock at my door and tell me what he says.
CLOWN God be with you, sir; I will.                    *Exit*
TITUS Come, Marcus, let us go. Publius, follow me.
                                                      *Exeunt*


# SCENE IV
## The same.

*Enter Saturninus and Tamora, and her two Sons.*
*Saturninus brings the arrows in his hand*
*that Titus shot at him*


SATURNINUS Why, lords, what wrongs are these! Was ever
    seen
    An emperor in Rome thus overborne,
    Troubled, confronted thus; and, for the extent
    Of equal justice, used in such contempt?
    My lords, you know, as know the mighty gods,
    However these disturbers of our peace
    Buzz in the people's ears, there naught has passed,
    But even with law, against the wilful sons
    Of old Andronicus. And whatever if
    His sorrows have so overwhelmed his wits?
    Shall we be thus afflicted in his wrath,
    His fits, his frenzy, and his bitterness?
    And now he writes to heaven for his redress.
    See, here's 'to Jove,' and this 'to Mercury';
    This 'to Apollo'; this 'to the god of war':
    Sweet scrolls to fly about the streets of Rome!
    What's this but libelling against the Senate
    And proclaiming our injustice everywhere?
    A goodly humour, is it not, my lords?

As who would say, in Rome no justice were.
But if I live, his feignèd madnesses
Shall be no shelter to these outrages;
But he and his shall know that justice lives
In Saturninus' health; who, if he sleeps,
He'll so awake as he in fury shall
Cut off the proudest conspirator that lives.
TAMORA My gracious lord, my lovely Saturnine,
    Lord of my life, commander of my thoughts,
    Calm you, and bear the faults of Titus' age,
    The effects of sorrow for his valiant sons,
    Whose loss has pierced him deep and scarred his heart;
    And rather comfort his distressèd plight
    Than prosecute the meanest or the best
    For these contempts. (*Aside*) Why, thus it shall become
    Clever Tamora to deceive them all.
    But, Titus, I have touched you to the quick;
    Your lifeblood out, if Aaron now is wise,
    Then is all safe, the anchor in the port.

*Enter Clown*

How now, good fellow? Would you speak with us?
CLOWN Yea, please, if your mistress-ship is emperial.
TAMORA Empress I am, but yonder sits the emperor.
CLOWN 'Tis he. God and Saint Stephen give you good day.
    I have brought you a letter and a couple of pigeons here.

*Saturninus reads the letter*

SATURNINUS Go take him away, and hang him at once.
CLOWN How much money must I have?
TAMORA Come, fellow, you must be hanged.
CLOWN Hanged? By our lady, then I have brought up a
    neck to a fair end.                                    *Exit*
SATURNINUS Despiteful and intolerable wrongs!

Shall I endure this monstrous villainy?
I know from whence this same device proceeds.
May this be borne as if his traitorous sons,
That died by law for murder of our brother,
Have by my means been butchered wrongfully?
Go drag the villain hither by the hair;
Not age nor honour shall shape privilege.
For this proud mock I'll be your slaughterman,
Sly frantic wretch, that helped to make me great
In hope yourself should govern Rome and me!

*Enter Aemilius*

What news with you, Aemilius?
AEMILIUS Arm, my lords! Rome never had more cause.
The Goths have gathered head, and with a body
Of high-resolvèd men, bent to the spoil,
They hither march in force, under conduct
Of Lucius, son to old Andronicus;
Who threats in course of this revenge to do
As much as ever Coriolanus did.
SATURNINUS Is warlike Lucius general of the Goths?
These tidings nip me, and I hang the head
As flowers with frost or grass beat down with storms.
Ay, now begin our sorrows to approach.
'Tis he the common people love so much;
Myself have often overheard them say,
When I have walkèd like a private man,
That Lucius' banishment was wrongfully,
And they have wished that Lucius were their emperor.
TAMORA Why should you fear? is not your city strong?
SATURNINUS Ay, but the citizens favour Lucius
And will revolt from me to succour him.
TAMORA King, be your thoughts imperious like your name.
Is the sun dimmed, that gnats do fly in it?
The eagle suffers little birds to sing,

And is not careful what they mean thereby,
Knowing that with the shadow of its wings
It can at pleasure stint their melody.
Even so may you the giddy men of Rome.
Then cheer your spirit; for know you, emperor,
I will enchant the old Andronicus
With words more sweet, and yet more dangerous,
Than baits to fish or clover stalks to sheep,
When as the one is wounded with the bait,
The other rotted with delicious feed.

SATURNINUS But he will not entreat his son for us.

TAMORA If Tamora entreats him, then he will;
For I can smooth, and fill his agèd ears
With golden promises, that, were his heart
Almost impregnable, his old ears deaf,
Yet should both ear and heart obey my tongue.
(*To Aemilius*) Go you before to be our ambassador;
Say that the emperor requests a parley
Of warlike Lucius, and appoint the meeting
Even at his father's house, the old Andronicus.

SATURNINUS Aemilius, do this message honorably,
And if he stands on hostage for his safety,
Bid him demand what pledge will please him best.

AEMILIUS Your bidding shall I do effectually.            *Exit*

TAMORA Now will I to that old Andronicus
And temper him with all the art I have,
To pluck proud Lucius from the warlike Goths.
And now, sweet emperor, be blithe again
And bury all your fear in my devices.

SATURNINUS Then go successfully, and plead to him.

                                                  *Exeunt*

# Act V

## SCENE I
### A plain near Rome.

*Enter Lucius, with an army of Goths*

LUCIUS Approvèd warriors and my faithful friends,
   I have receivèd letters from great Rome
   Which signify what hate they bear their emperor
   And how desirous of our sight they are.
   Therefore, great lords, be as your titles witness,
   Imperious, and impatient of your wrongs;
   And wherein Rome has done you any harm,
   Let him make treble satisfactiòn.
GOTH Brave slip sprung from the great Andronicus,
   Whose name was once our terror, now our comfort,
   Whose high exploits and honorable deeds
   Ungrateful Rome requites with foul contempt,
   Be bold in us: we'll follow where you lead,
   Like stinging bees in hottest summer's day,
   Led by their master to the flowered fields,
   And be avenged on cursèd Tamora.
GOTHS And as he says, so say we all with him.
LUCIUS I humbly thank him, and I thank you all.
   But who comes here, led by a lusty Goth?

*Enter a Goth, leading Aaron with his Child in his arms*

GOTH Renownèd Lucius, from our troops I strayed
   To gaze upon a ruinous monastery;
   And as I earnestly did fix my eye

Upon the wasted building, suddenly
I heard a child cry underneath a wall.
I made unto the noise, when soon I heard
The crying babe controlled with this discourse:
'Peace, tawny slave, half me and half your dame.
Did not your hue betray whose brat you are.
Had nature lent you but your mother's look,
Villain, you might have been an emperor:
But where the bull and cow are both milk-white,
They never do beget a coal-black calf.
Peace, villain, peace!' thus he berates the babe,
'For I must bear you to a trusty Goth,
Who, when he knows you are the empress' babe,
Will hold you dearly for your mother's sake.'
With this, my weapon drawn, I rushed upon him,
Surprised him suddenly, and brought him hither
To use as you think needful of the man.

LUCIUS O worthy Goth, this is the incarnate devil
That robbed Andronicus of his good hand:
This is the pearl that pleased your empress' eye;
And here's the base fruit of her burning lust.
Say, wall-eyed slave, whither would you convey
This growing image of your fiend-like face?
Why do you not speak? What, deaf? not a word?
A halter, soldiers! Hang him on this tree,
And by his side his fruit of bastardy.

AARON Touch not the boy, he is of royal blood.

LUCIUS Too like the sire for ever being good.
First hang the child, that he may see it sprawl!
A sight to vex the father's soul with all.
Get me a ladder.

*A ladder brought, which Aaron is made to climb*

AARON                Lucius, save the child,
And bear it from me to the empress.

If you do this, I'll show you wondrous things
That highly may advantage you to hear;
If you will not, befall what may befall,
I'll speak no more—but vengeance rot you all!
LUCIUS Say on; and if it please me what you speak,
Your child shall live, and I will see it nourished.
AARON And if it please you! why, assure you, Lucius,
'Twill vex your soul to hear what I shall speak;
For I must talk of murders, rapes, and massacres,
Acts of black night, abominable deeds,
Complots of mischief, treason, villainies
Ruthful to hear, yet piteously performed;
And this shall all be buried in my death
Unless you swear to me my child shall live.
LUCIUS Tell on your mind, I say your child shall live.
AARON Swear that he shall, and then I will begin.
LUCIUS Whom should I swear by? You believe no god.
That granted, how can you believe an oath?
AARON What if I do not? as indeed I do not.
Yet, for I know you are religiòus
And have a thing within you called conscience,
With twenty popish tricks and ceremonies
Which I have seen you careful to observe,
Therefore I urge your oath; because I know
An idiot holds his bauble for a god
And keeps the oath which by that god he swears.
To that I'll urge him: therefore you shall vow
By that same god, what god soever it be,
That you adore and have in reverence,
To save my boy, to nourish and bring him up,
Or else I will discover naught to you.
LUCIUS Even by my god I swear to you I will.
AARON First know you, I begot him on the empress.
LUCIUS O most insatiate and lustful woman!
AARON Tut, Lucius, this was but a deed of charity
To that which you shall hear of me anon:

'Twas her two sons that murdered Bassianus;
They cut your sister's tongue, and ravished her,
And cut her hands, and trimmed her as you saw.

LUCIUS O detestable villain! call you that trimming?

AARON Why, she was washed and cut and trimmed, and 'twas
Trim sport for them who had the doing of it.

LUCIUS O barbarous beastly villains like yourself!

AARON Indeed, I was their tutor to instruct them.
That lustful spirit had they from their mother,
As sure a card as ever won the set;
That bloody mind I think they learned of me,
As true a dog as ever fought at head.
Well, let my deeds be witness of my worth.
I trained your brethren to that guileful hole
Where the dead corpse of Bassianus lay.
I wrote the letter that your father found
And hid the gold within that letter mentioned,
Confederate with the queen and her two sons;
And what not done, that you have cause to rue,
Wherein I had no stroke of mischief in it?
I played the cheater for your father's hand,
And when I had it, drew myself apart
And almost broke my heart with extreme laughter.
I pried me through the crevice of a wall
When for his hand he had his two sons' heads,
Beheld his tears, and laughed so heartily
That both my eyes were rainy like to his.
And when I told the empress of this sport,
She swooned almost upon my pleasing tale
And for my tidings gave me twenty kisses.

GOTH What, can you say all this and never blush?

AARON Ay, like a black dog, as the saying is.

LUCIUS Are you not sorry for these heinous deeds?

AARON Ay, that I had not done a thousand more.
Even now I curse the day, and yet I think

Few come within the compass of my curse,
Wherein I did not some notorious ill:
As kill a man, or else devise his death;
Ravish a maid, or plot the way to do it;
Accuse some innocent, and perjure myself;
Set deadly enmity between two friends;
Make poor men's cattle break their necks;
Set fire on barns and haystacks in the night
And bid the owners quench them with their tears.
Oft have I digged up dead men from their graves
And set them upright at their dear friends' door
Even when their sorrow almost was forgot;
And on their skins, as on the bark of trees,
Have with my knife carved in Roman letters
'Let not your sorrow die, though I am dead.'
But I have done a thousand dreadful things
As willingly as one would kill a fly,
And nothing grieves me heartily indeed
But that I cannot do ten thousand more.
LUCIUS Bring down the devil, for he must not die
So sweet a death as hanging suddenly.

*Aaron is brought down from the ladder*

AARON If there are devils, would I were a devil,
To live and burn in everlasting fire,
If I might have your company in hell
But to torment you with my bitter tongue!
LUCIUS Sirs, stop his mouth and let him speak no more.

*Enter Aemilius*

GOTH My lord, there is a messenger from Rome
Desires to be admitted to your presence.
LUCIUS Let him come near.
Welcome, Aemilius: what's the news from Rome?

AEMILIUS Lord Lucius, and you princes of the Goths,
  The Roman emperor greets you all by me;
  And since he understands you are in arms,
  He craves a parley at your father's house,
  Willing you to demand your hostages,
  And they shall be immediately delivered.
GOTH What says our general?
LUCIUS Aemilius, let the emperor give his pledges
  Unto my father and my uncle Marcus,
  And we will come. March, away.                *Exeunt*

## SCENE II
### Before Titus' house.

*Enter Tamora and her two Sons, disguised*

TAMORA Thus, in this strange and sad habiliment,
  I will encounter with Andronicus,
  And say I am Revenge, sent from below
  To join with him and right his heinous wrongs.
  Knock at his study, where they say he keeps
  To ruminate strange plots of dire revenge.
  Tell him Revenge is come to join with him
  And work confusion on his enemies.

*They knock, and Titus opens his study door*

TITUS Who does molest my contemplatìon?
  Is it your trick to make me open the door,
  That so my sad decrees may fly away
  And all my study be to no effect?
  You are deceived; for what I mean to do
  See here in bloody lines I have set down;
  And what is written shall be executed.
TAMORA Titus, I am come to talk with you.

TITUS No, not a word; how can I grace my talk,
  Wanting a hand to give it that accord?
  You have the odds of me, therefore no more.
TAMORA If you did know me, you would talk with me.
TITUS I am not mad; I know you well enough.
  Witness this wretched stump, witness these crimson
    lines,
  Witness these trenches made by grief and care,
  Witness the tiring day and heavy night,
  Witness all sorrow, that I know you well
  For our proud empress, mighty Tamora.
  Is not your coming for my other hand?
TAMORA Know, you sad man, I am not Tamora;
  She is your enemy, and I your friend.
  I am Revenge, sent from the infernal kingdom
  To ease the gnawing vulture of your mind
  By working wrathful vengeance on your foes.
  Come down and welcome me to this world's light;
  Confer with me of murder and of death.
  There's not a hollow cave or lurking place,
  No vast obscurity or misty vale,
  Where bloody murder or detested rape
  Can couch for fear, but I will find them out;
  And in their ears tell them my dreadful name,
  Revenge, which makes the foul offender quake.
TITUS Are you Revenge? and are you sent to me
  To be a torment to my enemies?
TAMORA I am; therefore come down and welcome me.
TITUS Do me some service ere I come to you.
  Lo, by your side where Rape and Murder stand;
  Now give some assurance that you are Revenge:
  Stab them, or tear them on your chariot wheels,
  And then I'll come and be your wagoner
  And whirl along with you about the globe.
  Provide you two proper palfreys, black as jet,
  To hale your vengeful wagon swift away
  And find out murderers in their guilty caves.

And when your car is loaded with their heads,
I will dismount, and by your wagon wheel
Trot like a servile footman all day long,
Even from Hyperion's rising in the east
Until his very downfall in the sea;
And day by day I'll do this heavy task,
If you destroy Rapine and Murder there.

TAMORA These are my ministers and come with me.

TITUS Are they your ministers? what are they called?

TAMORA Rape and Murder; therefore callèd so
Because they take vengeance of such kind of men.

TITUS Good Lord, how like the empress' sons they are!
And you the empress! but we worldly men
Have miserable, mad, mistaking eyes.
O sweet Revenge, now do I come to you;
And, if one arm's embracement will content you,
I will embrace you in it by and by.                    *Exit*

TAMORA This closing with him fits his lunacy.
Whatever I forge to feed his brainsick humours
Do you uphold and maintain in your speeches,
For now he firmly takes me for Revenge.
And, being credulous in this mad thought,
I'll make him send for Lucius his son,
And while I at a banquet hold him sure,
I'll find some cunning practice out of hand
To scatter and disperse the giddy Goths,
Or at the least make them his enemies.
See, here he comes, and I must ply my theme.

*Enter Titus*

TITUS Long have I been forlorn, and all for you.
Welcome, dread Fury, to my woeful house.
Rapine and Murder, you are welcome too.
How like the empress and her sons you are!
Well are you fitted, had you but a Moor.

Could not all hell afford you such a devil?
For well I know the empress never moves
But in her company there is a Moor.
And, would you represent our queen aright,
It were convenient you had such a devil.
But welcome as you are: what shall we do?
TAMORA What would you have us do, Andronicus?
DEMETRIUS Show me a murderer, I'll deal with him.
CHIRON Show me a villain that has done a rape,
And I am sent to be revenged on him.
TAMORA Show me a thousand that have done you wrong,
And I will be revengèd on them all.
TITUS Look round about the wicked streets of Rome,
And when you find a man that's like yourself,
Good Murder, stab him; he's a murderer.
Go you with him, and when it is your chance
To find another that is like to you,
Good Rapine, stab him; he is a ravisher.
Go you with them; and in the emperor's Court
There is a queen, attended by a Moor.
Well shall you know her by your own proportion,
For up and down she does resemble you.
I pray you do on them some violent death;
They have been violent to me and mine.
TAMORA Well have you lessoned us; this shall we do.
But would it please you, good Andronicus,
To send for Lucius, your thrice-valiant son,
Who leads towards Rome a band of warlike Goths,
And bid him come and banquet at your house.
When he is here, even at your solemn feast,
I will bring in the empress and her sons,
The emperor himself, and all your foes,
And at your mercy shall they stoop and kneel,
And on them shall you ease your angry heart.
What says Andronicus to this device?
TITUS Marcus, my brother, 'tis sad Titus calls.

*Enter Marcus*

Go, gentle Marcus, to your nephew Lucius;
You shall enquire him out among the Goths.
Bid him repair to me and bring with him
Some of the chiefest princes of the Goths.
Bid him encamp his soldiers where they are.
Tell him the emperor and the empress too
Feast at my house, and he shall feast with them.
This do you for my love; and so let him,
As he regards his agèd father's life.

MARCUS This will I do and soon return again.          *Exit*

TAMORA Now will I hence about your business
    And take my ministers along with me.

TITUS Nay, nay, let Rape and Murder stay with me,
    Or else I'll call my brother back again
    And cleave to no revenge but Lucius.

TAMORA *(aside to her sons)* What say you, boys? will you
        abide with him
    While I go tell my lord the emperor
    How I have governed our determined jest?
    Yield to his humour, smooth and speak him fair,
    And tarry with him till I turn again.

TITUS *(aside)* I knew them all, though they supposed me
        mad,
    And will o'erreach them in their own devices,
    A pair of cursèd hellhounds and their dame.

DEMETRIUS Madam, depart at pleasure; leave us here.

TAMORA Farewell, Andronicus: Revenge now goes
    To lay a complot to betray your foes.

TITUS I know you do; and, sweet Revenge, farewell.

                                          *Exit Tamora*

CHIRON Tell us, old man, how shall we be employed?

TITUS Tut, I have work enough for you to do.
    Publius, come hither, Caius and Valentine.

*Enter Publius, Caius, and Valentine*

PUBLIUS What is your will?

TITUS Know you these two?

PUBLIUS The empress' sons, I take them, Chiron and
    Demetrius.

TITUS Fie, Publius, fie! You are too much deceived.
    The one is Murder, and Rape is the other's name;
    And therefore bind them, gentle Publius:
    Caius and Valentine, lay hands on them.
    Oft have you heard me wish for such an hour,
    And now I find it. Therefore bind them sure,
    And stop their mouths if they begin to cry.          *Exit*

CHIRON Villains, forbear! we are the empress' sons.

PUBLIUS And therefore do we what we are commanded.
    Stop close their mouths, let them not speak a word.
    Is he sure bound? look that you bind them fast.

*Enter Titus Andronicus with a knife, and*
*Lavinia with a basin*

TITUS Come, come, Lavinia; look, your foes are bound.
    Sirs, stop their mouths, let them not speak to me,
    But let them hear what fearful words I utter.
    O villains, Chiron and Demetrius!
    Here stands the spring whom you have stained with mud,
    This goodly summer with your winter mixed.
    You killed her husband, and for that vile fault
    Two of her brothers were condemned to death,
    My hand cut off and made a merry jest.
    Both her sweet hands, her tongue, and that more dear
    Than hands or tongue, her spotless chastity,
    Inhuman traitors, you constrained and forced.
    What would you say if I should let you speak?
    Villains, for shame you could not beg for grace.
    Hark, wretches, how I mean to martyr you.
    This one hand yet is left to cut your throats
    While Lavinia between her stumps does hold
    The basin that receives your guilty blood.

You know your mother means to feast with me,
And calls herself Revenge, and thinks me mad.
Hark, villains, I will grind your bones to dust,
And with your blood and it I'll make a paste;
And of the paste a pie-crust I will rear,
And make two pasties of your shameful heads,
And bid that strumpet, your unhallowed dam,
Like to the earth, swallow her own increase.
This is the feast that I have bid her to,
And this the banquet she shall surfeit on;
For worse than Philomel you used my daughter,
And worse than Progne I will be revenged.
And now prepare your throats. Lavinia, come,
Receive the blood; and when they are quite dead,
Let me go grind their bones to powder small
And with this hateful liquor temper it;
And in that paste let their vile heads be baked.
Come, come, be every one officioùs
To make this banquet, which I wish may prove
More stern and bloody than the Centaurs' feast.

*He cuts their throats*

So, now bring them in, for I'll play the cook
And see them ready when their mother comes.

*Exeunt*

## SCENE III
## The same.

*Enter Lucius, Marcus, and the Goths, with Aaron prisoner, and his Child in the arms of an Attendant*

LUCIUS Uncle Marcus, since 'tis my father's mind
That I repair to Rome, I am content.
GOTH And ours with yours, befall what fortune will.

LUCIUS Good uncle, take you in this barbarous Moor,
    This ravenous tiger, this accursèd devil.
    Let him receive no sustenance, fetter him,
    Till he is brought unto the empress' face
    For testimony of her foul proceedings.
    And see the ambush of our friends be strong;
    I fear the emperor means no good to us.
AARON Some devil whisper curses in my ear
    And prompt me that my tongue may utter forth
    The venomous malice of my swelling heart!
LUCIUS Away, inhuman dog, unhallowed slave!
    Sirs, help our uncle to convey him in.
                                        *Exeunt Goths with Aaron*
    The trumpets show the emperor is at hand.

        *Sound trumpets. Enter Emperor and Empress, with
            Aemilius, Tribunes, and others*

SATURNINUS What, has the firmament more suns than one?
LUCIUS What avails it you to call yourself a sun?
MARCUS Rome's emperor, and nephew, break the parley:
    These quarrels must be quietly debated.
    The feast is ready which the careful Titus
    Has ordainèd to an honorable end,
    For peace, for love, for league, and good to Rome.
    Please you therefore draw nigh and take your places.
SATURNINUS Marcus, we will.

        *A table brought in. Trumpets sounding, enter
        Titus like a cook, placing the dishes, and Lavinia
            with a veil over her face*

TITUS Welcome, my lord; welcome, dread queen;
    Welcome, you warlike Goths; welcome, Lucius;
    And welcome all: although the cheer is poor,
    'Twill fill your stomachs; please you eat of it.
SATURNINUS Why are you thus attired, Andronicus?

TITUS Because I would be sure to have all well
   To entertain your highness and your empress.
TAMORA We are beholding to you, good Andronicus.
TITUS And if your highness knew my heart, you were.
   My lord the emperor, resolve me this:
   Was it well done of rash Virginius
   To slay his daughter with his own right hand,
   Because she was enforced, stained, and deflowered?
SATURNINUS It was, Andronicus.
TITUS Your reason, mighty lord?
SATURNINUS Because the girl should not survive her shame,
   And by her presence still renew his sorrow.
TITUS A reason mighty, strong, and effectual;
   A pattern, precedent, and lively warrant
   For me, most wretched, to perform the like.
   Die, die, Lavinia, and your shame with you,
   And with your shame your father's sorrow die!

                                   *He kills her*

SATURNINUS What have you done, unnatural and unkind?
TITUS Killed her for whom my tears have made me blind.
   I am as woeful as Virginius was,
   And have a thousand times more cause than he
   To do this outrage; and it now is done.
SATURNINUS What, was she ravished? tell who did the
   deed.
TITUS Will it please you eat? will it please your highness
   feed?
TAMORA Why have you slain your only daughter thus?
TITUS Not I: 'twas Chiron and Demetrius,
   They ravished her and cut away her tongue;
   And they, 'twas they, that did her all this wrong.
SATURNINUS Go fetch them hither to us instantly.
TITUS Why, there they are, both bakèd in this pie,
   Whereof their mother daintily has fed,
   Eating the flesh that she herself has bred.
   'Tis true, 'tis true; witness my knife's sharp point!

*He stabs the Empress*

SATURNINUS Die, frantic wretch, for this accursèd deed!

*He stabs Titus*

LUCIUS Can the son's eye behold his father bleed?
There's measure for measure, death for a deadly deed!

*He stabs Saturninus*

MARCUS You sad-faced men, people and sons of Rome,
By uproar severed, as a flight of fowl
Scattered by winds and high tempestuous gusts,
O, let me teach you how to knit again
This scattered corn into one mutual sheaf,
These broken limbs again into one body.
ROMAN LORD Let Rome herself be death unto herself,
And she whom mighty kingdoms curtsy to,
Like a forlorn and desperate castaway,
Do shameful execution on herself,
Unless my frosty signs and chaps of age,
Grave witnesses of true experience,
Cannot induce you to attend my words.
(*To Lucius*) Speak, Rome's dear friend, as once our
    ancestor,
When with his solemn tongue he did discourse
To lovesick Dido's sad-attending ear
The story of that baleful burning night,
When subtle Greeks surprised King Priam's Troy.
Tell us what Sinon has bewitched our ears,
Or who has brought the fatal engine in
That gives our Troy, our Rome, the civil wound.
My heart is not compact of flint or steel;
Nor can I utter all our bitter grief,
But floods of tears will drown my oratory

And break my utterance, even in the time
When it should move you to attend me most,
And force you to commiseratiòn.
Here's Rome's young captain, let him tell the tale,
While I stand by and weep to hear him speak.
LUCIUS Then, gracious auditory, be it known to you
That Chiron and the damned Demetrius
Were they that murdered our emperor's brother,
And they it was that ravishèd our sister.
For their fell faults our brothers were beheaded,
Our father's tears despised, and basely cozened
Of that true hand that fought Rome's quarrel out
And sent her enemies unto the grave.
Lastly, myself unkindly banishèd,
The gates shut on me, and turned weeping out
To beg relief among Rome's enemies;
Who drowned their enmity in my true tears
And opened their arms to embrace me as a friend:
I am the turnèd-forth, be it known to you,
That have preserved her welfare in my blood
And from her bosom took the enemy's point,
Sheathing the steel in my adventurous body.
Alas, you know I am no braggart, I;
My scars can witness, dumb although they are,
That my report is just and full of truth.
But soft, I think I do digress too much,
Citing my worthless praise. O, pardon me!
For when no friends are by, men praise themselves.
MARCUS Now is my turn to speak. Behold the child:
Of this was Tamora deliverèd,
The issue of an irreligious Moor,
Chief architect and plotter of these woes.
The villain is alive in Titus' house,
And as he is to witness this is true.
Now judge what cause had Titus to revenge
These wrongs unspeakable, past patiènce,
Or more than any living man could bear.

Now you have heard the truth, what say you, Romans?
Have we done aught amiss, show us wherein,
And, from the place where you behold us pleading,
The poor remainder of Andronici
Will hand in hand all headlong hurl ourselves
And on the ragged stones beat forth our souls,
And make a mutual closure of our house.
Speak, Romans, speak, and if you say we shall,
Lo, hand in hand, Lucius and I will fall.
AEMILIUS Come, come, you reverent man of Rome,
And bring our emperor gently in your hand—
Lucius our emperor; for well I know
The common voice does cry it shall be so.
ALL Lucius, all hail, Rome's royal emperor!
MARCUS Go, go into old Titus' sorrowful house,
And hither hale that misbelieving Moor
To be adjudged some direful slaughtering death,
As punishment for his most wicked life.
                                        *Exeunt Attendants*
ALL Lucius, all hail, Rome's gracious governor!
LUCIUS Thanks, gentle Romans: may I govern so
To heal Rome's harms and wipe away her woe.
But, gentle people, give me aim awhile,
For nature puts me to a heavy task.
Stand all aloof; but, uncle, draw you near
To shed obsequious tears upon this trunk.
O, take this warm kiss on your pale cold lips,
These sorrowful drops upon your bloodstained face,
The last true duties of your noble son!
MARCUS Tear for tear, and loving kiss for kiss,
Your brother Marcus tenders on your lips.
O, were the sum of these that I should pay
Countless and infinite, yet would I pay them.
LUCIUS Come hither, boy; come, come and learn of us
To melt in showers: your grandsire loved you well.
Many a time he danced you on his knee,
Sung you asleep, his loving breast your pillow.

Many a story has he told to you,
And bid you bear his pretty tales in mind
And talk of them when he was dead and gone.

MARCUS How many thousand times have these poor lips,
When they were living, warmed themselves on yours!
O, now, sweet boy, give them their latest kiss.
Bid him farewell; commit him to the grave;
Do them that kindness, and take leave of them.

BOY O grandsire, grandsire! even with all my heart
Would I were dead, so might you live again!
O Lord, I cannot speak to him for weeping;
My tears will choke me if I open my mouth.

*Enter Attendants with Aaron*

ROMAN You sad Andronici, have done with woes.
Give sentence on this execrable wretch
That has been breeder of these dire events.

LUCIUS Set him breast-deep in earth, and famish him.
There let him stand and rave and cry for food.
If any one relieves or pities him,
For the offence he dies. This is our sentence.
Some stay to see him fastened in the earth.

AARON Ah, why should wrath be mute and fury dumb?
I am no baby, I, that with base prayers
I should repent the evils I have done;
Ten thousand worse than ever yet I did
Would I perform if I might have my will.
If one good deed in all my life I did,
I do repent it from my very soul.

LUCIUS Some loving friends convey the emperor hence,
And give him burial in his father's grave.
My father and Lavinia shall forthwith
Be closèd in our household's monument.
As for that ravenous tiger, Tamora,
No funeral rite, nor man in mourning weeds,
No mournful bell shall ring her burial;

But throw her forth to beasts and birds to prey.
Her life was beastly and devoid of pity,
And being dead, let birds on her take pity!
See justice done on Aaron, that damned Moor,
By whom our heavy haps had their beginning.
Then, afterwards, to order well the state,
That like events may ne'er it ruinate.                    *Exeunt*

# Pericles,
# Prince of Tyre

# INTRODUCTION

S hakespeare's partners, the Burbages, took over the Blackfriars theatre in 1608, with himself as part-owner. This small indoors theatre, with its more expensive select audience, demanded a new kind of play, while offering fresh opportunities, more stage scenery, music, lighting. Shakespeare responded to the challenge with something new—an old, episodic tale of sea-adventures, set in the archaic setting of John Gower, who serves to hold the various adventures together as Chorus. And the play had an immediate success; a pamphlet next year (1609) tells us:

> Amazed I stood to see a crowd
> Of civil throats stretched out so loud . . .
> So that I truly thought all these
> Came to see *Shore* or *Pericles*.

As usual Shakespeare took a subject ready to hand, from Gower's *Confessio Amantis,* perhaps prompted by the recent reprinting of the ancient tale in Lawrence Twyne's *The Pattern of Painful Adventures* only the year before (1607). In a sense old John Gower was there ready to hand too; for his monument dominated the church of St. Saviour's next the Globe in Southwark. Shakespeare shows in numerous references how conscious he was of monuments—and there was Gower, his head resting on his book. On the last day of December 1607 Shakespeare's actor-brother, Edmund, was buried in the church, with a knell presumably paid for by his now prosperous senior. The Venetian ambassador came to see the new play, and George Wilkins cashed in on its success with his novel—'the book of the play'—*The Painful Adventures of Pericles, Prince of Tyre.*

As frequently happened, the Company, to protect its playing profits, blocked the publication of the text—which turned out a sad loss for us. For, the next thing, misfortune struck: in July 1608 a severe outbreak of plague occurred, the theatres were closed for eighteen months, printing and publishing were alike disturbed. No doubt Shakespeare took refuge—as people did, who could—in the country. Once more we see how necessary it is to understand how the work of the time was conditioned by the circumstances of the time.

For, as the result, we have no good text of *Pericles:* this remarkable, experimental play is not so much a mere torso as a defaced monument. A publisher got hold of some text, much of it—principally, the first two Acts—put together by a reporter or two. It is all most provoking, and worse: occasionally one can observe a fustian line or two summing up the action, instead of the rich and devious development Shakespeare would have given it. The result is a whole library of profitless speculation where there is no certainty. And, as Wittgenstein adjures us—of that which is not known nothing is to be said.

One exception here, which illuminates Shakespeare's background and makes it more real to us, is something factual recently discovered by Mr. Roger Prior. Wilkins knew the Montjoies with whom Shakespeare had lodged in Silver Street, where he effected the betrothal of the daughter, on behalf of Madame Montjoie (evidently on confidential terms), to an apprentice of theirs. The young couple then lodged at Wilkins's unrespectable tavern in

Turnmill Street, which was frequented by theatre-folk. How things weave together, when one knows about them!— an ounce of fact worth a feather-bed of conjecture.

We need not go in detail into the complicated sea-adventures of Pericles, going back to the ancient romance of Apollonius of Tyre, popular with Elizabethans. Suffice it to say that sea ventures were much in the air with the Adventurers to Virginia, the voyages to America and even to India and the East—Mediterranean, Middle and Far East. The play starts off with the incest-theme, which propels Pericles off on his adventures, shipwreck, etc. This provided something new for the jaded taste of fashionable Jacobeans, and it shortly was taken up by other dramatists. Actually only a few years before there had been a sensational such case at the top of French society, in which the poor young brother and sister had been executed for their misdemeanour.[1]

The strongest scenes are the brothel scenes, in which Pericles's lost daughter, Marina, repels the onslaughts upon her virtue. These are convincingly realistic—evidently William Shakespeare knew the set-up in such interiors, common enough in Elizabethan London. More touching is the romantic recognition scene in which Pericles finds his daughter and wife, whom he had lost at sea. The title might well be Lost and Found—and in this the play forecasts the dominant theme of Shakespeare's last period, in particular *The Winter's Tale,* a masterpiece. It is hard to judge *Pericles* in its battered state; presumably Heming and Condell omitted it from their collected edition because they had not a satisfactory text. Or could the first two Acts have been another's?

All the same we recognise Shakespeare's indubitable hand, not least in the indirect grand language in which he

---

[1] cf Tancrède Martel, *Julien et Marguerite de Ravallet, 1582–1603.*

expresses simple things (bored with the simple and direct?)
Here is Pericles confronted by his lost daughter:

> You do look
> Like Patience gazing on kings' graves and smiling
> Extremity out of act.

Or again:

> your present kindness
> Makes my past miseries sports; you shall do well
> That on the touching of her lips I may
> Melt, and no more be seen.

What a way of putting it!—and yet, Shakespeare all over.

At Stratford in these years his mother, Mary Arden, died
in 1608. The year before, his intelligent elder daughter,
Susanna, had married a well-known doctor, John Hall.
From this time forward we find passages reflecting a medical
interest, like this:

> It is known I ever
> Have studied physic, through which secret art,
> By turning over authorities I have,
> Together with my practice, made familiar
> To me and to my aid the blest infusions
> That dwell in vegetives, in metals, stones.
> And I can speak of the disturbances
> That nature works and of its cures . . .

From earliest beginnings Shakespeare had known how to
put everything he came across to use.

Do we detect his characteristically superior note in
Pericles's comment on the fishermen drawing their net?—

How well this honest mirth becomes their labour!

We certainly detect his own characteristic words, never much used by other people, if at all: 'distain' for blemish, or 'misdread', or 'entreat'—so polite in its use. (We note it again in his last will.) Or even in such a usage as 'for that' instead of because. He was addicted to redundant 'thats', for that, if that, since that—no doubt partly useful for scansion; as also to 'the which'. This, though regular enough Elizabethan usage, was more common with him than with anyone. We have a piece of Elizabethan folklore in the belief that thunder stirs up the beds of eels; and he probably picked up the name of Valdez for his pirate, from that of the commander of the big ship Drake had captured from the Armada. The pimp, Boult, jokes—'What would you have me do? Go to the wars, where a man may serve seven years for the loss of a leg, and have not money enough in the end to buy him a wooden one?' This occurs so often in different forms that, joke as it is, it must represent what the author thought.

A regular reflection with him was that, to a blow of some kind, there is an offsetting advantage. It is some slight consolation that, with a ruined text as much of *Pericles* is, we need have no compunction about helping the reader over difficulties. Even ordinary editions of the play are reduced here and there to filling in evident gaps with phrases from Wilkins's 'book of the play.'

# CHARACTERS

GOWER, as Chorus

ANTIOCHUS, King of Antioch
PERICLES, Prince of Tyre
DAUGHTER of Antiochus
THALIARD, a lord of Antioch
HELICANUS ⎫
ESCANES ⎭ Lords of Tyre
CLEON, governor of Tarsus
DIONYZA, wife of Cleon
THREE FISHERMEN OF PENTAPOLIS
SIMONIDES, King of Pentapolis
THAISA, daughter of Simonides
MARSHAL
LYCHORIDA, a nurse
CERIMON, a lord of Ephesus
TWO SERVANTS of Ephesus
PHILEMON, servant of Cerimon
LEONINE, servant of Dionyza
MARINA, daughter of Pericles
PANDER
BAWD
BOULT, servant of the Pander and the Bawd
LYSIMACHUS, governor of Mytilene
DIANA, goddess of chastity

KNIGHTS, LORDS, LADIES, GENTLEMEN, ATTENDANTS,
SERVANTS, SAILORS, PIRATES, MESSENGERS

514

# Act I

## CHORUS

*Enter Gower*

GOWER

To sing a song that old was sung,
From ashes ancient Gower is come,
Assuming man's infirmities,
To glad your ear and please your eyes.
It has been sung at festivals,
On ember-eves and holidays,
And lords and ladies in their lives
Have read it for restoratives.
The purchase is to make men glorious,
   *Et bonum quo antiquius eo melius.*[1]
If you, born in these latter times
When wit's more ripe, accept my rhymes,
And that to hear an old man sing
May to your wishes pleasure bring,
I life would wish, and that I might
Waste it for you like taper-light.
This Antioch, then. Antiochus the Great
Built up this city for his chiefest seat,
The fairest in all Syria;
I tell you what my authors say.
This king unto him took a peer,
Who died and left a female heir,
So buxom, blithe, and full of face
As heaven had lent her all his grace;

_____
[1]The older a good thing the better it is.

With whom the father liking took,
And her to incest did provoke.
Bad child, worse father, to entice his own
To evil should be done by none;
But custom what they did begin
Was with long use accounted no sin.
The beauty of this sinful dame
Made many princes thither frame
To seek her as a bedfellow,
In marriage pleasures playfellow.
Which to prevent he made a law,
To keep her still and men in awe,
That whoso asked her for his wife,
His riddle told not, lost his life.
So for her many a man did die,
As yon grim looks do testify.
What now ensues, to the judgement of your eye—
I give my cause, who best can justify.                    *Exit*

# Act I

## SCENE I
## Antioch. The palace.

*Enter Antiochus, Pericles, and followers*

ANTIOCHUS
Young Prince of Tyre, you have at large received
The danger of the task you undertake?
PERICLES
I have, Antìochus, and with a soul
Emboldened with the glory of her praise
Think death no hazard in this enterprise.
ANTIOCHUS
Music!
Bring in our daughter, clothèd like a bride
For embracements even of Jove himself,
At whose conception, till Lucina reigned,
Nature this dowry gave; to glad her presence,
The senate-house of planets all did sit
To knit in her their best perfectiòns.

*Enter Antiochus's Daughter*

PERICLES
See where she comes, apparelled like the spring,
Graces her subjects, and her thoughts the king
Of every virtue gives renown to men;
Her face the book of praises, where is read
Nothing but rarest pleasures, as from thence
Sorrow was ever razed, and testy wrath

Could never be her mild companiòn.
You gods that made me man, and sway in love,
That have inflamed desïre in my breast
To taste the fruit of yon celestial tree
Or die in the adventure, be my help,
As I am son and servant to your will,
To compass such a boundless happiness!

ANTIOCHUS

Prince Pericles—

PERICLES

That would be son to great Antiochus.

ANTIOCHUS

Before you stands this fair Hesperides,
With golden fruit, but dangerous to be touched,
For deathlike dragons here affright you hard.
Her face, like heaven, entices you to view
Her countless glory, which desert must gain;
And which without desert because your eye
Presumes to reach, all the whole heap must die.
Yon sometime famous princes, like yourself,
Drawn by report, adventurous by desire,
Tell you with speechless tongues and semblance pale
That without covering, save yon field of stars,
Here they stand martyrs slain in Cupid's wars;
And with dead cheeks advise you to desist
For going on death's net, which none resist.

PERICLES

Antiochus, I thank you, who have taught
My frail mortality to know itself,
And by those fearful objects to prepare
This body, like to them, to what I must;
For death remembered should be like a mirror,
Who tells us life's but breath, to trust it error.
I'll make my will then, and as sick men do,
Who know the world, see heaven, but feeling woe
Catch not at earthly joys as once they did,

So I bequeath a happy peace to you
And all good men, as every prince should do;
My riches to the earth from whence they came,

*(to the Daughter)*

But my unspotted fire of love to you.
Thus ready for the way of life or death,
I wait the sharpest blow, Antiochus.

ANTIOCHUS
Scorning advice, read the conclusion then,
Which read and not expounded, 'tis decreed,
As these before you, you yourself shall bleed.

DAUGHTER
Of all tried yet, may you prove prosperous!
Of all tried yet, I wish you happiness.

PERICLES
Like a bold champion I assume the lists,
Nor ask advice of any other thought
But faithfulness and courage.

*He reads aloud*

THE RIDDLE

*I am no viper, yet I feed*
*On mother's flesh which did me breed.*
*I sought a husband, in which labour*
*I found that kindness in a father.*
*He's father, son, and husband mild;*
*I mother, wife, and yet his child.*
*How they may be, and yet in two,*
*As you will live, resolve it you.*

(*Aside*) Sharp physic is the last. But O you powers
That give heaven countless eyes to view men's acts,
Why cloud they not their sights perpetually,
If this is true which makes me pale to read it?
Fair glass of light, I loved you, and could still,
Were not this glorious casket stored with ill.
But I must tell you now my thoughts revolt;
For he's no man on whom perfections wait
That, knowing sin within, will touch the gate.
You are a fair viol, and your sense the strings,
Who, fingered to make man his lawful music,
Would draw heaven down and all the gods to hearken,
But, being played upon before your time,
Hell only dances at so harsh a chime.
In truth, I care not for you.

ANTIOCHUS
Prince Pericles, touch not, upon your life,
For that's an article within our law
As dangerous as the rest. Your time's expired;
Either expound now or receive your sentence.

PERICLES
Great King,
Few love to hear the sins they love to act.
'Twould upbraid yourself too near for me to tell it.
Who has a book of all that monarchs do,
He's more secure to keep it shut than shown,
For vice repeated is like the wandering wind,
Blows dust in others' eyes to spread itself.
And yet the end of all is bought thus dear,
The breath is gone, and the sore eyes see clear
To stop the air would hurt them. The blind mole casts
Humped hills towards heaven, to tell the earth is thronged
By man's oppression, and the poor worm does die for it.
Kings are earth's gods; in vice, their law's their will;
And if Jove strays, who dares say Jove does ill?
It is enough you know, and it is fit,

What being more known grows worse, to smother it.
All love the womb that their first being bred;
Then give my tongue like leave to love my head.
ANTIOCHUS   (aside)
  Heaven, that I had your head! He has found the meaning.
  But I will play with him.—Young Prince of Tyre,
  Though by the tenor of our strict edìct,
  Your exposition misinterpreting,
  We might proceed to cancel of your days—
  Yet hope, succeeding from so fair a tree
  As your fair self, does tune us otherwise.
  Forty days longer we do rèspite you,
  If by which time our secret is undone,
  This mercy shows we'll joy in such a son.
  And until then your entertainment be
  As does befit our honour and your worth.
                    *Exeunt. Pericles remains alone*
PERICLES
  How courtesy would seem to cover sin,
  When what is done is like an hypocrite,
  Which then is good in nothing but in sight.
  If it is true that I interpret false,
  Then were it certain you were not so bad
  As with foul incest to abuse your soul.
  Where now you're both a father and a son
  By your untimely claspings with your child,
  Which pleasures fit a husband, not a father.
  And she an eater of her mother's flesh
  By the defiling of her parents' bed;
  And both like serpents are, who, though they feed
  On sweetest flowers, yet they poison breed.
  Antioch, farewell, for wisdom sees those men
  Blush not in actions blacker than the night
  Will shun no course to keep them from the light.
  One sin, I know, another does provoke.
  Murder's as near to lust as flame to smoke.

Poison and treason are the hands of sin,
Ay, and the bucklers to put off the shame.
Then, lest my life is cropped to keep you clear,
By flight I'll shun the danger which I fear.                *Exit*

*Enter Antiochus*

ANTIOCHUS
He has found the meaning,
For which we mean to have his head.
He must not live to trumpet forth my infamy,
Nor tell the world Antiochus does sin
In such a loathèd manner.
And therefore instantly this prince must die,
For by his fall my honour must keep high.
Who attends us there?

*Enter Thaliard*

THALIARD                        Does your highness call?
ANTIOCHUS
Thaliard, you are of our chamber, Thaliard,
And our mind partakes its private actions
To your secrecy; and for your faithfulness
We will advance you, Thaliard.
Behold, here's poison, and here's gold.
We hate the Prince of Tyre, and you must kill him.
It fits you not to ask the reason why,
Because we bid it. Say, is it done?
THALIARD
My lord, it is done.
ANTIOCHUS                   Enough.

*Enter a Messenger*

Let your breath cool yourself, telling your haste.

MESSENGER    My lord, Prince Pericles is fled.        *Exit*

ANTIOCHUS    As you will live, fly after, and as an arrow
   shot from a well-experienced archer hits the mark his
   eye does level at, so you never return unless you say
   'Prince Pericles is dead.'

THALIARD    My lord, if I can get him within my pistol's
   length, I'll make him sure enough. So farewell to your
   highness.

ANTIOCHUS
   Thaliard, adieu.                            *Exit Thaliard*
              Till Pericles is dead,
   My heart can lend no succour to my head.          *Exit*


# SCENE II
## Tyre. The palace.

*Enter Pericles with his Lords*


PERICLES
   Let none disturb us.                     *Exeunt Lords*
              Why should this change of thoughts,
   The sad companion, dull-eyed melancholy,
   Be my so used a guest as not an hour
   In the day's glorious walk or peaceful night,
   The tomb where grief should sleep, can breed me quiet?
   Here pleasures court my eyes, and my eyes shun them,
   And danger, which I feared, is at Antioch,
   Whose arm seems far too short to hit me here.
   Yet neither pleasure's art can joy my spirits,
   Nor yet the other's distance comfort me.
   Then it is thus: the passions of the mind,
   That have their first conception by our dread,
   Have after-nourishment and life by care,
   And what was first but fear what might be done
   Grows older now and fears it is not done;

And so with me. The great Antiochus,
Against whom I am too little to contend,
Since he's so great can make his will his act,
Will think me speaking, though I swear to silence;
Nor does it profit me to say I honour
If he suspects I may dishonour him.
And what may make him blush in being known,
He'll stop the course by which it might be known.
With hostile forces he'll o'erspread the land,
And with the display of war will look so huge
Amazement shall drive courage from the state,
Our men be vanquished ere they do resist,
And subjects punished that never thought offence.
Which care of them, not pity of myself,
Who care no more but as the tops of trees
Which fence the roots they grow by and defend them,
Makes both my body pine and soul to languish,
And punish that before that he would punish.

*Enter Helicanus and the Lords*

FIRST LORD
  Joy and all comfort in your sacred breast!
SECOND LORD
  And keep your mind till you return to us
  Peaceful and comfortable.
HELICANUS
  Peace, peace, and give experience tongue.
  They do abuse the king that flatter him,
  For flattery is the bellows blows up sin;
  The thing then which is flattered, but a spark,
  To which that spur gives heat and stronger glowing;
  Whereas reproof, obedient and in order,
  Fits kings as they are men, for they may err.
  When Signor Sooth here does proclaim peace,
  He flatters you, makes war upon your life.

Prince, pardon me, or strike me if you please;
I cannot be much lower than my knees.

PERICLES

All leave us else. But let your cares o'erlook
What shipping and what ladings in our haven,
And then return to us.                    *Exeunt Lords*
                    Helicanus,
You have moved us. What see you in our looks?

HELICANUS

An angry brow, dread lord.

PERICLES

If there is such a dart in princes' frowns,
How durst your tongue move anger to our face?

HELICANUS

How dare the plants look up to heaven,
From whence they have their nourishment?

PERICLES

You know I have power to take your life from you.

HELICANUS

I have ground the axe myself. Do but strike the blow.

PERICLES

Rise, pray rise. Sit down. You are no flatterer;
I thank you for it, and heaven forbid
That kings should let their ears hear their faults
    hid.
Fit counsellor and servant for a prince,
Who by your wisdom make a prince your servant,
What would you have me do?

HELICANUS

To bear with patience such griefs
As you yourself do lay upon yourself.

PERICLES

You speak like a physician, Helicanus,
That ministers a potion unto me
That you would tremble to receive yourself.
Attend me then. I went to Antioch,

Where, as you know, against the face of death
I sought the purchase of a glorious beauty,
From whence an issue I might propagate
Are arms to princes and bring joys to subjects.
Her face was to my eye beyond all wonder,
The rest—hark in your ear—as black as incest.
Which by my knowledge found, the sinful father
Seemed not to strike, but smooth. But you know this,
'Tis time to fear when tyrants seem to kiss.
Which fear so grew in me I hither fled
Under the covering of a careful night
Which seemed my good protector; and, being here,
Bethought me what was past, what might succeed.
I knew him tyrannous, and tyrants' fears
Decrease not, but grow faster than the years.
Should he suspect, as no doubt he does,
That I should open to the listening air
How many worthy princes' bloods were shed
To keep his bed of blackness unlaid open,
To lop that doubt, he'll fill this land with arms,
And make pretence of wrong that I have done him;
When all for my—if I may call—offence
Must feel war's blow, which spares not innocence;
Which love to all, of which yourself are one,
Who now reproved me for it—

HELICANUS                          Alas, sir!

PERICLES
Drew sleep out of my eyes, blood from my cheeks,
Musings into my mind, with thousand doubts,
How I might stop this tempest ere it came.
And, finding little comfort to relieve them,
I thought it princely charity to grieve for them.

HELICANUS
Well, my lord, since you have given me leave to speak,
Freely will I speak. Antiochus you fear,
And justly too, I think, you fear the tyrant

Who either by public war or private treason
Will take away your life.
Therefore, my lord, go travel for a while,
Till then his rage and anger is forgotten
Or till the destinies do cut his thread of life.
Your rule direct to any; if to me,
Day serves not light more faithful than I'll be.

PERICLES
I do not doubt your faith,
But should he wrong my liberties in my absence?

HELICANUS
We'll mingle our bloods together in the earth,
From whence we had our being and our birth.

PERICLES
Tyre, I now look from you then, and to Tarsus
Intend my travel, where I'll hear from you,
And by whose letters I'll dispose myself.
The care I had and have of subjects' good
On you I lay, whose wisdom's strength can bear it.
I'll take your word for faith, not ask your oath;
Who shuns not to break one will crack both.
But in our orbs we'll live so round and safe
That time of both this truth shall never convince,
You showed a subject's shine, I a true prince.

*Exeunt*


# SCENE III
## The same.

*Enter Thaliard alone*

THALIARD    So this is Tyre, and this the Court. Here must
I kill King Pericles; and if I do it not, I am sure to be
hanged at home. 'Tis dangerous. Well, I perceive he was
a wise fellow and had good discretion that, being bidden

to ask what he would of the King, desired he might
know none of his secrets. Now do I see he had some
reason for it, for if a king bids a man be a villain, he's
bound by the indenture of his oath to be one. Hush!
Here come the lords of Tyre.

*Enter Helicanus and Escanes, with other lords*

HELICANUS
You shall not need, my fellow peers of Tyre,
Further to question me of your King's departure.
His sealed commission, left in trust with me,
Does speak sufficiently he's gone to travel.
THALIARD    *(aside)* How? the King gone?
HELICANUS
If further yet you will be satisfied
Why, as it were, unlicensed of your loves
He would depart, I'll give some light unto you.
Being at Antioch—
THALIARD    *(aside)* What from Antioch?
HELICANUS
Royal Antiochus, on what cause I know not,
Took some displeasure at him; at least he judged so.
And doubting lest he had erred or sinned,
To show his sorrow he'd correct himself;
So puts himself unto the shipman's toil,
With whom each minute threatens life or death.
THALIARD    *(aside)* Well, I perceive I shall not be hanged
now although I would; but since he is gone, the King's
seas must please; he escaped the land to perish at the
sea. I'll present myself.
Peace to the lords of Tyre!
HELICANUS
Lord Thaliard from Antiochus is welcome.

THALIARD
    From him I come
    With message unto princely Pericles,
    But since my landing I have understood
    Your lord has betaken himself to unknown travels.
    Now my message must return from whence it came.
HELICANUS
    We have no reason to desire it,
    Commended to our master, not to us.
    Yet, ere you shall depart, this we desire,
    As friends to Antioch, we may feast in Tyre.    *Exeunt*

## SCENE IV
## Tarsus. Cleon's house.

*Enter Cleon, Governor of Tarsus, with Dionyza, his wife,*
*and others*

CLEON
    My Dionyza, shall we rest us here
    And, by relating tales of others' griefs,
    See if it will teach us to forget our own?
DIONYZA
    That were to blow at fire in hope to quench it,
    For who digs hills because they do aspire
    Throws down one mountain to cast up a higher.
    O my distressed lord, even such our griefs are.
    Here they are but felt, and seen with mischief's eyes,
    But like to groves, being topped, they higher rise.
CLEON
    O Dionyza,
    Who wants food and will not say he wants it,
    Or can conceal his hunger till he famishes?
    Our tongues and sorrows force us to sound deep
    Our woes into the air, our eyes to weep,
    Till tongues fetch breath that may proclaim them louder,

That, if heaven slumbers while their creatures want,
They may awake their helpers to comfort them.
I'll then discourse our woes, felt several years,
And, wanting breath to speak, help me with tears.

DIONYZA

I'll do my best, sir.

CLEON

This Tarsus, o'er which I have the government,
A city on which plenty held full hand,
For riches strewed herself even in its streets,
Whose towers bore heads so high they kissed the clouds, ·
And strangers never beheld but wondered at;
Whose men and dames so strutted and adorned,
Like one another's glass to trim them by.
Their tables were stored full, to glad the sight,
And not so much to feed on as delight;
All poverty was scorned, and pride so great,
The name of help grew odious to repeat.

DIONYZA

O, it is too true!

CLEON

But see what heaven can do by this our change.
These mouths which but of late earth, sea, and air
Were all too little to content and please,
Although they gave their creatures in abundance,
As houses are defiled for want of use,
They are now starved for want of exercise.
Those palates which, not yet two summers younger,
Must have inventions to delight the taste
Would now be glad of bread and beg for it.
Those mothers who to nuzzle up their babes
Thought naught too delicate are ready now
To eat those little darlings whom they loved.
So sharp are hunger's teeth that man and wife
Draw lots who first shall die to lengthen life.
Here stands a lord and there a lady weeping;

Here many sink, yet those who see them fall
Have scarce strength left to give them burial.
Is not this true?

DIONYZA
Our cheeks and hollow eyes do witness it.

CLEON
O, let those cities that of plenty's cup
And her prosperities so largely taste
With their superfluous riots, hear these tears!
The misery of Tarsus may be theirs.

*Enter a Lord*

LORD
Where is the lord governor?

CLEON
Here.
Speak out your sorrows which you bring in haste,
For comfort is too far for us to expect.

LORD
We have descried, upon our neighbouring shore,
A stately sail of ships make hitherward.

CLEON
I thought as much.
One sorrow never comes but brings an heir
That may succeed as its inheritor,
And so in ours. Some neighbouring nation,
Taking advantage of our misery,
Has stuffed the hollow vessels with their power,
To beat us down, when are down already,
And make a conquest of unhappy me,
Wherein no glory's got to overcome.

LORD
That's the least fear, for by the semblance
Of their white flags displayed they bring us peace,
And come to us as favourers, not as foes.

CLEON
　　You speak like him untutored to repeat:
　　Who makes the fairest show means most deceit.
　　But bring they what they will and what they can,
　　What need we fear?
　　Our ground's the lowest and we are half-way there.
　　Go tell their general we attend him here,
　　To know for what he comes and whence he comes
　　And what he craves.
LORD
　　I go, my lord.                                      *Exit*
CLEON
　　Welcome is peace if he on peace insist;
　　If wars, we are unable to resist.

　　　　　　　*Enter Pericles with attendants*

PERICLES
　　Lord governor, for so we hear you are,
　　Let not our ships and number of our men
　　Be like a beacon fired to amaze your eyes.
　　We have heard your miseries as far as Tyre
　　And seen the desolation of your streets;
　　Nor come we to add sorrow to your tears,
　　But to relieve them of their heavy load.
　　And these our ships you happily may think
　　Are like the Trojan horse, were stuffed within
　　With bloody veins expecting overthrow,
　　Are stored with corn to make your needy bread
　　And give them life whom hunger starved half dead.
ALL
　　The gods of Greece protect you!
　　And we will pray for you.

　　　　　　　　*They kneel*

PERICLES              Arise, I pray you, rise.
   We do not look for reverence but for love,
   And harbourage for ourself, our ships, and men.
CLEON
   And that when any shall not gratify,
   Or pay you with unthankfulness in thought,
   Be it our wives, our children, or ourselves,
   The curse of heaven and men succeed their evils!
   Till when—but which I hope shall never be seen—
   Your grace is welcome to our town and us.
PERICLES
   Which welcome we'll accept, feast here awhile,
   Until our stars that frown lend us a smile.        *Exeunt*

# Act II

## CHORUS

*Enter Gower*

GOWER
  Here have you seen a mighty king
  His child, alas, to incest bring;
  A better prince and benign lord
  That will prove awful both in deed and word.
  Be quiet then as men should be
  Till he has passed necessity.
  I'll show you those in trouble's reign,
  Losing a mite, a mountain gain.
  The good in conversatiòn,
  To whom I give my benison,
  Is still at Tarsus, where each man
  Thinks all is writ be spoken can,
  And to remember what he does
  Builds his statue to make him glorious.
  But tidings to the contrary
  Are brought your eyes; what need speak I?

*Dumb show:*
*Enter at one door Pericles talking with Cleon. Enter at*
*another door a gentleman with a letter to Pericles. Pericles*
*shows the letter to Cleon. Pericles gives the messenger a*
*reward and knights him. Exit Pericles at one door and*
*Cleon at another*

Good Helicane that stayed at home,
Not to eat honey like a drone
From others' labours, he does strive
To kill the bad, keep good alive,
And to fulfil his prince's desire
Sends word of all that haps in Tyre.
How Thaliard came full bent with sin
And hid intent to murder him,
And that in Tarsus was not best
Longer for him to make his rest.
He, doing so, put forth to seas,
Where, when men are, there's seldom ease;
For now the wind begins to blow;
Thunder above and deeps below
Makes such unquiet that the ship
Should house him safe is wrecked and split,
And he, good prince, having all lost,
By waves from coast to coast is tossed.
All perishèd of man, of pelf,
Nor aught escapèd but himself;
Till Fortune, tired with doing bad,
Threw him ashore, to make him glad.
And here he comes. What shall be next,
Pardon old Gower—thus reads the text.                  *Exit*

# Act II

## SCENE I
Pentapolis. The sea-side.

*Enter Pericles, wet*

PERICLES
Yet cease your ire, you angry stars of heaven!
Wind, rain, and thunder, remember earthly man
Is but a substance that must yield to you,
And I, as fits my nature, do obey you.
Alas, the seas have cast me on the rocks,
Washed me from shore to shore, and left my breath
Nothing to think on but ensuing death.
Let it suffice the greatness of your powers
To have bereft a prince of all his fortunes,
And having thrown him from your watery grave
Here to have death in peace is all he'll crave.

*Enter three Fishermen*

FIRST FISHERMAN   What ho, Pilch!
SECOND FISHERMAN   Ha, come and bring away the nets!
FIRST FISHERMAN   What, Patchbreech, I say!
THIRD FISHERMAN   What say you, master?
FIRST FISHERMAN   Look how you stir now! Come away,
or I'll fetch you with a vengeance.
THIRD FISHERMAN   Faith, master, I am thinking of the
poor men that were cast away before us even now.
FIRST FISHERMAN   Alas, poor souls, it grieved my heart
to hear what pitiful cries they made to us to help them,
when, well-a-day, we could scarce help ourselves.

THIRD FISHERMAN    Nay, master, said not I as much when
I saw the porpoise how he bounced and tumbled? They
say they're half fish, half flesh. A plague on them, they
never come but I look to be washed. Master, I marvel
how the fishes live in the sea?

FIRST FISHERMAN    Why, as men do a-land: the great ones
eat up the little ones. I can compare our rich misers to
nothing so fitly as to a whale: he plays and tumbles,
driving the poor fry before him, and at last devours
them all at a mouthful. Such whales have I heard on
land who never leave gaping till they swallowed the
whole parish, church, steeple, bells, and all.

PERICLES    (aside) A pretty moral!

THIRD FISHERMAN    But, master, if I had been the sexton,
I would have been that day in the belfry.

SECOND FISHERMAN    Why, man?

THIRD FISHERMAN    Because he should have swallowed
me too, and when I had been in his belly I would have
kept such a jangling of the bells that he should never
have left till he cast bells, steeple, church, and parish
up again. But if the good King Simonides were of my
mind—

PERICLES    (aside) Simonides?

THIRD FISHERMAN    We would purge the land of these
drones that rob the bee of its honey.

PERICLES    (aside)
How from the finny subject of the sea
These fishers tell the infirmities of men,
And from their watery empire recollect
All that may men approve or men detect!—
Peace be at your labour, honest fishermen!

SECOND FISHERMAN    Honest, good fellow? What's that,
if it is a day fits you? Search out of the calendar, and
nobody look after it.

PERICLES
Nay, see the sea has cast upon your coast—

SECOND FISHERMAN  What a drunken knave was the
sea to cast you in our way!

PERICLES
A man whom both the waters and the wind,
In that vast tennis-court, has made the ball
For them to play upon entreats you pity him.
He asks of you that never used to beg.

FIRST FISHERMAN  No, friend, cannot you beg? Here's
them in our country of Greece get more with begging
than we can do with working.

SECOND FISHERMAN  Can you catch any fishes then?

PERICLES  I never practised it.

SECOND FISHERMAN  Nay then, you will starve, sure, for
here's nothing to be got nowadays unless you can fish
for it.

PERICLES
What I have been I have forgotten to know;
But what I am, want teaches me to think on:
A man frozen with cold; my veins are chill,
And have no more of life than may suffice
To give my tongue that heat to ask your help;
Which if you shall refuse, when I am dead,
Because I am a man, pray you see me buried.

FIRST FISHERMAN  Die, says he! Now gods forbid it if I
have a gown here! Come, put it on, keep you warm.
Now, on my word, a handsome fellow! Come, you shall
go home, and we'll have flesh for holidays, fish for
fastingdays, and moreover puddings and pancakes, and
you shall be welcome.

PERICLES  I thank you, sir.

SECOND FISHERMAN  Hark you, my friend, you said you
could not beg?

PERICLES  I did but crave.

SECOND FISHERMAN  But crave? Then I'll turn craver
too, and so I shall escape whipping.

PERICLES  Why, are your beggars whipped then?

SECOND FISHERMAN   O, not all, my friend, not all, for if all your beggars were whipped, I would wish no better office than to be beadle. But, master, I'll go draw up the net.                          *Exeunt Second and Third Fishermen*

PERICLES   *(aside)*
How well this honest mirth becomes their labour!

FIRST FISHERMAN   Hark you, sir, do you know where you are?

PERICLES   Not well.

FIRST FISHERMAN   Why, I'll tell you. This is called Pentapolis, and our king the good Simonides.

PERICLES   The good Simonides do you call him?

FIRST FISHERMAN   Ay, sir, and he deserves so to be called for his peaceable reign and good government.

PERICLES   He is a happy king, since he gains from his subjects the name of good by his government. How far is his Court distant from this shore?

FIRST FISHERMAN   Well, sir, half a day's journey. And I'll tell you, he has a fair daughter, and tomorrow is her birthday, and there are princes and knights come from all parts of the world to joust and tourney for her love.

PERICLES   Were my fortunes equal to my desires, I could wish to make one there.

FIRST FISHERMAN   O, sir, things must be as they may; and what a man cannot get, he may lawfully deal for his wife's soul.

*Enter the two Fishermen, drawing up a net*

SECOND FISHERMAN   Help, master, help! Here's a fish hangs in the net like a poor man's right in the law; it will hardly come out. Ha, plague on it, 'tis come at last, and 'tis turned to a rusty armour.

PERICLES
An armour, friends? I pray you let me see it.
Thanks, Fortune, that after all your crosses

You give me somewhat to repair myself;
And though it was my own, part of my heritage,
Which my dead father did bequeath to me,
With this strict charge, even as he left his life.
'Keep it, my Pericles; it has been a shield
Between me and death', and pointed to this brace,
'Because it saved me, keep it. In like necessity,
Which the gods protect you from, may it defend you.'
It kept where I kept, I so dearly loved it,
Till the rough seas, that spare not any man,
Took it in rage, though calmed have given it again.
I thank you for it. My shipwreck now's no ill,
Since I have what my father gave in his will.
FIRST FISHERMAN    What mean you, sir?
PERICLES
To beg of you, kind friends, this coat of worth,
For it was sometime armour to a king.
I know it by this mark. He loved me dearly,
And for his sake I wish the having of it,
And that you'd guide me to your sovereign's Court,
Where with it I may appear a gentleman.
And if then ever my low fortune is better,
I'll pay your bounties; till then rest your debtor.
FIRST FISHERMAN    Why, will you tourney for the lady?
PERICLES
I'll show the virtue I have borne in arms.
FIRST FISHERMAN    Why, take it, and the gods give you
good of it.
SECOND FISHERMAN    Ay, but hark you, my friend, it
was we that made up this garment through the rough
seams of the waters. There are certain condolements,
certain tips. I hope, sir, if you thrive, you'll remember
from whence you had them.
PERICLES
Believe it, I will.
By your furtherance I am clothed in steel,

And spite of all the plunder of the sea
This jewel holds the building on my arm.
Unto your value I will mount myself
Upon a courser, whose delightful steps
Shall make the gazer joy to see him tread.
Only, my friend, I yet am unprovided
Of a pair of breeches.

SECOND FISHERMAN    We'll sure provide. You shall have
my best gown to make you a pair, and I'll bring you to
the Court myself.

PERICLES
Then honour be but a goal to my will,
This day I'll rise, or else add ill to ill.                    *Exeunt*


# SCENE II
## Pentapolis. Before the Lists.

*Enter Simonides with Lords and attendants, and Thaisa*

SIMONIDES
Are the knights ready to begin the triumph?

FIRST LORD
They are, my liege,
And stay your coming to present themselves.

SIMONIDES
Return them we are ready; and our daughter here,
In honour of whose birth these triumphs are,
Sits here like beauty's child, whom Nature gat [got]
For men to see and, seeing, wonder at.

THAISA
It pleases you, my royal father, to express
My commendations great, whose merit's less.

SIMONIDES
It is fit it should be so, for princes are
A model which heaven makes like to itself.

As jewels lose their glory if neglected,
So princes their renowns if not respected.
It is now your honour, daughter, to entertain
The labour of each knight in his device.

THAISA
Which, to preserve my honour, I'll perform.

*The First Knight enters and passes by, his squire presenting
his shield to Thaisa*

SIMONIDES
Who is the first that does prefer himself?
THAISA
A knight of Sparta, my renownèd father,
And the device he bears upon his shield
Is a black Ethiop reaching at the sun.
The word, *Lux tua vita mihi.*[1]
SIMONIDES
He loves you well that holds his life of you.

*The Second Knight passes by*

Who is the second that presents himself?
THAISA
A prince of Macedon, my royal father,
And the device he bears upon his shield
Is an armed knight that's conquered by a lady.
The motto thus in Spanish, *Piu per dolcera che per
forza.*[2]

*The Third Knight passes by*

---

[1]Your light is life to me.
[2]More by gentleness than by force.

SIMONIDES
   And with the third?
THAISA            The third of Antioch,
   And his device a wreath of chivalry.
   The word, *Me pompae provexit apex*.[3]

*The Fourth Knight passes by*

SIMONIDES
   What is the fourth?
THAISA
   A burning torch that's turnèd upside down.
   The word, *Qui me alit me extinguit*.[4]
SIMONIDES
   Which shows that beauty has its power and will,
   Which can as well inflame as it can kill.

*The Fifth Knight passes by*

THAISA
   The fifth, a hand environèd with clouds,
   Holding out gold that's by the touchstone tried.
   The motto thus, *Sic spectanda fides*.[5]

*The Sixth Knight, Pericles, passes by*

SIMONIDES
   And what's the sixth and last, which the knight himself
   With such a graceful courtesy delivered?

---

[3]The honour of the contest drew me on.
[4]Who feeds me extinguishes me.
[5]Thus is faith to be tested.

THAISA
    He seems to be a stranger, but his present is
    A withered branch that's only green at top.
    The motto, *In hac spe vivo.*[6]

SIMONIDES
    A pretty moral,
    From the dejected state wherein he is,
    He hopes by you his fortunes yet may flourish.

FIRST LORD
    He had need mean better than his outward show
    Can any way speak in his just commend,
    For by his rusty outside he appears
    To have practised more the whiphand than the lance.

SECOND LORD
    He well may be a stranger, for he comes
    To an honoured triumph strangely furnishèd.

THIRD LORD
    And on set purpose let his armour rust
    Until this day, to scour it in the dust.

SIMONIDES
    Opinion's but a fool, that makes us scan
    By outward habit the true inward man.
    But stay, the knights are coming.
    We will withdraw into the gallery.                    *Exeunt*

*(Within) Great shouts, and all cry* 'The mean knight!'


# SCENE III
## Pentapolis. The palace.

*Enter Simonides, Thaisa, Pericles, and Knights from tilting,*
*with lords, ladies, Marshal, and attendants*

---

[6]In this hope I live.

SIMONIDES
    Knights,
    To say you are welcome is superfluous.
    To place upon the volume of your deeds,
    As in a title-page, your worth in arms,
    Is more than you expect, or more than is fit,
    Since every worth in show commends itself.
    Prepare for mirth, for mirth becomes a feast.
    You are princes and my guests.
THAISA    (to Pericles)
    But you, my knight and guest;
    To whom this wreath of victory I give,
    And crown you king of this day's happiness.
PERICLES
    It is more by fortune, lady, than my merit.
SIMONIDES
    Call it by what you will, the day is yours,
    And here, I hope, is none that envies it.
    In framing an artist, art has thus decreed,
    To make some good, but others to exceed,
    And you are her laboured scholar. Come, queen of the
        feast—
    For, daughter, so you are—here take your place.
    Marshal the rest as they deserve their grace.
KNIGHTS
    We are honoured much by good Simonides.
SIMONIDES
    Your presence glads our days; honour we love,
    For who hates honour hates the gods above.
MARSHAL
    Sir, yonder is your place.
PERICLES                        Some other is more fit.
FIRST KNIGHT
    Contend not, sir, for we are gentlemen
    Have neither in our hearts nor outward eyes
    Envied the great nor shall the low despise.

PERICLES
  You are right courteous knights.
SIMONIDES                    Sit, sir, sit.
  (*Aside*) By Jove, I wonder, that is king of thoughts,
  These meats resist me, he but thought upon.
THAISA    (*aside*)
  By Juno, that is queen of marriàge,
  All viands that I eat do seem unsavoury,
  Wishing him my meat. — Sure he's a gallant gentleman.
SIMONIDES
  He's but a country gentleman.
  He has done no more than other knights have done.
  He has broken a staff or so. So let it pass.
THAISA    (*aside*)
  To me he seems like diamond to glass.
PERICLES    (*aside*)
  Yon king's to me like my father's picture
  Which tells me in what glory once he was;
  Had princes sit like stars about his throne,
  And he the sun for them to reverence.
  None that beheld him but like lesser lights
  Did scant their crowns to his supremacy.
  Where now his son's like a glow-worm in the night,
  Which once had fire in darkness, none in light;
  Whereby I see that Time's the king of men.
  He's both their parent and he is their grave,
  And gives them what he will, not what they crave.
SIMONIDES
  What, are you merry, knights?
KNIGHTS
  Who can be other in this royal presence?
SIMONIDES
  Here with a cup that's stored unto the brim,
  As you do love, fill to your mistress' lips.
  We drink this health to you.
KNIGHTS                    We thank your grace.

SIMONIDES
Yet pause awhile.
Yon knight does sit too melancholy,
As if the entertainment in our Court
Had not a show might parallel his worth.
Note it not you, Thaisa?

THAISA
What is it to me, my father?

SIMONIDES
O, attend, my daughter:
Princes in this should live like gods above,
Who freely give to everyone that comes to honour them.
And princes not doing so are like the gnats,
Which make a sound, but killed are wondered at.
Therefore to make his entrance now more sweet,
Here, say we drink this standing-bowl of wine to him.

THAISA
Alas, my father, it befits not me
Unto a stranger knight to be so bold.
He may my proffer take for an offence,
Since men take women's gifts for impudence.

SIMONIDES
How?
Do as I bid you, or you'll move me else.

THAISA    *(aside)*
Now, by the gods, he could not please me better.

SIMONIDES
And furthermore tell him we desire to know of him
Of whence he is, his name, and parentage.

THAISA
The King my father, sir, has drunk to you.

PERICLES
I thank him.

THAISA
Wishing it so much blood unto your life.

PERICLES
   I thank both him and you, and pledge him freely.
THAISA
   And further he desires to know of you
   Of whence you are, your name, and parentage.
PERICLES
   A gentleman of Tyre, my name Pericles,
   My education been in arts and arms,
   Who, looking for adventures in the world,
   Was by the rough seas bereft of ships and men,
   And after shipwreck driven upon this shore.
THAISA
   He thanks your grace, names himself Pericles,
   A gentleman of Tyre,
   Who only by misfortune of the seas,
   Bereft of ships and men, cast on this shore.
SIMONIDES
   Now, by the gods, I pity his misfortune
   And will awake him from his melancholy.
   Come, gentlemen, we sit too long on trifles,
   And waste the time which looks for other revels.
   Even in your armours, as you are addressed,
   You will well become a soldiers' dance.
   I will not have excuse with saying this:
   Loud music is too harsh for ladies' heads,
   Since they love men in arms as well as beds.

*They dance*

   So, this was well asked, 'twas so well performed.
   Come, sir, here's a lady that wants breathing too,
   And I have heard you knights of Tyre
   Are excellent in making ladies trip,
   And that their measures are as excellent.
PERICLES
   In those that practise them they are, my lord.

SIMONIDES

  O, that's as much as you would be denied

  Of your fair courtesy.

*They dance*

      Unclasp, unclasp!

  Thanks, gentlemen, to all. All have done well,

  (*to Pericles*) But you the best.—Pages and lights, to conduct

  These knights unto their several lodgings.—

  Yours, sir, we give order be next our own.

PERICLES

  I am at your grace's pleasure.

SIMONIDES

  Princes, it is too late to talk of love,

  And that's the mark I know you level at.

  Therefore each one betake him to his rest;

  Tomorrow all for speeding do their best.     *Exeunt*

## SCENE IV
## Tyre. Helicanus's house.

*Enter Helicanus and Escanes*

HELICANUS

  No, Escanes, know this of me,

  Antiochus from incest lived not free.

  For which the most high gods not minding longer

  To withhold the vengeance that they had in store,

  Due to this heinous capital offence,

  Even in the height and pride of all his glory,

  When he was seated in a chariot

  Of an inestimable value, and his daughter with him,

  A fire from heaven came and shrivelled up

  Their bodies even to loathing. For they so stunk

  That all those eyes adored them ere their fall

  Scorn now their hand should give them burial.

ESCANES
  'Twas very strange.
HELICANUS          And yet but justice, for though
  This king was great, his greatness was no guard
  To bar heaven's shaft, but sin had its reward.
ESCANES
  'Tis very true.

*Enter two or three Lords*

FIRST LORD
  See, not a man in private conference
  Or council has respect with him but he.
SECOND LORD
  It shall no longer grieve without reproof.
THIRD LORD
  And cursed be he that will not second it.
FIRST LORD
  Follow me then. Lord Helicane, a word.
HELICANUS
  With me? And welcome. Happy day, my lords.
FIRST LORD
  Know that our griefs are risen to the top,
  And now at length they overflow their banks.
HELICANUS
  Your griefs? For what? Wrong not your prince you love.
FIRST LORD
  Wrong not yourself then, noble Helicane,
  But if the prince does live, let us salute him
  And know what ground's made happy by his breath.
  If in the world he lives we'll seek him out;
  If in his grave he rests we'll find him there.
  And be resolved he lives to govern us,
  Or dead, give us cause to mourn his funeral
  And leave us to our free election.

SECOND LORD
>Whose death indeed is strongest in our judgement,
>And knowing this kingdom is without a head,
>Like goodly buildings left without a roof,
>Soon fall to ruin—your noble self,
>That best know how to rule and how to reign,
>We thus submit unto, our sovereign.

ALL
>Live, noble Helicane!

HELICANUS
>Try honour's cause; forbear your suffrages.
>If you do love Prince Pèricles, forbear.
>Take I your wish, I leap into the seas,
>Where's hourly trouble, for a minute's ease.
>A twelvemonth longer let me entreat you
>Further to bear the absence of your king;
>If in which time expired he not returns,
>I shall with agèd patience bear your yoke.
>But if I cannot win you to this love,
>Go search like nobles, like noble subjects,
>And in your search spend your adventurous worth.
>Whom if you find, and win unto return,
>You shall like diamonds sit about his crown.

FIRST LORD
>To wisdom he's a fool that will not yield,
>And since Lord Helicane enjoins us now
>We with our travels will endeavour it.

HELICANUS
>Then you love us, we you, and we'll clasp hands.
>When peers thus knit, a kingdom ever stands. *Exeunt*

# SCENE V
## Pentapolis. The palace.

*Enter Simonides, reading a letter, at one door. The Knights*
*meet him*

FIRST KNIGHT
Good morrow to the good Simonides.
SIMONIDES
Knights, from my daughter this I let you know,
That for this twelvemonth she'll not undertake
A married life.
Her reason to herself is only known,
Which from her by no means can I get.
SECOND KNIGHT
May we not get access to her, my lord?
SIMONIDES
Faith, by no means. She has so strictly
Tied her to her chamber, that 'tis impossible.
One twelve moons more she'll wear Diana's livery.
This by the eye of Cynthia has she vowed
And on her virgin honour will not break it.
THIRD KNIGHT
Loath to bid farewell, we take our leaves. *Exeunt Knights*
SIMONIDES
So, they are well dispatched.
Now to my daughter's letter.
She tells me here she'll wed the stranger knight,
Or ever more to view nor day nor light.
'Tis well, mistress, your choice agrees with mine.
I like that well. Nay, how absolute she's in it,
Not minding whether I dislike or no.
Well, I do commend her choice,
And will no longer have it be delayed.
Soft, here he comes; I must dissemble it.

*Enter Pericles*

PERICLES
   All fortune to the good Simonides!
SIMONIDES
   To you as much, sir. I am beholding to you
   For your sweet music this last night. I do
   Protest my ears were never better fed
   With such delightful, pleasing harmony.
PERICLES
   It is your grace's pleasure to commend,
   Not my desert.
SIMONIDES          Sir, you are music's master.
PERICLES
   The worst of all her scholars, my good lord.
SIMONIDES
   Let me ask you one thing. What do you think
   Of my daughter, sir?
PERICLES              A most virtuous princess.
SIMONIDES
   And she is fair too, is she not?
PERICLES
   As a fair day in summer, wondrous fair.
SIMONIDES
   Sir, my daughter thinks very well of you;
   Ay, so well, that you must be her master,
   And she will be your scholar. Therefore, look to it.
PERICLES
   I am unworthy for her schoolmaster.
SIMONIDES
   She thinks not so; peruse this writing else.
PERICLES   (aside)
   What's here?
   A letter that she loves the knight of Tyre!
   It is the King's subtlety to have my life. —
   O, seek not to entrap me, gracious lord,
   A stranger and distressèd gentleman,

That never aimed so high to love your daughter,
But bent all offices to honour her.
SIMONIDES
You have bewitched my daughter,
And you are a villain.
PERICLES                    By the gods, I have not.
Never did thought of mine levy offence,
Nor ever did my actions yet commence
A deed might gain her love or your displeasure.
SIMONIDES
Traitor, you lie.
PERICLES               Traitor!
SIMONIDES                     Ay, traitor,
That thus disguised are stolen into my Court,
With the witchcraft of your actions to bewitch
The yielding spirit of my tender child.
PERICLES
Even in his throat, unless it is the King,
That calls me traitor, I return the lie.
SIMONIDES   (aside)
Now, by the gods, I do applaud his courage.
PERICLES
My actions are as noble as my thoughts,
That never relished of a base descent.
I came unto your Court for honour's cause,
And not to be a rebel to its state.
And he that otherwise accounts of me,
This sword shall prove he's honour's enemy.
SIMONIDES
No?
Here comes my daughter. She can witness it.

*Enter Thaisa*

PERICLES
Then, as you are as virtuous as fair,
Resolve your angry father if my tongue

Did ever solicit, or my hand subscribe
To any syllable that made love to you.

THAISA

Why, sir, say if you had, who takes offence
At that which would make me glad?

SIMONIDES

Yes, mistress, are you so peremptory?
(*Aside*) I am glad of it with all my heart.—
I'll tame you, I'll bring you in subjectiòn.
Will you, not having my consent,
Bestow your love and your affectiòns
Upon a stranger? (*aside*) who, for aught I know,
May be, nor can I think the contrary,
As great in blood as I myself—
A straggling Theseus born we know not where?
Therefore, hear you, mistress, either frame
Your will to mine—and you, sir, hear you,
Either be ruled by me, or I'll make you—
Man and wife.
Nay, come, your hands and lips must seal it too.
And being joined, I'll thus your hopes destroy,
And for further grief—God give you joy!
What, are you both pleased?

THAISA                                    Yes, if you love me, sir?

PERICLES

Even as my life my blood that fosters it.

SIMONIDES

What, are you both agreed?

PERICLES *and* THAISA

Yes, if it please your majesty.

SIMONIDES

It pleases me so well that I will see you wed;
And then, with what haste you can, get you to bed.

                                                *Exeunt*

# Act III

*Enter Gower*

GOWER
Now sleep has slakèd all the rout,
No din but snores about the house,
Made louder by the o'erfed breast
Of this most pompous marriage-feast.
The cat, with eyes of burning coal,
Now couches from the mouse's hole,
And crickets sing at the oven's mouth,
All the blither for their drouth.
Hymen has brought the bride to bed,
Where, by the loss of maidenhead,
A babe is moulded. Be attent,
And time that is so briefly spent
With your fine fancies quaintly eke.
What's dumb in show, I'll plainly speak.

*Dumb show:*
*Enter Pericles and Simonides at one door with attendants.*
*A messenger meets them, kneels, and gives Pericles a*
*letter. Pericles shows it to Simonides; the lords kneel to*
*him. Then enter Thaisa with child, with Lychòrida, a*
*nurse. The King shows her the letter; she rejoices. She*
*and Pericles take leave of her father and depart with*
*Lychorida. The rest go out.*

By many a dull and painful perch
Of Pericles the careful search,
By the four opposing coigns
Which the world together joins,
Is made with all due diligence
That horse and sail and high expense
Can speed the quest. At last from Tyre,
Fame answering the most strange inquire,
To the Court of King Simonides
Are letters brought, the tenor these:
Antiochus and his daughter dead,
The men of Tyrus on the head
Of Helicanus would set on
The crown of Tyre, but he will none.
The mutiny he hastes to oppress;
Says to them, if King Pericles
Comes not home in twice six moons,
He, obedient to their dooms,
Will take the crown. The sum of this,
Brought hither to Pentapolis,
Did ravish so the regions round,
And everyone with claps can sound
'Our heir-apparent is a king!
Who dreamed, who thought of such a thing?'
Brief, he must hence depart to Tyre.
His queen with child makes her desire—
Which who shall cross?—along to go.
Omit we all their dole and woe.
Lychòrida her nurse she takes,
And so to sea. Their vessel shakes
On Neptune's billow; half the flood
Has their keel cut; but fortune's mood
Varies again. The grisled north
Disgorges such a tempest forth
That, as a duck for life that dives,
So up and down the poor ship drives.

The lady shrieks and, well-a-near,
Does fall in travail with her fear.
And what ensues in this fell storm
Shall for itself itself perform.
I nill relate, action may
Conveniently the rest convey,
Which might not what by me is told.
In your imagination hold
This stage the ship, upon whose deck
The sea-tossed Pericles appears to speak. *Exit*

# Act III

## SCENE I
## A ship at sea.

*Enter Pericles on shipboard*

PERICLES
The god of this great vast rebuke these surges,
Which wash both heaven and hell. And you that have
Upon the winds command, bind them in brass,
Having called them from the deep! O, still
Your deafening, dreadful thunders, gently quench
Your nimble, sulphurous flashes! O, how, Lychorida,
How does my queen? You storm, venomously
Will you spit all yourself? The seaman's whistle
Is as a whisper in the ears of death,
Unheard. Lychorida! Lucina, O
Divinest patroness and midwife gentle
To those that cry by night, convey your deity
Aboard our dancing boat, make swift the pangs
Of my queen's travails! Now, Lychorida!

*Enter Lychorida with a baby*

LYCHORIDA
Here is a thing too young for such a place,
Who if it had knowledge would die as I
Am like to do. Take in your arms this piece
Of your dead queen.

561

PERICLES                How? How, Lychorida?
LYCHORIDA
   Patience, good sir, do not assist the storm.
   Here's all that is left living of your queen,
   A little daughter; for the sake of it,
   Be manly and take comfort.
PERICLES                      O you gods!
   Why do you make us love your goodly gifts
   And snatch them straight away? We here below
   Recall not what we give, and therein may
   Use honour with you.
LYCHORIDA                Patience, good sir,
   Even for this charge.
PERICLES                 Now, mild may be your life!
   For a more blusterous birth had never babe;
   Quiet and gentle your conditions! for
   You are the rudeliest welcome to this world
   That ever was prince's child. Happy what follows!
   You have as chiding a nativity
   As fire, air, water, earth, and heaven can make
   To herald you from the womb. Poor inch of nature!
   Even at the first your loss is more than can
   Your voyage quit, with all you can find here.
   Now the good gods throw their best eyes upon it.

*Enter two Sailors*

FIRST SAILOR   What courage, sir? God save you!
PERICLES
   Courage enough. I do not fear the storm;
   It has done to me the worst. Yet for the love
   Of this poor infant, this fresh new seafarer,
   I would it would be quiet.
FIRST SAILOR   Slack the bowlines there!—You will not,
   will you? Blow and split yourself.

SECOND SAILOR    But sea-room, if the brine and cloudy
  billow kiss the moon, I care not.
FIRST SAILOR    Sir, your queen must overboard. The sea
  works high, the wind is loud, and will not lie till the
  ship be cleared of the dead.
PERICLES    That is your superstition.
FIRST SAILOR    Pardon us, sir; with us at sea it has been
  ever observed, and we are strong in custom. Therefore
  briefly yield her, for she must overboard straight.
PERICLES
  As you think meet. Most wretched queen!
LYCHORIDA    Here she lies, sir.

  *She reveals the body of Thaisa*

PERICLES
  A terrible childbed have you had, my dear;
  No light, no fire; the unfriendly elements
  Forgot you utterly. Nor have I time
  To give you hallowed to your grave, but straight
  Must cast you, scarcely coffined, in the ooze,
  Where, for a monument upon your bones,
  And aye-remaining lamps, the belching whale
  And humming water must o'erwhelm your corpse,
  Lying with simple shells. O Lychorida,
  Bid Nestor bring me spices, ink and paper,
  My casket and my jewels. And bid Nicander
  Bring me the satin coffer. Lay the babe
  Upon the pillow. Hie you, while I say
  A priestly farewell to her. Suddenly, woman.
                                        *Exit Lychorida*
SECOND SAILOR    Sir, we have a chest beneath the hatches,
  caulked and bitumoned ready.
PERICLES
  I thank you. Mariner, say, what coast is this?
FIRST SAILOR    We are near Tarsus.

PERICLES
    Thither, gentle mariner,
    Alter your course for Tyre. When can you reach it?
FIRST SAILOR   By break of day, if the wind ceases.
PERICLES
    O, make for Tarsus!
    There will I visit Cleon, for the babe
    Cannot hold out to Tyre. There I'll leave it
    At careful nursing. Go your ways, good mariner;
    I'll bring the body immediately.        *Exeunt*

## SCENE II
## Ephesus. Cerimon's house.

*Enter Cerimon and Servants*

CERIMON   Philemon, ho!

*Enter Philemon*

PHILEMON   Does my lord call?
CERIMON
    Get fire and meat for these poor men.
    It has been a turbulent and stormy night. *Exit Philemon*
FIRST SERVANT
    I have been in many, but such a night as this
    Till now I never endured.
CERIMON   *(to First Servant)*
    Your master will be dead ere you return.
    There's nothing can be ministered to nature
    That can recover him. *(To Second Servant)* Give this to
      the apothecary
    And tell me how it works.     *Exeunt Servants*

*Enter two Gentlemen*

FIRST GENTLEMAN          Good morrow.
SECOND GENTLEMAN
  Good morrow to your lordship.
CERIMON                    Gentlemen,
  Why do you stir so early?
FIRST GENTLEMAN        Sir,
  Our lodgings, standing bleak upon the sea,
  Shook as the earth did quake.
  The very beams of the roof did seem to rend
  And all to topple. Pure surprise and fear
  Made me to quit the house.
SECOND GENTLEMAN
  That is the cause we trouble you so early;
  It is not our husbandry.
CERIMON            O, you say well.
FIRST GENTLEMAN
  But I much marvel that your lordship, having
  Rich things about you, should at these early hours
  Shake off the golden slumber of repose.
  It is most strange
  Nature should be so conversant with pain,
  Being thereto not compelled.
CERIMON                I held it ever
  Virtue and cunning were endowments greater
  Than nobleness and riches. Careless heirs
  May the two latter darken and expend,
  But immortality attends the former,
  Making a man a god. It is known I ever
  Have studied physic, through which secret art,
  By turning over authorities I have,
  Together with my practice, made familiar
  To me and to my aid the blest infusions
  That dwell in vegetives, in metals, stones.
  And I can speak of the disturbances
  That nature works and of its cures; which does give me
  A more content in course of true delight

Than to be thirsty after tottering honour,
Or tie my pleasure up in silken bags,
To please the fool and death.
SECOND GENTLEMAN          Your honour has
Through Ephesus poured forth your charity,
And hundreds call themselves your creatures, who
By you have been restored. And not your knowledge,
Your personal pain, but even your purse, still open,
Have built Lord Cerimon such strong renown
As time shall never—

*Enter servants with a chest*

FIRST SERVANT
So, lift there!
CERIMON          What's that?
FIRST SERVANT          Sir, even now
Did the sea toss up upon our shore this chest.
'Tis of some wreck.
CERIMON          Set it down, let's look upon it.
SECOND GENTLEMAN
'Tis like a coffin, sir.
CERIMON          Whatever it is,
It is wondrous heavy. Wrench it open straight.
If the sea's stomach is o'ercharged with gold,
'Tis a good gift of fortune it belches upon us.
SECOND GENTLEMAN
It is so, my lord.
CERIMON          How close 'tis caulked and bitumened!
Did the sea cast it up?
FIRST SERVANT
I never saw so huge a billow, sir,
As tossed it upon shore.
CERIMON          Wrench it open. Soft!
It smells most sweetly in my sense.

SECOND GENTLEMAN                    A delicate odour.
CERIMON
   As ever hit my nostril. So, up with it!
   O you most potent gods, what's here? A corpse?
SECOND GENTLEMAN
   Most strange!
CERIMON
   Shrouded in cloth of state, balmed and entreasured
   With full bags of spices! A passport too!
   Apollo, instruct me in the characters!

*He reads the scroll*

*Here I give to understand,*
*If e'er this coffin drives a-land,*
*I, King Pericles, have lost*
*This queen, worth all our mundane cost.*
*Who finds her, give her burying;*
*She was the daughter of a king.*
*Besides this treasure for a fee,*
*The gods requite his charity.*

   If you live, Pericles, you have a heart
   That ever cracks for woe. This chanced tonight.
SECOND GENTLEMAN
   Most likely, sir.
CERIMON                    Nay, certainly tonight,
   For look how fresh she looks. They were too rough
   That threw her in the sea. Make a fire within.
   Fetch hither all my boxes in my closet. *Exit a servant*
   Death may usurp on nature many hours,
   And yet the fire of life kindle again
   The overpressed spirits.

*Enter one with napkins and fire*

Well said, well said, the fire and cloths.

The rough and woeful music that we have,
Cause it to sound, beseech you.

*Music plays while Cerimon attends to Thaisa*

The viol once more! How you stir, you block!
The music there!

*Music again*

I pray you give her air.
Gentlemen, this queen will live!
Nature awakes. A warmth breathes out of her.
She has not been entranced above five hours.
See how she begins to blow into life's flower again.
FIRST GENTLEMAN
The heavens, through you, increase our wonder, and
Sets up your fame for ever.
CERIMON                    She is alive. Behold,
Her eyelids, cases to those heavenly jewels
Which Pericles has lost, begin to part
Their fringes of bright gold. The diamonds
Of a most praisèd water do appear
To make the world twice rich. Live,
And make us weep to hear your fate, fair creature,
Rare as you seem to be.

*She moves*

THAISA                    O dear Diana!
Where am I? Where's my lord? What world is this?
SECOND GENTLEMAN
Is not this strange?
FIRST GENTLEMAN    Most rare.

CERIMON
   Hush, my gentle neighbours.
   Lend me your hands. To the next chamber bear her.
   Get linen. Now this matter must be looked to,
   For her relapse is mortal. Come, come;
   And Aesculapius guide us.
                        *They carry her away. Exeunt*


## SCENE III
## Tarsus. Cleon's house.

*Enter Pericles with Cleon and Dionyza, and Lychorida with
                  the baby in her arms*

PERICLES
   Most honoured Cleon, I must needs be gone.
   My twelve months are expired, and Tyre now stands
   In a litigious peace. You and your lady
   Take from my heart all thankfulness. The gods
   Make up the rest upon you!
CLEON                         Your shakes of fortune,
   Though they haunt you mortally, yet glance
   Full wonderingly on us.
DIONYZA                O, your sweet queen!
   That the strict fates had pleased you had brought her
      hither,
   To have blessed my eyes with her.
PERICLES                         We cannot but obey
   The powers above us. Could I rage and roar
   As does the sea she lies in, yet the end
   Must be as it is. My gentle babe Marina,
   Whom, for she was born at sea, I have named so,
   Here I charge your charity with, leaving her
   The infant of your care, beseeching you

To give her princely training, that she may
Be mannered as she is born.

CLEON                 Fear not, my lord, but think
Your grace, that fed my country with your corn,
For which the people's prayers still fall upon you,
Must in your child be thought on. If neglect
Should therein make me vile, the common body
By you relieved would force me to my duty.
But if to that my nature needs a spur,
The gods revenge it upon me and mine
To the end of generation.

PERICLES             I believe you.
Your honour and your goodness teach me to it
Without your vows. Till she is married, madam,
By bright Diana, whom we honour, all
Unscissored shall this hair of mine remain,
Though I show will in it. So I take my leave.
Good madam, make me blessèd in your care
In bringing up my child.

DIONYZA             I have one myself,
Who shall not be more dear to my respect
Than yours, my lord.

PERICLES          Madam, my thanks and prayers.

CLEON
We'll bring your grace even to the edge of the shore,
Then give you up to the masked Neptune, and
The gentlest winds of heaven.

PERICLES             I will embrace
Your offer. Come, dearest madam. O, no tears,
Lychorida, no tears.
Look to your little mistress, on whose grace
You may depend hereafter. Come, my lord. *Exeunt*

## SCENE IV
### Ephesus. Cerimon's house.

*Enter Cerimon and Thaisa*

CERIMON

Madam, this letter, and some certain jewels,
Lay with you in your coffer, which are
At your command. Know you the character?

THAISA

It is my lord's.
That I was shipped at sea I well remember,
Even on my bearing time. But whether there
Delivered, by the holy gods,
I cannot rightly say. But since King Pericles,
My wedded lord, I never shall see again,
A vestal livery will I take me to,
And never more have joy.

CERIMON

Madam, if this you purpose as you speak,
Diana's temple is not distant far,
Where you may abide till your date expires.
Moreover, if you please, a niece of mine
Shall there attend you.

THAISA

My recompense is thanks, and that is all;
Yet my good will is great, though the gift is small.

                                          *Exeunt*

# Act IV

CHORUS

*Enter Gower*

GOWER
Imagine Pericles arrived at Tyre,
Welcomed and settled to his own desire.
His woeful queen we leave at Ephesus,
Unto Diana there's a votaress.
Now to Marina bend your mind,
Whom our fast-growing scene must find
At Tarsus, and by Cleon trained
In music's letters; who has gained
Of education all the grace,
Which makes her both the heart and place
Of general wonder. But, alack,
That monster envy, oft the wrack
Of earnèd praise, Marina's life
Seeks to take off by treason's knife.
And in this kind, our Cleon has
One daughter and a full-grown wench,
Even ripe for marriage-rite. This maid
Called Philoten, and it is said
For certain in our story she
Would ever with Marina be;
When she weaved the fine-drawn silk
With fingers long, small, white as milk;
Or when she would with sharp needle wound
The cambric, which she made more sound
By hurting it; or when to the lute

She sang, and made the night-bird mute,
That still records with moan; or when
She would with rich and constant pen
Bow to her mistress Dian. Still
This Philoten contends in skill
With absolute Marina. So
With dove of Paphos might the crow
Vie feathers white. Marina gets
All praises, which are paid as debts,
And not as given. This so darks
In Philoten all graceful marks
That Cleon's wife, with envy rare,
A present murderer does prepare
For good Marina, that her daughter
Might stand peerless by this slaughter.
The sooner her vile thoughts to stead,
Lychorida, our nurse, is dead,
And cursèd Dionyza hath
The pregnant instrument of wrath
Ready for this blow. The unborn event
I do commend to your content.
Only I carried wingèd time
Post on the lame feet of my rhyme,
Which never could I so convey
Unless your thoughts went on my way.
Dionyza does appear
With Leonine, a murderer.                        *Exit*

# Act IV

## SCENE I
## Tarsus. Near the sea-shore.

*Enter Dionyza with Leonine*

DIONYZA
  Your oath remember. You have sworn to do it.
  'Tis but a blow, which never shall be known.
  You can not do a thing in the world so soon
  To yield you so much profit. Let not conscience,
  Which is but cold, inflaming love in your bosom,
  Inflame too nicely; nor let pity, which
  Even women have cast off, melt you, but be
  A soldier to your purpose.
LEONINE                    I will do it—
  But yet she is a goodly creature.
DIONYZA
  The fitter then the gods should have her.
  Here she comes weeping for her only mistress' death.
  You are resolved?
LEONINE           I am resolved.

*Enter Marina with a basket of flowers*

MARINA
  No, I will rob Tellus of her weed
  To strew your green with flowers. The yellows, blues,
  The purple violets, and marigolds
  Shall as a carpet hang upon your grave
  While summer days do last. Ay me, poor maid,

Born in a tempest when my mother died,
This world to me is as a lasting storm,
Whirring me from my friends.

DIONYZA

How now, Marina? Why do you keep alone?
How chance my daughter is not with you?
Do not consume your blood with sorrowing;
Have you a nurse of me. Lord, how your feature's
Changed with this unprofitable woe!
Come, give me your flowers. On the sea-margin
Walk with Leonine. The air is quick there,
And it pierces and sharpens the stomach.
Come, Leonine. Take her by the arm, walk with her.

MARINA

No, I pray you. I'll not bereave you of your servant.

DIONYZA

Come, come.
I love the King your father and yourself
With more than foreign heart. We every day
Expect him here. When he shall come and find
Our paragon to all reports thus blasted,
He will repent the breadth of his great voyage,
Blame both my lord and me that we have taken
No care to your best courses. Go, I pray you.
Walk and be cheerful once again. Reserve
That excellent complexion which did steal
The eyes of young and old. Care not for me;
I can go home alone.

MARINA                    Well, I will go,
But yet I have no desire to it.

DIONYZA

Come, come, I know it is good for you.
Walk half an hour, Leonine, at the least.
Remember what I have said.

LEONINE

I warrant you, madam.

DIONYZA

I'll leave you, my sweet lady, for a while.

Pray walk softly, do not heat your blood.

What! I must have care of you.

MARINA                          My thanks, sweet madam.

*Exit Dionyza*

Is this wind westerly that blows?

LEONINE                             South-west.

MARINA

When I was born the wind was north.

LEONINE                          Was it so?

MARINA

My father, as nurse says, did never fear,

But cried 'Good seamen!' to the sailors, galling

His kingly hands haling ropes,

And, clasping to the mast, endured a sea

That almost burst the deck.

LEONINE

When was this?

MARINA

When I was born.

Never were waves nor wind more violent,

And from the ladder-tackle washes off

A canvas-climber. 'Ha!' says one, 'will you out?'

And with a dropping industry they skip

From stem to stern. The boatswain whistles, and

The master calls and trebles their confusion.

LEONINE

Come, say your prayers.

MARINA

What mean you?

LEONINE

If you require a little space for prayer,

I grant it. Pray; but be not tedious, for

The gods are quick of ear, and I am sworn
To do my work with haste.

MARINA                              Why will you kill me?

LEONINE
  To satisfy my lady.

MARINA
  Why would she have me killed?
  Now, as I can remember, by my faith,
  I never did her hurt in all my life.
  I never spoke bad word nor did ill turn
  To any living creature. Believe me, sure,
  I never killed a mouse, nor hurt a fly.
  I trod upon a worm against my will,
  But I wept for it. How have I offended,
  Wherein my death might yield her any profit,
  Or my life imply her any danger?

LEONINE
  My commission
  Is not to reason of the deed, but do it.

MARINA
  You will not do it for all the world, I hope.
  You are well-featured, and your looks foreshow
  You have a gentle heart. I saw you lately
  When you caught hurt in parting two that fought.
  Good truth, it showed well in you. Do so now.
  Your lady seeks my life; come you between,
  And save poor me, the weaker.

LEONINE                          I am sworn,
  And will dispatch.

                    *He seizes her*
                    *Enter Pirates*

FIRST PIRATE   Hold, villain!            *Leonine runs away*
SECOND PIRATE   A prize, a prize!

THIRD PIRATE   Half-shares, mates, half-shares. Come, let's have her aboard suddenly.

*Exeunt Pirates, carrying off Marina*

*Enter Leonine*

LEONINE
These roguing thieves serve the great pirate Valdes,
And they have seized Marina. Let her go.
There's no hope she will return. I'll swear she's dead,
And thrown into the sea. But I'll see further.
Perhaps they will but please themselves upon her,
Not carry her aboard. If she remain
Whom they have ravished must by me be slain.

*Exit*

# SCENE II
## Mytilene. A brothel.

*Enter the three Bawds*

PANDER   Boult!

BOULT   Sir?

PANDER   Search the market narrowly. Mytilene is full of gallants. We lost too much money this mart by being too wenchless.

BAWD   We were never so much out of creatures. We have but poor three, and they can do no more than they can do. And they with continual action are even as good as rotten.

PANDER   Therefore let's have fresh ones, whatever we pay for them. If there is not a conscience to be used in every trade, we shall never prosper.

BAWD   You say true. 'Tis not our bringing up of poor bastards—as I think, I have brought up some eleven—

BOULT    Ay, to eleven, and brought them down again. But shall I search the market?

BAWD    What else, man? The stuff we have, a strong wind will blow it to pieces, they are so pitifully sodden.

PANDER    You say true, there's two unwholesome, in conscience. The poor Transylvanian is dead that lay with the little baggage.

BOULT    Ay, she quickly pooped him; she made him roast meat for worms. But I'll go search the market.    *Exit*

PANDER    Three or four thousand sequins were as pretty a proportion to live quietly, and so give over.

BAWD    Why to give over, I pray you? Is it a shame to get when we are old?

PANDER    O, our credit comes not in like the commodity, nor the commodity wages not with the danger. Therefore, if in our youths we could pick up some pretty estate, it were not amiss to keep our door hatched. Besides, the sore terms we stand upon with the gods will be strong with us for giving over.

BAWD    Come, other sorts offend as well as we.

PANDER    As well as we? Ay, and better too; we offend worse. Neither is our profession any trade; it's no calling. But here comes Boult.

*Enter Boult with the Pirates and Marina*

BOULT    Come your ways, my masters. You say she's a virgin?

FIRST PIRATE    O, sir, we doubt it not.

BOULT    Master, I have gone through for this piece you see. If you like her, so. If not, I have lost my deposit.

BAWD    Boult, has she any qualities?

BOULT    She has a good face, speaks well, and has excellent good clothes. There's no farther necessity of qualities can make her be refused.

BAWD    What's her price, Boult?

BOULT    I cannot be reduced one farthing of a thousand
  pieces.
PANDER    Well, follow me, my masters; you shall have
  your money presently. Wife, take her in. Instruct her
  what she has to do, that she may not be raw in her
  entertainment.                    *Exeunt Pander and Pirates*
BAWD    Boult, take you the marks of her, the colour of her
  hair, complexion, height, her age, with warrant of her
  virginity, and cry 'He that will give most shall have her
  first.' Such a maidenhead were no cheap thing, if men
  were as they have been. Get this done as I command
  you.
BOULT    Performance shall follow.                    *Exit*
MARINA
  Alack that Leonine was so slack, so slow!
  He should have struck, not spoken. Or that these pirates,
  Not enough barbarous, had not overboard
  Thrown me to seek my mother!
BAWD    Why lament you, pretty one?
MARINA    That I am pretty.
BAWD    Come, the gods have done their part in you.
MARINA    I accuse them not.
BAWD    You are light into my hands, where you are likely
  to live.
MARINA
  The more my fault
  To escape his hands where I was likely to die.
BAWD    Ay, and you shall live in pleasure.
MARINA    No.
BAWD    Yes, indeed shall you, and taste gentlemen of all
  fashions. You shall fare well. You shall have the variety
  of all complexions. What, do you stop your ears?
MARINA    Are you a woman?
BAWD    What would you have me be, if I am not a woman?
MARINA    An honest woman, or not a woman.

BAWD   Law, whip the gosling. I think I shall have
something to do with you. Come, you're a young foolish
sapling, and must be bowed as I would have you.

MARINA   The gods defend me!

BAWD   If it pleases the gods to defend you by way of men,
then men must comfort you, men must feed you, men
stir you up. Boult's returned.

*Enter Boult*

Now, sir, have you cried her through the market?

BOULT   I have cried her almost to the number of her
hairs. I have drawn her picture with my voice.

BAWD   And I pray you tell me, how do you find the
inclination of the people, especially of the younger sort?

BOULT   Faith, they listened to me as they would have
hearkened to their father's testament. There was a
Spaniard's mouth watered, and he went to bed to her
very description.

BAWD   We shall have him here tomorrow with his best
ruff on.

BOULT   Tonight, tonight. But, mistress, do you know the
French knight, that cowers in the hams?

BAWD   Who, Monsieur Veroles?

BOULT   Ay, he. He offered to cut a caper at the proclamation,
but he made a groan at it, and swore he would see her
tomorrow.

BAWD   Well, well, as for him, he brought his disease
hither; here he does but renew it. I know he will come
under our roof to scatter his symptoms.

BOULT   Well, if we had of every nation a traveller, we
should lodge them with this sign.

BAWD   *(to Marina)* Pray you, come hither awhile. You
have fortunes coming upon you. Mark me. You must
seem to do that fearfully which you commit willingly;
despise profit where you have most gain. To weep that

you live as you do makes pity in your lovers. Seldom but that pity begets you a good opinion, and that opinion a mere profit.

MARINA     I understand you not.

BOULT     O, wake her up, mistress, wake her up. These blushes of hers must be quenched with some speedy practice.

BAWD     You say true, in faith, so they must, for your bride goes to that with shame which is her way to go with warrant.

BOULT     Faith, some do and some do not. But, mistress, if I have bargained for the joint—

BAWD     You may cut a morsel off the spit.

BOULT     I may so.

BAWD     Who should deny it? Come, young one. I like the manner of your garments well.

BOULT     Ay, by my faith, they shall not be changed yet.

BAWD     Boult, spend you that in the town. Report what a sojourner we have. You'll lose nothing by custom. When nature framed this piece, she meant you a good turn. Therefore say what a paragon she is, and you have the harvest out of your own report.

BOULT     I warrant you, mistress, thunder shall not so awake the beds of eels as my giving out her beauty stirs up the lewdly inclined. I'll bring home some tonight.

BAWD     *(to Marina)* Come your ways. Follow me.

MARINA

    If fires be hot, knives sharp, or waters deep,

    Untied I still my virgin knot will keep.

    Diana, aid my purpose!

BAWD     What have we to do with Diana? Pray you, will you go with us?                                              *Exeunt*

## SCENE III
### Tarsus. Cleon's house.

*Enter Cleon and Dionyza*

DIONYZA
Why are you foolish? Can it be undone?

CLEON
O Dionyza, such a piece of slaughter
The sun and moon never looked upon.

DIONYZA
I think you will turn a child again.

CLEON
Were I chief lord of all this spacious world,
I would give it to undo the deed. A lady
Much less in blood than virtue, yet a princess
To equal any single crown of the earth
In the justice of compare. O villain Leonine!
Whom you have poisoned too.
If you had drunk to him, it had been a kindness
Becoming well your fact. What can you say
When noble Pericles shall demand his child?

DIONYZA
That she is dead. Nurses are not the Fates.
To foster is not ever to preserve.
She died at night. I'll say so. Who can cross it?
Unless you play the impious innocent
And, for an honest reputation, cry out
'She died by foul play.'

CLEON                    O, go to! Well, well,
Of all the faults beneath the heavens, the gods
Do like this worst.

DIONYZA                    Be one of those that think
The petty wrens of Tarsus will fly hence
And open this to Pericles. I do shame

To think of what a noble strain you are,
And of how coward a spirit.
CLEON                          To such proceeding
Whoever but his approbation added,
Though not his prime consent, he did not flow
From honourable courses.
DIONYZA                   Be it so, then.
Yet none does know but you how she came dead,
And none can know, Leonine being gone.
She did blemish my child, and stood between
Her and her fortunes. None would look on her,
But cast their gazes on Marina's face,
While ours was blurted at, and held a slut,
Not worth the time of day. It pierced me through.
And though you call my course unnatural,
You not your child well loving, yet I find
It greets me as an enterprise of kindness
Performed to your sole daughter.
CLEON                          Heavens forgive it!
DIONYZA
And as for Pericles,
What should he say? We wept after her hearse,
And yet we mourn. Her monument
Is almost finished, and her epitaphs
In glittering golden characters express
A general praise to her, and care in us
At whose expense 'tis done.
CLEON                     You are like the harpy,
Which, to betray, do with your angel's face
Seize with your eagle's talons.
DIONYZA
You are like one that superstitiously
Do swear to the gods that winter kills the flies.
But yet I know you will do as I advise.          *Exeunt*

## SCENE IV
### Tarsus. Before the monument.

*Enter Gower*

GOWER
Thus time we waste, and long leagues make short,
Sail seas in cockles, have and wish but for't,
Working to take your imagination
From bourn to bourn, region to region.
By you being pardoned, we commit no crime
To use one language in each several clime
Where our scene seems to live. I do beseech you
To learn of me, who stand in the gaps to teach you
The stages of our story. Pericles
Is now again thwarting the wayward seas,
Attended on by many a lord and knight,
To see his daughter, all his life's delight.
Old Helicànus goes along. Behind
Is left to govern it, you bear in mind,
Old Èscanès, whom Hèlicànus late
Advanced in time to great and high estate.
Well-sailing ships and bounteous winds have brought
This king to Tarsus—think his pilot thought;
So with his steerage shall your thoughts grow on—
To fetch his daughter home, who first is gone.
Like motes and shadows see them move awhile;
Your ears unto your eyes I'll reconcile.

*Dumb show:*
*Enter Pericles at one door, Cleon and Dionyza at the other. Cleon shows Pericles the tomb, Pericles makes lamentation, puts on sackcloth, and in a passion departs. The rest go out.*

See how belief may suffer by foul show!
This borrowed passion stands for true old woe,
And Pericles, in sorrow all devoured,
With sighs shot through, and biggest tears o'ershowered,
Leaves Tarsus and again embarks. He swears
Never to wash his face, nor cut his hairs.
He puts on sackcloth, and to sea. He bears
A tempest which his mortal vessel tears,
And yet he rides it out. Now please you wit
The epitaph is for Marina writ
By wicked Dionyza.
> *The fairest, sweetest, and best lies here,*
> *Who withered in her spring of year.*
> *She was of Tyrus the King's daughter*
> *On whom foul death has made this slaughter.*
> *Marina was she called, and at her birth,*
> *Thetis being proud swallowed some part of the earth.*
> *Therefore the earth, fearing to be o'erflowed,*
> *Has Thetis' birth-child on the heavens bestowed.*
> *Wherefore she does, and swears she'll never stint,*
> *Make raging battery upon shores of flint.*
No visor does become black villainy
So well as soft and tender flattery.
Let Pericles believe his daughter's dead,
And bear his courses to be orderèd
By Lady Fortune, while our scene must play
His daughter's woe and heavy well-a-day
In her unholy service. Patience then,
And think you now are all in Mytilene.                *Exit*

## SCENE V
## Mytilene. Before the brothel.

*Enter two Gentlemen*

FIRST GENTLEMAN    Did you ever hear the like?

SECOND GENTLEMAN    No, and never shall do in such a place as this, she being once gone.

FIRST GENTLEMAN    But to have divinity preached there! Did you ever dream of such a thing?

SECOND GENTLEMAN    No, no. Come, I am for no more bawdy houses. Shall we go hear the vestals sing?

FIRST GENTLEMAN    I'll do anything now that is virtuous, but I am out of the road of rutting for ever.        *Exeunt*

## SCENE VI
## The brothel.

*Enter the three Bawds*

PANDER    Well, I had rather than twice the worth of her she had never come here.

BAWD    Fie, fie upon her! She's able to freeze the god Priapus and undo a whole generation. We must either get her ravished or be rid of her. When she should do for clients her business and do me the kindness of our profession, she has her quirks, her reasons, her master reasons, her prayers, her knees, that she would make a puritan of the devil if he should bargain for a kiss of her.

BOULT    Faith, I must ravish her, or she'll disfurnish us of all our cavaliers and make our swearers priests.

PANDER    Now, the pox upon her green-sickness for me!

BAWD   Faith, there's no way to be rid of it but by the way
to the pox. Here comes the Lord Lysimachus disguised.

BOULT   We should have both lord and loon if the peevish
baggage would but give way to customers.

*Enter Lysimachus*

LYSIMACHUS   How now, how a dozen of virginities?

BAWD   Now, the gods to bless your honour!

BOULT   I am glad to see your honour in good health.

LYSIMACHUS   You may so; it is the better for you that your
resorters stand upon sound legs. How now, wholesome
iniquity have you, that a man may deal with and defy
the surgeon?

BAWD   We have here one, sir, if she would—but there
never came her like in Mytilene.

LYSIMACHUS   If she'd do the deeds of darkness, you would
say.

BAWD   Your honour knows what it is to say well enough.

LYSIMACHUS   Well, call forth, call forth.

BOULT   For flesh and blood, sir, white and red, you shall
see a rose. And she were a rose indeed, if she had but—

LYSIMACHUS   What, pray?

BOULT   O, sir, I can be modest.

LYSIMACHUS   That dignifies the renown of a bawd no
less than it gives a good report to a number to be chaste.

*Exit Boult*

BAWD   Here comes that which grows to the stalk, never
plucked yet, I can assure you.

*Enter Boult with Marina*

Is she not a fair creature?

LYSIMACHUS    Faith, she would serve after a long voyage at sea. Well, there's for you.

*He gives her money*

Leave us.

BAWD    I beseech your honour, give me leave a word, and I'll have done immediately.

LYSIMACHUS    I beseech you, do.

BAWD    *(to Marina)* First, I would have you note this is an honourable man.

MARINA    I desire to find him so, that I may worthily note him.

BAWD    Next, he's the governor of this country, and a man whom I am bound to.

MARINA    If he governs the country, you are bound to him indeed, but how honourable he is in that I know not.

BAWD    Pray you, without any more virginal fencing, will you use him kindly? He will line your apron with gold.

MARINA    What he will do graciously, I will thankfully receive.

LYSIMACHUS    Have you done?

BAWD    My lord, she's not broken in yet; you must take some pains to work her to your control. Come, we will leave his honour and her together. Go your ways.

*Exeunt Pander, Bawd, and Boult*

LYSIMACHUS    Now, pretty one, how long have you been at this trade?

MARINA    What trade, sir?

LYSIMACHUS    Why, I cannot name it but I shall offend.

MARINA    I cannot be offended with my trade. Please you to name it.

LYSIMACHUS    How long have you been of this profession?

MARINA    Ever since I can remember.

LYSIMACHUS    Did you go to it so young? Were you a gamester at five, or at seven.

MARINA    Earlier too, sir, if now I am one.

LYSIMACHUS    Why, the house you dwell in proclaims you
to be a creature of sale.

MARINA    Do you know this house to be a place of such
resort, and will come into it? I hear say you are of
honourable parts and are the governor of this place.

LYSIMACHUS    Why, has your principal made known unto
you who I am?

MARINA    Who is my principal?

LYSIMACHUS    Why, your herb-woman; she that sets seeds
and roots of shame and iniquity. O, you have heard
something of my power, and so stand aloof for more
serious wooing. But I protest to you, pretty one, my
authority shall not see you, or else look friendly upon
you. Come, bring me to some private place. Come, come.

MARINA
If you were born to honour, show it now;
If put upon you, make the judgement good
That thought you worthy of it.

LYSIMACHUS
How's this? How's this? Some more. Be sage.

MARINA                                    For me
That am a maid, though most ungentle fortune
Have placed me in this sty, where since I came
Diseases have been sold dearer than physic—
That the gods
Would set me free from this unhallowed place,
Though they did change me to the meanest bird
That flies in the purer air!

LYSIMACHUS
I did not think you could have spoken so well,
Never dreamt you could.
Had I brought hither a corrupted mind,
Your speech had altered it. Hold, here's gold for you.
Persevere in that clear way you go,
And the gods strengthen you.

MARINA
  The good gods preserve you.
LYSIMACHUS
  For me, be you assured
  That I came with no ill intent; for to me
  The very doors and windows savour vilely.
  Fare you well. You are a piece of virtue, and
  I doubt not but your training has been noble.
  Hold, here's more gold for you.
  A curse upon him, die he like a thief,
  That robs you of your goodness! If you
  Do hear from me, it shall be for your good.

*Enter Boult*

BOULT    I beseech your honour, one piece for me.
LYSIMACHUS
  Off with you, you damnèd doorkeeper!
  Your house, but for this virgin that does prop it,
  Would sink and overwhelm you. Away!            *Exit*
BOULT    How's this? We must take another course with
  you. If your peevish chastity, which is not worth a
  breakfast in the cheapest country under the sky, shall
  undo a whole household, let me be gelded like a spaniel.
  Come your ways.
MARINA    Whither would you have me?
BOULT    I must have your maidenhead taken off, or the
  common hangman shall execute it. Come your ways.
  We'll have no more gentlemen driven away. Come your
  ways, I say.

*Enter Pander and Bawd*

BAWD    How now, what's the matter?
BOULT    Worse and worse, mistress. She has here spoken
  holy words to the Lord Lysimachus.

BAWD   O, abominable!

BOULT   She makes our profession as it were to stink before the face of the gods.

BAWD   Sure, hang her up for ever!

BOULT   The nobleman would have dealt with her like a nobleman, and she sent him away as cold as a snowball, saying his prayers too.

BAWD   Boult, take her away. Use her at your pleasure. Crack the glass of her virginity, and make the rest malleable.

BOULT   If she were a thornier piece of ground than she is, she shall be ploughed.

MARINA   Hark, hark, you gods!

BAWD   She conjures! Away with her! Would she had never come within my doors! Hang you! She's born to undo us. Will you not go the way of womenkind? Come up, my dish of chastity with rosemary and bays!

*Exeunt Pander and Bawd*

BOULT   Come, mistress, come your way with me.

MARINA   Whither will you have me?

BOULT   To take from you the jewel you hold so dear.

MARINA   Pray tell me one thing first.

BOULT   Come now, your one thing.

MARINA   What can you wish your enemy to be?

BOULT   Why, I could wish him to be my master, or rather my mistress.

MARINA
Neither of these are so bad as you are,
Since they do better you in their command.
You hold a place
For which the most tormented fiend of hell
Would not in reputation change. You are
The damnèd doorkeeper to every blackguard
That comes inquiring for his Tib.
To the choleric fisting of every rogue

Your ear is liable. Your food is such
As has been belched on by infected lungs.

BOULT   What would you have me do? go to the wars,
would you? where a man may serve seven years for the
loss of a leg, and have not money enough in the end to
buy him a wooden one?

MARINA
Do anything but this
You do. Empty old receptacles
Or common sewers of filth;
Serve by indenture to the common hangman.
Any of these ways are yet better than this,
For what you profess, a baboon, could he speak,
Would own a name too dear. That the gods
Would safely deliver me from this place!
Here, here's gold for you.
If your master would gain by me,
Proclaim that I can sing, weave, sew, and dance,
With other virtues which I'll keep from boast,
And I will undertake all these to teach.
I doubt not but this populous city will
Yield many scholars.

BOULT   But can you teach all this you speak of?

MARINA
Prove that I cannot, take me home again
And prostitute me to the basest groom
That does frequent your house.

BOULT   Well, I will see what I can do for you. If I can
place you, I will.

MARINA   But among honest women.

BOULT   Faith, my acquaintance lies little among them.
But since my master and mistress have bought you,
there's no going but by their consent. Therefore I will
make them acquainted with your purpose, and I doubt
not but I shall find them tractable enough. Come, I'll
do for you what I can. Come your ways.          *Exeunt*

# Act V

CHORUS

*Enter Gower*

GOWER
  Marina thus the brothel escapes, and chances
    Into an honest house, our story says.
  She sings like one immortal, and she dances
    As goddess-like to her admirèd lays.
  Deep clerks she dumbs, with her needle composes
    Nature's own shape, of bud, bird, branch, or berry,
  That even her art sisters the natural roses;
    Her linen, silk, twin with the rubied cherry;
  That pupils lacks she none of noble race,
    Who pour their bounty on her, and her gain
  She gives the cursèd bawd. Here we her place,
    And to her father turn our thoughts again,
  Where we left him on the sea. We there him lost,
    Where, driven before the winds, he is arrived
  Here where his daughter dwells; and on this coast
    Suppose him now at anchor. The city strived
  God Neptune's annual feast to keep; from whence
    Lysimachus our Tyrian ship espies,
  His banners sable, trimmed with rich expense;
    And to him in his barge with fervour hies.
  In your supposing once more put your sight;
    Of heavy Pericles, think this his bark;
  Where what is done in action, more if might,
    Shall be discovered. Please you sit and hark.

*Exit*

595

# Act V

## SCENE I
## On board Pericles' ship.

*Enter Helicanus, and two Sailors, one of Tyre and one of
Mytilene*

SAILOR OF TYRE   *(to Sailor of Mytilene)*
   Where is Lord Helicanus? He can resolve you.
   O, here he is.
   Sir, there is a barge put off from Mytilene,
   And in it is Lysimachus, the governor,
   Who craves to come aboard. What is your will?
HELICANUS
   That he have his. Call up some gentlemen.
SAILOR OF TYRE   Ho, gentlemen! My lord calls.

*Enter two or three Gentlemen*

FIRST GENTLEMAN   Does your lordship call?
HELICANUS   Gentlemen, there is one of worth would
   come aboard. I pray greet him fairly.
                                        *Exeunt Gentlemen*

*Enter Lysimachus and Lords, with the Gentlemen*

SAILOR OF MYTILENE   *(to Lysimachus)*
   Sir,
   This is the man that can in aught you would
   Resolve you.

LYSIMACHUS　Hail, reverend sir! The gods preserve you!

HELICANUS
　And you, to outlive the age I am,
　And die as I would do.

LYSIMACHUS　　　　　You wish me well.
　Being on shore, honouring Neptune's triumphs,
　Seeing this goodly vessel ride before us,
　I made to it to know of whence you are.

HELICANUS
　First, what is your place?

LYSIMACHUS　　　　　I am the governor
　Of this place you lie before.

HELICANUS　　　　　Sir,
　Our vessel is of Tyre; in it the King,
　A man who for these three months has not spoken
　To anyone, nor taken sustenance
　But to prorogue his grief.

LYSIMACHUS
　Upon what ground is his distemperature?

HELICANUS
　It would be too tedious to repeat,
　But the main grief springs from the loss
　Of a belovèd daughter and a wife.

LYSIMACHUS
　May we not see him?

HELICANUS　　　　　You may,
　But useless is your sight; he will not speak
　To any.

LYSIMACHUS
　Yet let me obtain my wish.

*Helicanus draws a curtain revealing Pericles lying on a*
*couch*

HELICANUS
    Behold him. This was a goodly person,
    Till the disaster that one mortal night
    Drove him to this.
LYSIMACHUS
    Sir King, all hail! The gods preserve you!
    Hail, royal sir!
HELICANUS
    It is in vain. He will not speak to you.
LORD
    Sir,
    We have a maid in Mytilene, I durst wager,
    Would win some words of him.
LYSIMACHUS                Well thought of.
    She questionless, with her sweet harmony
    And other chosen attractions, would allure,
    And make a battery through his deafened gates,
    Which now are midway stopped.
    She is all happy as the fairest of all,
    And with her fellow maids is now upon
    The leafy shelter that abuts against
    The island's side.                 *Exit Lord*
HELICANUS
    Sure, all effectless; yet nothing we'll omit
    That bears recovery's name. But since your kindness
    We have stretched thus far, let us beseech you
    That for our gold we may provision have;
    Wherein we are not destitute for want,
    But weary for the staleness.
LYSIMACHUS           O, sir, a courtesy
    Which if we should deny, the most just God
    For every bud would send a caterpillar,
    And so inflict our province. Yet once more
    Let me entreat to know at large the cause
    Of your king's sorrow.

HELICANUS
Sit, sir. I will recount it to you. But see,
I am forestalled.

*Enter Lord, with Marina and her companion*

LYSIMACHUS
O, here's the lady that I sent for.
Welcome, fair one! Is it not a goodly presence?
HELICANUS
She is a gallant lady.
LYSIMACHUS
She's such a one that, were I well assured
She came of a gentle kind and noble stock,
I'd wish no better choice, and think me rarely wed.
Fair one, all goodness that consists in beauty,
Expect even here, where is a kingly patient,
If your prosperous and special skill
Can draw him but to answer you in aught,
Your sacred physic shall receive such pay
As your desires can wish.
MARINA                        Sir, I will use
My utmost skill in his recovery, provided
That none but I and my companion maid
Are suffered to come near him.
LYSIMACHUS                           Come, let us leave her,
And the gods make her prosperous.

*They withdraw*
*Marina sings*

LYSIMACHUS   *(coming forward)*
Marked he your music?

MARINA No, nor looked on us.
LYSIMACHUS (*withdrawing*)
  See, she will speak to him.
MARINA
  Hail, sir! My lord, lend ear.
PERICLES
  Hum, ha!

*He pushes her away*

MARINA
  I am a maid,
  My lord, that never before invited eyes,
  But have been gazed on like a comet. She speaks,
  My lord, that maybe has endured a grief
  Might equal yours, if both were justly weighed.
  Though wayward fortune did malign my state,
  My derivation was from ancestors
  Who stood equivalent with mighty kings.
  But time has rooted out my parentage,
  And to the world and awkward casualties
  Bound me in servitude. (*Aside*) I will desist,
  But there is something glows upon my cheek,
  And whispers in my ear 'Go not till he speaks.'
PERICLES
  My fortunes—parentage—good parentage—
  To equal mine—was it not thus? What say you?
MARINA
  I said, my lord, if you did know my parentage,
  You would not do me violence.
PERICLES
  I do think so. Pray you, turn your eyes upon me.
  You're like something that—What countrywoman?
  Here of these shores?

MARINA                    No, nor of any shores,
   Yet I was mortally brought forth, and am
   No other than I appear.

PERICLES
   I am great with woe, and shall deliver weeping.
   My dearest wife was like this maid,
   And such a one my daughter might have been.
   My queen's square brows, her stature to an inch,
   As wand-like straight, as silver-voiced,
   Her eyes as jewel-like, and cased as richly,
   In pace another Juno;
   Who starves the ears she feeds, and makes them hungry
   The more she gives them speech. Where do you live?

MARINA
   Where I am but a stranger. From the deck
   You may discern the place.

PERICLES                    Where were you bred?
   And how achieved you these endowments which
   You make more rich to own?

MARINA
   If I should tell my history, it would seem
   Like lies disdained in the reporting.

PERICLES                    Pray speak.
   Falseness cannot come from you, for you look
   Modest as justice, and you seem a palace
   For the crowned truth to dwell in. I will believe you,
   And make my senses credit your relation
   To points that seem impossible, for you look
   Like one I loved indeed. What were your friends?
   Did you not say, when I did push you back—
   Which was when I perceived you—that you came
   From good descending?

MARINA                    So indeed I did.

PERICLES
   Report your parentage. I think you said
   You had been tossed from wrong to injury,

And that you thought your griefs might equal mine,
If both were opened.

MARINA                    Some such thing I said,
And said no more but what my thoughts
Did warrant me was likely.

PERICLES                    Tell your story.
If yours considered proves the thousandth part
Of my endurance, you are a man, and I
Have suffered like a girl; yet you do look
Like Patience gazing on kings' graves and smiling
Extremity out of act. What were your friends?
How lost you them? Your name, my most kind virgin?
Recount, I do beseech you. Come, sit by me.

MARINA
My name is Marina.

PERICLES          O, I am mocked,
And you by some incensèd god sent hither
To make the world to laugh at me.

MARINA                    Patience, good sir,
Or here I'll cease.

PERICLES          Nay, I'll be patient.
You little know how you do startle me
To call yourself Marina.

MARINA               The name
Was given me by one that had some power,
My father, and a king.

PERICLES               How, a king's daughter?
And called Marina?

MARINA              You said you would believe me,
But, not to be a troubler of your peace,
I will end here.

PERICLES     But are you flesh and blood?
Have you a working pulse? And are no fairy?
Motion? Well, speak on. Where were you born?
And wherefore called Marina?

MARINA                    Called Marina
  For I was born at sea.
PERICLES              At sea! what mother?
MARINA
  My mother was the daughter of a king;
  Who died the minute I was born,
  As my good nurse Lychorida has oft
  Delivered weeping.
PERICLES          O, stop there a little!
  This is the rarest dream
  That ever dull sleep did mock sad fools withal.
  This cannot be—my daughter—burièd!
  Well, where were you bred?
  I'll hear you more, to the bottom of your story,
  And never interrupt you.
MARINA              You scorn. Believe me
  It were best I did give over.
PERICLES              I will believe you
  By the syllable of what you shall deliver.
  Yet give me leave: how came you in these parts?
  Where were you bred?
MARINA
  The King my father did in Tarsus leave me,
  Till cruel Cleon with his wicked wife
  Did seek to murder me.
  And having wooed a villain to attempt it,
  Who having drawn to do it,
  A crew of pirates came and rescued me,
  Brought me to Mytilene. But, good sir,
  Whither will you have me? Why do you weep? It may
    be
  You think me an imposter. No, good faith!
  I am the daughter to King Pericles,
  If good King Pericles be.

PERICLES                    Ho, Helicanus!
HELICANUS
  Calls my lord?
PERICLES
  You are a grave and noble counsellor,
  Most wise in general. Tell me, if you can,
  What this maid is, or what is likely to be,
  That thus has made me weep.
HELICANUS                    I know not,
  But here's the regent, sir, of Mytilene
  Speaks nobly of her.
LYSIMACHUS          She never would tell
  Her parentage. Being demanded that,
  She would sit still and weep.
PERICLES
  O Helicanus, strike me, honoured sir,
  Give me a gash, put me to present pain,
  Lest this great sea of joys rushing upon me
  O'erbear the shores of my mortality
  And drown me with their sweetness. O, come hither,
  You that beget him that did you beget;
  You that were born at sea, buried at Tarsus,
  And found at sea again. O Helicanus,
  Down on your knees; thank the holy gods as loud
  As thunder threatens us. This is Marina.
  What was your mother's name? Tell me but that,
  For truth can never be confirmed enough,
  Though doubts did ever sleep.
MARINA                         First, sir, I pray,
  What is your title?
PERICLES
  I am Pericles of Tyre; but tell me now
  My drowned queen's name, as in the rest you said
  You have been god-like perfect, and you are
  The heir of kingdoms, and another life
  To Pericles your father.

MARINA

   Is it no more to be your daughter than
   To say my mother's name was Thàisa?
   Thàisa was my mother, who did end
   The minute I began.

PERICLES

   Now blessing on you! Rise; you are my child.
   Give me fresh garments. My own, Helicanus!
   She is not dead at Tarsus, as she would have been,
   By savage Cleon. She shall tell you all;
   When you shall kneel, and justify in knowledge
   She is your very princess. Who is this?

HELICANUS

   Sir, it is the governor of Mytilene
   Who, hearing of your melancholy state,
   Did come to see you.

PERICLES              I embrace you.

   Give me my robes. I am wild in my beholding.
   O, heavens bless my girl! But hark, what music?
   Tell Helicanus, my Marina, tell him
   Over, point by point, for yet he seems to doubt,
   How sure you are my daughter. But what music?

HELICANUS

   My lord, I hear none.

PERICLES             None?

   The music of the spheres! List, my Marina!

LYSIMACHUS

   It is not good to cross him; give him way.

PERICLES

   Rarest sounds! Do you not hear?

LYSIMACHUS            Music, my lord?

PERICLES

   I hear most heavenly music.
   It nips me unto listening, and thick slumber
   Hangs upon my eyes. Let me rest.

*He sleeps*

LYSIMACHUS
A pillow for his head. So, leave him all.
Well, my companion friends,
If this but answers to my just belief,
I will well remember you.          *Exeunt all but Pericles*

*Diana appears to Pericles in a vision*

DIANA
My temple stands in Ephesus. Hie you thither,
And do upon my altar sacrifice.
There, when my maiden priests are met together,
Before the people all,
Reveal how you at sea did lose your wife.
To mourn your crosses, with your daughter's, call,
And give them repetition to the life.
Perform my bidding, or you live in woe;
Do it, and happy, by my silver bow.
Awake, and tell your dream.                    *Exit*
PERICLES    *(waking)*
Celestial Dian, goddess argentine,
I will obey you. Helicanus!

*Enter Helicanus, Lysimachus, and Marina*

HELICANUS                    Sir?
PERICLES
My purpose was for Tarsus, there to strike
The inhospitable Cleon, but I am
For other service first. Toward Ephesus
Turn our blown sails. And soon I'll tell you why.
    *(To Lysimachus)*
Shall we refresh us, sir, upon your shore,
And give you gold for such provisìon

As our intents will need?

LYSIMACHUS                Sir,
With all my heart; and when you come ashore,
I have another suit.

PERICLES            You shall prevail,
Were it to woo my daughter, for it seems
You have been noble towards her.

LYSIMACHUS
Sir, lend me your arm.

PERICLES                Come, my Marina.            *Exeunt*


## SCENE II
## Ephesus. Before the temple.

*Enter Gower*


GOWER
Now our sands are almost run;
More a little, and then done.
This my last boon give me,
For such kindness must relieve me,
That you aptly will suppose
What pageantry, what deeds, what shows,
What minstrelsy, and pretty din
The regent made in Mytilene
To greet the King. So he thrived
That he is promised to be wived
To fair Marina, but in no wise
Till he had done his sacrifice
As Dian bade; whereto being bound,
The interim, pray you, all confound.
In feathered briefness sails are filled,
And wishes fall out as they're willed.
At Ephesus the temple see,
Our king, and all his company.

That he can hither come so soon
Is by your fancies' thankful doom.                    *Exit*

# SCENE III
# The temple.

*Enter on one side Thaisa and priestesses of Diana, Cerimon,
and other inhabitants of Ephesus; on the other side,
Pericles, Marina, Lysimachus, Helicanus, and Lords*

PERICLES
Hail, Dian! To perform your just command
I here confess myself the King of Tyre,
Who, frighted from my country, did wed
At Pentapolis the fair Thàisa.
At sea in childbed died she, but brought forth
A maid-child called Marina, who, O goddess,
Wears yet your silver livery. She at Tarsus
Was nursed with Cleon, whom at fourteen years
He sought to murder. But her better stars
Brought her to Mytilene; against whose shore
Riding, her fortunes brought the maid aboard us,
Where, by her own most clear remembrance, she
Made known herself my daughter.
THAISA                          Voice and favour!
You are, you are—O royal Pericles!

*She faints*

PERICLES
What means the nun? She dies! Help, gentlemen!
CERIMON
Noble sir,
If you have told Diana's altar true,
This is your wife.

PERICLES            Reverend appearer, no;
  I threw her overboard with these very arms.
CERIMON
  Upon this coast, I warrant you.
PERICLES                            Tis most certain.
CERIMON
  Look to the lady. O, she's but overjoyed.
  Early one blustering morn this lady was
  Thrown upon this shore. I opened the coffin,
  Found there rich jewels, recovered her, and placed her
  Here in Diana's temple.
PERICLES            May we see them?
CERIMON
  Great sir, they shall be brought you to my house,
  Whither I invite you. Look,
  Thaisa is recovered.
THAISA            O, let me look.
  If he is none of mine, my sanctity
  Will to my sense bend no licentious ear,
  But curb it, spite of seeing. O, my lord,
  Are you not Pericles? Like him you spoke,
  Like him you are. Did you not name a tempest,
  A birth, and death?
PERICLES            The voice of dead Thaisa!
THAISA
  That Thaisa am I,
  Supposèd dead and drowned.
PERICLES
  Immortal Dian!
THAISA        Now, I know you better:
  When we with tears departed Pentapolis,
  The King my father gave you such a ring.
PERICLES                        *Shows a ring.*
  This, this! No more, you gods; your present kindness
  Makes my past miseries sports; you shall do well
  That on the touching of her lips I may

Melt, and no more be seen. O, come, be buried
A second time within these arms.
MARINA                           My heart
Leaps to be gone into my mother's bosom.

*She kneels*

PERICLES
Look who kneels here; flesh of your flesh, Thaisa,
Your burden at the sea, and called Marina
For she was yielded there.
THAISA                        Blest, and my own!
HELICANUS    Hail, madam, and my queen!
THAISA                            I know you not.
PERICLES
You have heard me say, when I did fly from Tyre,
I left behind an ancient substitute.
Can you remember what I called the man?
I have named him oft.
THAISA                'Twas Helicanus then.
PERICLES
Still confirmation.
Embrace him, dear Thaisa, this is he.
Now do I long to hear how you were found,
How possibly preserved, and whom to thank,
Besides the gods, for this great miracle.
THAISA
Lord Cerimon, my lord; this man
Through whom the gods have shown their power; that
    can
From first to last resolve you.
PERICLES                        Reverend sir,
The gods can have no mortal officer
More like a god than you. Will you deliver
How this dead queen re-lives?

CERIMON                    I will, my lord.
　　Beseech you first, go with me to my house,
　　Where shall be shown you all was found with her,
　　How she came placed here in the temple;
　　No needful thing omitted.
PERICLES                    Pure Dian,
　　I bless you for your vision, and
　　Will offer night-oblations to you. Thaisa,
　　This prince, the fair betrothèd of your daughter,
　　Shall marry her at Pentapolis. And now,
　　This ornament,
　　Makes me look dismal, will I clip to form,
　　And what this fourteen years no razor touched,
　　To grace your marriage-day, I'll beautify.
THAISA
　　Lord Cerimon has letters of good credit, sir,
　　My father's dead.
PERICLES
　　Heavens make a star of him! Yet there, my queen,
　　We'll celebrate their nuptials, and ourselves
　　Will in that kingdom spend our following days.
　　Our son and daughter shall in Tyre now reign.
　　Lord Cerimon, we do our longing stay
　　To hear the rest untold. Sir, lead the way.          *Exeunt*


## EPILOGUE

*Enter Gower*


GOWER
　　In Antiochus and his daughter you have heard
　　Of monstrous lust the due and just reward;
　　In Pericles, his queen, and daughter seen,
　　Although assailed with fortune fierce and keen,
　　Virtue preserved from fell destruction's blast,

Led on by heaven, and crowned with joy at last.
In Helicanus may you well descry
A figure of truth, of faith, of loyalty.
In reverend Cerimon there well appears
The worth that learnèd charity aye wears.
For wicked Cleon and his wife, when fame
Had spread his cursèd deed to the honoured name
Of Pericles, to rage the city turn,
That him and his they in his palace burn.
The gods for murder seemèd to consent
To punish, although not done, but meant.
So on your patience evermore attending,
New joy wait on you! Here our play has ending.

*Exit*

# King John

# INTRODUCTION

K ing *John* is not one of Shakespeare's inspired plays. But that fact itself has its own interest for us, for it poses questions. When was it written? What is its character and place in the development of his work? Is it all of a piece, or does it show evidences of revision?

It is generally agreed that it is early work, and much of it has the naiveté for us of the patriotic plays that make up *Henry VI*—the slanging matches, the boasting and confrontations that Elizabethans loved—though it marks an improvement on those first works. It is less satisfactory than *Richard II*, most of it written before that, with which it has something in common, including a good deal of rhyme. On the other hand, there are passages of greater maturity in which the real Shakespeare comes through. Some of these point to revising about 1596, though the main body of the work was written earlier.

It was based upon an older play, *The Troublesome Reign of King John*, which was printed in 1591. Shakespeare adhered too closely to this work, re-writing as he went along, though he also consulted Holinshed's Chronicle as usual. I am in agreement with Professor C.J. Sisson as to the result: that the play was task-work and lacks spontaneity, 'the writing moreover is not all of a piece, and there are indications of revision in passages of greater maturity.'

The upshot is that the play is too long, with long speeches which can easily be shortened for modern production. Nevertheless the play has had its appeal on the stage: the part of Constance, mother of King John's nephew, was a favourite with the famous tragic actress, Mrs Siddons. This appeals less today—the part of a shrill denunciating Cassandra, analogous to Queen Margaret in *Henry VI*, though a stage further in development. The main human interest centres on the tragic fate of young Arthur, done out of his inheritance though supported by the French King at first, who then does a deal with King John ('Commodity'—accommodation). The uncle captures the boy in one of his swift ('expedient') moves—and, in historic fact, made away with him. In the play Shakespeare spares the King the murder and makes the boy leap to death from imprisonment within the castle walls. But he does not fail to twist the heart-strings in the scene where Hubert prepares to put out the boy's eyes, whose appeal for mercy frustrates the King's order.

The overwhelming sentiment of this scene, the boy's knowingness, may not be altogether to modern taste, though it never failed with less sophisticated audiences—though the medieval practice of blinding political prisoners is not unfamiliar today in the Middle East and India.

What made Shakespeare write into his re-writing of the fustian *Troublesome Reign* these affecting scenes and make the mother and son relationship central to the play—as they were not in historic fact or in his source?

In 1596 Shakespeare's only boy, the hope of carrying on his family name—Hamnet, called after neighbour Hamnet Sadler—died at Stratford. And in the play we find written in one of those passages with an affecting personal accent altogether different from the normal uninspired versification:

Grief fills the room up of my absent child,
Lies in his bed, walks up and down with me,

Puts on his pretty looks, repeats his words,
Remembers me of all his gracious parts,
Stuffs out his vacant garments with his form.

Another passage brings Stratford home to us, for in Henley
Street lived Hornby the blacksmith, and

I saw a smith stand with his hammer, thus,
While his iron did on the anvil cool,
With open mouth swallowing a tailor's news:
Who, with his shears and measure in his hand,
Standing on slippers which his nimble haste
Had falsely thrust upon contràry feet . . .

It is an authentic picture from country town life. Was
there a tailor living along that street too?
What supports the date 1596 for revision is this:

So, by a roaring tempest on the flood,
A whole armada of convicted sail
Is scattered and disjoined from fellowship.

That is precisely what happened with the second armada,
of 1596. Shakespeare knew his Latin; and the original 'convicted' comes from *convectus,* meaning gathered together.
It does *not* mean defeated, as editors take it to mean.
Shakespeare's phrase exactly describes the armada of 1596,
which was not defeated but scattered by a roaring tempest.
Hence I have modernised 'convicted' to the more correct in
meaning 'concerted'.

As we find regularly with the history plays, Shakespeare's
own inventions are the liveliest. Here, the Bastard Faulconbridge, supposedly a by-blow of Richard Coeur-de-
Lion, is best. A spirited, soldierly type, given to blowing
his own trumpet—Elizabethans never objected to that—
supplies the only humour and plays, in part, the Clown.
His joke is rather endearing:

> Grandam, I will pray—
If ever I remember to be holy.

And he is given some of the finest speeches in the play:

> Let not the world see fear and sad distrust
> Govern the motion of a kingly eye.
> Be stirring as the time; be fire with fire;
> Threaten the threatener, and outface the brow
> Of bragging horror. So shall inferior eyes,
> That borrow their behaviours from the great,
> Grow great by your example and put on
> The dauntless spirit of resolutiòn.

Still more with his famous exordium on Commodity—the spirit of self-interest that rules in the world, particularly of politics; the sense of expediency, of one's own advantage, convenience or accommodation:

> That smooth-faced gentleman, tickling Commodity,
> Commodity, the bias of the world—

to which the boy Arthur's interest is sacrificed, his mother driven demented.

> And why rail I on this Commodity?—
> Only because he has not wooed me yet.

This piece of candid self-knowledge is very Shakespearean: here he speaks to us across the stage in his own person.

His own profession is there, a constant term of reference in every play: here the citizens of Angiers

> stand securely on their battlements
> As in a theatre, whence they gape and point—

one sees them on the upper stage in a contemporary playhouse, or an upper balcony in an inn courtyard where plays were often performed. The contemporary world is present in the references to the 'muzzled bear', a common enough spectacle in the streets or at bear-baitings; a whole paragraph calls up the plague—disastrous in 1592–3; 'French inconstancy' was much in the public mind in the early 1590's. Shakespeare, very much the countryman, pops up in 'the jolly troop of huntsmen', and in the phrase about the predatory 'raven on a sick-fallen beast'—a countryman would know the habit of raven or carrion-crow, pecking the eyes out of a fallen animal.

We have a great deal of the kind of word-play the early Shakespeare was addicted to—simple puns being caught up to give another line; along with the curious conceits of which we find many examples in the Sonnets, especially those about hairs thought of as wires, 'wiry friends'.

In short everything shows that the basis of the play is early, and subsequently revised. It was first printed in the First Folio in 1623, apparently from the author's manuscript, which had not been tidied up for performance in the theatre. Shortening is not only permissible but desirable.

Also with modernisation: characteristic of early Shakespeare is the frequent use of redundant 'that'—if that, for that, because that; or the redundant 'an', meaning if, in frequent 'an if'. We have examples of plural subjects with singular verbs, and the curious frequency of the verb 'to be' used subordinately in phrases like 'he is arrived', 'he is come', where we should say he has come, etc. All this has been regularised. Why retain the original word 'owe', always used for own; or archaic words like module (image), tarre (spur on), scroyles (louts), coil (fuss); or 'angerly' for angrily? The word 'censure' was used more widely by Elizabethans to mean judgement or opinion; we use the word more restrictively. Similarly with the word 'cousin', used then

for a wider range of kinship; I have regularised this by
replacing it with 'nephew' where that is correct, or the
word 'kinsman', a word Shakespeare uses.

# CHARACTERS

KING JOHN
PRINCE HENRY, his son
EARL OF PEMBROKE
EARL OF SALISBURY
EARL OF ESSEX
LORD BIGOD
ROBERT FAULCONBRIDGE, son of Sir Robert Faulconbridge
Philip the BASTARD, his half-brother, bastard son of King
    Richard Coeur-de-lion
HUBERT, a follower of King John
JAMES GURNEY, servant to Lady Faulconbridge
PETER OF POMFRET, a prophet
PHILIP, King of France
LEWIS THE DAUPHIN
ARTHUR, Duke of Brittany, nephew of King John
DUKE OF AUSTRIA (Viscount of Limoges)
MELUN, a French lord
CHATILLON, ambassador from France to King John

CARDINAL PANDULPH, the Pope's legate

QUEEN ELEANOR, mother of King John
CONSTANCE, mother of Arthur
BLANCHE of Spain, niece of King John
LADY FAULCONBRIDGE, widow of Sir Robert Faulconbridge

Lords, citizens, Sheriff, officers, messengers, soldiers,
    attendants

# Act I

## SCENE I
### King John's palace.

*Enter King John, Queen Eleanor, Pembroke, Essex, and Salisbury, with Chatillon*

KING JOHN
Now say, Chatillon, what would France with us?

CHATILLON
Thus, after greeting, speaks the King of France,
In my behaviour, to the majesty,
The borrowed majesty, of England here.

QUEEN ELEANOR
A strange beginning—'borrowed majesty'!

KING JOHN
Silence, good mother. Hear the embassy.

CHATILLON
Philip of France, in right and true behalf
Of your deceasèd brother Geoffrey's son,
Arthur Plantagenet, lays most lawful claim
To this fair island and the territories,
To Ireland, Poitiers, Anjou, Touraine, Maine.
Desiring you to lay aside the sword
Which sways usurpingly these several titles,
And put the same into young Arthur's hand,
Your nephew and right royal sovereign.

KING JOHN
What follows if we disallow of this?

CHATILLON
    The proud control of fierce and bloody war,
    To enforce these rights so forcibly withheld.

KING JOHN
    Here have we war for war and blood for blood,
    Controlment for controlment. So answer France.

CHATILLON
    Then take my King's defiance from my mouth,
    The farthest limit of my embassy.

KING JOHN
    Bear mine to him, and so depart in peace.
    Be you as lightning in the eyes of France;
    For ere you can report I will be there,
    The thunder of my cannon shall be heard.
    So, hence! Be you the trumpet of our wrath
    And sullen presage of your own decay.
    An honourable conduct let him have.
    Pembroke, look to it. Farewell, Chatillon.

                *Exeunt Chatillon and Pembroke*

QUEEN ELEANOR
    What now, my son? Have I not ever said
    How the ambitious Constance would not cease
    Till she had kindled France and all the world
    Upon the right and party of her son?
    This might have been prevented and made whole
    With very easy arguments of love,
    Which now the rulers of two kingdoms must
    With fearful bloody issue arbitrate.

KING JOHN
    Our strong possession and our right for us.

QUEEN ELEANOR *(to King John)*
    Your strong possession much more than your right,
    Or else it must go wrong with you and me.
    So much my conscience whispers in your ear,
    Which none but heaven, and you and I, shall hear.

      *Enter a sheriff, who whispers to Essex*

ESSEX
> My liege, here is the strangest controversy,
> Come from the country to be judged by you,
> That ever I heard. Shall I produce the men?

KING JOHN
> Let them approach.                              *Exit sheriff*
> Our abbeys and our priories shall pay
> This expeditious charge.

*Enter Robert Faulconbridge and Philip, his bastard brother*

> What men are you?

BASTARD
> Your faithful subject I, a gentleman,
> Born in Northamptonshire, and eldest son,
> As I suppose, to Robert Faulconbridge,
> A soldier, by the honour-giving hand
> Of Coeur-de-lion knighted in the field.

KING JOHN
> What are you?

ROBERT FAULCONBRIDGE
> The son and heir to that same Faulconbridge.

KING JOHN
> Is that the elder, and are you the heir?
> You came not of one mother then, it seems.

BASTARD
> Most certain of one mother, mighty King—
> That is well known; and, as I think, one father.
> But for the certain knowledge of that truth
> I put you over to heaven, and to my mother;
> Of that I doubt, as all men's children may.

QUEEN ELEANOR
> Out on you, rude man! You do shame your mother,
> And wound her honour, with this disparagement.

BASTARD
> I, madam? No, I have no reason for it.

That is my brother's plea, and none of mine;
Which if he can then prove, he pops me out
At least from fair five hundred pound a year.
Heaven guard my mother's honour, and my land!

KING JOHN
A good blunt fellow! Why, being younger born,
Does he lay claim to your inheritance?

BASTARD
I know not why, except to get the land—
But once he slandered me with bastardy.
But whether I am as true begotten or no,
That still I lay upon my mother's head.
But that I am as well begotten, my liege—
Fair fall the bones that took the pains for me!—
Compare our faces and be judge yourself.
If old Sir Robert did beget us both
And was our father, and this son like him,
O old Sir Robert, father, on my knee
I give heaven thanks I was not like to thee!

KING JOHN
Why, what a madcap has heaven lent us here!

QUEEN ELEANOR (to King John)
He has a trick of Coeur-de-lion's face;
The accent of his tongue affects him too.
Do you not read some tokens of my son
In the large composition of this man?

KING JOHN (to Queen Eleanor)
My eye has well examinèd his parts
And finds them perfect Richard. (To Robert
        Faulconbridge) Fellow, speak.
What does move you to claim your brother's land?

BASTARD (aside)
Because he has a half-face like my father!
With half that face would he have all my land—
A half-faced groat, five hundred pound a year!

ROBERT FAULCONBRIDGE
  My gracious liege, when my father was alive,
  Your brother did employ my father much—
BASTARD (*aside*)
  Well, sir, by this you cannot get my land.
  Your tale must be how he employed my mother.
ROBERT FAULCONBRIDGE
  —And once dispatched him in an embassy
  To Germany, there with the Emperor
  To treat of high affairs touching that time.
  The advantage of his absence took the King
  And in the meantime sojourned at my father's,
  Where how he did prevail I shame to speak—
  But truth is truth. Large lengths of seas and shores
  Between my father and my mother lay,
  As I have heard my father speak himself,
  When this same lusty gentleman was got.
  Upon his death-bed he by will bequeathed
  His lands to me, and took it on his death
  That this, my mother's son, was none of his;
  And if he were, he came into the world
  Full fourteen weeks before the course of time.
  Then, good my liege, let me have what is mine,
  My father's land, as was my father's will.
KING JOHN
  Fellow, your brother is legitimate.
  Your father's wife did after wedlock bear him,
  And if she did play false, the fault was hers—
  Which fault lies on the hazards of all husbands
  That marry wives. Tell me, how if my brother,
  Who, as you say, took pains to get this son,
  Had of your father claimed this son for his?
  In truth, good friend, your father might have kept
  This calf, bred from his cow, from all the world;
  In truth he might. Then, if he were my brother's,
  My brother might not claim him, nor your father,
  Being none of his, refuse him. This concludes:

My mother's son did get your father's heir;
Your father's heir must have your father's land.

ROBERT FAULCONBRIDGE
Shall then my father's will be of no force
To dispossess that child which is not his?

BASTARD
Of no more force to dispossess me, sir,
Than was his will to get me, as I think.

QUEEN ELEANOR
Which had you rather be: a Faulconbridge,
And like your brother, to enjoy your land;
Or the reputed son of Coeur-de-lion,
Lord of your presence, and no land beside?

BASTARD
Madam, then if my brother had my shape
And I had his—Sir Robert's his, like him;
And if my legs were two such riding-rods,
My arms such eel-skins stuffed, my face so thin
That in my ear I durst not stick a rose
Lest men should say 'Look where three-farthings goes!'
And, to his shape, were heir to all this land—
Would I might never stir from off this place,
I'd give it every foot to have this face;
I would not be Sir Nob in any case!

QUEEN ELEANOR
I like you well. Will you forsake your fortune,
Bequeath your land to him, and follow me?
I am a soldier and now bound to France.

BASTARD
Brother, take you my land. I'll take my chance.
Your face has got five hundred pound a year,
Yet sell your face for fivepence and 'tis dear.
Madam, I'll follow you unto the death.

QUEEN ELEANOR
Nay, I would have you go before me thither.

BASTARD

Our country manners give our betters way.

KING JOHN

What is your name?

BASTARD

Philip, my liege, so is my name begun;
Philip, good old Sir Robert's wife's eldest son.

KING JOHN

From henceforth bear his name whose form you bear:
Kneel you down Philip, but rise more great—
Arise Sir Richard, and Plantagenet.

BASTARD

Brother, by the mother's side, give me your hand.
My father gave me honour, yours gave land.
Now blessèd be the hour, by night or day,
When I was got, Sir Robert was away!

QUEEN ELEANOR

The very spirit of Plantagenet!
I am your grandam, Richard. Call me so.

BASTARD

Madam, by chance but not by truth; what though?
Something about, a little from the right,
    In at the window, or else over the hatch;
Who dares not stir by day must walk by night,
    And have is have, however men do catch;
Near or far off, well won is still well shot,
And I am I, however I was begot.

KING JOHN

Go, Faulconbridge. Now have you your desire;
A landless knight makes you a landed squire.
Come, madam, and come, Richard, we must speed
For France, for France, for it is more than need.

BASTARD

Brother, adieu. Good fortune come to you,
For you were got in the way of honesty!

                              *Exeunt all but the Bastard*

A foot of honour better than I was,

But many a many foot of land the worse!
Well, now can I make any Joan a lady.
'Good-day, Sir Richard'—'God have mercy, fellow'—
And if his name is George, I'll call him Peter;
For new-made honour does forget men's names—
'Tis too respective and too sociable
For your conversion. Now your traveller,
He and his toothpick at my worship's mess,
And when my knightly stomach is sufficed,
Why then I suck my teeth and catechize
My pickèd man of countries: 'My dear sir'—
Thus, leaning on my elbow, I begin—
'I shall beseech you'—that is question now.
And then comes answer like an alphabet:
'O sir,' says answer, 'at your best command;
At your employment, at your service, sir.'
'No sir,' says question, 'I, sweet sir, at yours.'
And so, ere answer knows what question would,
Saving in dialogue of compliment,
And talking of the Alps and Apennines,
The Pyrenean and the River Po,
It draws toward supper in conclusion so.
But this is worshipful society,
And fits the mounting spirit like myself;
For he is but a bastard to the time
That does not smack of fashion and regard.
And so am I—whether I smack or no,
And not alone in habit and device,
Exterior form, outward accoutrement,
But from the inward motion—to deliver
Sweet, sweet, sweet poison for the age's tooth.
Which, though I will not practise to deceive,
Yet to avoid deceit I mean to learn;
For it shall strew the footsteps of my rising.
But who comes in such haste in riding robes?

What woman-post is this? Has she no husband
That will take pains to blow a horn before her?

*Enter Lady Faulconbridge and James Gurney*

O me, it is my mother! How now, good lady?
What brings you here to court so hastily?
LADY FAULCONBRIDGE
Where is that slave your brother? Where is he
That holds in chase my honour up and down?
BASTARD
My brother Robert? Old Sir Robert's son?
Colbrand the Giant, that same mighty man?
Is it Sir Robert's son that you seek so?
LADY FAULCONBRIDGE
Sir Robert's son?—Ay, you unreverend boy,
Sir Robert's son. Why scorn you at Sir Robert?
He is Sir Robert's son, and so are you.
BASTARD
James Gurney, will you give us leave a while?
GURNEY
Good leave, good Philip.
BASTARD                          Philip?—Sparrow! James,
There's toys abroad. Soon I'll tell you more.
                                        *Exit Gurney*
Madam, I was not old Sir Robert's son.
Sir Robert might have eaten his part in me
Upon Good Friday and never broken his fast.
Sir Robert could do well—indeed, to confess
He could get me, Sir Robert could not do it!
We know his handiwork. Therefore, good mother,
To whom am I beholding for these limbs?
Sir Robert never helped to make this leg.
LADY FAULCONBRIDGE
Have you conspirèd with your brother too,

That for your own gain should defend my honour?
What means this scorn, you most unmannerly knave?

BASTARD

Knight, knight, good mother, Basilisco-like!
What! I am dubbed, I have it on my shoulder.
But, mother, I am not Sir Robert's son.
I have disclaimed Sir Robert and my land;
Legitimation, name, and all are gone.
Then, good my mother, let me know my father;
Some proper man, I hope. Who was it, mother?

LADY FAULCONBRIDGE

Have you denied yourself a Faulconbridge?

BASTARD

As faithfully as I deny the devil.

LADY FAULCONBRIDGE

King Richard Coeur-de-lion was your father.
By long and vehement suit I was seduced
To make room for him in my husband's bed.
Heaven lay not my transgression to your charge!
You are the issue of my dear offence,
Which was so strongly urged past my defence.

BASTARD

Now by this light, were I to get again,
Madam, I would not wish a better father.
Some sins do bear their privilege on earth,
And so does yours. Your fault was not your folly.
Needs must you lay your heart at his dispose,
Subjected tribute to commanding love,
Against whose fury and unmatchèd force
The aweless lion could not wage the fight,
Nor keep his princely heart from Richard's hand.
He that perforce robs lions of their hearts
May easily win a woman's. Ay, my mother,
With all my heart I thank you for my father.
Who lives and dares but say you did not well
When I was got, I'll send his soul to hell.

Come, lady, I will show you to my kin,
    And they shall say, when Richard me begot,
If you had said him nay, it had been sin.
    Who says it was, he lies—I say 'twas not!

*Exeunt*

# Act II

## SCENE I
## Before the walls of Angiers.

*Enter on one side King Philip of France, Lewis the Dauphin, Constance, Arthur, lords, and soldiers; on the other side the Duke of Austria and soldiers*

KING PHILIP
Before Angiers well met, brave Austria.
Arthur, that great forerunner of your blood,
Richard, that robbed the lion of his heart
And fought the holy wars in Palestine,
By this brave duke came early to his grave.
And for amends to his posterity,
At our importuning hither is come
To spread his colours, boy, in your behalf,
And to rebuke the usurpatiòn
Of your unnatural uncle, English John.
Embrace him, love him, give him welcome hither.

ARTHUR
God shall forgive you Coeur-de-lion's death
The rather that you give his offspring life,
Shadowing their right under your wings of war.
I give you welcome with a powerless hand,
But with a heart full of unstainèd love.
Welcome before the gates of Angiers, Duke!

KING PHILIP
A noble boy! Who would not do you right!

AUSTRIA
Upon your cheek lay I this zealous kiss,

As seal to this indenture of my love:
That to my home I will no more return
Till Angiers and the right you have in France,
Together with that pale, that white-faced shore—
Whose foot spurns back the ocean's roaring tides
And coops from other lands her islanders—
Even till that England, hedged in with the main,
That water-wallèd bulwark, still secure
And confident from foreign purposes,
Even till that utmost corner of the west
Salutes you for her king. Till then, fair boy,
Will I not think of home, but follow arms.

CONSTANCE
O, take his mother's thanks, a widow's thanks,
Till your strong hand shall help to give him strength
To make a more requital to your love.

AUSTRIA
The peace of heaven is theirs that lift their swords
In such a just and charitable war.

KING PHILIP
Well then, to work! Our cannon shall be bent
Against the brows of this resisting town.
Call for our chiefest men of discipline,
To choose the plots of best advantages.
We'll lay before this town our royal bones,
Wade to the market-place in Frenchmen's blood,
But we will make it subject to this boy.

CONSTANCE
Stay for an answer to your embassy,
Lest unadvised you stain your swords with blood.
My Lord Chatillon may from England bring
That right in peace which here we urge in war,
And then we shall repent each drop of blood
That hot rash haste so indirectly shed.

*Enter Chatillon*

KING PHILIP
  A wonder, lady! Lo, upon your wish,
  Our messenger Chatillon has arrived.
  What England says, say briefly, gentle lord;
  We coldly pause for you. Chatillon, speak.
CHATILLON
  Then turn your forces from this paltry siege
  And stir them up against a mightier task.
  England, impatient of your just demands,
  Has put himself in arms. The adverse winds,
  Whose leisure I have stayed, have given him time
  To land his legions all as soon as I.
  His marches are making swiftly for this town,
  His forces strong, his soldiers confident.
  With him along is come the Mother-Queen,
  An Ate, stirring him to blood and strife;
  With her her niece, the Lady Blanche of Spain;
  With them a bastard of the King's deceased.
  And all the unsettled humours of the land—
  Rash, inconsiderate, fiery voluntaries,
  With ladies' faces and fierce dragons' spleens—
  Have sold their fortunes at their native homes,
  Bearing their birthrights proudly on their backs,
  To make a hazard of new fortunes here.
  In brief, a braver choice of dauntless spirits
  Than now the English bottoms have waft over
  Did never float upon the swelling tide
  To do offence and harm in Christendom.

*A drum beats*

  The interruption of their churlish drums
  Cuts off more circumstance. They are at hand—
  To parley or to fight! Therefore prepare!
KING PHILIP
  How much unlooked-for is this swift arrival.

AUSTRIA
　　By how much unexpected, by so much
　　We must awake endeavour for defence;
　　For courage mounts with the occasiòn.
　　Let them be welcome then. We are prepared!

*Enter King John, Queen Eleanor, Blanche, the Bastard,*
*lords, and soldiers*

KING JOHN
　　Peace be to France—if France in peace permits
　　Our just and lineal entrance to our own.
　　If not, bleed France, and peace ascend to heaven,
　　While we, God's wrathful agent, do correct
　　Their proud contempt that beat his peace to heaven.
KING PHILIP
　　Peace be to England—if then war returns
　　From France to England, there to live in peace.
　　England we love, and for that England's sake
　　With burden of our armour here we sweat.
　　This toil of ours should be a work of yours;
　　But you from loving England are so far
　　That you have underwrought its lawful king,
　　Cut off the sequence of posterity,
　　Outfacèd infant state, and done a rape
　　Upon the maiden virtue of the crown.
　　Look here upon your brother Geoffrey's face.
　　These eyes, these brows, were moulded out of his;
　　This little abstract does contain that large
　　Which died in Geoffrey; and the hand of time
　　Shall draw this brief into as huge a volume.
　　That Geoffrey was your elder brother born,
　　And this his son. England was Geoffrey's right,
　　And this is Geoffrey's. In the name of God
　　How comes it then that you are called a king,
　　When living blood does in these temples beat
　　Which own the crown that you have overmastered?

KING JOHN
> From whom have you this great commission, France,
> To draw my answer from your articles?

KING PHILIP
> From that supernal judge that stirs good thoughts
> In any breast of strong authority
> To look into the blots and stains of right.
> That judge has made me guardian to this boy:
> Under whose warrant I impeach your wrong
> And by whose help I mean to chastise it.

KING JOHN
> Alas, you do usurp authority.

KING PHILIP
> Excuse it is to beat usurping down.

QUEEN ELEANOR
> Who is it you do call usurper, France?

CONSTANCE
> Let me make answer: your usurping son.

QUEEN ELEANOR
> Out, insolent! Your bastard shall be king
> That you may be a queen and check the world.

CONSTANCE
> My bed was ever to your son as true
> As yours was to your husband; and this boy
> Liker in feature to his father Geoffrey
> Than you and John in manners—being as like
> As rain to water or devil to his dam!
> My boy a bastard! By my soul, I think
> His father never was so true begotten.
> It cannot be, if you then were his mother.

QUEEN ELEANOR
> There's a good mother, boy, that blots your father.

CONSTANCE
> There's a good grandam, boy, that would blot you.

AUSTRIA
> Peace!

BASTARD Hear the crier!

AUSTRIA                    What the devil are you?

BASTARD

    One that will play the devil, sir, with you,

    If he may catch your hide and you alone.

    You are the hare of whom the proverb goes,

    Whose valour plucks dead lions by the beard.

    I'll smoke your skin-coat if I catch you right!

    Fellow, look to it! In faith I will, in faith!

BLANCHE

    O, well did he become that lion's robe

    That did disrobe the lion of that robe!

BASTARD

    It lies as sightly on the back of him

    As great Alcides' shoes upon an ass.

    But, ass, I'll take that burden from your back,

    Or lay on that shall make your shoulders crack.

AUSTRIA

    What cracker is this same that deafens our ears

    With this abundance of superfluous breath?

    King Philip, determine what we shall do straight.

KING PHILIP

    Women and fools, break off your conference!

    King John, this is the very sum of all:

    England and Ireland, Anjou, Touraine, Maine,

    In right of Arthur do I claim of you.

    Will you resign them and lay down your arms?

KING JOHN

    My life as soon! I do defy you, France.

    Arthur of Brittany, yield you to my hand,

    And out of my dear love I'll give you more

    Than ever the coward hand of France can win.

    Submit you, boy.

QUEEN ELEANOR Come to your grandam, child.

CONSTANCE

    Do, child, go to its grandam, child.

Give grandam kingdom, and its grandam will
Give it a plum, a cherry, and a fig.
There's a good grandam.
ARTHUR                          Good my mother, peace!
I would that I were low laid in my grave.
I am not worth this trouble that's made for me.
QUEEN ELEANOR
His mother shames him so, poor boy, he weeps.
CONSTANCE
Now shame upon you, whether she does or no!
His grandam's wrongs, and not his mother's shames,
Draw those heaven-moving pearls from his poor eyes,
Which heaven shall take in nature of a fee—
Ay, with these crystal beads heaven shall be bribed
To do him justice and revenge on you.
QUEEN ELEANOR
You monstrous slanderer of heaven and earth!
CONSTANCE
You monstrous injurer of heaven and earth!
Call not me slanderer! You and yours usurp
The dominations, royalties, and rights,
Of this oppressèd boy. Your older son's son
Is unfortunate in nothing but in you.
Your sins are visited on this poor child;
The canon of the law is laid on him,
Being but the second generation
Removèd from your sin-conceiving womb.
KING JOHN
Bedlam, have done!
CONSTANCE            I have but this to say:
That he is not only plaguèd for her sin,
But God has made her sin and her the plague
On this removèd issue, plagued for her
And with her plague; her sin his injury,
Her injury the beadle to her sin,

All punished in the person of this child,
And all for her. A plague upon her!

QUEEN ELEANOR
You unadvisèd scold, I can produce
A will that bars the title of your son.

CONSTANCE
Ay, who doubts that! A will, a wicked will!
A woman's will, a cankered grandam's will!

KING PHILIP
Peace, lady! Pause, or be more temperate.
It ill beseems this presence to cry aim
To these ill-tunèd repetitiòns.
Some trumpet summon hither to the walls
These men of Angiers. Let us hear them speak
Whose title they admit, Arthur's or John's.

*A trumpet sounds*
*Enter Hubert upon the walls*

HUBERT
Who is it that has warned us to the walls?

KING PHILIP
'Tis France, for England.

KING JOHN                        England, for itself.
You men of Angiers, and my loving subjects—

KING PHILIP
You loving men of Angiers, Arthur's subjects,
Our trumpet called you to this gentle parley—

KING JOHN
For our advantage; therefore hear us first.
These flags of France, that are advancèd here
Before the eye and prospect of your town,
Have hither marched to your endamagement.
The cannons have their bowels full of wrath,
And ready mounted are they to spit forth
Their iron indignation against your walls.

All preparation for a bloody siege
And merciless proceeding by these French
Confronts your city's eyes, your winking gates.
And but for our approach those sleeping stones,
That as a waist do girdle you about,
By the compulsion of their ordnance now
By this time from their fixèd beds of lime
Had been dishabited, and wide havoc made
For bloody power to rush upon your peace.
But on the sight of us your lawful King,
Who painfully, with expeditious march,
Have brought a countercheck before your gates,
To save unscratched your city's threatened cheeks,
Behold, the French, amazed, allow a parley.
And now, instead of bullets wrapped in fire,
To make a shaking fever in your walls,
They shoot but calm words folded up in smoke,
To make a faithless error in your ears.
Which trust accordingly, kind citizens,
And let us in—your King, whose laboured spirits,
Forwearied in this action of swift speed,
Craves harbourage within your city walls.

KING  PHILIP
When I have said, make answer to us both.
Lo, in this right hand, whose protectiòn
Is most divinely vowed upon the right
Of him it holds, stands young Plantagenet,
Son to an elder brother of this man,
And king over him and all that he enjoys.
For this downtrodden equity we tread
In warlike march these greens before your town,
Being no further enemy to you
Than the constraint of hospitable zeal
In the relief of this oppressèd child
Religiously provokes. Be pleasèd then
To pay that duty which you truly owe

To him that owns it, namely this young prince.
And then our arms, like to a muzzled bear,
Save in aspect, has all offence sealed up.
Our cannons' malice vainly shall be spent
Against the invulnerable clouds of heaven;
And with a blessèd and unvexed retirement
With unhacked swords and helmets all unbruised,
We will bear home that lusty blood again
Which here we came to spout against your town,
And leave your children, wives, and you, in peace.
But if you foolishly pass our proffered offer,
'Tis not the roundness of your old-faced walls
Can hide you from our messengers of war,
Though all these English and their discipline
Were harboured in their rude circumference.
Then tell us, shall your city call us lord
In that behalf which we have challenged it,
Or shall we give the signal to our rage
And stalk in blood to our possessiòn?

HUBERT
In brief, we are the King of England's subjects;
For him, and in his right, we hold this town.

KING JOHN
Acknowledge then the King, and let me in.

HUBERT
That can we not. But he that proves the King,
To him will we prove loyal. Till that time
Have we rammed up our gates against the world.

KING JOHN
Does not the crown of England prove the King?
And if not that, I bring you witnesses,
Twice fifteen thousand hearts of England's breed—

BASTARD (aside)
Bastards and else!

KING JOHN
—To verify our title with their lives.

KING PHILIP

As many and as well-born bloods as those—

BASTARD *(aside)*

Some bastards too!

KING PHILIP

—Stand in his face to contradict his claim.

HUBERT

Till you compound whose right is worthiest,
We, for the worthiest, hold the right from both.

KING JOHN

Then God forgive the sin of all those souls
That to their everlasting residence,
Before the dew of evening fall, shall fleet,
In dreadful trial of our kingdom's king.

KING PHILIP

Amen, amen! Mount, chevaliers! To arms!

BASTARD

Saint George, that killed the dragon, and ever since
Sits on his horseback at my hostess' door,
Teach us some fence! *(To Austria)* Sir, were I at home
At your den, master, with your lioness,
I would set an ox-head to your lion's hide,
And make a monster of you.

AUSTRIA                          Peace! No more.

BASTARD

O, tremble, for you hear the lion roar!

KING JOHN

Up higher to the plain, where we'll set forth
In best appointment all our regiments.

BASTARD

Speed then, to take advantage of the field.

KING PHILIP

It shall be so. And at the other hill
Command the rest to stand. God and our right!

*Exeunt all but Hubert*

*Enter the Herald of France, with trumpeters, to the gates*

FRENCH HERALD
    You men of Angiers, open wide your gates
    And let young Arthur Duke of Brittany in,
    Who by the hand of France this day has made
    Much work for tears in many an English mother,
    Whose sons lie scattered on the bleeding ground,
    Many a widow's husband grovelling lies,
    Coldly embracing the discoloured earth.
    And victory with little loss does play
    Upon the dancing banners of the French,
    Who are at hand, triumphantly displayed,
    To enter conquerors and to proclaim
    Arthur of Brittany England's king and yours.

*Enter English Herald with trumpeters*

ENGLISH HERALD
    Rejoice, you men of Angiers, ring your bells!
    King John, your king and England's, does approach,
    Commander of this hot malicious day.
    Their armours that marched hence so silver-bright
    Hither return all gilt with Frenchmen's blood.
    There stuck no plume in any English crest
    That is removèd by a staff of France;
    Our colours do return in those same hands
    That did display them when we first marched forth,
    And like a jolly troop of huntsmen come
    Our lusty English, all with purpled hands,
    Dyed in the dying slaughter of their foes.
    Open your gates and give the victors way.
HUBERT
    Heralds, from off our towers we might behold,
    From first to last, the onset and retirement
    Of both your armies; whose equality

By our best eyes cannot be truly judged.
Blood has bought blood and blows have answered blows,
Strength matched with strength and power confronted
    power.
Both are alike, and both alike we like.
One must prove greatest; while they weigh so even,
We hold our town for neither, yet for both.

*Enter on one side King John, Queen Eleanor, Blanche, the
Bastard, lords, and soldiers; on the other side King Philip,
the Dauphin, Austria, lords, and soldiers*

KING JOHN
France, have you yet more blood to cast away?
Say, shall the current of our right run on,
Whose passage, vexed with your impediment,
Shall leave its native channel and over-swell,
With course disturbed, even your confining shores,
Unless you let its silver water keep
A peaceful progress to the oceàn?
KING PHILIP
England, you have not saved one drop of blood,
In this hot trial, more than we of France;
Rather, lost more. And by this hand I swear,
That sways the earth this climate overlooks,
Before we will lay down our just-borne arms,
We'll put you down—against whom these arms we bear
Or add a royal number to the dead,
Gracing the scroll that tells of this war's loss
With slaughter coupled to the name of kings.
BASTARD
Ha, majesty! How high your glory towers
When the rich blood of kings is set on fire!
O, now does death line his dead chaps with steel;
The swords of soldiers are his teeth, his fangs.
And now he feasts, mousing the flesh of men,

In undetermined differences of kings.
Why stand these royal fronts amazèd thus?
Cry slaughter, Kings! Back to the stainèd field,
You equal potents, fiery-kindled spirits!
Then let confusion of one part confirm
The other's peace. Till then, blows, blood, and death!

KING JOHN
Whose party do the townsmen yet admit?

KING PHILIP
Speak, citizens, for England. Who's your king?

HUBERT
The King of England, when we know the King.

KING PHILIP
Know him in us, that here hold up his right.

KING JOHN
In us, that are our own great deputy
And bear possession of our person here,
Lord of our presence, Angiers, and of you.

HUBERT
A greater power than we denies all this.
And, till it is undoubted, we do lock
Our former scruple in our strong-barred gates;
Kings of our fear, until our fears, resolved,
Are by some certain king purged and deposed.

BASTARD
By heaven, these louts of Angiers flout you, Kings,
And stand securely on their battlements
As in a theatre, whence they gape and point
At your industrious scenes and acts of death.
Your royal presences, be ruled by me:
Do like the factions of Jerusalem,
Be friends awhile, and both conjointly bend
Your sharpest deeds of malice on this town.
By east and west let France and England mount
Their battering cannon chargèd to the mouths,
Till their soul-fearing clamours have brawled down

The flinty ribs of this contemptuous city.
I'd play incessantly upon these jades,
Even till unfencèd desolatiòn
Leaves them as naked as the vulgar air.
That done, dissever your united strengths
And part your mingled colours once again;
Turn face to face and bloody point to point.
Then, in a moment, fortune shall call forth
Out of one side her happy miniòn,
To whom in favour she shall give the day,
And kiss him with a glorious victory.
How like you this wild counsel, mighty states?
Smacks it not something of the policy?

KING JOHN
Now, by the sky that hangs above our heads,
I like it well! France, shall we knit our powers
And lay this Angiers even with the ground,
Then after fight who shall be king of it?

BASTARD (to King Philip)
Now if you have the mettle of a king,
Being wronged as we are by this peevish town,
Turn you the mouth of your artillery,
As we will ours, against these saucy walls.
And when we have then dashed them to the ground,
Why, then defy each other, and pell-mell
Make work upon ourselves, for heaven or hell.

KING PHILIP
Let it be so. Say, where will you assault?

KING JOHN
We from the west will send destructiòn
Into this city's bosom.

AUSTRIA
I from the north.

KING PHILIP            Our thunder from the south
Shall rain their drift of bullets on this town.

BASTARD (*aside*)

 O prudent discipline! From north to south
 Austria and France shoot in each other's mouth.
 I'll stir them to it. Come, away, away!

HUBERT

 Hear us, great Kings! Grant us a while to stay,
 And I shall show you peace and fair-faced league,
 Win you this city without stroke or wound,
 Rescue those breathing lives to die in beds
 That here come sacrifices for the field.
 Persèver not, but hear me, mighty Kings!

KING JOHN

 Speak on with favour. We are bent to hear.

HUBERT

 That daughter there of Spain, the Lady Blanche,
 Is niece to England. Look upon the years
 Of Lewis the Dauphin and that lovely maid.
 If lusty love should go in quest of beauty,
 Where should he find it fairer than in Blanche?
 If zealous love should go in search of virtue,
 Where should he find it purer than in Blanche?
 If love ambitious sought a match of birth,
 Whose veins bound richer blood than Lady Blanche?
 Such as she is, in beauty, virtue, birth,
 Is the young Dauphin every way complete.
 If not completed, say he is not she;
 And she again wants nothing, to name want,
 If want it is not that she is not he.
 He is the half part of a blessèd man,
 Left to be finishèd by such as she;
 And she a fair divided excellence,
 Whose fullness of perfection lies in him.
 O, two such silver currents, when they join,
 Do glorify the banks that bound them in;
 And two such shores to two such streams made one,
 Two such controlling bounds, shall you be, Kings,
 To these two princes, if you marry them.

This union shall do more than battery can
To our fast-closèd gates. For at this match,
With swifter spirit than powder can enforce,
The mouth of passage shall we fling wide open
And give you entrance. But without this match,
The sea enragèd is not half so deaf,
Lions more confident, mountains and rocks
More free from motion, no, not death himself
In mortal fury half so pèremptòry,
As we to keep this city.

BASTARD (*aside*)                    Here's a stay
That shakes the rotten carcass of old death
Out of his rags! Here's a large mouth, indeed,
That spits forth death and mountains, rocks and seas,
Talks as familiarly of roaring lions
As maids of thirteen do of puppy-dogs.
What cannoneer begot this lusty blood?
He speaks plain cannon—fire and smoke and bounce;
He gives the bastinado with his tongue.
Our ears are cudgelled; not a word of his
But buffets better than a fist of France.
Zounds! I was never so bethumped with words
Since I first called my brother's father dad!

QUEEN ELEANOR (*to King John*)
Son, list to this conjunction, make this match;
Give with our niece a dowry large enough.
For by this knot you shall so surely tie
Your now unsured assurance to the crown
That yon green boy shall have no sun to ripen
The bloom that promises a mighty fruit.
I see a yielding in the looks of France;
Mark how they whisper. Urge them while their souls
Are capable of this ambitiòn,
Lest zeal, now melted by the windy breath
Of soft petitions, pity, and remorse,
Cool and congeal again to what it was.

HUBERT
> Why answer not the double majesties
> This friendly treaty of our threatened town?

KING PHILIP
> Speak England first, that has been forward first
> To speak unto this city. What say you?

KING JOHN
> If the Dauphin there, your princely son,
> Can in this book of beauty read 'I love',
> Her dowry shall weigh equal with a queen.
> For Anjou and fair Touraine, Maine, Poitiers,
> And all that we upon this side the sea—
> Except this city now by us besieged—
> Find liable to our crown and dignity,
> Shall gild her bridal bed and make her rich
> In titles, honours, and promotiòns,
> As she in beauty, education, blood,
> Holds hand with any princess of the world.

KING PHILIP
> What say you, boy? Look in the lady's face.

LEWIS THE DAUPHIN
> I do, my lord. And in her eye I find
> A wonder, or a wondrous miracle,
> The shadow of myself formed in her eye;
> Which, being but the shadow of your son,
> Becomes a sun and makes your son a shadow.
> I do protest I never loved myself
> Till now infixèd I beheld myself
> Drawn in the flattering table of her eye.

*He whispers with Blanche*

BASTARD (*aside*)
> Drawn in the flattering table of her eye!
>> Hanged in the frowning wrinkle of her brow
> And quartered in her heart! He does espy

Himself love's traitor. This is pity now,
That, hanged and drawn and quartered, there should be
In such a love so vile a lout as he.

BLANCHE (*to Lewis*)
My uncle's will in this respect is mine.
If he sees aught in you that makes him like,
That anything he sees which moves his liking,
I can with ease translate it to my will.
Or if you will, to speak more properly,
I will enforce it easily to my love.
Further I will not flatter you, my lord,
That all I see in you is worthy love,
Than this: that nothing do I see in you,
Though churlish thoughts themselves should be your judge,
That I can find should merit any hate.

KING JOHN
What say these young ones? What say you, my niece?

BLANCHE
That she is bound in honour ever to do
What you in wisdom ever agree to say.

KING JOHN
Speak then, Prince Dauphin. Can you love this lady?

LEWIS THE DAUPHIN
Nay, ask me if I can refrain from love;
For I do love her most unfeignedly.

KING JOHN
Then do I give Volquessen, Touraine, Maine,
Poitiers, and Anjou, these five provinces,
With her to you; and this addition more,
Full thirty thousand marks of English coin.
Philip of France, if you are pleased with this,
Command your son and daughter to join hands.

KING PHILIP
It likes us well. Young princes, close your hands.

AUSTRIA

    And your lips too—for I am well assured
    That I did so when I was first assured.

KING PHILIP

    Now, citizens of Angiers, open your gates;
    Let in that amity which you have made.
    For at Saint Mary's chapel presently
    The rites of marriage shall be solemnized.
    Is not the Lady Constance in this troop?
    I know she is not, for this match made up
    Her presence would have interrupted much.
    Where are she and her son? Tell me, who knows.

LEWIS THE DAUPHIN

    She is sad and passionate at your highness' tent.

KING PHILIP

    And, by my faith, this league that we have made
    Will give her sadness very little cure.
    Brother of England, how may we content
    This widow-lady? In her right we came,
    Which we, God knows, have turned another way,
    To our own advantage.

KING JOHN             We will heal up all,

    For we'll create young Arthur Duke of Brittany
    And Earl of Richmond; and this rich fair town
    We make him lord of. Call the Lady Constance;
    Some speedy messenger bid her repair
    To our solemnity. I trust we shall,
    If not fill up the measure of her will,
    Yet in some measure satisfy her so
    That we shall stop her exclamatiòn.
    Go we as well as haste will suffer us
    To this unlooked-for, unpreparèd pomp.

                    *Exeunt all but the Bastard*

BASTARD

    Mad world! Mad kings! Mad compositiòn!
    John, to stop Arthur's title in the whole,

Has willingly departed with a part;
And France, whose armour conscience buckled on,
Whom zeal and charity brought to the field
As God's own soldier, rounded in the ear
With that same purpose-changer, that sly devil,
That broker that ever breaks the pate of faith,
That daily break-vow, he that wins of all,
Of kings, of beggars, old men, young men, maids—
Who, having no external thing to lose
But the word 'maid', cheats the poor maid of that—
That smooth-faced gentleman, tickling commodity.
Commodity, the bias of the world—
The world, which of itself is balanced well,
Made to run even upon even ground,
Till this advantage, this vile-drawing bias,
This sway of motion, this commodity,
Makes it take head from all indifferency,
From all direction, purpose, course, intent,
And this same bias, this commodity,
This bawd, this broker, this all-changing word,
Clapped on the outward eye of fickle France,
Has drawn him from his own determined aid,
From a resolved and honourable war,
To a most base and vile-concluded peace.
And why rail I on this commodity?
Only because he has not wooed me yet;
Not that I have the power to clutch my hand
When his fair angels would salute my palm;
But that my hand, as unattempted yet,
Like a poor beggar rails so on the rich.
Well, while I am a beggar, I will rail
And say there is no sin but to be rich;
And being rich, my virtue then shall be
To say there is no vice but beggary.
Since kings break faith upon commodity,
Gain, be my lord—for I will worship thee!

# Act III

## SCENE I
### The French King's tent.

*Enter Constance, Arthur, and Salisbury*

CONSTANCE
Gone to be married? Gone to swear a peace?
False blood to false blood joined! Gone to be friends?
Shall Lewis have Blanche, and Blanche those provinces?
It is not so; you have misspoken, misheard.
Be well advised, tell over your tale again.
It cannot be; you do but say it is so.
I trust I may not trust you, for your word
Is but the vain breath of a common man.
Believe me, I do not believe you, man;
I have a king's oath to the contrary.
You shall be punished for thus frightening me,
For I am sick and capable of fears,
Oppressed with wrongs, and therefore full of fears,
A widow, husbandless, subject to fears,
A woman, naturally born to fears.
And, though you now confess you did but jest,
With my vexed spirits I cannot take a truce,
But they will quake and tremble all this day.
What do you mean by shaking of your head?
Why do you look so sadly on my son?
What means that hand upon that breast of thine?
Why holds your eye that lamentable tear,
Like a proud river peering over its bounds?
Are these sad signs confirmers of your words?

Then speak again—not all your former tale,
But this one word, whether your tale is true.

SALISBURY
As true as I believe you think them false
That give you cause to prove my saying true.

CONSTANCE
O, if you teach me to believe this sorrow,
Teach you this sorrow how to make me die!
And let belief and life encounter so
As does the fury of two desperate men
Who in the very meeting fall and die.
Lewis marry Blanche! O boy, then where are you?
France friend with England, what becomes of me?
Fellow, be gone! I cannot brook your sight.
This news has made you a most ugly man.

SALISBURY
What other harm have I, good lady, done,
But spoken the harm that is by others done?

CONSTANCE
Which harm within itself so heinous is
As it makes harmful all that speak of it.

ARTHUR
I do beseech you, madam, be content.

CONSTANCE
If you that bid me be content were grim,
Ugly and slanderous to your mother's womb,
Full of unpleasing blots and sightless stains,
Lame, foolish, crookèd, swart, a misfit,
Patched with foul moles and eye-offending marks,
I would not care, I then would be content,
For then I should not love you; no, nor you
Become your great birth, nor deserve a crown.
But you are fair, and at your birth, dear boy,
Nature and fortune joined to make you great.
Of nature's gifts you may with lilies boast
And with the half-blown rose. But fortune, O,

She is corrupted, changed, and won from you;
She adulterates hourly with your uncle John,
And with her golden hand has plucked on France
To tread down fair respect of sovereignty,
And made his majesty the bawd to theirs.
France is a bawd to fortune and King John,
That strumpet fortune, that usurping John!
Tell me, you fellow, is not France forsworn?
Envenom him with words, or get you gone
And leave those woes alone which I alone
Am bound to underbear.

SALISBURY                             Pardon me, madam,
   I may not go without you to the Kings.

CONSTANCE
   You may, you shall. I will not go with you.
   I will instruct my sorrows to be proud,
   For grief is proud and makes its owner stoop.

*She seats herself on the ground*

   To me and to the state of my great grief
   Let kings assemble; for my grief's so great
   That no supporter but the huge firm earth
   Can hold it up. Here I and sorrows sit;
   Here is my throne. Bid kings come bow to it.

*Exit Salisbury with Arthur*

*Enter King John, King Philip, Queen Eleanor, Lewis the*
*Dauphin, Blanche, the Bastard, Austria, and attendants*

KING PHILIP
   'Tis true, fair daughter; and this blessèd day
   Ever in France shall be kept festival.
   To solemnize this day the glorious sun
   Stays in its course and plays the alchemist,
   Turning with splendour of its precious eye

The meagre cloddy earth to glittering gold.
The yearly course that brings this day about
Shall never see it but a holiday.

CONSTANCE (*rising*)
A wicked day, and not a holy day!
What has this day deserved, what has it done,
That it in golden letters should be set
Among the high tides in the calendar?
Nay, rather turn this day out of the week,
This day of shame, oppression, perjury.
Or, if it must stand still, let wives with child
Pray that their burdens may not fall this day,
Lest their hopes be ominously crossed.
But on this day let seamen fear no wreck;
No bargains break that are not this day made;
This day all things begun come to ill end,
Yea, faith itself to hollow falsehood change!

KING PHILIP
By heaven, lady, you shall have no cause
To curse the fair proceedings of this day.
Have I not pawned to you my majesty?

CONSTANCE
You have beguiled me with a counterfeit
Resembling majesty, which, being touched and tried,
Proves valueless. You are forsworn, forsworn!
You came in arms to spill my enemies' blood,
But now in arms you strengthen it with yours.
The grappling vigour and rough frown of war
Are cold in amity and painted peace,
And our oppression has made up this league.
Arm, arm, you heavens, against these perjured Kings!
A widow cries; be husband to me, heavens.
Let not the hours of this ungodly day
Wear out the day in peace; but, ere sunset,
Set armèd discord between these perjured Kings.
Hear me! O, hear me!

AUSTRIA                    Lady Constance, peace!
CONSTANCE
  War! War! No peace! Peace is to me a war.
  O Limoges! O Austria! You do shame
  That bloody spoil. You slave, you wretch, you coward!
  You little valiant, great in villainy!
  You ever strong upon the stronger side!
  You fortune's champion, that do never fight
  But when her humorous ladyship is by
  To teach you safety! You are perjured too,
  And sooth up greatness. What a fool are you,
  A ramping fool, to brag and stamp and swear
  Upon my party! You cold-blooded slave!
  Have you not spoken like thunder on my side,
  Been sworn my soldier, bidding me depend
  Upon your stars, your fortune, and your strength,
  And do you now fall over to my foes?
  You wear a lion's hide! Doff it for shame,
  And hang a calf's-skin on those cowardly limbs.
AUSTRIA
  O that a man should speak those words to me!
BASTARD
  And hang a calf's-skin on those cowardly limbs.
AUSTRIA
  You dare not say so, villain, for your life!
BASTARD
  And hang a calf's-skin on those cowardly limbs.
KING JOHN
  We like not this; you do forget yourself.

*Enter Cardinal Pandulph*

KING PHILIP
  Here comes the holy legate of the Pope.
CARDINAL PANDULPH
  Hail, you anointed deputies of heaven!

To you, King John, my holy errand is.
I Pandulph, of fair Milan Cardinal,
And from Pope Innocent the legate here,
Do in his name religiously demand
Why you against the church, our holy mother,
So wilfully do kick; and force perforce
Keep Stephen Langton, chosen Archbishop
Of Canterbury, from that holy see.
This, in our foresaid Holy Father's name,
Pope Innocent, I do demand of you.

KING JOHN
What earthy name to interrogatòries
Can tax the free breath of a sacred king?
You can not, Cardinal, devise a name
So slight, unworthy, and ridiculous,
To charge me to an answer, as the Pope.
Tell him this tale, and from the mouth of England
Add thus much more: that no Italian priest
Shall tithe or toll in our dominions.
But as we, under God, are supreme head,
So, under him, that great supremacy
Where we do reign we will alone uphold,
Without the assistance of a mortal hand.
So tell the Pope, all reverence set apart
To him and his usurped authority.

KING PHILIP
Brother of England, you blaspheme in this.

KING JOHN
Though you, and all the kings of Christendom,
Are led so grossly by this meddling priest,
Dreading the curse that money may buy out;
And by the merit of vile gold, dross, dust,
Purchase corrupted pardon of a man,
Who in that sale sells pardon from himself—
Though you and all the rest, so grossly led,
This juggling witchcraft with revènue cherish,

Yet I alone, alone do me oppose
Against the Pope, and count his friends my foes.

CARDINAL PANDULPH
Then, by the lawful powèr that I have,
You shall stand cursed and excommunicate,
And blessèd shall he be that does revolt
From his allegiance to a heretic.
And meritorious shall that hand be called,
Canonizèd and worshipped as a saint,
That takes away by any secret course
Your hateful life.

CONSTANCE			O, lawful let it be
That I have room with Rome to curse awhile!
Good father Cardinal, cry you 'Amen'
To my keen curses; for without my wrong
There is no tongue has power to curse him right.

CARDINAL PANDULPH
There's law and warrant, lady, for my curse.

CONSTANCE
And for mine too; when law can do no right,
Let it be lawful that law bars no wrong.
Law cannot give my child his kingdom here,
For he that holds his kingdom holds the law.
Therefore, since law itself is perfect wrong,
How can the law forbid my tongue to curse?

CARDINAL PANDULPH
Philip of France, on peril of a curse,
Let go the hand of that arch-heretic,
And raise the power of France upon his head,
Unless he does submit himself to Rome.

QUEEN ELEANOR
Look you pale, France? Do not let go your hand.

CONSTANCE
Look to it, devil, lest now France repents,
And by disjoining hands, hell loses a soul.

AUSTRIA
    King Philip, listen to the Cardinal.
BASTARD
    And hang a calf's-skin on his cowardly limbs.
AUSTRIA
    Well, ruffian, I must pocket up these wrongs
    Because—
BASTARD    Your breeches best may carry them.
KING JOHN
    Philip, what say you to the Cardinal?
CONSTANCE
    What should he say, but as the Cardinal?
LEWIS THE DAUPHIN
    Bethink you, father, for the difference
    Is purchase of a heavy curse from Rome,
    Or the light loss of England for a friend.
    Forgo the easier.
BLANCHE                That's the curse of Rome.
CONSTANCE
    O Lewis, stand fast! The devil tempts you here
    In likeness of a new, untrimmèd bride.
BLANCHE
    The Lady Constance speaks not from her faith,
    But from her need.
CONSTANCE        O, if you grant my need,
    Which only lives but by the death of faith,
    That need must needs infer this principle,
    That faith would live again by death of need.
    O then, tread down my need, and faith mounts up;
    Keep my need up, and faith is trodden down.
KING JOHN
    The King is moved, and answers not to this.
CONSTANCE (to King Philip)
    O, be removed from him, and answer well!
AUSTRIA
    Do so, King Philip; hang no more in doubt.

BASTARD
  Hang nothing but a calf's-skin, most sweet lout.
KING PHILIP
  I am perplexed, and know not what to say.
CARDINAL PANDULPH
  What can you say but will perplex you more,
  If you stand excommunicate and cursed?
KING PHILIP
  Good reverend father, make my person yours,
  And tell me how you would bestow yourself.
  This royal hand and mine are newly knit,
  And the conjunction of our inward souls
  Married in league, coupled and linked together
  With all religious strength of sacred vows.
  The latest breath that gave the sound of words
  Was deep-sworn faith, peace, amity, true love
  Between our kingdoms and our royal selves.
  And even before this truce, but new before,
  No longer than we well could wash our hands
  To clap this royal bargain up of peace,
  Heaven knows, they were besmeared and overstained
  With slaughter's pencil, where revenge did paint
  The fearful difference of incensèd kings.
  And shall these hands, so lately purged of blood,
  So newly joined in love, so strong in both,
  Unyoke this seizure and this kind accord?
  Play fast and loose with faith? So jest with heaven,
  Make such inconstant children of ourselves,
  As now again to snatch our palm from palm,
  Unswear faith sworn, and on the marriage-bed
  Of smiling peace to march a bloody host,
  And make a riot on the gentle brow
  Of true sincerity? O holy sir,
  My reverend father, let it not be so!
  Out of your grace, devise, ordain, impose
  Some gentle order, and then we shall be blessed
  To do your pleasure and continue friends.

CARDINAL PANDULPH
    All form is formless, order orderless,
    Save what is opposite to England's love.
    Therefore to arms! Be champion of our church,
    Or let the church, our mother, breathe her curse,
    A mother's curse, on her revolting son.
    France, you may hold a serpent by the tongue,
    An angry lion by the mortal paw,
    A fasting tiger safer by the tooth,
    Than keep in peace that hand which you do hold.
KING PHILIP
    I may disjoin my hand, but not my faith.
CARDINAL PANDULPH
    So make you faith an enemy to faith,
    And like a civil war set oath to oath,
    Your tongue against your tongue. O, let your vow
    First made to heaven, first be to heaven performed,
    That is, to be the champion of our church.
    What since you swore is sworn against yourself
    And may not be performèd by yourself.
    For that which you have sworn to do amiss
    Is not amiss when it is truly done;
    And being not done, where doing tends to ill,
    The truth is then most done not doing it.
    The better act of purposes mistaken
    Is to mistake again; though indirect,
    Yet indirection thereby grows direct,
    And falsehood falsehood cures, as fire cools fire
    Within the scorchèd veins of one new burned.
    It is religion that does make vows kept,
    But you have sworn against religiòn
    By what you swear against the thing you swear,
    And make an oath the surety for your truth
    Against an oath! The truth you are unsure
    To swear, swears only not to be forsworn—
    Else what a mockery should it be to swear!

But you do swear only to be forsworn,
And most forsworn to keep what you do swear.
Therefore your later vow, against your first,
Is in yourself rebellion to yourself;
And better conquest never can you make
Than arm your constant and your nobler parts
Against these giddy loose suggestiòns.
Upon which better part our prayers come in,
If you will grant them. But if not, then know
The peril of our curses light on you
So heavy as you shall not shake them off,
But in despair die under their black weight.

AUSTRIA
Rebellion, flat rebellion!

BASTARD                        Will it not be—
Will not a calf's-skin stop that mouth of yours?

LEWIS THE DAUPHIN
Father, to arms!

BLANCHE            Upon your wedding-day?
Against the blood that you have marrièd?
What, shall our feast be kept with slaughtered men?
Shall braying trumpets and loud churlish drums,
Clamours of hell, be measures to our pomp?
O husband, hear me! Ay, alas, how new
Is 'husband' in my mouth! Even for that name,
Which till this time my tongue did never pronounce,
Upon my knee I beg, go not to arms
Against my uncle.

CONSTANCE            O, upon my knee,
Made hard with kneeling, I do pray to you,
You virtuous Dauphin, alter not the sentence
Forethought by heaven.

BLANCHE
Now shall I see your love! What motive may
Be stronger with you than the name of wife?

CONSTANCE

That which upholds him then that you upholds,
His honour! O, your honour, Lewis, your honour!

LEWIS THE DAUPHIN

I muse your majesty does seem so cold,
When such profound respects do pull you on!

CARDINAL PANDULPH

I will denounce a curse upon his head.

KING PHILIP

You shall not need. England, I will fall from you.

CONSTANCE

O fair return of banished majesty!

QUEEN ELEANOR

O foul revolt of French inconstancy!

KING JOHN

France, you shall rue this hour within this hour.

BASTARD

Old Time the clock-setter, that bald sexton Time,
Is it as he wills? Well then, France shall rue.

BLANCHE

The sun's o'ercast with blood; fair day, adieu!
Which is the side that I must go with then?
I am with both; each army has a hand,
And in their rage, I having hold of both,
They whirl asunder and dismember me.
Husband, I cannot pray that you may win;
Uncle, I needs must pray that you may lose.
Father, I may not wish the fortune yours;
Grandam, I will not wish your wishes thrive.
Whoever wins, on that side shall I lose—
Assurèd loss, before the match is played!

LEWIS

Lady, with me, with me your fortune lies.

BLANCHE

There where my fortune lives, there my life dies.

KING JOHN

Nephew, go now and draw our force together.

Exit the Bastard

France, I am burned up with inflaming wrath—
A rage whose heat has this condition,
That nothing can allay, nothing but blood,
The blood, and dearest-valued blood, of France.

KING PHILIP

Your rage shall burn you up, and you shall turn
To ashes, ere our blood shall quench that fire.
Look to yourself, you are in jeopardy!

KING JOHN

No more than he that threatens. To arms let's hie!

Exeunt

## Scene II
## Before Angiers.

*Alarums, excursions. Enter the Bastard, with Austria's head*

BASTARD

Now, by my life, this day grows wondrous hot.
Some airy devil hovers in the sky
And pours down mischief. Austria's head lie there,
While Philip breathes.

*Enter King John, Arthur, and Hubert*

KING JOHN

Hubert, keep this boy. Philip, make up!
My mother is assailèd in our tent,
And taken, I fear.

BASTARD          My lord, I rescued her;
Her highness is in safety, fear you not.
But on, my liege! For very little pains
Will bring this labour to a happy end.          *Exeunt*

## Scene III
## The same.

*Alarums, excursions, retreat. Enter King John, Queen*
*Eleanor, Arthur, the Bastard, Hubert, lords, and soldiers*

KING JOHN (*to Queen Eleanor*)
　So shall it be—your grace shall stay behind,
　And strongly guarded. (*To Arthur*) Nephew, look not
　　sad!
　Your grandam loves you, and your uncle will
　As dear be to you as your father was.
ARTHUR
　O, this will make my mother die with grief!
KING JOHN (*to the Bastard*)
　Nephew, away for England! Haste before,
　And ere our coming see you shake the bags
　Of hoarding abbots; imprisoned angels[1]
　Set at liberty. The fat ribs of peace
　Must by the hungry now be fed upon.
　Use our commission in its utmost force.
BASTARD
　Bell, book, and candle shall not drive me back
　When gold and silver beck me to come on.
　I leave your highness. Grandam, I will pray—
　If ever I remember to be holy—
　For your fair safety. So I kiss your hand.
QUEEN ELEANOR
　Farewell, gentle kinsman.
KING JOHN                    Kinsman, farewell.
　　　　　　　　　　　　　　　　*Exit the Bastard*
QUEEN ELEANOR
　Come hither, little kinsman. Hark, a word.

---

[1]A pun on the coin, worth ten shillings.

*She takes Arthur aside*

KING JOHN

    Come hither, Hubert. O my gentle Hubert,
    We owe you much! Within this wall of flesh
    There is a soul counts you her creditor,
    And with advantage means to pay your love;
    And, my good friend, your voluntary oath
    Lives in this bosom, dearly cherishèd.
    Give me your hand. I had a thing to say,
    But I will fit it with some better tune.
    By heaven, Hubert, I am almost ashamed
    To say what good respect I have of you.

HUBERT

    I am much bounden to your majesty.

KING JOHN

    Good friend, you have no cause to say so yet,
    But you shall have; and creep time never so slow,
    Yet it shall come for me to do you good.
    I had a thing to say—but let it go.
    The sun is in the heaven, and the proud day,
    Attended with the pleasures of the world,
    Is all too wanton and too full of toys
    To give me audience. If the midnight bell
    Did with its iron tongue and brazen mouth
    Sound on into the drowsy race of night;
    If this same were a churchyard where we stand,
    And you possessèd with a thousand wrongs;
    Or if that surly spirit, melancholy,
    Had baked your blood, and made it heavy, thick,
    Which else runs tickling up and down the veins,
    Making that idiot, laughter, keep men's eyes
    And strain their cheeks to idle merriment,
    A passion hateful to my purposes;
    Or if then you could see me without eyes,
    Hear me without your ears, and make reply

Without a tongue, using thought alone,
Without eyes, ears, and harmful sound of words;
Then, in despite of brooded watchful day,
I would into your bosom pour my thoughts.
But, ah, I will not. Yet I love you well,
And, by my troth, I think you love me well.

HUBERT
So well that what you bid me undertake,
Though my death were adjunct to my act,
By heaven, I would do it.

KING JOHN                        Do not I know you would?
Good Hubert! Hubert, Hubert, throw your eye
On yon young boy. I'll tell you what, my friend,
He is a very serpent in my way,
And wheresoever this foot of mine does tread
He lies before me. Do you understand me?
You are his keeper.

HUBERT              And I'll keep him so
That he shall not offend your majesty.

KING JOHN
Death.

HUBERT My lord.

KING JOHN        A grave.

HUBERT                        He shall not live.

KING JOHN                                Enough.
I could be merry now. Hubert, I love you.
Well, I'll not say what I intend for you.
Remember. Madam, fare you well.
I'll send those troops over to your majesty.

QUEEN ELEANOR
My blessing go with you.

KING JOHN                        For England, nephew, go.
Hubert shall be your man, attend on you
With all true duty. On toward Calais, ho!

                                                *Exeunt*

# Scene IV
## The French King's tent.

*Enter King Philip, the Dauphin,*
*Cardinal Pandulph, and attendants*

KING PHILIP

So, by a roaring tempest on the flood,
A whole armada of concerted sail
Is scattered and disjoined from fellowship.

CARDINAL PANDULPH

Courage and comfort! All shall yet go well.

KING PHILIP

What can go well, when we have run so ill?
Are we not beaten? Is not Angiers lost?
Arthur taken prisoner? Divers dear friends slain?
And bloody England into England gone,
O'erbearing interruption, spite of France?

LEWIS THE DAUPHIN

What he has won, that has he fortified.
So hot a speed, with such advice disposed,
Such temperate order in so fierce a cause,
Does want example. Who has read or heard
Of any kindred action like to this?

KING PHILIP

Well could I bear that England had this praise,
So we could find some pattern of our shame.

*Enter Constance*

Look who comes here! A grave unto a soul,
Holding the eternal spirit, against her will,
In the vile prison of afflicted breath.
I pray you, lady, go away with me.

CONSTANCE

Lo! Now—now see the issue of your peace!

KING PHILIP
    Patience, good lady. Comfort, gentle Constance.
CONSTANCE
    No, I defy all counsel, all redress,
    But that which ends all counsel, true redress—
    Death! Death, O amiable, lovely death!
    You odoriferous stench! Sound rottenness!
    Arise forth from the couch of lasting night,
    You hate and terror to prosperity,
    And I will kiss your detestable bones,
    And put my eyeballs in your vaulty brows,
    And ring these fingers with your household worms,
    And stop this gap of breath with fulsome dust,
    And be a carrion monster like yourself.
    Come, grin on me, and I will think you smile
    And kiss you as your wife. Misery's love,
    O, come to me!
KING PHILIP       O fair affliction, peace!
CONSTANCE
    No, no, I will not, having breath to cry!
    O that my tongue were in the thunder's mouth!
    Then with a passion would I shake the world,
    And rouse from sleep that dread anatomy
    Which cannot hear a lady's feeble voice,
    Which scorns an ordinary invocation.
CARDINAL PANDULPH
    Lady, you utter madness, and not sorrow.
CONSTANCE
    You are not holy to belie me so!
    I am not mad. This hair I tear is mine.
    My name is Constance. I was Geoffrey's wife.
    Young Arthur is my son, and he is lost!
    I am not mad—I would to heaven I were,
    For then more like I should forget myself!
    O, if I could, what grief should I forget!
    Preach some philosophy to make me mad,

And you shall be canònized, Cardinal.
For, being not mad, but sensible of grief,
My reasonable part produces reason
How I may be delivered of these woes,
And teaches me to kill or hang myself.
If I were mad, I should forget my son,
Or madly think a babe of clouts were he.
I am not mad—too well, too well I feel
The different plague of each calamity.

KING PHILIP

Bind up those tresses! O, what love I note
In the fair multitude of those her hairs!
Where but by chance a silver drop has fallen,
Even to that drop ten thousand wiry friends
Do glue themselves in sociable grief,
Like true, inseparable, faithful loves,
Sticking together in calamity.

CONSTANCE

To England, if you will.

KING PHILIP                    Bind up your hairs.

CONSTANCE

Yes, that I will; and wherefore will I do it?
I tore them from their bonds, and cried aloud,
'O that these hands could so redeem my son
As they have given these hairs their liberty!'
But now I envy them their liberty,
And will again commit them to their bonds,
Because my poor child is a prisoner.
And, father Cardinal, I have heard you say
That we shall see and know our friends in heaven.
If that is true, I shall see my boy again;
For since the birth of Cain, the first male child,
To him that did but yesterday suspire,
There was not such a gracious creature born.
But now will canker-sorrow eat my bud
And chase the native beauty from his cheek,

And he will look as hollow as a ghost,
As dim and meagre as an ague's fit,
And so he'll die. And, rising so again,
When I shall meet him in the court of heaven
I shall not know him. Therefore never, never
Must I behold my pretty Arthur more.

CARDINAL PANDULPH
You hold too heinous a respect of grief.

CONSTANCE
He talks to me that never had a son.

KING PHILIP
You are as fond of grief as of your child.

CONSTANCE
Grief fills the room up of my absent child,
Lies in his bed, walks up and down with me,
Puts on his pretty looks, repeats his words,
Remembers me of all his gracious parts,
Stuffs out his vacant garments with his form;
Then have I reason to be fond of grief?
Fare you well. Had you such a loss as I,
I could give better comfort than you do.
I will not keep this form upon my head
When there is such disorder in my wits
O Lord! My boy, my Arthur, my fair son!
My life, my joy, my food, my all the world!
My widow-comfort, and my sorrows' cure!          *Exit*

KING PHILIP
I fear some outrage, and I'll follow her.          *Exit*

LEWIS THE DAUPHIN
There's nothing in this world can make me joy.
Life is as tedious as a twice-told tale,
Vexing the dull ear of a drowsy man,
And bitter shame has spoiled the sweet world's taste,
That it yields naught but shame and bitterness.

CARDINAL PANDULPH
Before the curing of a strong disease,

Even in the instant of repair and health,
The fit is strongest. Evils that take leave,
On their departure most of all show evil.
What have you lost by losing of this day?

LEWIS THE DAUPHIN
All days of glory, joy, and happiness.

CARDINAL PANDULPH
If you had won it, certainly you had.
No, no. When fortune means to men most good
She looks upon them with a threatening eye.
'Tis strange to think how much King John has lost
In this which he accounts so clearly won.
Are not you grieved that Arthur is his prisoner?

LEWIS THE DAUPHIN
As heartily as he is glad he has him.

CARDINAL PANDULPH
Your mind is all as youthful as your blood.
Now hear me speak with a prophetic spirit;
For even the breath of what I mean to speak
Shall blow each dust, each straw, each little rub,
Out of the path which shall directly lead
Your foot to England's throne. And therefore mark:
John has seized Arthur, and it cannot be
That while warm life plays in that infant's veins
The misplaced John should entertain an hour,
One minute, nay, one quiet breath, of rest.
A sceptre snatched with an unruly hand
Must be as boisterously maintained as gained;
And he that stands upon a slippery place
Makes nice of no vile hold to stay him up.
That John may stand, then Arthur needs must fall.
So be it—for it cannot be but so.

LEWIS THE DAUPHIN
But what shall I gain by young Arthur's fall?

CARDINAL PANDULPH
You, in the right of Lady Blanche your wife,
May then make all the claim that Arthur did.

LEWIS THE DAUPHIN
  And lose it, life and all, as Arthur did.

CARDINAL PANDULPH
  How green you are and fresh in this old world!
  John lays you plots; the times conspire with you—
  For he that steeps his safety in true blood
  Shall find but bloody safety and untrue.
  This act, so evilly borne, shall cool the hearts
  Of all his people, and freeze up their zeal,
  That none so small advantage shall step forth
  To check his reign, but they will cherish it.
  No natural exhalation in the sky,
  No scope of nature, no distempered day,
  No common wind, no customèd event,
  But they will pluck away its natural cause
  And call them meteors, omens ill, and signs,
  Abortives, prophecies, and tongues of heaven,
  Plainly denouncing vengeance upon John.

LEWIS THE DAUPHIN
  Maybe he will not touch young Arthur's life,
  But hold himself safe in his imprisonment.

CARDINAL PANDULPH
  O sir, when he shall hear of your approach,
  If then young Arthur is not gone already,
  Even at that news he dies. And then the hearts
  Of all his people shall revolt from him,
  And kiss the lips of unacquainted change,
  And pick strong matter of revolt and wrath
  Out of the bloody fingers' ends of John.
  I think I see this trouble all on foot;
  And, O, what better matter breeds for you
  Than I have named! The bastard Faulconbridge
  Is now in England ransacking the church,
  Offending charity. If but a dozen French
  Were there in arms, they would be as a call

To train ten thousand English to their side,
Or as a little snow, tumbled about,
Anon becomes a mountain. O noble Dauphin,
Go with me to the King. It is wonderful
What may be wrought out of their discontent,
Now that their souls are topfull of offence.
For England, go! I will whet on the King.

LEWIS THE DAUPHIN

Strong reasons make strange actions! Let us go.
If you say ay, the King will not say no.

*Exeunt*

# Act IV

## SCENE I
### A room in a castle.

*Enter Hubert and executioners*

HUBERT
Heat me these irons hot, and look you stand
Within the arras. When I strike my foot
Upon the bosom of the ground, rush forth
And bind the boy whom you shall find with me
Fast to the chair. Be heedful. Hence, and watch!
EXECUTIONER
I hope your warrant will bear out the deed.
HUBERT
Uncleanly scruples! Fear not you. Look to it!

*The executioners withdraw*

Young lad, come forth; I have to say with you.

*Enter Arthur*

ARTHUR
Good morrow, Hubert.
HUBERT                          Good morrow, little prince.
ARTHUR
As little prince, having so great a title
To be more prince, as may be. You are sad.
HUBERT
Indeed, I have been merrier.

ARTHUR                              Mercy on me!
  I think nobody should be sad but I.
  Yet I remember, when I was in France,
  Young gentlemen would be as sad as night
  Only for pleasure. By my christendom,
  If I were out of prison and kept sheep,
  I should be as merry as the day is long.
  And so I would be here, but I suspect
  My uncle practises more harm to me.
  He is afraid of me and I of him.
  Is it my fault that I was Geoffrey's son?
  No, indeed it is not; and I would to heaven
  I were your son, so you would love me, Hubert.
HUBERT *(aside)*
  If I talk to him, with his innocent prattle
  He will awake my mercy, which lies dead.
  Therefore I will be sudden, and dispatch.
ARTHUR
  Are you sick, Hubert? You look pale today.
  In truth, I would you were a little sick,
  That I might sit all night and watch with you.
  I warrant I love you more than you do me.
HUBERT *(aside)*
  His words do take possession of my bosom.

*He shows Arthur the warrant*

  Read here, young Arthur. *(Aside)* How now, foolish tears!
  Turning pitiless torture out of door!
  I must be brief, lest resolution drop
  Out at my eyes in tender womanish tears.
  Can you not read it? Is it not fairly written?
ARTHUR
  Too fairly, Hubert, for so foul effect.
  Must you with hot irons burn out both my eyes?

HUBERT
   Young boy, I must.
ARTHUR                          And will you?
HUBERT                                        And I will.
ARTHUR
   Have you the heart? When your head did but ache,
   I knit my handkerchief about your brows—
   The best I had, a princess wrought it me—
   And I did never ask it you again.
   And with my hand at midnight held your head,
   And, like the watchful minutes to the hour,
   Now and then cheered up the heavy time,
   Saying 'What lack you?', and 'Where lies your grief?',
   Or 'What good love may I perform for you?'.
   Many a poor man's son would have lain still
   And never have spoken a loving word to you;
   But you at your sick service had a prince.
   Nay, you may think my love was crafty love,
   And call it cunning. Do then, if you will.
   If heaven is pleased that you must use me ill,
   Why then you must. Will you put out my eyes—
   These eyes that never did, nor ever shall,
   So much as frown on you?
HUBERT                            I have sworn to do it,
   And with hot irons must I burn them out.
ARTHUR
   Ah, none but in this iron age would do it!
   The iron of itself, though heat red-hot,
   Approaching near these eyes, would drink my tears
   And quench its fiery indignatiòn
   Even in the matter of my innocence;
   Nay, after that, consume away in rust,
   But for containing fire to harm my eye.
   Are you more stubborn-hard than hammered iron?
   For if an angel should have come to me
   And told me Hubert should put out my eyes,
   I would not have believed him—no tongue but Hubert's!

*Hubert stamps his foot*

HUBERT
    Come forth!

*The executioners enter with cord and irons*

                    Do as I bid you do.

ARTHUR
    O, save me, Hubert, save me! My eyes are out
    Even with the fierce looks of these bloody men.

HUBERT
    Give me the iron, I say, and bind him here.

ARTHUR
    Alas, what need you be so boisterous-rough?
    I will not struggle; I will stand stone-still.
    For heaven's sake, Hubert, let me not be bound!
    Nay, hear me, Hubert! Drive these men away,
    And I will sit as quiet as a lamb.
    I will not stir, nor flinch, nor speak a word,
    Nor look upon the iron angrily.
    Thrust but these men away, and I'll forgive you,
    Whatever torment you do put me to.

HUBERT
    Go stand within. Leave me alone with him.

EXECUTIONER
    I am best pleased to be forth from such a deed.

                                    *Exeunt executioners*

ARTHUR
    Alas, I then have chidden away my friend!
    He has a stern look, but a gentle heart.
    Let him come back, that his compassion may
    Give life to yours.

HUBERT                      Come, boy, prepare yourself.

ARTHUR
    Is there no remedy?

HUBERT                    None, but to lose your eyes.

ARTHUR

O heaven, that there were but a mote in yours,
A grain, a dust, a gnat, a wandering hair,
Any annoyance in that precious sense.
Then feeling what small things are boisterous there,
Your vile intent must needs seem horrible.

HUBERT

Is this your promise? Go to, hold your tongue!

ARTHUR

Hubert, the utterance of a brace of tongues
Must needs want pleading for a pair of eyes.
Let me not hold my tongue. Let me not, Hubert!
Or, Hubert, if you will, cut out my tongue,
So I may keep my eyes. O, spare my eyes,
Though to no use but still to look on you!
Lo, by my faith, the instrument is cold
And would not harm me.

HUBERT                        I can heat it, boy.

ARTHUR

No, in good truth; the fire is dead with grief,
Being created for comfort, to be used
In undeserved extremes. See else yourself.
There is no malice in this burning coal;
The breath of heaven has blown its spirit out,
And strewed repentant ashes on its head.

HUBERT

But with my breath I can revive it, boy.

ARTHUR

Then if you do, you will but make it blush
And glow with shame of your proceedings, Hubert.
Nay, it perchance will sparkle in your eyes,
And, like a dog that is compelled to fight,
Snatch at his master that does spur him on.
All things that you should use to do me wrong
Deny their office. Only you do lack

That mercy which fierce fire and iron extend—
Creatures of note for mercy-lacking uses.

HUBERT
Well, see to live. I will not touch your eye
For all the treasure that your uncle owns;
Yet am I sworn, and I did purpose, boy,
With this same very iron to burn them out.

ARTHUR
O, now you look like Hubert. All this while
You were disguisèd.

HUBERT                                  Peace! No more. Adieu.
Your uncle must not know but you are dead.
I'll fill these doggèd spies with false reports;
And, pretty child, sleep doubtless and secure
That Hubert, for the wealth of all the world,
Will not offend you.

ARTHUR                          O heaven! I thank you, Hubert.

HUBERT
Silence! No more. Go closely in with me.
Much danger do I undergo for thee.

                                                                *Exeunt*


# SCENE II
## King John's palace.

*Enter King John, Pembroke, Salisbury, and other lords*


KING JOHN
Here once again we sit, once again crowned,
And looked upon, I hope, with cheerful eyes.

PEMBROKE
This 'once again', but that your highness pleased,
Was once superfluous. You were crowned before,
And that high royalty was never plucked off,
The faiths of men never stainèd with revolt;

Fresh expectation troubled not the land
With any longed-for change or better state.

SALISBURY

Therefore, to be possessed with double pomp,
To guard a title that was rich before,
To gild refinèd gold, to paint the lily,
To throw a perfume on the violet,
To smooth the ice, or add another hue
Unto the rainbow, or with taper-light
To seek the beauteous eye of heaven to garnish,
Is wasteful and ridiculous excess.

PEMBROKE

But that your royal pleasure must be done,
This act is as an ancient tale new told,
And in the last repeating troublesome,
Being urgèd at a time unseasonable.

SALISBURY

In this the antique and well noted face
Of plain old form is much disfigurèd;
And, like a shifted wind unto a sail,
It makes the course of thoughts to fetch about,
Startles and frights consideratiòn,
Makes sound opinion sick and truth suspected,
For putting on so new a fashioned robe.

PEMBROKE

When workmen strive to do better than well,
They do confound their skill in covetousness;
And oftentimes excusing of a fault
Does make the fault the worse by the excuse,
As patches set upon a little breach
Discredit more in hiding of the fault
Than did the fault before it was so patched.

SALISBURY

To this effect, before you were new crowned,
We breathed our counsel. But it pleased your highness
To overbear it, and we are all well pleased,

Since all and every part of what we would
Does make a stand at what your highness will.

KING JOHN

Some reasons of this double coronation
I have possessed you with, and think them strong;
And more, more strong, the lesser is my fear,
I shall indue you with. Meantime but ask
What you would have reformed that is not well,
And well shall you perceive how willingly
I will both hear and grant you your requests.

PEMBROKE

Then I, as one that am the tongue of these
To sound the purposes of all their hearts,
Both for myself and them—but, chief of all,
Your safety, for which indeed myself and them
Bend their best studies—heartily request
The enfranchisement of Arthur. Whose restraint
Does move the murmuring lips of discontent
To break into this dangerous argument:
If what in rest you have in right you hold,
Why then your fears—which, as they say, attend
The steps of wrong—should move you to mew up
Your tender kinsman, and to choke his days
With barbarous ignorance, and deny his youth
The rich advantage of good exercise.
That the time's enemies may not have this
To grace occasions, let it be our suit,
That you have bid us ask, his liberty.
Which for our goods we do no further ask
Than whereupon our weal, on you depending,
Counts it your weal he has his liberty.

*Enter Hubert*

KING JOHN

Let it be so. I do commit his youth
To your direction. Hubert, what news with you?

*He takes Hubert aside*

PEMBROKE

   This is the man should do the bloody deed;
   He showed his warrant to a friend of mine.
   The image of a wicked heinous fault
   Lives in his eye; that close aspèct of his
   Does show the mood of a much troubled breast,
   And I do fearfully believe it is done,
   What we so feared he had a charge to do.

SALISBURY

   The colour of the King does come and go
   Between his purpose and his consciènce,
   Like heralds between two dreadful armies set.
   His passion is so ripe it needs must break.

PEMBROKE

   And when it breaks, I fear will issue thence
   The foul corruption of a sweet child's death.

KING JOHN *(coming forward)*

   We cannot hold mortality's strong hand.
   Good lords, although my will to give is living,
   The suit which you demand is gone and dead.
   He tells us Arthur is deceased tonight.

SALISBURY

   Indeed we feared his sickness was past cure.

PEMBROKE

   Indeed we heard how near his death he was,
   Before the child himself felt he was sick.
   This must be answered—either here or hence.

KING JOHN

   Why do you bend such solemn brows on me?
   Think you I bear the shears of destiny?
   Have I commandment on the pulse of life?

SALISBURY

   It is apparent foul play; and it is shame

That greatness should so grossly offer it.
So thrive it in your game! And so, farewell.

PEMBROKE
Stay yet, Lord Salisbury. I'll go with you,
And find the inheritance of this poor child,
His little kingdom of a forcèd grave.
That blood which owned the breadth of all this isle,
Three foot of it does hold—bad world the while!
This must not be thus borne; this will break out
To all our sorrows, and ere long, I fear.
     *Exeunt Pembroke, Salisbury, and the other lords*

KING JOHN
They burn in indignation. I repent.
There is no sure foundation set on blood,
No certain life achieved by others' death.

*Enter a Messenger*

A fearful eye you have. Where is that blood
That I have seen inhabit in those cheeks?
So foul a sky clears not without a storm;
Pour down your weather—how goes all in France?

MESSENGER
From France to England; never such a power
For any foreign preparatiòn
Was levied in the body of a land.
The copy of your speed is learned by them;
For when you should be told they do prepare,
The tidings comes that they have all arrived.

KING JOHN
O, where has our intelligence been drunk?
Where has it slept? Where is my mother's care,
That such an army could be drawn in France
And she not hear of it?

MESSENGER              My liege, her ear

Is stopped with dust. The first of April died
Your noble mother; and, as I hear, my lord,
The Lady Constance in a frenzy died
Three days before. But this from rumour's tongue
I idly heard; if true or false I know not.

KING JOHN
Withhold your speed, dreadful occasiòn!
O, make a league with me till I have pleased
My discontented peers. What! Mother dead?
How wildly then walks my estate in France!
Under whose conduct came those powers of France
That you for truth give out are landed here?

MESSENGER
Under the Dauphin.

*Enter the Bastard and Peter of Pomfret*

KING JOHN                You have made me giddy
With these ill tidings. (*To the Bastard*) Now, what says
    the world
To your proceedings? Do not seek to stuff
My head with more ill news, for it is full.

BASTARD
But if you are afraid to hear the worst,
Then let the worst unheard fall on your head.

KING JOHN
Bear with me, kinsman, for I was amazed
Under the tide; but now I breathe again
Aloft the flood, and can give audience
To any tongue, speak it of what it will.

BASTARD
How I have sped among the clergymen
The sums I have collected shall express.
But as I travelled hither through the land,
I find the people strangely fantasied,
Possessed with rumours, full of idle dreams,

Not knowing what they fear, but full of fear.
And here's a prophet that I brought with me
From forth the streets of Pomfret, whom I found
With many hundreds treading on his heels;
To whom he sung, in rude harsh-sounding rhymes,
That, ere the next Ascension Day at noon,
Your highness should deliver up your crown.

KING JOHN
You idle dreamer, wherefore did you so?

PETER OF POMFRET
Foreknowing that the truth will fall out so.

KING JOHN
Hubert, away with him! Imprison him;
And on that day at noon whereon he says
I shall yield up my crown, let him be hanged.
Deliver him to safety and return,
For I must use you.

               *Exit Hubert with Peter of Pomfret*
               O my gentle kinsman,
Hear you the news abroad, who have arrived?

BASTARD
The French, my lord—men's mouths are full of it.
Besides, I met Lord Bigod and Lord Salisbury,
With eyes as red as new-enkindled fire,
And others more, going to seek the grave
Of Arthur, whom they say is killed tonight
On your suggestion.

KING JOHN            Gentle kinsman, go,
And thrust yourself into their companies.
I have a way to win their loves again;
Bring them before me.

BASTARD           I will seek them out.

KING JOHN
Nay, but make haste! The better foot before!
O, let me have no subject enemies,
When adverse foreigners affright my towns

With dreadful pomp of stout invasiòn.
Be Mercury, set feathers to your heels,
And fly like thought from them to me again.
KING JOHN

BASTARD
The spirit of the time shall teach me speed.          *Exit*
KING JOHN
Spoken like a sprightful gentleman!
(*To the Messenger*)
Go after him; for he perhaps shall need
Some messenger between me and the peers;
And be you he.
MESSENGER          With all my heart, my liege.          *Exit*
KING JOHN
My mother dead!

*Enter Hubert*

HUBERT
My lord, they say five moons were seen tonight—
Four fixèd, and the fifth did whirl about
The other four in wondrous motiòn.
KING JOHN
Five moons?
HUBERT          Old men and beldames in the streets
Do prophesy upon it dangerously.
Young Arthur's death is common in their mouths,
And when they talk of him they shake their heads
And whisper one another in the ear.
And he that speaks does grip the hearer's wrist,
While he that hears makes fearful actiòn,
With wrinkled brows, with nods, with rolling eyes.
I saw a smith stand with his hammer, thus,
While his iron did on the anvil cool,
With open mouth swallowing a tailor's news;
Who, with his shears and measure in his hand,
Standing on slippers which his nimble haste

Had falsely thrust upon contràry feet,
Told of many thousand warlike French
That were embattled now and ranked in Kent.
Another lean unwashed artificer
Cuts off his tale and talks of Arthur's death.

KING JOHN
Why seek you to possess me with these fears?
Why urge you so oft young Arthur's death?
Your hand has murdered him; I had a mighty cause
To wish him dead, but you had none to kill him.

HUBERT
No had, my lord! Why, did you not provoke me?

KING JOHN
It is the curse of kings to be attended
By slaves that take their humours for a warrant
To break within the bloody house of life,
And on the winking of authority
To understand a law, to know the meaning
Of dangerous majesty, when perchance it frowns
More upon humour than advised respect.

HUBERT
Here is your hand and seal for what I did.

KING JOHN
O, when the last account between heaven and earth
Is to be made, then shall this hand and seal
Witness against us to damnatiòn!
How oft the sight of means to do ill deeds
Makes deeds ill done! Had not you been by,
A fellow by the hand of nature marked,
Noted, and signed to do a deed of shame,
This murder had not come into my mind.
But, taking note of your abhorred aspèct,
Finding you fit for bloody villainy,
Apt, liable to be employed in danger,
I faintly broke with you of Arthur's death;
And you, to be endearèd to a king,

Made it no conscience to destroy a prince.
HUBERT
My lord—
KING JOHN
Had you but shaken your head or made a pause
When I spoke darkly what I purposèd,
Or turned an eye of doubt upon my face,
As bid me tell my tale in èxpress words,
Deep shame had struck me dumb, made me break off,
And those your fears might have wrought fears in me.
But you did understand me by my signs
And did in signs again parley with sin;
Yea, without stop, did let your heart consent,
And consequently your rude hand to act
The deed which both our tongues held vile to name.
Out of my sight, and never see me more!
My nobles leave me, and my state is threatened
Even at my gates, with ranks of foreign powers,
Nay, in the body of this fleshly land,
This kingdom, this confine of blood and breath,
Hostility and civil tumult reign
Between my conscience and my nephew's death.
HUBERT
Arm you against your other enemies;
I'll make a peace between your soul and you.
Young Arthur is alive. This hand of mine
Is yet a maiden and an innocent hand,
Not painted with the crimson spots of blood.
Within this bosom never entered yet
The dreadful motion of a murderous thought;
And you have slandered nature in my form,
Which, howsoever rude exteriorly,
Is yet the cover of a fairer mind
Than to be butcher of an innocent child.
KING JOHN
Does Arthur live? O, haste you to the peers!

Throw this report on their incensèd rage
And make them tame to their obedience.
Forgive the comment that my passion made
Upon your features, for my rage was blind,
And foul imaginary eyes of blood
Presented you more hideous than you are.
O, answer not, but to my closet bring
The angry lords with all expedient haste.
I conjure you but slowly—run more fast!                *Exeunt*

## SCENE III
### Before a castle.

*Enter Arthur on the walls*

ARTHUR
The wall is high, and yet will I leap down.
Good ground, be pitiful and hurt me not!
There's few or none do know me; if they did,
This ship-boy's semblance has disguised me quite.
I am afraid—and yet I'll venture it.
If I get down, and do not break my limbs,
I'll find a thousand shifts to get away.
As good to die and go as die and stay.

*He leaps down*

O me! My uncle's spirit is in these stones!
Heaven take my soul, and England keep my bones!
                                                       *He dies*

*Enter Pembroke, Salisbury, and Bigod*

SALISBURY
Lords, I will meet him at Saint Edmundsbury.

It is our safety, and we must embrace
This gentle offer of the perilous time.

PEMBROKE

Who brought that letter from the Cardinal?

SALISBURY

The Count Melun, a noble lord of France,
Whose private notice of the Dauphin's love
Is much more general than these lines import.

BIGOD

Tomorrow morning let us meet him then.

SALISBURY

Or rather then set forward; it will be
Two long days' journey, lords, before we meet.

*Enter the Bastard*

BASTARD

Once more today well met, distempered lords!
The King by me requests your presence straight.

SALISBURY

The King has dispossessed himself of us;
We will not line his thin bestainèd cloak
With our pure honours, nor attend the foot
That leaves the print of blood wherever it walks.
Return and tell him so! We know the worst.

BASTARD

Whatever you think, good words, I think, were best.

SALISBURY

Our griefs, and not our manners, reason now.

BASTARD

But there is little reason in your grief.
Therefore more reason you had manners now.

PEMBROKE

Sir, sir, impatience has its privilege.

BASTARD

'Tis true—to hurt its master, no man else.

SALISBURY
  This is the prison.

  *He sees Arthur's body*

  What is he lies here?

PEMBROKE
  O death, made proud with pure and princely beauty!
  The earth had not a hole to hide this deed.

SALISBURY
  Murder, as hating what himself has done,
  Does lay it open to urge on revenge.

BIGOD
  Or, when he doomed this beauty to a grave,
  Found it too precious-princely for a grave.

SALISBURY
  Sir Richard, what think you? You have beheld.
  Or have you read, or heard, or could you think,
  Or do you almost think, although you see,
  That you do see? Could thought, without this object,
  Form such another? This is the very top,
  The height, the crest, or crest unto the crest,
  Of murder's arms. This is the bloodiest shame,
  The wildest savagery, the vilest stroke,
  That ever wall-eyed wrath or staring rage
  Presented to the tears of soft remorse.

PEMBROKE
  All murders past do stand excused in this.
  And this, so sole and so unmatchable,
  Shall give a holiness, a purity,
  To the yet-unbegotten sin of times,
  And prove a deadly bloodshed but a jest,
  Exampled by this heinous spectacle.

BASTARD
  It is a damnèd and a bloody work,

The graceless action of a heavy hand—
If it should be the work of any hand.
SALISBURY
If it should be the work of any hand!
We had a kind of light what would ensue.
It is the shameful work of Hubert's hand,
The practice, and the purpose, of the King—
From whose obedience I forbid my soul,
Kneeling before this ruin of sweet life,
And breathing to this breathless excellence
The incense of a vow, a holy vow;
Never to taste the pleasures of the world,
Never to be infected with delight,
Nor cònversant with ease and idleness,
Till I have set a glory to this hand
By giving it the worship of revenge.
PEMBROKE *and* BIGOD
Our souls religiously confirm your words.

*Enter Hubert*

HUBERT
Lords, I am hot with haste in seeking you.
Arthur does live; the King has sent for you.
SALISBURY
O, he is bold, and blushes not at death!
Be gone, you hateful villain! Get you gone!
HUBERT
I am no villain.
SALISBURY            Must I rob the law?

*He draws his sword*

BASTARD
Your sword is bright, sir; put it up again.
SALISBURY
Not till I sheathe it in a murderer's skin.

HUBERT

> Stand back, Lord Salisbury, stand back, I say!
> By heaven, I think my sword's as sharp as yours.
> I would not have you, lord, forget yourself,
> Nor tempt the danger of my true defence;
> Lest I, by marking of your rage, forget
> Your worth, your greatness, and nobility.

BIGOD

> Out, dunghill! Dare you brave a nobleman?

HUBERT

> Not for my life; but yet I dare defend
> My innocent life against an emperor.

SALISBURY

> You are a murderer.

HUBERT                                   Do not prove me so;

> Yet I am none. Whose tongue so'er speaks false,
> Not truly speaks; who speaks not truly, lies.

PEMBROKE

> Cut him to pieces!

BASTARD                    Keep the peace, I say.

SALISBURY

> Stand by, or I shall gall you, Faulconbridge.

BASTARD

> You were better gall the devil, Salisbury.
> If you but frown on me, or stir your foot,
> Or teach your hasty spleen to do me shame,
> I'll strike you dead. Put up your sword betime,
> Or I'll so maul you and your toasting-iron
> That you shall think the devil is come from hell.

BIGOD

> What will you do, renownèd Faulconbridge?
> Second a villain and a murderer?

HUBERT

> Lord Bigod, I am none.

BIGOD                             Who killed this prince?

HUBERT

    'Tis not an hour since I left him well.

    I honoured him, I loved him, and will weep

    My date of life out for his sweet life's loss.

SALISBURY

    Trust not those cunning waters of his eyes,

    For villainy is not without such tears,

    And he, long traded in it, makes it seem

    Like rivers of remorse and innocence.

    Away with me, all you whose souls abhor

    The uncleanly savours of a slaughter-house;

    For I am stifled with this smell of sin.

BIGOD

    Away toward Bury, to the Dauphin there!

PEMBROKE

    There tell the King he may inquire us out.

                 *Exeunt Pembroke, Salisbury, and Bigot*

BASTARD

    Here's a good world! Knew you of this fair work?

    Beyond the infinite and boundless reach

    Of mercy, if you did this deed of death,

    Are you damned, Hubert.

HUBERT

    Do but hear me, sir—

BASTARD              Ha! I'll tell you what.

    You are damned as black—nay, nothing is so black;

    You are more deep damned than Prince Lucifer;

    There is not yet so ugly a fiend of hell

    As you shall be, if you did kill this child.

HUBERT

    Upon my soul—

BASTARD          If you did but consent

    To this most cruel act, do but despair;

    And if you want a cord, the smallest thread

    That ever spider twisted from her womb

    Will serve to strangle you. A rush will be a beam

    To hang you on; or would you drown yourself,

Put but a little water in a spoon
And it shall be as all the oceàn,
Enough to stifle such a villain up.
I do suspect you very grievously.

HUBERT
If I in act, consent, or sin of thought
Be guilty of the stealing that sweet breath
Which was embounded in this beauteous clay,
Let hell want pains enough to torture me.
I left him well.

BASTARD              Go, bear him in your arms.
I am amazed, I think, and lose my way
Among the thorns and dangers of this world.
How easy do you take all England up!
From forth this morsel of dead royalty
The life, the right and truth, of all this realm
Is fled to heaven; and England now is left
To tug and scramble and to part by the teeth
The unowned interest of proud-swelling state.
Now for the bare-picked bone of majesty
Does doggèd war bristle its angry crest
And snarls here in the gentle eyes of peace.
Now powers from home and discontents at home
Meet in one line; and vast confusion waits,
As does a raven on a sick-fallen beast,
The imminent decay of wrested pomp.
Now happy he whose cloak and girdle can
Hold out this tempest. Bear away that child
And follow me with speed; I'll to the King.
A thousand businesses are brief in hand,
And heaven itself does frown upon the land.     *Exeunt*

# Act V

## SCENE I
### King John's palace.

*Enter King John, Cardinal Pandulph, and attendants*

KING JOHN *(giving the crown to Cardinal Pandulph)*
    Thus have I yielded up into your hand
    The circle of my glory.
CARDINAL PANDULPH *(returning the crown)*
                Take again
    From this my hand, as holding of the Pope
    Your sovereign greatness and authority.
KING JOHN
    Now keep your holy word. Go meet the French,
    And from his holiness use all your power
    To stop their marches before we are inflamed.
    Our discontented counties do revolt;
    Our people quarrel with obedience,
    Swearing allegiance and the love of soul
    To stranger blood, to foreign royalty.
    This inundation of mistempered humour
    Rests by you only to be assuaged.
    Then pause not, for the present time's so sick
    That present medicine must be ministered,
    Or overthrow incurable ensues.
CARDINAL PANDULPH
    It was my breath that blew this tempest up,
    Upon your stubborn usage of the Pope.
    But since you are a gentle convertite,
    My tongue shall hush again this storm of war

And make fair weather in your blustering land.
On this Ascension Day, remember well,
Upon your oath of service to the Pope,
Go I to make the French lay down their arms.          *Exit*

KING JOHN
Is this Ascension Day? Did not the prophet
Say that before Ascension Day at noon
My crown I should give off? Even so I have!
I did suppose it should be on constraint,
But, heaven be thanked, it is but voluntary.

*Enter the Bastard*

BASTARD
All Kent has yielded—nothing there holds out
But Dover Castle; London has received,
Like a kind host, the Dauphin and his powers.
Your nobles will not hear you, but are gone
To offer service to your enemy;
And wild amazement hurries up and down
The little number of your doubtful friends.

KING JOHN
Would not my lords return to me again
After they heard young Arthur was alive?

BASTARD
They found him dead and cast into the streets,
An empty casket, where the jewel of life
By some damned hand was robbed and taken away.

KING JOHN
That villain Hubert told me he did live.

BASTARD
So, on my soul, he did, for aught he knew.
But wherefore do you droop? Why look you sad?
Be great in act, as you have been in thought;
Let not the world see fear and sad distrust
Govern the motion of a kingly eye.

Be stirring as the time; be fire with fire;
Threaten the threatener, and outface the brow
Of bragging horror. So shall inferior eyes,
That borrow their behaviour from the great,
Grow great by your example and put on
The dauntless spirit of resolution.
Away, and glister like the god of war
When he intends to honour the battlefield.
Show boldness and aspiring confidence!
What, shall they seek the lion in his den,
And fright him there? And make him tremble there?
O, let it not be said! Forage, and run
To meet displeasure farther from the doors,
And grapple with him ere he comes so nigh.

KING JOHN
The legate of the Pope has been with me,
And I have made a happy peace with him;
And he has promised to dismiss the powers
Led by the Dauphin.

BASTARD                    O inglorious league!
Shall we, upon the footing of our land,
Send fair-play orders and make compromise,
Accommodation, parley, and base truce
To arms invasive? Shall a beardless boy,
A cockered silken wanton, brave our fields
And flesh his spirit in a warlike soil,
Mocking the air with colours idly spread,
And find no check? Let us, my liege, to arms!
Perhaps the Cardinal cannot make your peace;
Or, if he does, let it at least be said
They saw we had a purpose of defence.

KING JOHN
Have you the ordering of this present time.

BASTARD
Away, then, with good courage! Yet, I know,
Our party may well meet a prouder foe.          *Exeunt*

## SCENE II
### The French camp.

*Enter, in arms, Lewis the Dauphin, Melun, Pembroke,*
*Salisbury, Bigod, and soldiers*

LEWIS THE DAUPHIN
  My Lord Melun, let this be copied out,
  And keep it safe for our remembrance.
  Return the precedent to these lords again,
  That, having our fair order written down,
  Both they and we, perusing o'er these notes,
  May know wherefore we took the sacrament,
  And keep our faiths firm and inviolable.
SALISBURY
  Upon our sides it never shall be broken.
  And, noble Dauphin, albeit we swear
  A voluntary zeal and an unurged faith
  To your proceedings, yet believe me, prince,
  I am not glad that such a sore of time
  Should seek a plaster by contemned revolt,
  And heal the inveterate canker of one wound
  By making many. O, it grieves my soul
  That I must draw this metal from my side
  To be a widow-maker! O, and there
  Where honourable rescue and defence
  Cry out upon the name of Salisbury!
  But such is the infection of the time
  That, for the health and physic of our right,
  We cannot deal but with the very hand
  Of stern injustice and confusèd wrong.
  Is it not pity, O my grievèd friends,
  That we, the sons and children of this isle,
  Were born to see so sad an hour as this?
  Wherein we step after a stranger, march
  Upon her gentle bosom, and fill up

Her enemies' ranks—I must withdraw and weep
Upon the spot of this enforcèd cause—
To grace the gentry of a land remote,
And follow unacquainted colours here?
What, here? O nation, that you could remove!
That Neptune's arms, which circle you about,
Would bear you from the knowledge of yourself
And grapple you unto a pagan shore—
Where these two Christian armies might combine
The blood of malice in a vein of league,
And not to spend it so unneighbourly!

LEWIS THE DAUPHIN
A noble temper do you show in this,
And great affections wrestling in your bosom
Do make an earthquake of nobility.
O, what a noble combat have you fought
Between compulsion and a brave respect!
Let me wipe off this honourable dew
That silverly does progress on your cheeks.
My heart has melted at a lady's tears,
Being an ordinary inundatiòn,
But this effusion of such manly drops—
This shower, blown up by tempest of the soul—
Startles my eyes, and makes me more amazed
Than had I seen the vaulty top of heaven
Figured quite o'er with burning meteors.
Lift up your brow, renownèd Salisbury,
And with a great heart heave away this storm.
Commend these waters to those baby eyes
That never saw the giant world enraged,
Nor met with fortune other than at feasts,
Full warm of blood, of mirth, of gossiping.
Come, come; for you shall thrust your hand as deep
Into the purse of rich prosperity
As Lewis himself. So, nobles, shall you all,
That knit your sinews to the strength of mine.

*A trumpet sounds*

And even there, I think, an angel spoke.

*Enter Cardinal Pandulph*

Look where the holy legate comes apace,
To give us warrant from the hand of heaven,
And on our actions set the name of right
With holy breath.
CARDINAL  PANDULPH
                              Hail, noble prince of France!
The next is this: King John has reconciled
Himself to Rome; his spirit has come in
That so stood out against the holy church,
The great metropolis and see of Rome.
Therefore your threatening colours now wind up,
And tame the savage spirit of wild war,
That, like a lion fostered up at hand,
It may lie gently at the foot of peace
And be no further harmful than in show.
LEWIS  THE  DAUPHIN
Your grace shall pardon me, I will not back.
I am too high-born to be made use of thus,
To be a secondary at control,
Or useful servingman and instrument
To any sovereign state throughout the world.
Your breath first kindled the dead coal of wars
Between this chastised kingdom and myself,
And brought in matter that should feed this fire;
And now 'tis far too huge to be blown out
By that same weak wind which enkindled it.
You taught me how to know the face of right,
Acquainted me with interest to this land,
Yea, thrust this enterprise into my heart;
And come you now to tell me John has made

His peace with Rome? What is that peace to me?
I, by the honour of my marriage-bed,
After young Arthur, claim this land for mine;
And now it is half conquered must I back
Because John has made his peace with Rome?
Am I Rome's slave? What penny has Rome borne,
What men provided, what munition sent,
To underprop this action? Is it not I
That undergo this charge? Who else but I,
And such as to my claim are liable,
Sweat in this business and maintain this war?
Have I not heard these islanders shout out
'Vive le roi!' as I have coasted their towns?
Have I not here the best cards for the game
To win this easy match played for a crown?
And shall I now give o'er the yielded set?
No! No, on my soul, it never shall be said!

CARDINAL PANDULPH
You look but on the outside of this work.

LEWIS THE DAUPHIN
Outside or inside, I will not return
Till my attempt so much be glorified
As to my ample hope was promisèd
Before I drew this gallant head of war,
And called these fiery spirits from the world
To outlook conquest and to win renown
Even in the jaws of danger and of death.

*A trumpet sounds*

What lusty trumpet thus does summon us?

*Enter the Bastard*

BASTARD
According to the fair play of the world,

Let me have audience; I am sent to speak.
My holy lord of Milan, from the King
I come, to learn how you have dealt for him;
And, as you answer, I do know the scope
And warrant limited unto my tongue.

CARDINAL PANDULPH

The Dauphin is too wilful-opposite,
And will not temporize with my entreaties.
He flatly says he'll not lay down his arms.

BASTARD

By all the blood that ever fury breathed,
The youth says well! Now hear our English King,
For thus his royalty does speak in me:
He is prepared, and reason too he should.
This apish and unmannerly approach,
This harnessed masque and unadvisèd revel,
This unhaired sauciness and boyish troops,
The King does smile at; and is well prepared
To whip this dwarfish war, these pigmy arms,
From out the circle of his territories.
That hand which had the strength, even at your door,
To cudgel you and make you leap the hatch,
To dive like buckets in concealèd wells,
To crouch in litter of your stable planks,
To lie like pawns locked up in chests and trunks,
To hug with swine, to seek sweet safety out
In vaults and prisons, and to thrill and shake
Even at the crying of your nation's crow,
Thinking this voice an armèd Englishman—
Shall that victorious hand be feebled here
That in your chambers gave you chastisement?
No! Know the gallant monarch is in arms
And like an eagle o'er his eyrie towers
To souse annoyance that comes near his nest.
And you degenerate, you ingrate rebels,
You bloody Neroes, ripping up the womb

Of your dear mother England, blush for shame!
For your own ladies and pale-visaged maids,
Like Amazons, come tripping after drums,
Their thimbles into armèd gauntlets change,
Their needles to lances, and their gentle hearts
To fierce and bloody inclinatiòn.

LEWIS THE DAUPHIN
There end your challenge and turn your face in peace.
We grant you can outscold us. Fare you well!
We hold our time too precious to be spent
With such a brabbler.

CARDINAL PANDULPH Give me leave to speak.

BASTARD
No, I will speak.

LEWIS THE DAUPHIN
              We will attend to neither.
Strike up the drums, and let the tongue of war
Plead for our interest and our being here.

BASTARD
Indeed, your drums, being beaten, will cry out—
And so shall you, being beaten. Do but start
An echo with the clamour of your drum,
And even at hand a drum is ready braced
That shall reverberate all as loud as yours.
Sound but another, and another shall,
As loud as yours, rattle the heavens' ear
And mock the deep-mouthed thunder. For at hand—
Not trusting to this halting legate here,
Whom he has used rather for sport than need—
Is warlike John. And in his forehead sits
A bare-ribbed death, whose office is this day
To feast upon whole thousands of the French.

LEWIS THE DAUPHIN
Strike up our drums to find this danger out.

BASTARD
And you shall find it, Dauphin, do not doubt.      *Exeunt*

# SCENE III
## The battlefield.

*Alarums. Enter King John and Hubert*

KING JOHN
How goes the day with us? O, tell me, Hubert.

HUBERT
Badly, I fear. How fares your majesty?

KING JOHN
This fever that has troubled me so long
Lies heavy on me. O, my heart is sick!

*Enter a Messenger*

MESSENGER
My lord, your valiant kinsman, Faulconbridge,
Desires your majesty to leave the field
And send him word by me which way you go.

KING JOHN
Tell him, toward Swineshead, to the abbey there.

MESSENGER
Be of good comfort; for the great supply
That was expected by the Dauphin here
Was wrecked three nights ago on Goodwin Sands.
This news was brought to Richard but even now.
The French fight coldly, and retire themselves.

KING JOHN
Ay me! This tyrant fever burns me up,
And will not let me welcome this good news.
Set on toward Swineshead. To my litter straight;
Weakness possesses me, and I am faint.          *Exeunt*

# SCENE IV
## The same.

*Enter Salisbury, Pembroke, and Bigod*

SALISBURY
  I did not think the King so stored with friends.
PEMBROKE
  Up once again! Put spirit in the French;
  If they miscarry, we miscarry too.
SALISBURY
  That misbegotten devil, Faulconbridge,
  In spite of spite, alone upholds the day.
PEMBROKE
  They say King John, sore sick, has left the field.

*Enter Melun, wounded*

MELUN
  Lead me to the rebels of England here.
SALISBURY
  When we were happy we had other names.
PEMBROKE
  It is the Count Melun.
SALISBURY                      Wounded to death.
MELUN
  Fly, noble English, you are bought and sold.
  Unthread the rude eye of rebellion,
  And welcome home again discarded faith.
  Seek out King John and fall before his feet;
  For if the French are lords of this loud day,
  He means to recompense the pains you take
  By cutting off your heads. Thus has he sworn,
  And I with him, and many more with me,
  Upon the altar at Saint Edmundsbury;
  Even on that altar where we swore to you
  Dear amity and everlasting love.

SALISBURY
    May this be possible? May this be true?
MELUN
    Have I not hideous death within my view,
    Retaining but a quantity of life,
    Which bleeds away, even as a form of wax
    Resolving from its figure against the fire?
    What in the world should make me now deceive,
    Since I must lose the use of all deceit?
    Why should I then be false, since it is true
    That I must die here, and live hence by truth?
    I say again, if Lewis does win the day,
    He is forsworn if ever those eyes of yours
    Behold another daybreak in the east.
    But even this night—whose black contagious breath
    Already smokes about the burning crest
    Of the old, feeble, and day-wearied sun—
    Even this ill night, your breathing shall expire,
    Paying the fine of rated treachery
    Even with a treacherous fine of all your lives,
    If Lewis by your assistance wins the day.
    Commend me to one Hubert, with your King.
    The love of him, and this respect besides,
    Because my grandsire was an Englishman,
    Awakes my conscience to confess all this.
    In lieu whereof, I pray you bear me hence
    From forth the noise and rumour of the field,
    Where I may think the remnant of my thoughts
    In peace, and part this body and my soul
    With contemplation and devout desires.
SALISBURY
    We do believe you now; and bless my soul
    But I do love the favour and the form
    Of this most fair occasion, by which now
    We will untread the steps of damnèd flight,

And like a bated and retirèd flood,
Leaving our rankness and irregular course,
Stoop low within those bounds we have o'erlooked,
And calmly run on in obedience
Even to our ocean, to our great King John.
My arm shall give you help to bear you hence;
For I do see the cruel pangs of death
Right in your eye. Away, my friends! New flight,
And happy newness, that intends old right!

*Exeunt*


# SCENE V
## The French camp.

*Enter Lewis the Dauphin and attendants*

LEWIS THE DAUPHIN
The sun of heaven, I thought, was loth to set,
But stayed and made the western sky to blush,
When English measured backward their own ground
In faint retreat! O, bravely came we off,
When with a volley of our needless shot,
After such bloody toil, we bid good night,
And wound our tottering colours clearly up,
Last in the field, and almost lords of it.

*Enter a Messenger*

MESSENGER
Where is my prince, the Dauphin?
LEWIS THE DAUPHIN                        Here. What news?
MESSENGER
The Count Melun is slain. The English lords
By his persuasion are again fallen off,
And your supply, which you have wished so long,
Is cast away and sunk on Goodwin Sands.

LEWIS THE DAUPHIN
  Ah, foul, shrewd news! Curse your very heart!
  I did not think to be so sad tonight
  As this has made me. Who was he that said
  King John did fly an hour or two before
  The stumbling night did part our weary forces?
MESSENGER
  Whoever spoke it, it is true, my lord.
LEWIS THE DAUPHIN
  Well, keep good quarter and good care tonight!
  The day shall not be up so soon as I
  To try the fair adventure of tomorrow.            *Exeunt*

# SCENE VI
## Near Swineshead abbey.

*Enter the Bastard and Hubert, separately*

BASTARD
  Who's there? Speak, ho! Speak quickly, or I shoot.
HUBERT
  A friend. What are you?
BASTARD                          Of the part of England.
HUBERT
  Whither do you go?
BASTARD
  What's that to you?
HUBERT                 Why may not I demand
  Of your affairs as well as you of mine?
BASTARD
  Hubert, I think.
HUBERT                You have a perfect thought.
  I will upon all hazards well believe
  You are my friend that know my tongue so well.
  Who are you?

BASTARD          Whom you will; and if you please,
  You may befriend me so much as to think
  I come one way of the Plantagenets.
HUBERT
  Unkind remembrance! You and endless night
  Have done me shame. Brave soldier, pardon me
  That any accent breaking from your tongue
  Should escape the true acquaintance of my ear.
BASTARD
  Come, come! No compliment, what news abroad?
HUBERT
  Why, here walk I in the black brow of night
  To find you out.
BASTARD                 Brief, then; and what's the news?
HUBERT
  O my sweet sir, news fitting to the night—
  Black, fearful, comfortless, and horrible.
BASTARD
  Show me the very wound of this ill news;
  I am no woman, I'll not swoon at it.
HUBERT
  The King, I fear, is poisoned by a monk;
  I left him almost speechless, and broke out
  To acquaint you with this evil, that you might
  The better arm you to the sudden time
  Than if you had at leisure known of this.
BASTARD
  How did he take it? Who did taste to him?
HUBERT
  A monk, I tell you, a resolvèd villain,
  Whose bowels suddenly burst out. The King
  Yet speaks, and peradventure may recover.
BASTARD
  Whom did you leave to tend his majesty?
HUBERT
  Why, know you not? The lords are all come back,

And brought Prince Henry in their company,
At whose request the King has pardoned them,
And they are all about his majesty.

BASTARD
Withhold your indignation, mighty heaven,
And tempt us not to bear above our power!
I'll tell you, Hubert, half my force this night,
Passing these flats, are taken by the tide—
These Lincoln Washes have devourèd them;
Myself, well mounted, hardly have escaped.
Away before! Conduct me to the King;
I fear he will be dead before I come.                    *Exeunt*


# SCENE VII
## The orchard at Swineshead.

*Enter Prince Henry, Salisbury, and Bigod*

PRINCE HENRY
It is too late. The life of all his blood
Is touched corruptibly, and his pure brain,
Which some suppose the soul's frail dwelling-house,
Does by the idle comments that it makes
Foretell the ending of mortality.

*Enter Pembroke*

PEMBROKE
His highness yet does speak, and holds belief
That, being brought into the open air,
It would allay the burning quality
Of that strong poison which assailèd him.

PRINCE HENRY
Let him be brought into the orchard here.    *Exit Bigod*
Does he still rage?

PEMBROKE            He is more patient
  Than when you left him. Even now he sang.
PRINCE HENRY
  O vanity of sickness! Fierce extremes
  In their continuance will not feel themselves.
  Death, having preyed upon the outward parts,
  Leaves them unusable. His siege is now
  Against the mind, which he does prick and wound
  With many legions of strange fantasies,
  Which, in their throng and press to that last hold,
  Confound themselves. 'Tis strange that death should
    sing.
  I am the cygnet to this pale faint swan
  Who chants a doleful hymn to his own death,
  And from the organ-pipe of frailty sings
  His soul and body to their lasting rest.
SALISBURY
  Be of good comfort, prince; for you are born
  To set a form upon that muted mass
  Which he has left so shapeless and so rude.

*King John is brought in by attendants*

KING JOHN
  Ay, marry, now my soul has elbow-room;
  It would not out at windows nor at doors.
  There is so hot a summer in my bosom
  That all my bowels crumble up to dust.
  I am a scribbled form, drawn with a pen
  Upon a parchment, and against this fire
  Do I shrink up.
PRINCE HENRY How fares your majesty?
KING JOHN
  Poisoned—ill fare! Dead, forsaken, cast off;
  And none of you will bid the winter come

To thrust its icy fingers in my maw;
Nor let my kingdom's rivers take their course
Through my burned bosom; nor entreat the north
To make its bleak winds kiss my parchèd lips
And comfort me with cold. I do not ask you much—
I beg cold comfort; and you are so strait
And so ungrateful you deny me that.

PRINCE HENRY
O that there were some virtue in my tears
That might relieve you!

KING JOHN                    The salt in them is hot.
Within me is a hell, and there the poison
Is as a fiend confined to tyrannize
On unreprievable, condemnèd blood.

*Enter the Bastard*

BASTARD
O, I am scalded with my violent motion
And spleen of speed to see your majesty!

KING JOHN
O nephew, you are come to set my eye!
The tackle of my heart is cracked and burnt,
And all the shrouds wherewith my life should sail
Are turnèd to one thread, one little hair.
My heart has one poor string to stay it by,
Which holds but till your news be utterèd;
And then all this you see is but a clod
And image of confounded royalty.

BASTARD
The Dauphin is preparing hitherward,
Where God does know how we shall answer him!
For in a night the best part of my force
As I upon advantage did remove,
Was in the Washes all unwarily
Devourèd by the unexpected flood.          *King John dies*

SALISBURY

You breathe these dead news in as dead an ear.
My liege! My lord! But now a king, now thus!

PRINCE HENRY

Even so must I run on, and even so stop.
What surety of the world, what hope, what stay,
When this was now a king, and now is clay?

BASTARD

Are you gone so? I do but stay behind
To do the office for you of revenge,
And then my soul shall wait on you to heaven,
As it on earth has been your servant ever.
Now, now, you stars that move in your right spheres,
Where are your powers? Show now your mended faiths,
And instantly return with me again
To push destruction and perpetual shame
Out of the weak door of our fainting land.
Straight let us seek, or straight we shall be sought;
The Dauphin rages at our very heels.

SALISBURY

It seems you know not, then, so much as we.
The Cardinal Pandulph is within at rest,
Who half an hour since came from the Dauphin,
And brings from him such offers of our peace
As we with honour and respect may take,
With purpose presently to leave this war.

BASTARD

He will the rather do it when he sees
Ourselves well-sinewèd to our defence.

SALISBURY

Nay, it is in a manner done already;
For many carriages he has dispatched
To the sea-side, and put his cause and quarrel
To the disposing of the Cardinal.
With whom yourself, myself, and other lords,
If you think meet, this afternoon will post
To consummate this business happily.

BASTARD

    Let it be so. And you, my noble prince,
    With other nobles that may best be spared,
    Shall wait upon your father's funeral.

PRINCE HENRY

    At Worcester must his body be interred,
    For so he willed it.

BASTARD                   Thither shall it then.

    And happily may your sweet self put on
    The lineal state and glory of the land!
    To whom, with all submission, on my knee,
    I do bequeath my faithful services
    And true subjection everlastingly.

SALISBURY

    And the like tender of our love we make,
    To rest without a spot for evermore.

PRINCE HENRY

    I have a kind soul that would give thanks,
    And knows not how to do it but with tears.

BASTARD

    O, let us pay the time but needful woe,
    Since it has been beforehand with our griefs.
    This England never did, and never shall,
    Lie at the proud foot of a conqueror
    But when it first did help to wound itself.
    Now these her princes are come home again,
    Come the three corners of the world in arms
    And we shall shock them! Naught shall make us rue
    If England to itself does rest but true!       *Exeunt*